The Flatbush Journal of Jewish Law and Thought

Volume 19 / Summer 2015

A publication of
Hakirah, Inc.
www.Hakirah.org

Ḥakirah
The Flatbush Journal of Jewish Law and Thought
Volume 19 / Summer 2015

Introduction

After the destruction of European Jewry in the previous century, the last 70 years have seen a rebirth of the Jewish people, both in Israel as a result of the establishment of the state and in the United States primarily as a result of the influx of the remnant of European Jewry. Against all predictions, the Torah communities in these two centers have emerged in recent years as Jewry's most vibrant elements. In the past decades other segments of Jewry have begun to fade, while Orthodoxy continues to thrive. With this growth, however, comes the responsibility to be involved not only with the spiritual needs of *Klal Yisrael,* but also with its material ones. As other segments of American Jewry diminish not only in numbers but also in their inclination to stand up for Jewish values and the Jewish State, our opening article asks "Who Will Support the State of Israel?" Other articles in this issue deal with the impact of some of the dramatic changes that have occurred within Jewry during these last seventy years and Orthodoxy's attitude towards these changes. A Hebrew article looks at a famous essay by Rav Yitzḥak Hutner and gives a new, more nuanced interpretation of his stance on Zionism. With Israel's return to their land, one Halakhah article asks whether the laws regarding "Mourning the *Ḥurban* in a Rebuilt Jerusalem" still apply, while another, "Acknowledging a Miracle with a Berachah," asks whether the time has come to make a *berakhah* upon seeing Jerusalem's Kidron Valley.

Menachem Elon, the recently deceased Orthodox justice of Israel's Supreme Court, tried to integrate traditional halakhah with modern legal systems within Israel's court system. A Hebrew article takes a close look at one of his cases to evaluate his methodology. In our *History of Halakhah* section, "The Intersection of Halakhah and Science in Medical Ethics: The approach of Rabbi Eliezer Waldenberg" looks at the halakhic method of Israel's most influential *posek* in the realm of science and medicine. Also in our *History of Halakhah* section, "Can a Ger Tzedek be appointed Parnass" looks back to the 17th Century to another newly formed Jewish society, which grew, in part, as a result of an influx of *anusim* from Spain. In addition to providing a glimpse of the challenges of this time, the article introduces us to the work of halakhic authorities little known in our day.

A second focus of this issue is modern analysis of the words of the Rishonim. As is often the case, Rambam's words come in for special attention. In "Further Reflections on Classification of Mishneh Torah: Real Answers to Real Problems," an academic scholar takes on a challenge by Prof. Haym Soloveitchik to explain several anomalies in Rambam's organization of *Mishneh Torah.* In "The Sin of ADU," the authors use statistical analyses to corroborate Rambam's heretofore puzzling assertion about a well-known rule concerning the onset of Rosh Hashanah. And, in "Pikuach Nefesh for a Ger Toshav" the author claims that a careful reading of Ramban and Rambam is necessary to establish their position on this controversial issue. Two additional articles focus on other Rishonim. "Divine Providence and Natural Forces: Conflict or Harmony?" looks to Ramban and other Rishonim to unravel their positions on one of the major principles of Judaism. "Some Aspects of Originality in the Responsa of R. Simeon Duran" is a study of Tashbetz's *teshuvo*t that reveals his creative leanings. Two other articles demonstrate how factors other than careful reading of the sources influence interpretations of halakhah and halakhic decisions. In "The History of an Interpretation of Sixteen Drops of Wine at the Seder," the author shows how modern sensibilities eclipsed the reason given by Rishonim for an ancient custom. And in "The Silkscreen Sefer Torah," the author makes an argument for the use of a new, less expensive methodology for writing *Sifrei Torah* and posits an explanation as to why a method supported by one of America's leading *poskim* was so forcefully opposed.

We are pleased to welcome Dov Friedberg to our Board of Directors. Dov earned his PhD at the University of Toronto and is the author of *"Crafting the 613 Commandments: Maimonides on the Enumeration, Classification, and Formulation of the Scriptural Commandments"* (Brighton: Academic Studies Press, 2014) and of various articles on the Bible and Maimonides.

Special thanks to all those who worked hard to make this edition of *Ḥakirah* a reality, including Ari Bornstein and Nina Ackerman Indig, copy-editing; Tuvia Ganz, cover design and production; and Chaim Lam, design and maintenance of our Web page, www.Hakirah.org.

It is our continuing hope that the articles in this journal will stimulate thought, study and discussion, and inspire other members of the public to contribute their own insights. The articles we print thus reflect a wide range of opinion and do not necessarily reflect the views of our Editorial Board. ☙

Instructions for Contributors

Ḥakirah, The Flatbush Journal of Jewish Law and Thought, publishes original, interesting, well-researched and well-organized manuscripts that provide new or profound insights into areas of Jewish *halakhah* and *hashkafah.*

Manuscripts should be in Microsoft Word format and sent as an email attachment to HakirahFlatbush@msn.com. Short references—for example, to a Biblical verse or to a page within the Talmud—should be embedded directly into the text of the manuscript. Longer references should be inserted electronically as footnotes, rather than endnotes.

The author's name should not appear on the manuscript, as it is the Journal's policy to forward the articles for evaluation without disclosing the author's identity. On a separate cover sheet include your name, a short bio, an abstract of your article, your telephone number, fax number, and e-mail address.

After reviewing and accepting your manuscript, we are likely to request clarification of certain points. A revised electronic copy of your manuscript will then be required.

To encourage a wide variety of contributors, the Journal accepts articles employing the Hebrew transliteration style of either *Encyclopedia Judaica* or *ArtScroll.* If you have no preference we suggest you follow the pronunciation rules used by the *Encyclopedia Judaica.* Words in languages other than English should always be italicized, unless the foreign words have become part of the English language.

For more information about writing an article for *Ḥakirah* see <www.Hakirah.org\HakirahGuideToWriting.pdf>. ☙

LETTERS TO THE EDITOR

Molad Zaqen

In "Molad Zaqen and Islamic Scientific Innovation," *Ḥakirah*, Vol. 18, Rabbi Ari Storch seeks to relate the establishment of the *deḥiyyot Molad Zaqen* to Islamic observations of the visibility of the moon around the globe made at the end of the first millennium.

Rabbi Storch begins, "The contemporary Hebrew calendar is a lunar one that sets the first day of the year based on the *molad*, the time of a lunar conjunction."

It is essential to understand what these terms mean.

Molad

Three relationships collectively define the Molad:

A) Rabban Gamliel's statement of Synodic Interval: אין חדושה של לבנה פחותה מעשרים ותשעה יום ומחצה ושני שלישי שעה ושבעים ושלשה חלקים.
B) The tradition of the *Molad* of *Tohu*, *BaHaRad*, 2-5-204, a mathematical constant that melds the analog of the lunar cycle to the moon and enables calculation of the calendar from knowledge of the Hebrew Year.
C) *GUHADZaT* (גוחאדזט), a mnemonic that relates to, and links the months in the Hebrew year in a way to sync the moon with the Sun, i.e., 3-6-8-11-14-17-19.

This series, or at least a subset of it, should be familiar to every *gabai*. It is used to announce the *Molad* at each *Shabbat Mevorkhim*. Traditionally it has been thought that the use of this series began with Hillel II in 358 CE.

From the Gemara, *Ḥulin* 95b we learn of Shmuel's ability to calculate the Molad: כתב שדר ליה עיבורא דשיתין שני, He sent [R' Yoḥanan] the calendar for the next 60 years. אמר השתא חושבנא בעלמא ידעת [R' Yoḥanan's curt reply], He only knows mere calculations.

Precisely true, the *Molad* is only a calculation.

Lunar Conjunction

The Lunar Conjunction, as we now understand it, after much relatively recent science, is an exact physical reality. NASA has provided 6 millennia of lunar phase data for use by historians. This means we know the time of each Conjunction back through the *Molad* of *Tohu*, Monday, September 7, 3761 BCE (Gregorian).

Rabbi Storch gives a definition. "A lunar conjunction is defined as when the moon is aligned with the earth and sun in such a way that all its light is reflected toward the sun, rendering it invisible to those on earth."

A reasonable definition—but was it *Ḥazal's* understanding? At the time of *Ḥazal* there was a geocentric view of the Solar System. Today with our heliocentric view we understand that much of the perceived motions of the Sun and Moon are the result of the revolution of the Earth. This results in symmetry between the last time we see the Old Moon (just before a sunrise) and the first time we see the New Moon (just after a sunset). This means that the minimum period the moon is invisible is 36 hours, and not the 24 hours cited in the Gemora. Normally the moon is invisible for 60 hours and occasionally 84 hours, confirming Rabban Gamliel's expertise on the moon: פעמים שבא בארוכה ופעמים שבא בקצרה.

Many Rabbis thought that the time of the *Molad* was at the time of the Conjunction. They knew by observation that the moon could not be seen at the *Molad* nor could it be seen at the Conjunction.

Rabban Gamliel's Synodic Interval is within half a second of the astronomers' value, but combined with *BaHaRad* and *GUHADZaT* it is still, on average, 5 hours and 17 minutes after the value of the Conjunction for values related to the Molad of Tishrei, within the Common Era.

From the mathematical parameters it was *BaHaRad* that positioned the *Molad.* Had *Molad* of *Tohu* (2-5-204) been 1-23-975 then the *Molad* would have been on average equal to the Conjunction. Incidentally, had the *Molad* of *Tohu* been 4-5-204, two days later, then we would, on average, see the New Moon on the *Molad* of *Tishrei.*

The *Molad* is not the Conjunction—but if the *Molad* is not the Conjunction then what is it?

Etymologically the word *Molad* means birth. Contemporary astronomers consider the birth of the moon to be the Conjunction that they can calculate and detect but not see with the naked eye. Ancient peoples kept lunar calendars based upon the first appearance of the moon after a substantial period of darkness. To this day this is the prime modus operandi of the Muslims to establish the start of their new months. So why didn't Ḥazal set the parameters of *Molad* to track the New Moon? I discuss this in my book, *Sod Ha'ibur.*

The Real Raison D'être of the *Deḥiyyah Molad Zaqen*

According to my study of the years subject to the *Deḥiyyah Molad Zaqen,* the moon will not be seen until two days after the day of the Molad—thus not visible anywhere on earth. This is what Dr. Irv Bromberg of the University of Toronto on his calendar-related website states, "Traditionally, this postponement [*Deḥiyyah Molad Zaqen*] was considered necessary to ensure the visibility of the New Moon on the first day of Rosh Hashanah. In reality, it doesn't ensure that." This could be true only on those minority of days that the *Deḥiyyah Molad Zaqen* is followed by the *Deḥiyyah Lo ADU Rosh.*

In my book I show that approximately 74% of the time the New Moon cannot be seen on the day of the Molad of Tishrei nor the day after. Another surprising fact is also revealed. Of the 74%, only 70% are what I call two-day discrepancies, 4% are three-day discrepancies. Three-day discrep-ancies are characterized with the conditions described in Yerushalmi, *RH* 2:4:

> רבי חייה רבה הילך לאורו של ישן ארבעת מיל רבי אבון משדי עלוי צררין ואמר לה לא תבהית בני מריך ברמשא אנן בעיין תיתחמי מיכא ואת מיתחמי מיכא מיד איתבלע מן קומוי.

R' Ḥiyya the Great walked by the light of the Old Moon for four miles. Rabbi Abun threw pebbles at [the Old Moon] and said to it: "Do not upset the children of your Master, tonight we have to see you from this side [i.e., the New Moon], but you are seen from here [the Old Moon is still visible]."

A compelling confirmation of the relationships I have just revealed is attested by four dates, two embedded in history and two inferred by history, all of which are proven in my book to be dates with a three-day discrepancy.

358 CE, as mentioned, is traditionally the date of adoption of the Hebrew Calendar in use today. The date is in the source. Yet lunar science will confirm the Old Moon was very visible the morning before Rosh Hashanah (the *Molad* of Tishrei).

835 CE, the letter of the Exilarch, is discussed by Sacha Stern. In my book I show this letter too was the result of the very visible Old Moon before Rosh Hashanah.

198 CE, using lunar science, the date is consistent with known fact of the R' Ḥiyya incident. Indeed it is consistent with and confirms the veracity of the story itself.

120 CE, using lunar science, the date is consistent with the life of Rabban Gamliel and his conflict with R' Yehoshua.

In all of the dates the *Molad* would have been deferred by the *Deḥiyyah Molad Zaqen* and prevented the visible Old Moon, the appearance of which belied the establishment of Rosh Hashanah based on actual witnessed testimony.

Richard Fiedler
Author, *Sod Ha'ibur*

Ari Storch responds:

As Mr. Fiedler theorizes, the contemporary *molad* is an average and not an actual conjunction, but this is irrelevant to my article. My article was not based on the contemporary usage of the word *molad*; rather, it was based on Talmudic texts. The contemporary usage of the word *molad* is entirely different from the way the Talmudic passages treat it. I explicitly mentioned my intention to focus on the Talmudic definition when citing a dispute between the *Rishonim* and the Rambam on p. 182. Citing to contemporaneous definitions of *molad*, cannot be used with the pre-calendar discussions in the Talmud.

This new theory's presentation of *molad* is certainly creative, but is flawed. This new theory extrapolates the definition of *molad* from the contemporary system and works backwards. But the current *molad* did not exist in the time period this new theory attempts to analyze. Writing for Bar Ilan University, Yaaqov Loewinger proves that the *molad* in current use was most in synch with the astronomical reality in the 4th century—the traditional date for the introduction of the calendar. <http://www.biu.ac.il/JH/Parasha/veethca/lev.html>. Just as the *molad* has subsequently drifted from being perfectly aligned, it drifts when projecting the calendar back through history to the centuries prior to its introduction. It is therefore no surprise that the theoretical *molad* did not synchronize with any astronomical event during Rabban Gamliel's lifetime; this was centuries before the contemporary *molad* was created. Instead of redefining *molad* to some unknown and nondescript lunar position, the more reasonable approach is that our tradition is based on the historic reality of the 4th century when the calendar was introduced. At that time the *molad* aligned with actual conjunctions. The new theory cites Dr. Bromberg of the University of Toronto in its support, but Dr. Bromberg actually mentions that the *molad* corresponded to the average conjunction during the 4th. <http://individual.utoronto.ca/kalendis/hebrew/molad.htm>. Thus, it is clear one cannot project the calendar to a time before its inception as this new theory does.

This disconnect between the time periods before and after the introduction of the calendar emanates from the Talmudic texts themselves, something that this new theory seems to recognize but ignores. In establishing the Talmudic definition of *molad*, Mr. Fiedler writes, "This means that the minimum period the moon is invisible is for 36 hours, and not the 24 hours cited in the Gemara." Somehow Mr. Fiedler attempts to give a Talmudic definition while simultaneously refuting it. He then resorts to using a system he attributes to Rabban Gamliel. The problem with this is that no Talmudic text attributes *molad* to Rabban Gamliel and it is incorrect to do so. The Talmud does not use the word *molad* within Rabban Gamliel's methodology of determining the months; rather, it intentionally uses the word *ḥiddushah*. This is because Rabban Gamliel was working within a system where the *beit din* would determine the months based on the sighting of the moon and not the conjunctions. It is plausible that Rabban Gamliel estimated the *moladot* to determine the first sightings, but that is not the Talmud's concern. Additionally, this new theory essentially must state that Rabban Gamliel's definitions were abandoned by the Talmud and then somehow resurrected at a later point in time. Such an assertion requires significant proof. The simpler approach is more intuitive and is the one the Talmud itself presents with its terminology; the two incompatible systems worked under different parameters. The Talmud itself demonstrates that there are two systems with two definitions.

A concern not addressed by this new theory, and its fatal flaw, is the overwhelming evidence that *molad zaqen* was not introduced until the 9th century. This new theory is predicated on *molad zaqen's* presence prior to the 9th century; yet, as mentioned in the article, there is an abundance of evidence that it did not exist until that time. The new theory presents the dates of the *molad* of Tishrei for four years to support his idea: 120, 198, 358, and 835. Not only was *molad zaqen* not practiced during this time, but two of the dates were prior to the calendar itself! The years 120 and 198 predate the calendar and *molad zaqen*, or the underlying reason behind it, cannot have been present. The new theory contends that *molad zaqen* is to ensure that the sighting of the moon occurs on Rosh Hashanah, but during this time period, Rosh Hashanah was declared by the sighting of the moon itself. The date of Rosh Hashanah would not be pushed off due to its nonoccurrence on the date the moon was sighted because witnesses would present themselves to the *beit din* and testify that they had sighted the moon prior to the declaration of Rosh Hashanah. The year 835 is also an interesting date to use as proof because, as mentioned in my article, we have a written testimonial from the Exilarch that *molad zaqen* was not implemented in that year. The only year left is 358, the first of the calendar, and I am unsure as to any symbolism this has. Thus, this new theory is incompatible with Talmudic passages because it is predicated on a calendrical component that was nonexistent at the time, *molad zaqen*. Based on the scientific, Talmudic, and historical evidence, I fail to see Mr. Fiedler's position on this subject.

ଔ

Who Will Support the State of Israel?

By: HESHEY ZELCER

It is difficult to overstate the importance of United States support for the State of Israel. Since 2011 the United States has provided Israel with over three billion dollars of aid each year,[1] and it allows Israel to use this money to purchase the latest and most sophisticated United States military equipment. The United States also shares intelligence with Israel and is the only superpower that has consistently used its veto power to block anti-Israel resolutions at the United Nations.

Why does the United States shower these gifts upon the State of Israel?[2] There are various reasons. One is that the American people have been consistently pro-Israel. A second factor is that the Jewish people are the largest non-Christian religious group in the Unites States and could potentially tip the scale for one political candidate over another. A third is that Jewish organizations successfully lobby the United States Congress for the State of Israel.[3]

Should one or more of these dynamics change for the worse, United States aid to Israel would likely decline and the very fate of Israel could be in danger. It is always difficult to predict what will happen, but if we examine current demographic and social trends we notice that all three legs of support are weakening: Israel's reputation is under attack at American universities, eroding American public opinion. The number of non-Orthodox Jews, who have been in the forefront of lobbying on behalf of Israel, is on the decline. And finally, while Jews are currently the largest

---

1 Sharp, *US Foreign Aid to Israel.* See the second page, *Summary*. See also *Appendix B. Bilateral Aid to Israel*, p. 29.

2 Aid to Israel also benefits the United States. Israel is a powerful and dependable ally in a volatile and unstable Middle East. In addition, Israeli battlefield experience with and upgrades to American weapons help the United States improve its military equipment and battlefield tactics.

3 Sharp, *US Foreign Aid to Israel*, states, "For decades, the United States and Israel have maintained strong bilateral relations based on a number of factors, including robust domestic U.S. support for Israel and its security; shared strategic goals in the Middle East; a mutual commitment to democratic values… U.S. officials and many lawmakers have long considered Israel to be a vital partner in the region…"

Heshey Zelcer, CEO of *Ḥakirah*, has published books and articles on Jewish law, philosophy, history and liturgy.

non-Christian religious denomination in the country, by 2050 Muslims are projected to be more numerous.[4]

The Changing Jewish Demographic

In 2002 and 2011 the UJA-Federation studied the Jewish population of the "Eight-County New York Area," which includes the five boroughs of New York City as well as Nassau, Suffolk and Westchester. This area contains the greatest concentration of Jewish people in the United States.[5]

The study showed that since 2002 Jewish population growth has been driven not by immigration, but by high birthrates among the Orthodox, especially the Ḥaredim, whose birth rate is at least three times that associated with non-Orthodox Jewish New Yorkers. In fact, ninety percent of the growth in Jewish population has been among the Orthodox.

The strong growth of the Orthodox Jewish population is true also on a national level. A Pew report in 2013 showed that Orthodox Jews are much younger and tend to have much higher fertility rates than the overall population: 4.1 children among the Orthodox Jews compared with 1.9 children per Jewish adult overall. In the past, high fertility in the US Orthodox community was at least partially offset by attrition, but the retention rate of the Orthodox seems to be improving.[6]

Intermarriage too is not a problem among the Orthodox. By contrast, among Jews in general 44% have a non-Jewish spouse, including nearly six-in-ten of those married in 2000 or later.[7]

Jewish Sociologist Steven M. Cohen sums it up as follows: "Every year, the Orthodox population has been adding 5,000 Jews. The non-Orthodox population has been losing 10,000 Jews."[8]

Both the UJA regional reports and the Pew national studies paint a rosy picture for American Orthodoxy and a pessimistic one for the non-Orthodox.[9] This bodes ill for the State of Israel because Orthodox Jews

---

4 Lipka, *Muslims Expected to Surpass Jews.*

5 Cohen, Ukeles and Miller, *Jewish Community Study of NY: 2011,* pp. 19–30.

6 Cooperman, *Eight Facts about Orthodox Jews,* section 2.

7 Cooperman, *Eight Facts about Orthodox Jews,* section 6.

8 Nathan-Kazis, *Orthodox Population Grows Faster.*

9 The UJA "Eight-County New York Area" study shows the change in the number of Jews from 2002 to 2011: Orthodox increased from 27% to 32%, Conservative declined from 23% to 18%, and Reform declined from 24% to 20%. The Pew reports from 2007 and 2015 show that nationally, Orthodox increased from 10% to 14%, Conservative decreased from 31% to 22%, and Reform increased from 43% to 44%.

have not been doing their share in supporting Israel, and the most dynamic subgroup of Ḥaredi Orthodoxy—as we explain below—is hesitant to openly identify with the State of Israel and has not yet gotten into the habit of advocating for the Jewish state.

Practical Ḥaredim

Pollsters understand that the Ḥaredi community is not monolithic. They have learned to correctly subdivide Ḥaredim into Hasidic and Yeshivish. When it comes to the balance of Orthodox Jews, however, they tend to lump them into a single category called Modern Orthodox. This is unfortunate as it conceals an important trend in the Orthodox world. There is a very large, successful and growing group of Orthodox Jews that we label Practical Ḥaredim, practical in their approach to secular education and to the State of Israel.

The Ḥaredim who are identifiable by their black hats, beards and long dark jackets, those who are truly Hasidic or Yeshivish, tend to have a negative attitude toward secular education and advocate many years of post–high school Talmud study for their male children. Their attitude toward the State of Israel is mostly hostile and at best ambivalent.

Modern Orthodox Jews, on the other hand, those who pray in Young Israel or Orthodox Union–type synagogues, send their children to Zionist schools and summer camps, view secular education as an ideal, and openly and enthusiastically support the State of Israel.

Practical Ḥaredim fit into neither of the above categories. They appreciate that Israel exists, they love to visit it but they do not openly identify with it. They go to college not because secular knowledge is an ideal but because they need to make a living. They send their children to yeshivot whose rabbis are Hasidic or Yeshivish and who ignore the Jewish state. Their yeshivot teach secular education as mandated by the government and the parents want their children to master the secular curriculum. When they graduate high school the sons generally go to a yeshiva in Israel for a year or two to study Talmud full-time. The daughters might attend seminary for a year to strengthen their Jewish education and *hashkafa*, religious outlook. Viewing secular education as a means to a good profession, Practical Ḥaredim often send their children to Touro,[10] a predominantly Jewish university where male and female students are segregated. When they marry they tend to pray in small synagogues, *shteiblich*, whose

10 In New York City (the Five Boroughs) Practical Ḥaredim often send their children to Touro College. Outside New York City they are more likely to attend a university in their local area.

rabbis are usually Hasidic or Yeshivish. The men can generally be identified by their clean-shaven look and by the black hats they wear on the Sabbath.

Practical Ḥaredim are now the predominant Orthodox group in Flatbush, Queens and Staten Island and are beginning to dominate areas in the Five Towns of Long Island as well.

Practical Ḥaredim are active in their community. They help raise money for their yeshivot and they support social service organizations such as Chai Lifeline, Hatzolah, Bonei Olam, etc.. To date, however, Practical Ḥaredim have not openly identified with the State of Israel.[11] They have not been active politically on behalf of Israel and they have not offered up money for its support. Open any issue of the Flatbush Jewish Journal (FJJ) and you will find pages and pages of ads for people being honored by various Jewish organizations. You will not, however, find an ad for anyone being honored by an organization that supports the State of Israel, such as Friends of Israel Defense Forces (FIDF). When Practical Ḥaredim do get involved politically it is usually for the interests of their own community, such as tuition tax credits.

Why Americans are Pro-Israel

To help keep America pro-Israel it is necessary to understand which Americans care about Israel and why.

American support for the State of Israel began at Israel's very founding. Despite warnings from his Secretary of State, President Harry Truman recognized the State of Israel a mere 11 minutes after Israel declared its existence as a state.[12] The recognition was widely popular with the American people: a Gallup poll in June of 1948 showed that almost three times as many Americans sympathized with the Jews in Israel as sympathized with the Arabs.[13]

American Christian Zionism, however, began much earlier. In 1891 the Methodist lay leader William Blackstone presented a petition signed by four hundred predominantly non-Jewish Zionists to President Benjamin Harrison. It called on the United States to use its good offices to convene a congress of European powers to induce the Ottoman Empire

---

11 While 79% of Modern Orthodox Jews say that caring about Israel is an essential part of being Jewish, only 45% of Ḥaredim say the same. See, Lipka, *Controversy Over New Israeli Law.*

12 Holbrooke, *Washington's Battle over Israel's Birth.*

13 Mead, *The New Israel and the Old*, p. 29.

to turn Palestine over to the Jews. The signatories included the chief justice of the Supreme Court, the Speaker of the House of Representatives, the chairs of the House Ways and Means Committee and the House Foreign Affairs Committee, the future president William McKinley and mayors of many large American cities. At that time the Jewish community in the United States was neither large nor powerful and there was no Jewish lobby advocating for a Jewish state.[14]

Since the founding of the State of Israel there has never been a Gallup poll showing more Americans sympathizing with the Arabs than with the Israelis. Why are Americans sympathetic to Israel? There are a variety of reasons. For one, Israel is a democracy.[15] There is also a residue of guilt among many Christians for the two millennia of Christian persecution of Jews. Since Nostra Aetate in the mid-1960s, for example, the Catholic Church has owned up to its past and has taken concrete actions to change its attitude toward the Jews, and by extension the State of Israel.

Christian Zionists can be divided into two groups: A) Prophetic Christian Zionists, who support the Jewish return to their homeland as a fulfillment of biblical prophecy. With the ingathering of the Jews to their homeland, Prophetic Christian Zionists wait for the eschatological end and the second coming of their messiah. B) Progressive Christian Zionists, who see the Jewish return to their homeland as the continuation of a divine plan to build a better world through human progress. God, working through history, is restoring and emancipating the Jews who had previously been repressed and degraded.[16]

Prophetic Christian Zionists also see the United States as the New Canaan. Just as Israel receives the bounty from God when they observe His commandments, Christian Zionists believe they receive God's bounty in the New Canaan, the United States, when they do what is right and proper in God's eyes. They take very seriously the verse in Genesis concerning the descendants of Abraham, "I will bless those who bless you" (12:2). They believe that for Christians to receive God's bounty they must support the Jews, the descendants of Abraham.[17]

The Christians who most exemplify the Prophetic Christian Zionist outlook are the evangelicals and the fundamentalists, who take the bible literally. Evangelicalism is a transdenominational movement within Protestant Christianity whose adherents believe in the centrality of the

---

14 Mead, *The New Israel and the Old*, p. 32.

15 Sharp, *US Foreign Aid to Israel,* p. 1.

16 Mead, *The New Israel and the Old*, p. 31.

17 Mead, *The New Israel and the Old*, p. 33.

"born again" experience in receiving salvation. They believe in the authority of the Bible as God's revelation to humanity, and they share a strong commitment to sharing the Christian message.

In the United States, support for the State of Israel among evangelical Christians is stronger even than among the Jews. A Pew study asked, "Was Israel given to the Jewish people by God?" 40% of Jews answered yes as opposed to 44% of the US general public, 55% of Christians, and 82% of white Evangelicals. Only Orthodox Jews had a higher percentage, 84 (Ultra-Orthodox/Ḥaredim 81%, Modern Orthodox 90%.)[18]

Roughly 25%[19] of the population in the United States identify themselves as evangelicals. Pat Robertson, a renowned evangelical and a former Southern Baptist minister, writes about Israel, "We are with you in your struggle. We are with you as a wave of anti-Semitism is engulfing the earth. We are with you despite ... the incredible hostile resolutions of the United Nations. We are with you despite the threats and ravings of Wahhabi Jihadists, Hezbollah thugs, and Hamas assassins."[20]

The Threat from American Universities

There is a serious problem on American universities. Pro-Israel students share depressing tales of being bullied by professors, insulted by roommates and put down by supposed friends for supporting Israel.

This should not be surprising. There are various college campus groups that organize campaigns to delegitimize and paint a negative image of Israel. The most prominent of these groups are the Muslim Student Association (MSA) and Students for Justice in Palestine (SJP). One or more anti-Israel groups have a presence on approximately 330 typically high-profile university campuses across the country. The intent of these organizations is to stigmatize the State of Israel as the embodiment of racism, colonialism and imperialism.[21]

To date, the negative effect of these organizations has been partially balanced by Hillel, which has chapters on 363 campuses, and by national pro-Israel organizations, which have representatives at 273 universities.

---

18 See, Lipka, *More Evangelicals than Jews Say God Gave Israel to the Jewish People.* This correlates with another Pew question regarding emotional attachment to Israel: 30% of American Jews say they are very attached, as compared to 55% of ultra-Orthodox Jews, and 77% of Modern Orthodox Jews. See, Cooperman, *Eight Facts About Orthodox Jews,* section 7.

19 See, "America's Changing Religious Landscape," *Pew Research Center.*

20 Robertson, *Why Evangelicals Support Israel.*

21 Bard and Dawson, *Israel and the Campus*, p. 8.

Better still, although 330 universities contain anti-Israel groups, the vast majority of the roughly 4,000 universities in the country do not.

Despite anxiety about a growing boycott, divestment, and sanction (BDS) movement, its effect so far is manageable. While a few American universities did adopt BDS resolutions, not a single university has divested from Israel, and many university presidents have made it clear they would oppose such moves.[22] Furthermore, in May 2015 the Illinois House joined the state's senate in unanimously passing an anti-BDS bill that would prevent the state's pension fund from investing in companies that boycott Israel. The state's governor, Bruce Rauner, has pledged to sign the bill, and pro-Israel advocates see it as a model for other states as well.[23]

There is no question, however, that Israel is less popular among university students than it is among the American population at large. Many students have serious questions about Israel's peaceful intentions and about its human rights record.

To combat anti-Israel hate groups on the campuses, the American-Israeli Cooperative Enterprise (AICE) suggests we provide every Jewish college student with an Israel toolkit to help educate them about Israel, and to teach them to effectively communicate their knowledge. AICE also suggests we teach college students mature Zionism that includes Israel, warts and all, but make sure the students first understand the basic facts about the Middle East.[24]

The more serious problem on campus is the politically left-leaning professors, found mostly in the humanities and social science departments.[25] Unlike students, those professors have both power and presumed knowledge. What they transmit in their classrooms affects not only what their students believe, but also the overall climate on campus.[26]

College officials are often reluctant to interfere with anti-Israel bias on their campuses even when such bias borders on anti-Semitism. Saudi Arabia and other Arab governments give generously to American universities. Campus Watch reports, "In 1986, Saudi arms dealer Adnan Khashoggi donated $5 million toward a sports center to be named after

---

22 Medina and Lewin, *Campus Debates on Israel.*

23 Kontorovich, *Illinois Passes Historic Anti-BDS Bill.* See also, Kontorovich, *South Carolina Passes Historic Anti-Boycott Law.*

24 Bard and Dawson, *Israel and the Campus*, p. 38.

25 The vast majority of professors in humanities and social sciences identify themselves on the left of the political spectrum. See, "A Burning Campus," *The David Project*, pp. 22-23.

26 Bard and Dawson, *Israel and the Campus*, p. 4.

him at American University. Since then, grants for endowed chairs in Islamic studies and Middle Eastern studies centers have popped up at the University of California/Santa Barbara; Columbia University; Rice University; University of Arkansas; University of California in Los Angeles; and the University of California/Berkeley, among many others."[27]

Organizations involved in pro-Israel advocacy on campus believe it is less effective to fight anti-Israel voices on campus, and more productive to build pro-Israel support; not to counter the negative but to promote the positive; to make new friends on campus rather than to teach Israel supporters how to debate. They also recommend that we "...demand universities provide the best 'product' possible—which includes open classrooms, fair syllabi, thoughtful and thought-provoking professors, a safe campus environment psychologically, not just physically."[28]

Another way to counter left-leaning professors is to encourage universities to offer more courses on Modern Israel. Universities should also be encouraged to invite Israeli visiting professors. This has not always worked out, however, as visiting professors are often more interested in advancing in their profession than on focusing on Israel advocacy in their limited time in the United States.[29]

We should also capitalize on the minority communities that are our natural allies on campus. These include Indian Americans, who see American Jews as a model for minority success in the United States; India, which has a strong entrepreneurial culture and has its own problems with Islamist terrorism; South Korea, which has a large and growing evangelical population; and China, which has an affinity for Jewish culture and Israel.[30]

It is also important to establish chairs in Israel studies at universities. This, of course, requires donors with deep pockets. Other than at Yeshiva University, there are not many chairs of Israel studies dedicated by Orthodox Jews.

Taglit-Birthright Israel

To counter left-wing hatred of Israel on campus, we should support organizations that have proven to instill love, admiration and advocacy for Israel among college students.

---

27 Duin, *Saudis Give Big to US Colleges.*

28 "A Burning Campus," *The David Project*, p. 3.

29 Bard and Dawson, *Israel and the Campus*, p. 40.

30 "A Burning Campus," *The David Project*, p. 33.

Taglit-Birthright Israel was inaugurated in 1999, and since its inception it has sponsored 10-day educational trips to Israel for more than 400,000 Jewish college students from across the globe (two thirds from the United States). The goal of Birthright Israel is to help participants feel closer to Israel and their Jewish heritage. As a side benefit it has also helped pump $825 million into Israel's economy.

A study by Brandeis University[31] concluded that Birthright Israel has been successful in meeting its goals: 77% of participants are married to a Jewish spouse (as opposed to 51% of non-participants), 66% view raising children Jewish as very important (as opposed to 49% of non-participants), and 51% feel very much connected to Israel (as opposed to 35% of non-participants.) Participants were also more likely to celebrate the Sabbath, be a synagogue member, keep kosher, attend Jewish religious services, and make charitable donations to Jewish or Israeli causes.[32]

The success of Birthright Israel has led to another pro-Israel experiment on college campuses. Covenant Journey, a new organization announced in May 2015, hopes to provide Christian students what Birthright Israel offers Jewish students. Funded by politically conservative Jews and Christians, Covenant Journey plans to bring 250 Christian students to Israel by the end of the summer, and thousands more in the coming years. According to the organization's founder, the results from a recently concluded pilot project were encouraging. A participant explained, "I grew to love Israel by reading my Old Testament, but after visiting Israel, it gave me a push to act for Israel." While it does not officially take a stance on the Israeli-Palestinian conflict, Covenant Journey stresses the security risks faced by Israel, and it highlights the plight of Christians across the Arab world.[33]

AIPAC and Pro-Israel PACs

AIPAC was founded a few short years after the birth of Israel but did not achieve prominence until the mid-70s. It now has more than 100,000 members and seventeen regional offices.[34]

---

31 Saxe, *The Impact of Taglit-Birthright Israel.*

32 Projects that help turn the Birthright Israel enthusiasm into a lifelong commitment include: One Table which sponsors Friday night Shabbat meals for Birthright alumni; and Bring Israel Home in which participants in Israeli and Jewish activities earn points toward a Jewish weekend retreat.

33 Guttman, *Introducing Birthright for Evangelical Christians.*

34 "How We Work," *AIPAC.*

AIPAC's purpose is to lobby US Congress on issues and legislation related to Israel and to ensure that bipartisan support remains strong.[35] While pro-Israel interest groups rank 31 in dollars spent,[36] the annual AIPAC Policy Conference is the largest gathering of the pro-Israel movement; over 16,000 delegates attended the 2015 conference.[37] In 1997, Fortune Magazine ranked AIPAC as the second most powerful influence group in Washington DC, second only to the American Association of Retired People (AARP).

AIPAC is not a political action committee and does not donate to any political campaigns. Approximately 50 of about 80 pro-Israel PACs, however, are operated by AIPAC officials. The largest and most prominent of these PACs, which donates money to political candidates in the United States, is NORPAC.

Between 2000 and 2004 the 50 members of AIPAC's board donated an average of $72,000 each to campaigns and political action committees.[38] Contributions from pro-Israel PACs often constitute roughly 10 to 15% of a typical congressional campaign budget.

Unfortunately, until a few years ago, Orthodox Jews of Brooklyn, Queens and Staten Island had almost no involvement in AIPAC. Orthodox Jews need to become more active in reaching out to their local politicians to express their concern for the safety and well-being of the State of Israel. Political candidates welcome contributions but they also pay attention to the will of their constituents.

Encouraging Signs

There are some encouraging signs that Practical Ḥaredim are beginning to take some responsibility for the security and well-being of the State of Israel.

Nathan Guttman[39] writing in the Forward reports that a new breed of Orthodox Jews whom he labels Modern Ultra-Orthodox are beginning to give money to political candidates who are pro-Israel and who espouse conservative family values. According to the report, Dr. Richard Roberts, an Orthodox Jew from Lakewood, NJ, gave $750,000 to a pro-Romney super-PAC, and another million dollars to yet another Republican super

---

35 As we go to press David Horowitz reports that a recent survey by Frank Luntz shows that Israel is losing the Democrats and that it can no longer claim bipartisan US support.

36 "Top Interest Groups," *OpenSecrets.*

37 Frankel, *A Beautiful Friendship.*

38 Frankel, *A Beautiful Friendship.*

39 Guttman, *How Orthodox Money Is Reshaping Republican Politics.*

PAC. Roberts is not the only Orthodox Jew mentioned in the article and the Republican Party is starting to recognize the importance of Orthodox Jewish contributors.

There was another encouraging sign. This one did not include millions of dollars in contributions, but it was a display of Practical Ḥaredim going public with their pro-Israel sentiments. On Israel Independence Day in 2014 about 300 Practical Ḥaredim gathered in Bais Moshe Shmiel, a *shteible* in Flatbush headed by a hasidic rebbe, to express *hakarat hatov*, appreciation to God, for the State of Israel. The session was introduced by Shlomo Sprecher, a prominent physician and scholar residing in Flatbush. A representative of AIPAC spoke about Israel advocacy, and the guest speaker at the event was Malcolm Hoenlein, the executive vice chairman of the Conference of Presidents of Major American Jewish Organizations.[40]

In yet another step in the right direction, AIPAC events are now all glatt kosher, and policy conferences that had usually begun on Sundays now also include a Shabbaton on the previous day that has expanded to include about 600 people. Yarmulkes of all kinds (and even some hats) are now visible at these conferences and there are *minyanim* for attending delegates. AIPAC under the leadership of a past president, Howard Friedman, an Orthodox Jew, has recognized the importance of recruiting Orthodox Jews to their organization.

Conclusion

Demographic studies show that while the non-Orthodox population is declining, Orthodoxy is on the rise.

As these demographic trends gain momentum it will become ever more important for Orthodox Jews to invest their time and money to help mold public opinion on university campuses, and to lobby the United States Congress on behalf of the State of Israel.

In winning the demographic war, Orthodoxy will no longer have the luxury of focusing on itself. It will need to assume a leading role in support of the Jewish state. ❧

40 Zelcer, *Is This a Turning Point?*

Bibliography

The bibliographic entries below end with a short description within parentheses. These are used within the footnotes to reference the works. We have not included URLs as each work can be found by Googling it.

Bard, Mitchell and Dawson, Jeff. "Israel and the Campus: The Real Story," *The American-Israeli Cooperative Enterprise.* (Bard and Dawson, *Israel and the Campus*).

Bard, Mitchell G. "Myths and Facts: A Guide to the Arab-Israeli Conflict," *The American-Israeli Cooperative Enterprise.* (Bard, *Myths and Facts*).

Cohen, Steven and Ukeles, Jacob and Miller, Ron. "Jewish Community Study of New York: 2011 Comprehensive Report," *UJA Federation of New York.* (Cohen, Ukeles and Miller, *Jewish Community Study of NY: 2011*).

Cooperman, Alan. "Eight facts about Orthodox Jews from the Pew Research survey," *Pew Research Center*, October 17, 2013. (Cooperman, *Eight Facts About Orthodox Jews*).

Duin, Julia. "Saudis Give Big to U.S. Colleges," *Campus Watch.* (Duin, *Saudis Give Big to US Colleges*).

Frankel, Glenn. "A Beautiful Friendship," *The Washington Post*, July 16, 2006. (Frankel, *A Beautiful Friendship*).

Guttman, Nathan. "How Orthodox Money Is Reshaping Republican Politics," *Forward*, May 4, 2015. (Guttman, *How Orthodox Money is Reshaping Republican Politics*).

Holbrooke, Richard. "Washington's Battle Over Israel's Birth," *WashingtonPost.com*, May 7, 2008. (Holbrooke, *Washington's Battle over Israel's Birth*).

Horovitz, David. "Israel losing Democrats, 'can't claim bipartisan US support,' top pollster warns," *The Times of Israel*, July, 5, 2015.

Kontorovich, Eugene. "Illinois passes historic anti-BDS bill, as Congress mulls similar moves," *The Washington Post*, May 18, 2015. (Kontorovich, *Illinois Passes Historic Anti-BDS Bill*).

Kontorovich, Eugene. "South Carolina passes historic anti-boycott law," *The Washington Post*, June 5, 2015. (Kontrovich, *South Carolina passes historic anti-boycott law*).

Matthews, Cynthia. "Introducing Birthright for Evangelical Christians," *Forward*, May 17, 2015. (Guttman, *Introducing Birthright for Evangelical Christians*).

Mead, Walter Russell. "The New Israel and the Old," *Foreign Affairs*, July/August 2008. (Mead, *The New Israel and the Old*).

Medina, Jennifer and Lewin, Tamar. "Campus Debates of Israel Drive a Wedge between Jews and Minorities," *International New York Times*, May 9, 2015. (Medina and Lewin, *Campus Debates on Israel*).

Lipka, Michael. "Controversy over new Israeli law highlights growing ultra-Orthodox population," *Pew Research Center*, March 13, 2014. (Lipka, *Controversy Over New Israeli Law*).

Lipka, Michael. "More white evangelicals than American Jews say God gave Israel to the Jewish People," *Pew Research Center*, October 3, 2013. (Lipka, *More Evangelicals than Jews Say God Gave Israel to the Jewish People*).

Lipka, Michael. "Muslims expected to surpass Jews as second-largest U.S. religious group," *Pew Research Center*, April 14, 2015. (Lipka, *Muslims Expected to Surpass Jews*).

Nathan-Kazis, Josh. "Orthodox Population Grows Faster Than First Figures in Pew Jewish America Study," *Forward*, November 12, 2013. (Nathan-Kazis, *Orthodox Population Grows Faster*).

Robertson, Pat. "Why Evangelical Christians Support Israel." (Robertson, *Why Evangelicals Support Israel*).

Saxe, Leonard; Fishman, Shira; Shain, Michelle; Wright, Graham; Hecht, Shahar. "Young Adults and Jewish Engagement: The Impact of Taglit-Birthright Israel," *Brandeis University: Maurice and Marilyn Cohen Center for Modern Jewish Studies*, November 2013. (Saxe, *The Impact of Taglit-Birthright Israel*).

Sharp, Jeremy M. "U.S. Foreign Aid to Israel," *Congressional Research Service*, April 11, 2014. (Sharp, *US Foreign Aid to Israel*).

Zelcer, Heshey. "Is This a Turning Point? Gratitude in Flatbush," *Emes Ve-Emunah*, May 11, 2014. (Zelcer, *Is This a Turning Point?*).

"A Burning Campus? Rethinking Israel Advocacy at America's Universities and Colleges," *The David Project*, 2012. ("A Burning Campus," *The David Project*).

"America's Changing Religious Landscape," *Pew Research Center*, May 12, 2015. ("America's Changing Religious Landscape," *Pew Research Center*).

"Top Interest Groups Giving to Members of Congress, 2014 Cycle," *OpenSecrets.org*. ("Top Interest Groups," *Open Secrets*).

Further Reflections on Classification of Mishneh Torah: Real Answers to Real Problems

By: LAWRENCE KAPLAN

This essay, a response to Haym Soloveitchik's essay "Classification of *Mishneh Torah*: Problems Real and Imaginary," recently published in *Collected Essays: Volume* II (Oxford: Littman Library, 2014), pp. 369–377, is based on a lecture I gave at the Annual Conference of the Association for Jewish Studies, Boston, Massachusetts, December 2003, in response to the original Hebrew version of the essay, "Hirhurim 'al Miyyuno shel ha-Rambam be-Mishneh Torah: Be'ayot Amitiyot u-Medummot," *Maimonidean Studies* 4 (2000), 107–115. Professor Soloveitchik was present in the audience. I altered and considerably expanded my original lecture in light of further study on my part, recent scholarship, and some differences between the Hebrew and English versions of Soloveitchik's essay. Soloveitchik's revisions are referred to and discussed below in notes 21, 37, and 46. See, as well, his "Preface" to *Collected Essays II*, p. viii, for his policy regarding revisions to his previously printed essays. All page numbers in the body of my text refer to Soloveitchik's English essay.

Issues of Classification

Haym Soloveitchik begins his incisive and stimulating essay "Classification of *Mishneh Torah*: Problems Real and Imaginary" by drawing two contrasts between the approach to the study of the *Mishneh Torah* by Talmudic scholars and historians. First, "Talmudic scholars...are concerned with specific rulings, and if the meaning of a ruling is not affected in any way by its position in the text, they generally ignore the context. Historians,

---

Lawrence J. Kaplan received his BA from Yeshiva College, his MA and PhD from Harvard University, and his rabbinical ordination from Rabbi Isaac Elchanan Theological Seminary. He has taught at McGill University since 1972, and is currently Professor of Rabbinics and Jewish Philosophy in its Department of Jewish Studies. In 2013 he was a Polonsky Fellow at the Oxford Centre for Hebrew and Jewish Studies.

on the other hand, attempt to understand the system as a whole, the principles of its arrangement and organization" (367). Second, while Talmudic scholars "from the days of the scholars of Lunel in the closing decade of the twelfth century down to our own days" (367) have advanced our understanding of the *Mishneh Torah* by subjecting it to questioning, scrutiny, and query, "Maimonidean scholarship" has tended to substitute "sing[ing] the praises of the *Mishneh Torah*" (367) for such scrutiny and query. One must then combine modern Maimonidean scholarship's concern with the *Mishneh Torah*'s "principles of … arrangement and organization" (367) with the traditional rabbinic approach to its study, which, "without fear or favoritism, questions whatever in the work appears to be problematic." As Soloveitchik notes, "It is through such questioning and only through such that we will be able to arrive at a deeper understanding of Maimonides' teachings.[1]

To be sure, as Soloveitchik's rather vague reference to "Maimonidean scholarship" indicates, many distinguished twentieth-century scholars, among them Boaz Cohen, Isaac Herzog, Chaim Tchernowitz, Lawrence Berman, and Isadore Twersky, preceded Soloveitchik in addressing many of the issues raised by the original system of classification Maimonides constructed for his encyclopedic work, and seeking to understand that system's logic,[2] but, so Soloveitchik suggests, they tended to gloss over

---

1 The last two quotes are from Soloveitchik's Hebrew essay, p. 106.

2 Boaz Cohen, "Classification of the Law: *Mishneh Torah*," *JQR*, 1935, pp. 519–540; Isaac Herzog, "The Order of the Books in *Mishneh Torah*" (Hebrew), in *Rabbeinu Moshe ben Maimon*, ed. Yehudah Leib Fishman (Jerusalem, 1935), pp. 257–264; Chaim Tchernowitz (Rav Tzair), *Toledoth ha-Poskim: History of the Jewish Codes* (Hebrew) New York: The Jubilee Committee, I, 1946; Lawrence V. Berman, "The Structure of the Commandments of the Torah in the Thought of Maimonides," *Studies in Jewish Religious and Intellectual History in Honor of Alexander Altmann*, eds. S. Stein and R. Loewe (Tuscaloosa Ala., 1979), pp. 51–66; and Isadore Twersky, *Introduction to the Code of Maimonides (Mishneh Torah)* (New Haven and London: Yale University Press, 1980), pp. 238–323. Since the appearance of Soloveitchik's Hebrew essay in *Maimonidean Studies*, further studies of Maimonides' classification in the *Mishneh Torah* have appeared: Joseph Tabory, "The Structure of *Mishneh Torah*," in *Traditions of Maimonideanism*, ed. Carlos Fraenkel (Leiden and Boston: Brill, 2009), pp. 51–71; Shamma Friedman, "*Mishneh Torah*: ha-Ḥibbur ha-Gadol" (Hebrew), in *Birkat Moshe: Jubilee Volume in Honor of Rabbi Nahum Eliezer Rabinowitz* (Ma'aleh Adumim: Ma'aliyyot, 2012), pp. 361–368; Asher Benzion Buchman, "The Order of the Books of the *Mishneh Torah*" (Hebrew), *Ḥakirah* 18 (2014), pp. 5–26 (Hebrew numbering); and David Gillis, *Reading Maimonides' Mishneh Torah* (Oxford: Littman Library, 2014), pp. 72–76, 86, 239–260, 319–324, and *passim*. One key question dividing these scholars is the

certain problematic aspects of Maimonides' classification.[3] Soloveitchik points to three types of problems raised by that classification: "problems in the placements of units (i.e., "Laws of X") within a book, problems within the units themselves, and at times, even problems in the internal organization of sub-units" (369). After detailing several problems from all three categories, Soloveitchik concludes, "it is only through solving these and like problems that we will be able to understand the methodology of Maimonides' halakhic classification."[4]

Soloveitchik himself in a subsequent essay, "*Mishneh Torah*: Polemic and Art,"[5] addressed one example of problems in the organization of units, namely the internal organization of *Hilkhot Shabbat*, but otherwise left all the questions he raised unanswered. This paper will take up, if only in part, Soloveitchik's tacit invitation. I will limit myself to the first category, that is, "problems in the placements of units within a book."[6]

How does one determine whether or not a placement of a set of laws in the *Mishneh Torah* is prima facie problematic? First there is the issue, as Soloveitchik notes, of the fit of a unit (i.e., "Laws of X") with the theme of the book of which it forms a part. Maimonides himself calls attention to this issue when offering justifications as to why the "Laws of Circumcision" are placed in the *Book of Love* and the "Laws of Mourning" in the *Book of Judges*.

Second, there is the problem of the tension between, to use Twersky's terms, "overall macroscopic classification and internal microscopic unity,"[7] that is, "between an inner-directed unity of a given section and external integration of this section with the thematic structure and rationale of the whole book in which it is found."[8] Often a unit will contain

---

extent to which Maimonides' scheme of classification in the *Mishneh Torah* breaks with that of the *Mishnah*.

3 Soloveitchik is not being entirely fair here to earlier scholarship. Thus, while Twersky in his magisterial work *Introduction to the Code of Maimonides* certainly "sings the praises of the *Mishneh Torah*," in his chapter on "Classification" (pp. 238–323) he takes ample note, as we shall see, of "stresses and strains in the system" (p. 281)," unexplained difficulties or cruxes in classification" (p. 282), "unexplained trouble spots" (p. 283), and the like.

4 Again, this quote is from Soloveitchik's Hebrew essay, p. 115.

5 "*Mishneh Torah*: Polemic and Art," in Jay M. Harris, ed., *Maimonides 800 Years After: Essays on Maimonides and His Influence* (Cambridge, Mass., 2007), 327–343 [republished in Soloveitchik, *Collected Essays: Volume* II, 387–395].

6 To be precise, Soloveitchik's examples refer not to units ("Laws of X"), but, as we shall immediately see, to sub-units.

7 Twersky, *Introduction*, pp. 291-292.

8 Twersky, *Introduction*, pp. 292-293.

several related topics, say topics *a*, *b*, and *c*, of which, to cite Twersky, only "the first [topic] establishes a thematic link to the book in which it is found."[9] That is, while topics *b* and *c* are related to topic *a*, neither *b* nor *c*, unlike *a*, is related to the book's theme. Thus, again to cite Twersky, while the unit itself forms "an independent and self-contained entity, full integration on both levels is not forthcoming."[10] One might say that topics *b* and *c*, despite their lack of connection with the theme of the book in which they are found, are included in the book by virtue of their being "piggybacked" onto topic *a*, to which they are internally connected.

Among the examples offered by Twersky of this are the "Laws of First Fruits (*bikkurim*) and Other Gifts Offered to the Priests Outside the Sanctuary," in the *Book of Seeds*. As Twersky notes, "the laws of *bikkurim* constitute only one third of the unit, while the bulk is devoted to other non-agricultural gifts, such as setting apart a cake of dough for the priest, giving him parts of an animal, and redeeming a first born son."[11] *Bikkurim* is the opening topic of this unit "in order to warrant the unit's integration into the agricultural *Book of Seeds*,"[12] while the other topics, despite their non-agricultural nature, are included in the unit, alongside *bikkurim*, by virtue of their common character of being gifts offered to the priests outside the sanctuary. In this situation a set of laws could be viewed as problematic only if, in addition to lacking any thematic link to the book in which it is found, it also is not linked in any integral way to the main theme of the unit itself.

Even if the placement of a set of laws in the *Mishneh Torah* is prima facie problematic, the problem can be viewed as a real one, Soloveitchik correctly argues, only if "one can suggest a more appropriate locus" for that set of laws (368). For example, Soloveitchik maintains, while the placement of the "Laws of Mourning" in the *Book of Judges* not only is problematic, but Maimonides himself is aware of and refers to its problematic nature, one cannot criticize his choice of placement, for there isn't any better place in the *Mishneh Torah* into which it can be fit (p. 368).[13]

---

9 Twersky, *Introduction*, p. 291.

10 Twersky, *Introduction*, p. 291.

11 Twersky, *Introduction*, p. 291.

12 Twersky, *Introduction*, p. 291.

13 In truth, as Moshe Halbertal has shown, "further consideration of the placement anomaly [of the "Laws of Mourning" in the *Book of Judges*] provides an indication of how Maimonides understood mourning. It also can account for the organization of the material on mourning and several halakhic decisions related to it." After explaining and elaborating upon his contention, Halbertal concludes that precisely the apparently problematic placement of the "Laws of Mourning" may

In this light, Soloveitchik takes note of two problems regarding the placement of a set of laws in the *Mishneh Torah.* In both cases Soloveitchik argues that the set of laws in the unit in question is, indeed, not linked in any integral way to the main theme of the unit itself, the theme that gives the unit its name, and, even more so, lacks any thematic link to the book in which it is found. Moreover, Soloveitchik contends, in both cases "a more appropriate locus" for that set of laws can be suggested.

I, to the contrary, will argue that in each case: 1) the internal links between the set of laws in question and the main theme of the unit in which it is found are much stronger than Soloveitchik would have us believe; 2) that even if one wishes to argue that the links to which I will point are not sufficiently strong by themselves to justify including that set of laws in the unit in question, the set of laws, in truth, *is* thematically linked to the book in which it is found;[14] and 3) no "more appropriate locus" in the *Mishneh Torah* for that set of laws can be suggested.

First Problem

The first problem Soloveitchik raises is the placement of the laws of lost property *('Avedah)* together with the laws of robbery (*Gezelah*) in the *Book of Torts* (*Nezikin*).

Soloveitchik writes:

The *Book of Torts* (*Nezikin*) treats all the laws dealing with a breach of law or the duty of care, such as theft, robbery, murder, and personal and property damages. Obviously, you will say; why, however, are the laws of lost property *(avedah)* in the *Book of Torts*? Why has Maimonides created a unit "Laws of Robbery and Lost Property" ("Gezelah ve-'Avedah")? If the

---

serve as an example of "the linkage in *Mishneh Torah* between an original organizational structure and a new conceptual understanding of important halakhic principles." See Halbertal, *Maimonides: Life and Thought* (Princeton and Oxford: Princeton University *Press*, 2014), pp. 236–243. More recently, Gillis, *Reading Maimonides' Mishneh Torah*, pp. 319–324, advances the (to my knowledge) novel idea that there are links between the "Laws of Mourning" and the following and concluding unit of the *Mishneh Torah*, the "Laws of Kings and Wars." While I do not find most of the connections Gillis draws particularly persuasive, his link (p. 321) between Maimonides' statement in *Laws of Mourning* 13:11 that death is *minhago shel olam*, the ordinary course of the world, and his statement in *Laws of Kings and Wars* 12:1 that even with the advent of the Messiah *olam ke-minhago noheg*, the world runs its ordinary course, strikes me as suggestive.

14 In one of the two cases, as we shall see, the set of laws is thematically linked to the *original* form of the book in which it is found.

reply be made that someone who does not return lost property is viewed as a robber (*gazlan*),[15] there is the counter that someone who did not pay his workers is equally a robber. Maimonides, however, does not place the laws of hire in the *Book of Torts*. The same holds true of bailments. Conversion of a bailment is robbery, but the laws of bailment are not found in the *Book of Torts*. Correctly so. The fact that the breach of certain obligations by either employer or bailee constitutes robbery turns neither bailment nor hire into a sub-unit of *Torts*.

One may contend that both in robbery and lost property there is a common religious obligation of returning the lost or stolen object (*hashavah*), and this imperative yokes the two together. Why then should one not combine the laws of the Sabbath with those of the festivals (*yom tov*), for both share a common denominator of abstention from work? One might respond that the definitions of work on the Sabbath and on *yom tov* differ from one another: on *yom tov* cooking is permitted, on the Sabbath it is forbidden, and thus the two cannot be combined. Such an argument must answer an obvious question: does this difference outweigh the differences that exist between the obligation of returning lost property and that of returning stolen objects? Truth to tell, there is little in common between these two obligations other than the word *hashavah*. In lost property there is no actual "obligation to return." The obligation is to publicize the find, so that the rightful owner can come to recover his property. After having placed the poster in the public square or the notice in the newspaper, the finder can settle down in his easy chair, never budging until the owner of the lost property rings him up. Not so the thief or the robber. He must actively seek out the owners, and even if they be found in the "lands of the Medes and the Persians," he must travel there and return the stolen object to them.

If the existence of a common religious imperative, in this case that of *hashavah*, suffices to justify placement in the same category in Mishneh Torah, then why not position the laws regulating the Nazirite (*nazir*) alongside those regulating the leper (*metsora*)? Both share a common injunction against shaving. Why shouldn't one combine *halanat sakhar*, *halanat ha-met*, and *halanat kodashim* (*notar*), as they all have a common injunction of *lo talin*? The simple answer is that other than this shared characteristic no member of either group has anything in common with the others. The same holds true for robbery (*Gezelah*) and lost property (*avedah*).

---

15 This suggestion was made by Boaz Cohen, "Classification of the Law," p. 538, n. 68. "These laws [robbery and lost property] are put together because if one fails to return a lost object he violates the prohibition of *lo tigzol* (*Gezelah va-'Avedah* 11:2)."

What alternative placement can be offered for the laws of lost property? Could it be located with equal plausibility outside the *Book of Torts*? I suggest the *Book of Acquisition* (*Kinyan*), alongside the laws of *hefker* (abandoned or ownerless property) and *nikhsei ha-ger*, as, indeed, is found in the *Tur* and the *Shulḥan 'Arukh*. (369-370)

I reply:

Soloveitchik's main point, to which I shall return, that the laws of lost property (*'Avedah)*, inasmuch as they do not involve a tort, do not belong in the *Book of Torts*, alongside the laws of theft, robbery, murder, and personal and property damages, is well taken. However the series of objections he raises against there being any substantive links, any internal connections, between the laws of robbery and the laws of lost property strike me as forced and unconvincing.

With reference to the contention "that both in robbery and lost property there is a common religious obligation of returning the lost or stolen object (*hashavah*), and this imperative yokes the two together," Soloveitchik, as we have seen, responds:

> Truth to tell, there is little in common between these two obligations other than the word *hashavah*. In lost property there is no actual "obligation to return." The obligation is to publicize the find, so that the rightful owner can come to recover his property. After having placed the poster in the public square or the notice in the newspaper, the finder can settle down in his easy chair, never budging until the owner of the lost property rings him up. Not so the thief or the robber. He must actively seek out the owners, and even if they be found in the "lands of the Medes and the Persians," he must travel there and return the stolen object to them.

But is it the case that "there is little in common between these two obligations other than the word *hashavah*"? I wonder how it is that Soloveitchik passes over the central feature that lost property and stolen objects have in common, to wit, that while they still belong to the owner (*shelo*), they are not in his possession (*einam birshuto*), but in the possession of another. The duty of *hashavah* in both the case of a stolen and that of a lost object stems from this fundamental reality, and, according to Maimonides, it places upon the finder of the lost object or the robber the duty to see that the object is restored to its lawful owner in its original condition.

In this connection, Soloveitchik exaggerates the distinctions between the duty of *hashavah* with regard to a robber returning a stolen object and that duty with regard to a finder returning a lost one. First, the duty of a robber to return a stolen object is not as demanding as Soloveitchik would have us believe. Soloveitchik states that "the thief or the robber… must actively seek out the owners, and even if they be found in the 'lands of the Medes and the Persians,' he must travel there and return the stolen object to them." In truth, however, as Maimonides, basing himself on the Talmud, definitively rules:

> If one robs another, even if he denies it, seeing that he did not take an oath, he need not, upon subsequent confession of guilt, chase after the owner to return to him the money in his possession. But the money may remain in the possession of the robber until the owner comes to take what is his.
>
> If, however, one has denied under oath a robbery …he is obligated to pursue the owner to make restitution to him, even if the latter be on the isles of the sea. For the owner will have abandoned hope of recovery, seeing that the robber has already taken an oath, and he will not return to demand it from him. (*Gezelah va-'Avedah* 7:9)

It is clear from Maimonides' rationale for his ruling that the obligation to "actively seek out the owners" is not an integral part of the robber's duty of *hashavah*, but takes effect only as a result of the owner's abandonment of hope of recovery precipitated by the robber's having denied his robbery under oath. Indeed, many eminent authorities infer from Maimonides' rationale that even if a robber denied his robbery under oath, if he succeeded in notifying the owner—say by e-mail—that he wished to make restitution to him, he need not actively seek him out, but "the money may remain in [his] possession … until the owner comes to take what is his."[16]

Nor, on the other hand, is the finder's duty with respect to the lost object quite as undemanding as Soloveitchik portrays it. Soloveitchik colorfully states, "After having placed the poster in the public square or the notice in the newspaper, the finder can settle down in his easy chair, never budging until the owner of the lost property rings him up." Really? At the very least, as Maimonides makes very clear, the finder will have to budge from that easy chair every now and then in order to take care of the object and make sure it does not deteriorate, so that it might be restored to its owner in its original condition. As Maimonides rules, "The finder must pay attention to the lost article and inspect it, so that it will not become spoiled and ruined over the course of time. As the verse states: "And you shall return it to him" (Deut. 22:2). See to it that the article will in fact be

16 See the authorities cited in the *Mafteaḥ* of the Frankel Rambam, ad loc.

returned intact" (*Gezelah va-'Avedah* 13:11).[17] Just consider the lost animals specified by the Bible—the ox, the sheep, the ass—and try to imagine their finder caring for them from his easy chair.... I, for one, would not wish to set foot in his house!

Thus, contrary to Soloveitchik's claim, the two obligations of returning a stolen object and returning a lost one have much in common. Which is precisely why Maimonides refers to the religious obligation of returning the lost or stolen object, both in his short enumeration of the commandments in the Introduction to the *Mishneh Torah* and in the listing of commandments in the heading preceding the "Laws of Robbery and Lost Property" as commandments of *hashavah* ("le-hashiv et ha-gezelah"; "le-hashiv et ha-'Avedah"). And we should not forget that Maimonides' listing and definition of the 613 commandments serves as a primary organizing principle in the *Mishneh Torah* on the unit level.[18]

In addition to the fundamental commandments of *hashavah* regarding both lost property and stolen objects, there are other internal connections between these two categories, most significantly, the critical role that *yeush*

---

17 If the reply be made that the duty of care is derived from Deut. 22:2 and thus is distinct from the commandment to return the lost object whose source is Deut. 22:1, one may counter that, as Rabbi Kenneth Schiowitz suggested to me in private conversation, though the duty of care derives from a different verse than the commandment to return the lost object, it may be not a separate obligation, but an expansion of the duty of *hashavah* set forth in Deut. 22:1. As Rabbi Schiowitz put it to me, "even though the *makor* (source) may be different, that does not mean that it is a separate *ḥiyyuv* (obligation)." In any event, be these conceptual distinctions as they may, Soloveitchik's minimalist description of the duty incumbent upon the finder of a lost object is certainly misleading. One should also note that the Talmud speaks of the finder of the lost object, if he knows who the owner is, *physically* returning the lost object to the owner's domain and thereby freeing himself from any liability for its theft or loss. Indeed, to cite the lucid summary of the eminent twentieth-century rabbinic authority Rabbi Isaac Herzog, "the duty of *haḥzarah*, returning or restoring the lost object to its owner" involves "*netilah*, the duty of taking charge of the found object. If the finder knows to whom the *Avedah* belongs, if, for instance, he came across a cow, known to him, visibly straying, it is his duty to take charge of it until he has brought it to the owner's *reshuth* or premises, a place where it would be reasonably safe. If the owner is unknown to him, it is his duty first to take the found object into his own custody and then to make the matter public (*hakrazah*)." See Isaac Herzog, *The Main Institutions of Jewish Law*, Vol. I (London and New York: Soncino Press, 1965), p. 308.

18 In a comment he made after the lecture I gave at the 2003 Annual Conference of the Association for Jewish Studies (referred to in the Introduction to this essay), Professor Bernard Septimus placed great stress on this point.

(abandonment) plays in both areas. One also ought to note how in chapter six of *Gezelah va-'Avedah* Maimonides skillfully weaves together laws from both these two areas. Finally, I would point to the close connection, already noted by both the *Kesef Mishneh* and (in particular) the *Maggid Mishneh*, between *Gezelah va-'Avedah* 6:2 in the section dealing with robbery and *Gezelah va-'Avedah* 11:10 in the section dealing with lost objects.

As we saw, Soloveitchik queries:

> If the existence of a common religious imperative, in this case that of *hashavah*, suffices to justify placement in the same category in Mishneh Torah, then why not position the laws regulating the Nazirite (*nazir*) alongside those regulating the leper (*metsora*)? Both share a common injunction against shaving. Why shouldn't one combine *halanat sakhar*, *halanat ha-met*, and *halanat kodashim* (*notar*), as they all have a common injunction of *lo talin*?[19]

---

19 Actually, it does not appear to be the case that, for Maimonides, there is an injunction of *lo talin* common to all three areas. In the Short Enumeration of the Commandments in the Introduction to the *Mishneh Torah*, Maimonides with reference to a supposed general prohibition on *halanat kodashim*, in negative commandments 117–120 refers to the prohibitions as "lo totir." Only in negative commandment 116 does he refer to the prohibition of "le-haniaḥ eimurei ha-Pesaḥ 'ad she-yipaslu be-linah." (Note though that in the *Book of Commandments*, negative commandment 116, Maimonides uses the Hebrew word "notar" and not "linah.") In his list of commandments preceding the "Laws of the Paschal Offering" Maimonides, consistent with his language in the Short Enumeration, lists four prohibitions: "she-lo talin eimurav," "she-lo yash'ir mimenu le-boker," "she-lo yash'ir mi-Pesaḥ sheni le-boker," and "she-lo yash'ir me-hagigat 'arb'ah 'asar 'ad yom shelisihi." Similarly consistent with his language in the Short Enumeration, Maimonides in his list of commandments preceding the "Laws of Invalid Offerings" refers to the prohibition of "she-lo yotir kodashim le-aḥar zemanam." With reference to *sekhar sakhir*, in the Short Enumeration, negative commandment 238, Maimonides refers to "lo le-aḥer pe'ulat sakhir," though the verse he cites states "lo talin pe'ulat sakhir." Again, consistent with his language in the Short Enumeration, Maimonides in his list of commandments preceding the "Laws of Hiring" refers to the prohibition of "she-lo ye'aḥer sekhar sakhir le-aḥar zemano." (Note, incidentally, that regarding the biblical source of this prohibition, Maimonides appears to have changed his mind. In the *Book of Commandments* and the Short Enumeration the source of the prohibition is Lev. 19:13, while in the *Laws of Hiring* 11:1 its source is Deut. 24:15.) Only with reference to *halanat ha-met* does Maimonides, both in the Short Enumeration, negative commandment 66 and in his list of commandments preceding the "Laws of Sanhedrin," describe the prohibition as being one of "lo talin." What sub-

He correctly replies: "The simple answer is that other than this shared characteristic no member of either group has anything in common with the others," But, it follows from my analysis that, contrary to Soloveitchik's conclusion, the same does *not* "hold true for *gezelah* and *'avedah*."[20]

---

stantive conclusions, if any, ought to be drawn from these terminological variations of Maimonides is, obviously, beyond the scope of this note. I have only sought to show that Soloveitchik's remark about "a common injunction of '"lo talin"' is not warranted by the evidence.

20 As we saw, in response to the argument that "in robbery and lost property there is a common religious obligation of returning the lost or stolen object (*hashavah*), and this imperative yokes the two together," Soloveitchik queries: "Why then should one not combine the laws of the Sabbath with those of the festivals (*yom tov*), for both share a common denominator of abstention from work? One might respond that the definitions of work on the Sabbath and on *yom tov* differ from one another: on *yom tov* cooking is permitted, on the Sabbath it is forbidden, and thus the two cannot be combined. Such an argument must answer an obvious question: does this difference outweigh the differences that exist between the obligation of returning lost property and that of returning stolen objects?" One may concede Soloveitchik's point that the difference in the definitions of work on the Sabbath and on *yom tov* does not outweigh the differences that exist between the obligation of returning lost property and that of returning stolen objects (though in light of my discussion I am not certain on that point), but offer other reasons as to why Maimonides did not combine the laws of the Sabbath with those of *yom tov*. First there is the issue of length. The "Laws of Sabbath" in its present form is, alongside "The Laws of Sale," the largest unit in the *Mishneh Torah*, consisting of thirty chapters. Had Maimonides combined the laws of the Sabbath with those of the festivals, the result would have been a monstrously large unit of thirty-eight chapters. Maimonides may have felt that there can be too much of a good thing. *Gezelah va-'Avedah* consists of eighteen chapters. Perhaps more important, Maimonides, for practical reasons and perhaps also influenced here by order of the *Mishnah*, decided to have the "Laws of Sabbath" followed by the "Laws of *'Eruvin*," laws that pertain only to the Sabbath and not to *yom tov*. (To be more precise, *'eruvei ḥatzerot*, the subject of Chapters 1-5 of "The Laws of *'Eruvin*," pertain only to the Sabbath and *Yom Kippur*, while *'eruvei teḥumin*, the subject of Chapters 6-8, pertain as well to *yom tov*. See *'Eruvin* 8:4.) "The Laws of *'Eruvin*," in turn, are followed by the "Laws of *Shevitat 'Asor*," Maimonides' unique and provocative formulation (discussed by such eminent contemporary rabbinic authorities as Rabbis Yosef Dov Soloveitchik and Yitzhak Hutner) for the laws of *Yom Kippur* regarding both the prohibition of work and of eating and drinking. The definition of work on Yom Kippur, of course, is the same as the definition of work on the Sabbath and differs from the definition of work on *yom tov*. In sum, if, first, we take into account the already extreme length of the "Laws of Sabbath," and if, second, we look at the "Laws of Sabbath" not in isolation but as the first of a series of thematically

Still, granted these internal links of robbery and lost property, Soloveitchik's main query as to what the laws of lost property are doing in the *Book of Torts,* alongside all the laws dealing with a breach of law or the duty of care, such as theft, robbery, murder, and personal and property damages remains unanswered. As Maimonides states in the Introduction to the *Mishneh Torah*, the *Book of Torts* (*Nezikin*) includes only those commandments "bein adam la-ḥavero, ve-yesh bahen hezek teḥilah," "those commandments between man and man that involve a tort to begin with." However, while finding lost property imposes a commandment between man and man upon the finder, namely, the obligation of returning the lost property to the owner, it does not "involve a tort to begin with."

Where, then, should the laws of lost property be placed? What would be a "more appropriate locus"? As we saw, Soloveitchik suggests that they should be included in "the *Book of Acquisition* (*Kinyan*), together with the laws of *hefker* (abandoned or ownerless property) and *nikhsei ha-ger* [in the laws of *Taking Possession and Gifts* (*Zekhiyyah u-Matannah*)], as, indeed, is found in the *Tur* and the *Shulḥan 'Arukh*."[21] Of course, it is true that *if* the owner of the lost object abandons hope for its recovery, *then* the object becomes ownerless and can be acquired by the finder without *da`at makneh* (resolve on the part of the one who is transferring ownership of the object). It seems to me, however, that this focus on acquisition, again relevant only if the owner abandons hope, ignores what is important for Maimonides about *'avedah*, namely, its *bein adam la-havero* aspect, that is to repeat, that the finding of a lost object under ordinary circumstances imposes upon the finder a commandment of *hashavah*, of returning the lost object, however one chooses to define it. And, again, we must emphasize that Maimonides uses the commandments connected with a particular area of law as a primary organizing principle in the *Mishneh Torah.* Note that Maimonides in the Introduction to the *Mishneh Torah* states that the *Book of Acquisition* (*Kinyan*) "includes the commandments of buying and

related units, the reasons that Maimonides did not combine the laws of the Sabbath with those of *yom tov* become evident. The broader point is that since there are many considerations that went into Maimonides' decisions as to whether or not to conjoin two themes, the fact that a certain consideration does not prevail in a certain unit does not necessarily mean that it should not prevail in another unit, and vice versa.

21 While in his English essay Soloveitchik introduces this suggestion with the appropriately modest "I suggest," in the essay's earlier Hebrew version Soloveitchik advances the suggestion with much greater certainty: "nireh she-ha-teshuvah meḥuveret ke-simlah," "the answer would appear to be as clear as day" (109).

selling." Note, particularly, that there are no commandments at all associated with the "Laws of Taking Possession and Gifts" (*Zekhiyyah u-Matannah*)—one of the four out of eighty-three units for which this is so.[22] Rather, Maimonides states, "the subject matter of these laws is to know the law regarding the person who takes possession of an ownerless article, how he acquires it and the means whereby he acquires it, and [to know] the law governing one who gives a gift and one who receives, and which gift is retracted and which is not." Do the laws governing lost property really belong, then, in the "Laws of Taking Possession and Gifts" (*Zekhiyyah u-Mattanah*) in the *Book of Acquisition* (*Kinyan*)? Well, maybe. But I would suggest that a much more appropriate place would be for these laws to be a separate unit in the *Book of Judgments* (*Mishpatim*), which, as Maimonides states in the Introduction to the *Mishneh Torah*, includes commandments "bein adam la-ḥavero bi-she'ar ha-dinin sh'ein bi-teḥilahtan hezek," "those commandments between man and man regarding the other laws that do not involve a tort to begin with." Be that as it may, Soloveitchik's fundamental question as to what the laws of lost property are doing in the *Book of Torts* (*Nezikin*) remains unanswered.

But there is, I would suggest, a tacit assumption underlying this query, namely, that Maimonides *first* divided the *Mishneh Torah* into books and *then* subdivided it into units, determining the nature of the units in terms of how they would fit into the books. But an examination of the history of the composition of the *Mishneh Torah*, as determined from a reading of the Introduction to the *Book of Commandments* and the Introduction to the *Mishneh Torah*, indicates that originally Maimonides just intended to divide the *Mishneh Torah* into *halakhot*, groups of laws; the division of the work into 14 books took place at a later stage in its composition. As Herbert Davidson has noted, "Maimonides does not appear to have regarded the division into fourteen books as essential to his plan, since he does not mention it when describing the projected structure of the code in the *Book of Commandments*—he may not even have decided on it yet—or when outlining the structure at the beginning of the code itself."[23]

Thus in his discussion of the structure of the *Mishneh Torah* in his Introduction to the Book *of Commandments*, Maimonides writes:

---

22 The other three are "The Laws of Vessels," "The Laws of Neighbors," and the "Laws of Agents and Partners." It is interesting that three of these four units are in the *Book of Acquisition*. This has already been noted by Twersky, *Introduction*, p. 260, n. 46.

23 Herbert Davidson, *Moses Maimonides: The Man and his Work* (Oxford and New York: Oxford University Press, 2005), p. 213.

> And it appeared to me that the best way to divide the book would be to replace the tractates of the Mishnah with groups of laws (*Halakhot*), for example *Hilkhot Sukkah*, *Hilkhot Lulav*, *Hilkhot Tefillin*, *Hilkhot Mezuzah*, and *Hilkhot Tzitzit*. And that I would divide each general category into chapters and paragraphs (*halakhot*), as the *Mishnah* had done. For example: in *Hilkhot Tefillin* there would be Chapter 1, Chapter 2, Chapter 3, and Chapter 4, and each chapter would be divided into paragraphs, so that it will be easy for anyone who so wishes to know it by heart.

Nary a mention here of any books.

Even more telling—and here I am elaborating on Davidson—an examination of the Introduction to the *Mishneh Torah* reveals that it consists of two distinct strata. The first and earlier stratum extends from the beginning of the Introduction to the short enumeration of the 613 commandments, followed by a brief discussion of the authority of the rabbinic commandments, and concluding with "Ve-'al derekh zeh kol mitzvah u-mitzvah she-hu mi-divrei sofrim, beyn 'aseh, beyn lo ta'aseh," "And this is the case regarding every rabbinic commandment, whether it is a positive or a negative commandment." This stratum also includes the very last sentence of the Introduction "ve-'atah atḥil le-va'er mishhpetei kol mitzvah u-mitzvah, ve-khol ha-dinin ha-niglalin 'imah mei-'inyeneha 'al seder ha-halakhot be-'ezrat Shadai." "And now I will begin to explain the rules of each and every commandment, and all the laws are connected with it in its various aspects, following the order of the halakhot, with the help of God." Again, in this early stratum, as in his Introduction to the Book *of Commandments*, there is no mention of books. We just saw that in the very last sentence of this stratum there is no mention of books. Similarly, in the body of the first stratum, just before the short enumeration of the 613 commandments, Maimonides writes, "Ve-ra'iti leḥalek ḥibbur zeh halakhot halakhot bekhol `inyan ve- `inyan, ve-aḥalek et ha-halakhot li-perakim she-be-oto 'inyan, ve-khol perek u-perek aḥalek oto li-halakhot ketanot, kedei she-yehu sedurin be- 'al peh," "And I saw fit to divide this work into units (*Halakhot*) for each and every subject, and to divide the units into chapters, and to divide each chapter into small paragraphs (*halakhot*), so that they may be all be memorized." The similarity between this statement and the one cited just above from the *Book of Commandments* is evident.

The second stratum consists of the section immediately following Maimonides' discussion of the authority of the rabbinic commandments. It begins with "Ve-ra'iti le-ḥalek ḥibbur zeh le-`arba`a 'asar sefarim," "And I saw fit to divide this work into fourteen books," continues with a list of those fourteen books and the subject matter of the commandments each book contains, and then proceeds to give a complete table of contents, enumerating all the fourteen books together with all their halakhot and all the commandments in each halakhah, introducing the table of contents with "Ve-zeh hu ḥilluk halakhot shel ḥibbur zeh lefi 'inyenei ha-sefarim; ve-ḥilluk ha-mitzvot lefi 'inyenei ha-halakhot," "And this is the division of the halakhot of this book in accordance with the subject matter of the books, and the division of the commandments according to the subject matter of the *Halakhot*," and concluding it with the statement "Ve-nimtzeu kol ha-halakhot shel arba'a 'asar sefer shalosh u-shemonim halakhot," "Thus the total of all the *Halakhot* of [these] fourteen books is eighty-three *Halakhot*."

Indeed, readers who will perform the simple exercise of excising the second stratum from the introduction will not notice that anything is missing. It is, thus, clear that Maimonides spliced the later stratum dealing with the books into the earlier stratum dealing with halakhot just before the earlier stratum's very last sentence.[24]

It appears that Maimonides, in order to make the *Mishneh Torah* less atomistic, changed his original plans in two ways. First, such units as *shofar*, *lulav* and *sukkah*, which, as the Introduction to the *Book of Commandments* indicates, had originally been intended to be separate units, were grouped by him into a single unit. A *genizah* fragment indicates that Maimonides had originally planned that the "Laws of Borrowing" (*She'eilah*) be an independent unit, but then decided to combine it with the "Laws of Deposits" (*Pikkadon*).[25] And second, he decided to divide the work as a whole into a few overarching parts, namely, *Sefarim*, corresponding to the Mishnah's *Sedarim*.

When exactly did the Maimonides decide to divide the *Mishneh Torah* into *Sefarim*? The evidence is not clear. Perhaps some will say that this

---

24 Twersky, *Introduction*, notes this, but does not seem to appreciate its full significance. "The elemental division of the *Mishneh Torah* into fourteen books, the real core of his classification, is mentioned for the first time, quite unobtrusively, in what looks like a postscript to the Mishneh Torah introduction" (p. 260). As we have seen, however, "the elemental division of the *Mishneh Torah* into fourteen books" was, to begin with, *not* "the real core of his classification," and its first mention in what I have referred to as the second and later stratum of the introduction does not just "look... like a postscript," but, indeed, is a postscript.

25 See *Keta'im mi-Sefer Yad ha-Ḥazakah le-Rabbenu Moshe ben Maimon*, ed. *Samuel Atlas* (London, 1940), p. 43; reprinted with the notes of Moshe Lutzky as an addendum to the fifth volume of the Schulsinger edition of the *Mishneh Torah* (New York, 1947), p. 14.

division took place at a relatively early stage of the *Mishneh Torah*'s composition before Maimonides had begun any intensive work on the *Halakhot.* Indeed, I tend to think that this is the case. Nevertheless, my impression is that Maimonides focused mainly on crafting individual units that would possess inner thematic coherence, and that the issue of the integration of the unit's theme into the overall theme of the book of which it forms a part was often secondary.[26] Perhaps we may envisage Maimonides as moving from unit to book to unit and back again.

Be this as it may, as evidence from the *Genizah* indicates, even *after* Maimonides decided to divide the *Mishneh Torah* into *Sefarim,* he was still unclear as to the exact number of *Sefarim* and their contents. More important—and this is the critical point—the evidence indicates that at a relatively late stage of composition the *Book of Torts* did not exist as a separate book![27]

The *Book of Judgments* (*Mishpatim*) is the thirteenth book of the *Mishneh Torah* in its final version. It includes, as noted earlier, those commandments "bein adam la-ḥavero bi-she'ar ha-dinin sh'ein bi-teḥilahtan hezek,"

---

26 Here the example, discussed earlier in the text, of the "Laws of First Fruits (*bikkurim*) and Other Gifts Offered to the Priests Outside the Sanctuary," in the *Book of Seeds* is instructive. An examination of the first chapter of this unit, which presents a sweeping survey of all twenty-four priestly gifts, indicates that Maimonides views the gifts offered to the priests outside the sanctuary as a unit, consisting of six gifts, from which it follows that his singling out *bikkurim* from the other gifts in the title "Laws of First Fruits (*bikkurim*) and Other Gifts Offered to the Priests Outside the Sanctuary" is a rather awkward and makeshift attempt to establish some link between the unit and the agricultural *Book of Seeds.* Note, in this connection, that in the *Laws of Firstlings* (*Bekhorot*) 1:7 Maimonides refers back to the *Laws of First Fruits and Other Gifts Offered to the Priests Outside the Sanctuary* 11:9 and 12:14, but terms the unit there the "Laws of Gifts Offered to the Priests" (*Matennot Kehunah*). Further evidence that Maimonides primarily thought in terms of the inner thematic coherence of the individual unit and that the issue of the integration of the unit's theme into the overall theme of the book of which it forms a part was often secondary may be provided by Maimonides' elaborate internal cross-referencing in the body of the *Mishneh Torah.* An examination of this cross-referencing reveals that there are some two hundred or so cross-references to *Halakhot*, e.g., "as we have explained in *Hilkhot* so and so," "as we will explain in *Hilkhot* so and so," and the like. There are exactly *eight* references to Books (*Sefarim*). Seven are internal cross-references: "As we have explained in this book;" only one is a cross-reference to another book: "As we have explained in the fifth Book (*Sefer Hamishi*)." Note in the latter instance that the book lacks a title.

27 When I refer to "a relatively late stage of composition," the emphasis should be on the word "relatively." See below, note 29.

"those commandments between man and man regarding the other laws that do not involve a tort to begin with," and consists of five units (*Halakhot*) in the following order: "Hiring" (*Sekhirut*), "Borrowing and Deposits" (*She'eilah u-Fikkadon*), "Lenders and Borrowers" (*Malveh ve-Loveh*), "Litigation" (*To'en ve-Nit'an*) and "Inheritances" (*Naḥalot*). However, this was not Maimonides' original plan.

The *Genizah* fragment, TS 10 K8, f.1 (University Library, Cambridge) (see Figures 1 and 2) is a single page in Maimonides' own hand, containing a draft of the very first page of the *Book of Judgments* (*Mishpatim*) in its original form.[28] Here the *Book of Judgments* is not the thirteenth book of the *Mishneh Torah*, but the eleventh book (*Sefer Ahad 'Asar*). Moreover, it does not consist of five but of fourteen units (*Halakhot*), though Maimonides does not list them. Finally, and perhaps most important, the first unit (*Halakhah*) is not "Hiring" (*Sekhirut*), but "Torts" (*Nezikin*), which title Maimonides at some subsequent point crossed out, replacing it with its present title "Torts Committed by one's Property" (*Nizke Mamon*). As is clear, however, from the manuscript, the basic contents of this unit, whether titled "Torts" (*Nezikin*) or "Torts Committed by one's Property" (*Nizke Mamon*), were always the same as they are now, treating of four commandments: the law of the ox, the law of the pit, the law of the grazing animal, and the law of fire.[29]

What does this fragment, then, tell us about the intention of the Maimonides at this stage? I believe the answer is clear. As we saw earlier, there is a conceptual connection, in Maimonides' view, between the *Book of Torts* and the *Book of Judgments* in their present forms. The *Book of Torts* in its present form includes those commandments "bein adam la-ḥavero, ve-yesh bahen hezek teḥilah," "those commandments between man and man that involve damage to begin with," while the *Book of Judgments* in its present form includes those commandments "bein adam la-ḥavero bi-she'ar ha-dinin sh'ein bi-teḥilahtan hezek," "those commandments between man and man regarding the other laws that do not involve a tort to begin

---

28 See Elazar Hurvitz "Seridim Nosafim le-Sefer Mishneh Torah le-ha-Rambam," *Hadorom* 38 (1973), pp. 22-23, 38.

29 Note, though, that the order of the commandments in the fragment differs from the order of the commandments in the final published version of *Nizke Mamon*. Moreover, Maimonides in the fragment significantly revises the text of the very first halakhah—alas, the only halakhah preserved—striking out the phrase "eḥad ha-behemah, ve-eḥad ha-ḥayyah, ve-eḥad ha-'ofot," and inserting in its stead "she-harei mamonam hizik," the phrase found in the final version. All this would appear to indicate that what we have here is an early draft.

הרב אלעזר הורביץ 38

עמוד ה

University Library, Cambridge, TS 10 K8, f.1

הרב אלעזר הורביץ 22

העתקה — עמוד ה

ספר אחד עשר והוא ספר משפטים
הלכותיו ארבע עשרה וזה הוא סדורן... כתב...
נמצאו כל המצוות בו (?)

נזקי ממון
הלכות ~~נזיקים~~

יש בכללן ארבע מצוות עשה וזה הוא פרטן ה
א׳ דין השור ג׳ דין הבור ב׳ דין ההבער
ד׳ דין הבערה וביא[ור] מצוות אלו בפרקים אלו

פרק ראשון

כל נפש חיה שהיא ברשותו שלאדם שהזיקה
שהרי ממונם הזיק
הבעלים חייבין לשלם, ~~אחד הבהמה ואחד~~ י
~~החיה ואחד העופות~~ שנ׳ כי יגוף שור איש
את שור רעהו וכו׳ אחד השור ואחד שאר

with." Maimonides' original plan, then, was that there be *not* a separate *Book of Torts*, but one massive *Book of Judgments* that would include *all* mitzvot "bein adam la-ḥavero," *all* "the commandments between man and man," whether "yesh bahen hezek teḥilah," or "ein bi-teḥilahtan hezek," that is, irrespective of whether or not they involve a tort to begin with.[30]

Soloveitchik's question as to "why … are the laws of lost property *(avedah)* in the *Book of Torts*?" is now resolved. When Maimonides conjoined the Laws of Lost Property with those of Robbery there was no *Book of Torts*![31] Maimonides conjoined these two sets of laws because of

30 Hurvitz, "Seridim Nosafim," p. 32, suggests that the original *Book of Judgments* included nor only the *Book of Torts* and the *Book of Judgments*, but also the *Book of Acquisition*. This is highly doubtful. First, as we have seen, there is a conceptual connection between the *Book of Torts* and the *Book of Judgments* in their present form, the current *Book of Torts* containing those mitzvot "bein adam le-ḥavero ve-yesh bahen hezek teḥilah," the current *Book of Judgments* containing those mitzvot "bein adam le-ḥavero bi-she'ar ha-dinin sh'ein bi-teḥilahtan hezek." One can, then, imagine an original *Book of Judgments* that would include *all* mitzvot "bein adam le-ḥavero," *all* "the commandments between man and man," whether "yesh bahen hezek teḥilah," or "ein bi-teḥilahtan hezek," that is, irrespective of whether or not they involve a tort to begin with. But there is no conceptual connection between the *Book of Torts* and the *Book of Judgments*, on the one hand, and the *Book of Acquisition* on the other. How could one imagine, then, a *Book of Judgments* that in addition to including *all* mitzvot "bein adam le-ḥavero," would also include the laws of buying and selling? Possible, but unlikely. Second, according to Maimonides' draft, the *Book of Judgments* in its original form consisted not of five but of fourteen units (*Halakhot*). The *Book of Torts* and the *Book of Judgments* in their present form contain a total of ten units. One can explain the reduction from fourteen units to ten by Maimonides' practice of combining what had been originally intended to be independent units, for example, as we have seen, his decision to combine the "Laws of Borrowing" with the "Laws of Deposits," though both had originally been intended to be independent units. However, the *Book of Torts,* the *Book of Judgments*, and the *Book of Acquisition* in their present form contain a total of fifteen units. Given Maimonides' practice of combining what had been originally intended to be independent units, one would, then, have expected an original *Book of Judgments* that included the *Book of Torts*, the *Book of Judgments*, and the *Book of Acquisition* in their present form to have consisted of much more than fourteen units.

31 In light of the undeniable evidence provided by Maimonides' draft, we must unequivocally reject Twersky's claim (*Introduction*, p. 308) that "as best as can be determined …there is no indication that Maimonides considered alternate arrangements of the fourteen books…The underlying fourteen-book sequence is a constant." (I should note that Twersky's bibliography includes Hurvitz's, "Seridim Nosafim le-Sefer Mishneh Torah le-ha-Rambam.") Indeed, one wonders whether Maimonides had originally intended that the *Book of Temple Service*

the internal connections between them indicated earlier, and he included this combined unit in the *Book of Judgments*, which included all *mitzvot bein adam la-havero,* whether "yesh bahen hezek teḥilah," like *Gezelah*, or "ein bi-teḥilahtan hezek," like *'Avedah*. It was only sometime *after* completing a draft of the unit of *Gezelah* va-*'Avedah* that Maimonides decided to split the *Book of Judgments* into two, thereby creating a new *Sefer*, the *Book of*

(*Abodah*) and the *Book of Sacrifices* (*Korbanot*) be one book and decided to split it into two books only at a later stage of composition, so as to avoid an inordinately large book. (The *Book of Temple Service* contains nine units, while the *Book of Sacrifices* contains six units. Had they been combined into one book, that book would have contained fifteen units, by far exceeding the number of units in what is now the largest book of the *Mishneh Torah*, the *Book of Seasons* (*Zemanim*), which contains ten units.) Note that according to Maimonides' Introduction to the *Mishneh Torah* there is a conceptual connection between the *Book of Temple Service*, which includes, among other things, "the commandments concerning… the regular communal sacrifices," and the *Book of Sacrifices*, which includes "the commandments concerning the sacrifices brought by a private individual," just as there is a conceptual connection between the *Book of Torts* and the *Book of Judgments*—and, as we saw, the latter were originally intended to be one book. That the *Book of Temple Service* (*Abodah*) and the *Book of Sacrifices* (*Korbanot*) were originally intended to be one book would help account for a certain overlap between them. Indeed, Twersky himself describes the *Book of Sacrifices* as "a direct continuation of the preceding [book]" (p. 267). Still there is no textual evidence supporting this suggestion, and unless further evidence is forthcoming, it must remain in the realm of conjecture. For a different approach to the issue of Maimonides' division of the laws of sacrifices into two books, see Tabory, "The Structure of *Mishneh Torah*," pp. 62-63. I should note that Gillis in *Reading Maimonides' Mishneh Torah* argues that the division of the *Mishneh Torah* into fourteen books, the first ten books dealing with commandments between man and God and the last four dealing with commandments between man and his fellow, is of profound philosophical—indeed cosmic—significance. To cite him, "the first ten books with their exalted themes are parallel to the ten orders of angels, or to the nine spheres plus the agent intellect, and, like them, are ordered hierarchically, while the mundane last four books are parallel to the four elements of matter" (pp. 3-4). I believe that the facts I have brought to light, namely, that 1) the division of the *Mishneh Torah* into books was, to begin with, not part of Maimonides' scheme of classification, and 2) that even when Maimonides decided to divide the *Mishneh Torah* into books, the division into exactly fourteen books in their current sequence was not fixed in stone, tend to undercut Gillis' provocative claim. But this matter requires a separate discussion.

Torts.[32] Naturally he put *Gezelah* va-*'Avedah* in the newly created *Book of Torts.*[33]

---

32 Maimonides' decision to remove the units dealing with torts from the original *Book of Judgments* and create an independent *Book of Torts* explains, in my view, why Maimonides in the *Genizah* fragment containing the draft of the very first page of the *Book of Judgments* (*Mishpatim*) in its original form crossed out "Torts" (*Nezikin*) and replaced it with its present title, "Torts Committed by Chattel" (*Nizke Mamon*). I would suggest that Maimonides was already considering creating an independent *Book of Torts* (*Nezikin*), and he did not want to have both a unit and a book called *Nezikin*. Note that nowhere in the *Mishneh Torah* are a unit and the book it is part of called by the same name. However, both Elazar Hurvitz, "Seridim Nosafim," p. 32, and Shamma Friedman, "*Mishneh Torah*: ha-Ḥibbur ha-Gadol," p. 362, argue that the change of name indicates a change in content. Aside from all the other problems with their suggestions, which I will discuss immediately, their suggestions must be rejected because, as I have indicated, it is clear from the manuscript that the basic contents of this unit were always the same as they are now, treating of four commandments: the law of the ox, the law of the pit, the law of the grazing animal, and the law of fire. Hurvitz suggests that *Hilkhot Nezikin*, the "Laws of Torts," originally contained all five units of what is now *Sefer Nezikin*, the *Book of Torts*: "Torts Committed by Chattel" (*Nizke Mamon*), "Theft" (*Genevah*)," "Robbery and Lost Property" (*Gezelah va-'Avedah*), "Wounding and Torts" (*Ḥovel u-Mazzik*), and "Murder and Preservation of Life" (*Rotzeaḥ u-Shemirat Nefesh*). That Maimonides ever considered such a unit, covering such a wide variety of laws and containing (based on the total number of chapters in the current five units) sixty-two (!) chapters, more than twice as much as the thirty chapters contained in the "Laws of Sabbath" and the "Laws of Sale," the largest units in the *Mishneh Torah*, is, to say the least, extremely unlikely on the face of it. This is not to mention that Maimonides' beginning with such a monstrously large unit and then breaking it down into smaller units goes completely against what we have seen to be his standard procedure of combining smaller units to form larger ones. Friedman suggests that *Hilkhot Nezikin*, the "Laws of Torts," originally contained the laws about a person who damaged another's property, and not just the laws about damages committed by chattel. Maimonides removed the laws about a person who damages another's property (*mazzik*) and combined them with the laws about a person who wounds his fellow (*hovel*) to create the unit "Wounding and Torts" (*Ḥovel u-Mazzik*). Friedman's explanation is more plausible than Hurvitz's, but still unacceptable. First, if one assumes, as I do, that the contents of the units *Nezikin* (as it was originally called) or *Nizke Mamon* (the new name Maimonides gave it) and *Ḥovel u-Mazzik* were always the same as they are now, we have a neat symmetry: the first unit contains (and always contained) the laws of damages by chattel, whether to property or to people, while the second unit contains (and always contained) the laws of damages committed by a person, whether to property or to people. However, according to Friedman, the first unit originally contained the laws of damages by chattel, whether to property or to people, as well

If there is a problem, it is a different and much weaker one. Not Soloveitchik's question as to why the Maimonides conjoined the Laws of Lost Property with those of Robbery to begin with. That question has just been answered. But one can ask how come when Maimonides in the *final* draft of the *Mishneh Torah* decided to divide the original *Book of Judgments* into two books—one being the *Book of Torts* containing only those mitzvot "bein adam la-ḥavero ve-yesh bahen hezek teḥilah," the other the current *Book of Judgments* containing only those mitzvot "bein adam la-ḥavero bi-she'ar ha-dinin sh'ein bi-teḥilahtan hezek"—he did not *at that point* detach the laws of *'Avedah* from *Gezelah*, place *'Avedah* as a separate unit in

---

as the laws of damages committed by a person to property, while the second unit originally contained only the laws regarding a person wounding his fellow. Second, it is difficult to see how Maimonides could originally have contemplated separating the laws regarding a person wounding another from the laws regarding a person damaging another's property, since Maimonides in his heading to the "Laws of Wounding and Torts" states that the administration of the laws concerning a person who wounds his fellow and the laws concerning a person who damages another's property constitutes a single positive commandment. (Note, however, that Positive Commandment 236, in both the *Book of Commandments* and the Short Enumeration of the Commandments, refers to the administration of the laws concerning a person who wounds his fellow. But as Maimonides explains in his discussion in the *Book of Commandments*, this commandment, by extension, takes in all the laws of monetary fines for damages (*kenasot*), including, in addition to the fundamental case of damages caused by a person to his fellow, also the cases of damages caused by a person to an animal or an animal to a person. It should follow from this that Chapters 10 and 11 of *Nizke Mamon*, dealing with an ox that kills a person, really belong in *Ḥovel u-Mazzik*.) But again, the main argument against Hurvitz's and Friedman's suggestions regarding the conjoining of the laws of robbery with the laws of lost property is that it is clear from the draft of the first page of the original *Book of Judgments* that the basic contents of the "Laws of Damages by Chattel," whatever the change in the unit's name, were always the same as they are now.

33 It is strange that while Soloveitchik, p. 373, refers to Maimonides' draft of the first page of the "Laws of borrowing and Deposits" (see note 25), he never refers to this draft of the first page of the original *Book of Judgments*, despite its relevance to the question he poses regarding Maimonides' conjoining the laws of lost property with the laws of robbery. Perhaps even stranger is that though Friedman ("*Mishneh Torah*: ha-Ḥibbur ha-Gadol," p. 362), as we saw in the previous note, *does* refer to Maimonides' draft of the first page of the original *Book of Judgments*, he does so only in connection with Maimonides' changing the name of its original first unit from *Nezikin* to *Nizke Mamon*, and despite the fact that he struggles to answer Soloveitchik's question, he evidently fails to appreciate how that draft could have enabled him to—at least in my view—easily answer it.

Book of Judgments, and do the necessary restructuring and rewriting of both units? I think the simple answer in a word or, to be more precise, in two words is—human nature. After all, as we saw, when Maimonides decided to divide the *Mishneh Torah* into *Sefarim*, he spliced the section dealing with *Sefarim* into his Introduction to the *Mishneh Torah*, which originally dealt only with the units (*Halakhot*), and did not rewrite the earlier stratum at all. Consider, in particular, the last sentence of the Introduction, which, as we saw, is from the earlier stratum. "Ve-'atah atḥil le-va'er mishpetei kol mitzvah u-mitzvah, ve-khol ha-dinin ha-niglalin 'imah mei-'inyeneha 'al seder ha-halakhot be-'ezrat Shadai," "And now I will begin to explain the rules of each and every commandment, and all the laws that are connected with it in its various aspects, following the order of the units, with the help of God." How much effort would it have required for Maimonides to rewrite this sentence and insert a reference to the *Sefarim* into it? Yet he did not do it.

There is a well-known *halakhah* that even though a *kinyan*, a formal act of transfer, is required to pass value or money to another party, *meḥilah*, waiver, that is, an agreement to release another party from a debt, does not require a *kinyan*, since, as Rabbi Isaac Herzog observes, "it is an agreement for something passive, and sheer mental assent conveyed by word of mouth is quite sufficient."[34] As we all know, when we are working on a major project, we wish, to begin with, to make it as perfect, as ideal, as possible. However, when we have worked on something for a long time and at a very late stage of the project, when we have essentially completed the work, we decide to make one easily accomplished structural change, and we then realize that that change in turn requires of us, if we want things to be ideal, further major restructuring and rewriting—well that is another story. And this is an age of word processing! In such circumstances it does not require that much mental assent to passively let things remain as they are.

Perhaps the reader will object that that is true for ordinary human beings like ourselves, but we are speaking here about Maimonides, the great eagle, *ha-nesher ha-gadol*. All I can say is: "even so." Of course, Maimonides kept on revising the *Mishneh Torah* throughout the rest of his life. But those were substantive halakhic revisions of individual rulings. There is evidence that, to cite Herbert Davidson, "Perhaps Maimonides was so eager to finish his immense project that he neglected, as writers often do,

---

34 See Isaac Herzog, *The Main Institutions of Jewish Law*, Vol. II (London and New York: Soncino Press, 1967), p. 115.

to go back a tedious final time and submit his code to one more editing."[35] Moreover, Maimonides might have thought to himself that in addition to the restructuring and rewriting that would be necessitated by his detaching *'Avedah* from *Gezelah* and presenting them both as separate units, such detaching would fly in the face of his goal of combining units instead of multiplying them.

One thing I believe. Had Maimonides clearly decided to have two separate *Sefarim*, the *Book of Torts* containing only those commandments "bein adam la-ḥavero ve-yesh bahen hezek teḥilah," and the *Book of Judgments*, as it is in its present form, containing only those commandments "bein adam la-ḥavero bi-she'ar ha-dinin sh'ein bi-teḥilahtan hezek," *before* he started working on *Gezelah va-'Avedah*, *Gezelah* would, of course, have been, as it is now, in the *Book of Torts*, perhaps combined with *Genevah*, while *'Avedah* most probably would have been a separate unit in the *Book of Judgments*, or—much less likely—in "Zekhiyyah u-Matannah" in the *Book of Acquisition*, as Soloveitchik suggests. I do not believe that under those circumstances Maimonides would have combined *'Avedah* with *Gezelah* in the *Book of Torts*, despite the links connecting them.

Second Problem

The second problem Soloveitchik raises is the placement of the laws of conversion (*gerut*) in "Laws of Forbidden Sexual Relations" *(Issurei Biah)* in *Sefer Kedushah*, the *Book of Holiness*.

---

35 Davidson, *Moses Maimonides*, p. 231; see also Eliav Schochetman, "Makkat mardut be-Mishnat ha-Rambam—Gishah Ḥadashah le-Sugyat ha-Hashmatot be-Mishneh Torah la-Rambam," *Meḥkarim be-Halakhah u-ve-Maḥshevet Yisrael: Jubilee Volume in Honor of Rabbi Professor Emanuel Rackman*, ed. Moshe Beer (Ramat-Gan: Bar-Ilan University, 1994), pp. 91–119. Davidson's main argument in support of his view that the *Mishneh Torah* lacked a final editing is "the occasions on which, rather than polishing and clarifying the rulings he records, [Maimonides] simply repeats statements or phrases verbatim from classic sources that even… readers fully adept in rabbinic law will fail to understand unless they happen to remember the precise context in the classic sources from which Maimonides draws" (p. 231). One minor stylistic indication of this absence of a final editing may be found in the slight variations in the names of its units found in Maimonides' cross references. (See above, note 26.) Thus, for example, as a computer word search or perusal of Volume 4 (containing the letter ה) of David Assaf, *Concordance to the Mishneh Torah*, Haifa, 1978, will indicate, Maimonides alternates between "Mekhirah" and "Mekaḥ u-Memkar," "Issure Bi'ah" and "Bi'ot Asurot," and "Ma'akhalot Asurot" and "Issure Ma'akhlot"; consistently refers to "Hilkhot Malveh ve-Loveh" as "Hilkhot Halva'ah"; and once (*Avot ha-Tume'ot* 15:4) even refers to "Tume'at Tzara'at" as "Nega'im." (In the last case Maimonides, perhaps instinctively, seems to have reverted to the Mishnaic name.)

Soloveitchik writes:

Maimonides places the laws of conversion (*gerut*) in "Laws of Forbidden Sexual Relations" ("Issurei Biah"). True, conversion (plus marriage) permits a sexual relationship between a Jew and a former Gentile. However, is the purpose and r*aison d'etre* of conversion to permit sexual intercourse? Conversion would have fit more properly in any one of three places in the *Book of Knowledge* (*Madda'*): (1) At the end of "Laws of the Fundamentals of Faith" ("Yesodei ha-Torah"), which treats recognizing and acknowledging the one sole God. If the erasure of the Divine Name (*meḥikat ha-shem*) has its place in *Yesodei ha-Torah*, surely conversion, the classic recognition and acknowledgment of God, has an equal claim. (2) After "Laws of Idolatry" ("Avodah Zarah"). Conversion would serve as a perfect foil to the denial of God discussed here. Doubly so, as Maimonides opened the laws of *avodah ẓarah* with his famous portrait of Abraham, who began as an idolater and after a forty-year quest arrived at the recognition of the true God. Moreover, Abraham is viewed as the father of all converts. Rounding off the laws of idolatry with the opening theme would give that section a literary unity, something that Maimonides was eminently aware of. (3) Lastly, they could have been placed at the end of "Laws of Repentance," concluding the *Book of Knowledge* with conversion, for reasons I shall soon point out.

Had the laws of conversion been placed in the *Book of Knowledge*, the problems of the location of the laws of circumcision would have been solved, for circumcision is an essential component of conversion and the two fit naturally side by side. Indeed they are so found in the *Tur* and the *Shulḥan 'Arukh*. The issue goes deeper. Maimonides was wont to end each book of the *Mishneh Torah* with a peroration, and, when possible, to link one book to the next. This makes the ending of the *Book of Knowledge* with conversion and circumcision especially appealing, as he could have melded various section of that book into a memorable ending that linked up with the coming *Book of Adoration* (*Ahavah*). He could have joined conversion and circumcision with his famous remarks about Abraham's long quest for the true God in "Laws of Idolatry" and fused them with his ending of "Laws of Repentance ("Teshuvah") and the timeless words he wrote to Obadiah the proselyte in approximately this fashion:

> על פי הדעה וההכרה תהיה האהבה, אם מעט מעט ואם הרבה הרבה. ומי ששטט בדעתו כמו אותו איתן עד שהכיר את בוראו ונכספה נפשו לאהוב את ה', ורדף אחריו והלך בדרך הקודש עד שנכנס תחת כנפי השכינה, הרי הוא מבניו של אברהם אבינו, שבבריתו נכנס, שנאמר אב המון גויים נתתיך, ועליו אמר הכתוב, זרע אברהם אוהבי.

> According to the understanding and recognition will be the love. If [the former is] little, [so will the latter be] little; if [the former is] great, [so will the latter be] great. And he whose mind began to reflect about the world as did that titan [Abraham] until he came to recognize his creator and his soul longed for the love of God, and he pursued Him and went in the path of holiness until he came under the wings of the *Shekhinah*, he is indeed a son of Abraham our father, for he [the searcher-convert] has entered into his [i.e. Abraham's] covenant for it is written [Gen. 17:4] "thou shalt be the father of many nations"; and about him the verse was said [Isaiah [Isa.41:8], "[he is] of the seed of Abraham who did love me." (pp. 370–372)

I reply:

Just as Soloveitchik minimizes the connections between the laws of lost property and those of robbery, so he minimizes the connections between the laws of conversion and the broader rubric of the "Laws of Forbidden Sexual Relations." Soloveitchik writes as if the only connection between conversion and the laws governing forbidden sexual relations is that "conversion (plus marriage) permits a sexual relationship between a Jew and a former Gentile." In fact, as Soloveitchik knows at least as well as I, conversion raises a host of issues with regard to forbidden sexual relations, to which Maimonides devotes ten paragraphs, "Laws of Forbidden Sexual Relations" 14:10–19, a full quarter of the two chapters ("Laws of Forbidden Sexual Relations" Chapters 13-14) devoted to conversion. As Maimonides points out, since there is a halakhic principle that a convert is like a newborn child, on a biblical level all the incest prohibitions to which a gentile is subject lapse upon his conversion. However, Maimonides continues, "the Sages forbade this matter, so that people should not say that they [the converts] have exchanged a severe form of holiness for a light form of holiness" (*Laws of Forbidden Sexual Relations* 14:12). This, in turn, raises a whole slew of complex legal issues, for example the differences between paternal and maternal relatives, which Maimonides treats in the following halakhot. The bottom line is that there is a deep connection between the laws of conversion and the "Laws of Forbidden Sexual Relations."

Reply may be made that even granted this deep legal connection, it, in itself, cannot justify placing the laws of conversion in the "Laws of Forbidden Sexual Relations," since the issues that conversion raises with regard to forbidden sexual relations, important as they may be, do not touch on conversion's essence, namely, that the convert "enter into the covenant, take shelter under the wings of the *Shekhinah*, and accept upon himself the yoke of the Torah" (*Laws of Forbidden Sexual Relations* 13:4).

This is true. I would suggest, then, that in order to fully understand Maimonides' placing the laws of conversion in the "Laws of Forbidden Sexual Relations," it does not suffice, as I have done until now, to move from conversion to its implications with regard to forbidden sexual relations. What is necessary is to reverse the procedure and move from the laws of forbidden sexual relations in general to conversion. What is the purpose, the *telos*, of these laws?

It is the name of the book in which the "Laws of Forbidden Sexual Relations" are to be found, the *Book of Holiness*, that provides us with the answer. On one level the holiness referred to is the holiness of *perishut*, the separation from and disciplining of one's physical desires. Thus Maimonides concludes the "Laws of Forbidden Foods" with the ringing declaration, "Whoever is careful concerning these matters brings an additional measure of holiness and purity to his soul and purges his soul for the sake of the Holy One, blessed be He, as the verse states, 'And you shall make yourselves holy and you shall be holy, for I am holy' (Lev. 11:44)" (Laws of Forbidden Foods 17:32). Similarly, at the end of the "Laws of Forbidden Sexual Relations" Maimonides declares, "Therefore it is proper for a person to subjugate his natural inclination with regard to this matter [the matter of forbidden sexual relations] and train himself in extra holiness, pure thought, and correct understanding so that he will be guarded against them" (*Laws of Forbidden Sexual Relations* 22:20).

But in the Introduction to the *Mishneh Torah*, Maimonides offers a related but very different explanation regarding the nature of the holiness referred to in the *Book of Holiness*.

> The fifth book: I will include in it the commandments of *forbidden* sexual relations and forbidden foods. For it is through these two matters that the Omnipresent sanctified us and separated us from the nations, through [the laws of] forbidden sexual relations and forbidden foods. And in connection with both, it [i.e., Scripture] states, "And I will separate you from the nations" (Lev. 20:26, following the laws of forbidden foods) "that I have separated you from the nations" (Lev. 20:24, following the laws of forbidden sexual relations).

It should be noted that this is the only instance where Maimonides, in explaining his division of the *Mishneh Torah* into fourteen books, cites biblical verses.

Maimonides' linkage of the holiness of *perishut* and the holiness of Israel is to be found as well in the *Guide* 3:8 in the context of Maimonides' explanation of "the serious prohibition that exists among us against obscene language."

> This also is necessary. For speaking with the tongue is one of the properties of a human being and a benefit that is granted to him and by which he is distinguished....Now this benefit granted us with a view to perfection in order that we learn and teach should not be used with a view to the greatest deficiency and utter disgrace, so that one says what the ignorant and sinful Gentiles say in their songs and their stories, suitable for them but not for those to whom it has been said: "And you shall be unto Me a kingdom of priests and a holy nation" (Exod.19:6). And whoever has applied his thought or his speech to some of the stories concerning that sense which is a disgrace to us [the sense of touch], so that he thought more about drink or copulation than needful or recited songs about these matters, has made use of the benefit granted to him, applying and utilizing it to commit an act of disobedience with regard to Him who has granted this benefit and to transgress His orders.[36]

Given, then, this tight link between the holiness of abstinence and the holiness of Israel, it ought to come as no surprise that the laws of conversion whereby converts separate themselves from the nations, accept upon themselves the yoke of the commandments, and attain the holiness of Israel should be in the "Laws of Forbidden Sexual Relations," which laws treat of matters of personal status *and which laws, by strictly disciplining the sexual desires of all Israelites, including converts, thereby sanctify them and separate them from the nations.*[37]

---

36 On the other hand, Maimonides in the *Guide* 3:32 states that "God sent Moses our Master to make out of us a 'kingdom of priests and a holy nation' (Exod. 19:6)—through the knowledge of Him, may He be exalted." However, for Maimonides, knowledge of God and abstention from forbidden sexual relations are two sides of the same coin. Thus Maimonides states in *Laws of Forbidden Sexual Relations* 22:21 that the way to achieve sexual purity (*tahorah gedolah*) is to "turn one's self and one's thought to words of Torah and to broaden one's mind in wisdom, for thoughts about forbidden sexual relations are to be found only in the heart of one empty of wisdom. And concerning wisdom it is stated, 'love's doe, a graceful gazelle...you should always obsessively dote on her' (Prov. 5:19)."

37 In a footnote Soloveitchik observes that there is a possible justification for Maimonides' placement of the laws of conversion in Hilkhot *Issurei Biah* that some may wish to put forward, but dismisses that proffered justification as entirely inadequate.

> Reply cannot be made that these laws are located in the *Book of Holiness, Kedushah*. For this term is not used by Maimonides in the same sense as "the sanctity of the Temple." The root meaning of *kadosh* is "separated," "set apart from," "taboo." It is used here in the sense of voluntary abstinence,

I believe I have offered a satisfactory reason as to why Maimonides placed the laws of conversion in the "Laws of Forbidden Sexual Relations," and therefore I need not explain why he did not place them elsewhere. But even if readers are not satisfied with my explanation, they must bear in mind Soloveitchik's principle that "one cannot object to the [ap-

---

> pursuant to the language of *Torat Kohanim* (Lev.19:2) "Thou shalt be holy"—you should abstain from forbidden intercourse (*'arayot*) in the sense of *Perishut*, separation from one's physical desires. Maimonides saw "holiness" as restraint in food and sex, the two basic animal drives of man. For this reason the *Book of Holiness* consists of, and only of, the laws of *kashrut* ("Ma'akhalot Assurot" and "Sheḥitah") and those of forbidden sexual relations ("Issurei Bi'ah"). (371, n. 4)

This note is perplexing. What is the point of the "reply" that Soloveitchik is countering? Even if "holiness" were used by Maimonides in the same sense as "the sanctity of the Temple," how would this observation serve to explain why Maimonides included the laws of conversion in the "Laws of Forbidden Sexual Relations"? A look at the beginning of this note in Soloveitchik's original Hebrew essay may serve to dispel our perplexity. There he writes:

> Do not seek to reply that these laws are located in the *Book of Holiness* (*Kedushah*), for this term, holiness, in the name of the book does not refer to holiness in the sense of the "holiness of Israel" or "the holiness of the Temple." (p. 110. note 4)

The rest of the note is the same in the Hebrew version as it is in the English one.

Here let me raise a point of personal privilege. Professor Soloveitchik delivered a version of his paper as a talk at an AJS Conference a number of years *prior* to the publication of the Hebrew version of his essay. After the conference, in conversation with Professor Soloveitchik, I tentatively suggested that the solution to his query rests in the connection between the meaning of holiness in the title of the *Book of Holiness* and the holiness of Israel. (At the time, Maimonides' statement precisely to this effect in the Introduction to the *Mishnah Torah* had slipped my mind.) I, of course, said nothing about the holiness of the Temple. What possibly could have been its relevance? Indeed, at my AJS lecture in 2003, Professor Soloveitchik confirmed that he wrote the note in the Hebrew version of his essay in response to my suggestion. However, as I point out in the body of my paper and, indeed, as I already pointed out in my lecture, an examination of Maimonides Introduction to the *Mishneh Torah* speedily reveals that it is not just I who links the holiness in the title of the *Book of Holiness* with the holiness of Israel, but also, and obviously first and foremost, Maimonides himself. It is unfortunate that Soloveitchik's version of the note in his later English essay thoroughly obscures the point and relevance of my original suggestion contained in the note in its original Hebrew version, which, to repeat, turns out to be amply confirmed by the words of the master himself.

parently problematic] placement of a set of laws, a halakhic field, in *Mishneh Torah* unless one can suggest a more appropriate locus." Are any of the three places in the *Book of Knowledge* (*Madda'*) that Soloveitchik suggests for the laws of conversion "a more appropriate locus"? I think not.

First it must be noted that there is no thematic connection between the laws of conversion and the *Book of Knowledge* as a whole. In his Introduction to the *Mishneh Torah* Maimonides characterize the units found in the *Book of Knowledge* as containing commandments "that are the fundamental principles of the religion of Moses and that a person must know at the very outset." But a moment's reflection should suffice to indicate that the laws of conversion, unlike the "Laws of the Foundations of the Torah," "the Laws of Idolatry," "the Laws of Moral Dispositions," "the Laws of the Study of the Torah," and the "Laws of Repentance," cannot be characterized as belonging to the class of commandments or as containing regulations "that are the fundamental principles of the religion of Moses and that a person must know at the very outset." The fact that a convert, as part of his conversion, has to be informed about the fundamental principles of religion does not suffice to make the laws of conversion themselves fundamental principles of religion. All the categories of laws in the *Book of Knowledge* are binding on everyone (or at least, as in the case of Torah study, on all males) at every moment of their lives. By contrast, conversion is a one-time ritual procedure, applicable, by definition, only to the convert. As a result, if I am an ordinary Jew who is not a member of a rabbinic court, I can live my life very well without knowing the laws of conversion. Of course, for Maimonides, I ought to know the laws of conversion, just as I ought to know, say, the "Laws of Things Prohibited for the Altar" (*Issure Mizbeaḥ*). But the bottom line remains that conversion is not one of the "fundamental principles of the religion of Moses ... that a person must know at the very outset," and, therefore, its laws do not thematically belong in the *Book of Knowledge.*

Given, then, this lack of connection between the laws of conversion and the theme of *Book of Knowledge* as a whole, the only way they could be included in the book would be if these laws were internally connected to one of the primary topics of the units constituting that book. This is precisely what Soloveitchik suggests. But is he correct?

Underlying Soloveitchik's suggestions, I would argue, are misconceptions regarding both Maimonides' view of the essence of conversion and his image of Abraham, misconceptions that render Maimonides' view of conversion too universalistic and his image of Abraham too particularistic.

With reference to conversion, it is an oversimplification to refer to conversion as "the classic recognition and acknowledgment of God." Recognition and acknowledgment of God are much more universal in character than conversion, which is of a more particularistic nature. After all, Maimonides says concerning the Muslims, "elu ha-Yishme`elim … me-yaḥadim la-El yiḥud ke-rauy, yiḥud she-ein bo dofi," "these Ishmaelites profess God's unity in a proper and flawless manner,"[38] and, it need not be said, Muslims are non-Jews who never converted. Similarly the resident alien "has accepted upon himself not to worship idols together [with a commitment to observe] the other commandments that the descendants of Noah were commanded to observe" (*Laws of Forbidden Sexual Relations* 14:7), but that acceptance does not thereby make the resident alien [*ger toshav*] into a righteous convert [*ger tzedek*]. Maimonides, as we already saw, clearly states that the essence of conversion is the convert's "enter[ing] into the covenant, tak[ing] shelter under the wings of the *Shekhinah*, and accept[ing]… the yoke of the Torah." To be sure, as Maimonides famously emphasizes, all prospective converts must be "informed at length about the fundamental principles of the [Jewish] religion, namely, the unity of the Divine Name and the prohibition of idol worship" (*Laws of Forbidden Sexual Relations* 14:2), but this acknowledgment of those fundamental principles, that is, this recognition of God's unity and abandonment of idolatry, forms *part* the convert's acceptance of the yoke of the Torah. Conversion, thus, is first and foremost entry into the Jewish covenant with God and acceptance of the Mosaic Law, but, of course, for Maimonides, that covenant and that Law possess universal significance.[39]

Conversely, Soloveitchik's hypothetical Maimonidean peroration, as eloquent as it may be, draws an overly particularistic portrait of Abraham that scants the universal aspects of Maimonides' genuine portrait of Abraham. With reference to Maimonides' "timeless" letter to Obadiah the proselyte: included there among "the disciples of Abraham" are not only "all those who will convert in the future," but also "all those who profess the unity of God's Name, as it is prescribed in the Torah."[40] That is, not only native-born Jews and converts are the disciples of Abraham, but

---

38 Yitzhak Shailat, *Iggerot ha-Rambam*, Vol. 1 (Jerusalem: Ma'aliyyot Press, 1987), p. 238.

39 For further discussion, see James Diamond, *Converts, Heretics, and Lepers: Maimonides and the Outsider* (Notre Dame, Indiana: University of Notre Dame Press, 2007), pp. 11–31; and Menachem Kellner, *Maimonides on Judaism and the Jewish People* (Albany: SUNY Press, 1991), pp. 49–57, 61–63. I believe, however, that Kellner scants the more particularist features of Maimonides' conception of conversion.

40 Shailat, *Iggerot ha-Rambam*, Vol. 1, p. 234.

Gentiles are as well, if they profess God's unity in a proper fashion.[41] Indeed, it is striking that in his codification of the laws of conversion in the *Mishneh Torah* Maimonides does not speak of Abraham.

Maimonides' portrait of Abraham in the three places he refers to him in the *Book of Knowledge*—the *Laws of Idolatry* 1:3, the *Laws of Moral Dispositions* 1:7 and the *Laws of Repentance* 10:2—is even more universalistic. A number of points ought to be noted. First on a negative note, Maimonides *never* in the *Book of Knowledge* refers to any covenant that God made with Abraham.[42] Second, the community founded by Abraham, as described in *Laws of Idolatry* 1:3 (and, not so incidentally, in the *Guide* 1:63, 2:39, and 3:29 as well), is *not* the Jewish people. Rather the Abrahamic community is a universal community of knowledge, "a people who knows God." It consists of both Abraham's "pious posterity" *and* his spiritual disciples, and consequently lacks both ethnic and political boundaries.[43] Finally, Abraham is consistently presented as a *hakham*, a sage, whose teachings are based on reason and knowledge. The Abraham of the *Laws of Idolatry* 1:3 arrived at knowledge of the one true God on the basis of his own reason; he realized that idolatry was wrong through his understanding of the nature of the average man; and he spread the knowledge of the one true God via proclamation, exhortation, and above all, teaching. Abraham in this extended description is not referred to as a prophet, and Maimonides conspicuously omits to say that God spoke to him, even where a

---

41 See Lawrence Kaplan, "Maimonides on the Singularity of the Jewish People," in DAAT 15 (1979), p. xix, particularly n. 26. My reading is supported by Diamond, *Converts, Heretics, and Lepers*, p. 232, n. 15.

42 Indeed, in the *Book of Knowledge* Maimonides avoids referring to the covenant between God and Israel. In *Laws of Repentance* 9:1 he mentions incidentally "the words of the covenant," and in *Laws of the Foundations of the Torah* 8:1 he cites a verse referring to the covenant. (This citation of Deut. 5:3 is strange, since it appears to be both superfluous and beside the point.) It is striking that in *Laws of Moral Dispositions* 6:4, the one paragraph in the *Book of Knowledge* where Maimonides mentions the convert, he describes him as having "entered under the wings of the Shekhinah" (*nikhnas taḥat kanfei ha-Shekhinah*), silently, but no less pointedly, omitting mention of his entry into the covenant. Note especially that Maimonides in *Laws of Forbidden Sexual Relations* 13:4 uses the verbs "nikhnas," "enter," in relation to the covenant, and "le-histofef," "to take shelter" in connection with being under the wings of the *Shekhinah*. It is as if in *Laws of Moral Dispositions* 6:4 Maimonides plays with our expectations, using the verb normally used to signify entry into the covenant to signify rather entry under the wings of the *Shekhinah*.

43 I have drawn here from my essay "Maimonides on the Singularity of the Jewish People," p. xvi.

mention of such a divine message would seem to be called for. Similarly, Maimonides in the *Laws of Moral Dispositions* 1:7 refers to the middle path as the path of God that Abraham followed and that he taught to his children. But this middle path in 1:4 of that unit is clearly identified as the path of the wise. Again, there is no indication in this chapter that Abraham learned about this path through divine revelation. Finally, in the *Laws of Repentance* 10:2 Abraham is the model of the person who has reached the level of service of God out of love, a level that is identified there with attaining the heights of wisdom, a level that flows from, as Maimonides states in 10:6 there, the passionate and unrelenting study and knowledge of the sciences that enable a person to understand his Maker to the extent of his ability.[44]

Now that I have set forth Maimonides' view regarding the essence of conversion and his view of Abraham as found in the *Book of Knowledge*, I am in a position to return to and examine Soloveitchik's claim that there are three places in that book that would each serve as "a more appropriate locus" for the laws of conversion than the "Laws of Forbidden Sexual Relations."

With reference to Soloveitchik's first two suggestions: Had Maimonides' definition of conversion included a reference to the recognition and acknowledgment of the great Name of God, that would indeed have constituted good grounds for including the laws of conversion as part of the "Laws of the Foundations of the Torah," alongside the laws regarding the sanctification of the Divine Name (*kiddush ha-Shem*) in chapter 5 and the laws regarding the erasure of the Divine Name (*meḥikat ha-shem*) in chapter 6. Or, again, had Maimonides' definition of conversion included a reference to the rejection of idolatry, that would have constituted good grounds for the laws of conversion serving as the conclusion of the "Laws of Idolatry." But, as we have seen, Maimonides defines conversion as the convert's "enter[ing] into the covenant, tak[ing] shelter under the wings of the *Shekhinah*, and accept[ing]… the yoke of the Torah"—the convert's

44 For more on Maimonides' portrait of Abraham in general and in the *Book of Knowledge* in particular, see Kaplan, "Maimonides on the Singularity of the Jewish People," pp. x-xxi; Diamond, *Converts, Heretics, and Lepers*, pp. 15–20; Kellner, *Maimonides' Confrontation with Jewish Mysticism* (Oxford: Littman Library, 2006), pp. 77–83; David Hartman, "Pilosophiah ve-Halakhah ki-Shenei Derakhim le-Hitmodedut 'im 'Avodah Zarah be-Mishnat ha-Rambam," *Jerusalem Studies in Jewish Thought* 3:1 (1988), pp. 319–33; and Masha Turner, "Avraham Avinu be-Haguto shel ha-Rambam," in *Avraham Avi ha-Ma'aminim*, eds. M. Halamish, H. Kasher, and A. Ravitzky (Ramat-Gan: Bar-Ilan University Press, 2002), pp. 143–154.

recognition of God and his rejection of idolatry forming *part* of his acceptance of the yoke of the Torah. Thus while one cannot say that there are no links between the laws of conversion and either the "Laws of the Foundations of the Torah" or "Laws of Idolatry," they are not nearly as strong as Soloveitchik suggests.

Moreover, if we shift our focus from the units of the *Book of Knowledge* to the book itself, Maimonides' understanding of the essence of conversion constitutes good grounds for *not* including the laws of conversion in either of these two units. For since, in Maimonides' view, an integral part of the very definition of conversion is entry into the covenant—indeed, Maimonides refers to the covenant four times at the beginning of his discussion of the laws of conversion in chapter 13 of the "Laws of Forbidden Sexual Relations"[45]—and since, as we have seen, Maimonides very deliberately chooses not to mention either Israel's covenant with God or Abraham's covenant with God in the *Book of Knowledge*, neither the "Laws of the Foundations of the Torah" nor the "Laws of Idolatry," both of which are, after all, units in the *Book of Knowledge*, can serve as appropriate loci for the laws of conversion.

This last point can also serve to explain why Soloveitchik's third suggestion, namely that the laws of conversion could have been placed at the end of "Laws of Repentance," thereby concluding the *Book of Knowledge*, must also be rejected. Indeed, what for Soloveitchik is a plus, namely, that "had the laws of conversion been placed in the *Book of Knowledge*, the problem of the location of the laws of circumcision would have been solved, for circumcision is an essential component of conversion and the two fit naturally side by side," for Maimonides would be a minus. For, if as we have argued, Maimonides had good reason not to include the laws of conversion in *any* of the units of the *Book of Knowledge*, he had even better reason not to include the laws of circumcision in *any* of its units. For, as we have seen, Maimonides very deliberately chooses not to mention Abraham's covenant with God in the *Book of Knowledge*, while he concludes the "Laws of Circumcision" with an eloquent peroration about the *thirteen* covenants that God established with Abraham with regard to the covenant of circumcision, citing each of the relevant thirteen biblical texts containing the word "berit." Perhaps Maimonides' placement of the "Laws of Circumcision" in the *Book of Love* is problematic, but he certainly knew

45 But, as I pointed out in note 41, it does not appear at all in *Laws of Moral Dispositions* 6:4, the one paragraph in the *Book of Knowledge* where Maimonides mentions the convert.

what he was doing when he did *not* place those laws in the *Book of Knowledge*.[46]

Turning to the internal level, as we saw with reference to the placement of the laws of conversion in either the "Laws of the Foundations of the Torah" or the "Laws of Idolatry," the links between the laws of conversion and the "Laws of Repentance" are not nearly as strong as Soloveitchik suggests. Indeed, is there any intrinsic connection between conversion and repentance? Can the conversion, say, of a *ger toshav* be viewed as a form of repentance? Of course, the conversion of a pagan to Judaism

---

46 It should be noted that Soloveitchik in his Hebrew essay advanced a somewhat different third suggestion regarding the locus of the laws of conversion in the *Book of Knowledge*. There he writes, "He-ḥatimah shel *Sefer ha-Madda* be-Hilkhot Gerut ve-Milah kime`at mitbakeshet me-eleha," "That the *Book of Knowledge* should conclude with [a separate unit] the 'Laws of Conversion and Circumcision' is almost self-evident" (p. 110). That is, as opposed to his present third suggestion that the laws of conversion and circumcision should form part of the "Law of Repentance," in his Hebrew essay Soloveitchik suggests that these laws should be a separate independent unit, following the "Laws of Repentance" and thus forming the concluding unit of the book. However, in light of my observations in this essay—I already made this point in my AJS lecture—Soloveitchik's original suggestion, rather than being "kime`at mitbakeshet me-eleha," "almost self-evident," is, in truth, "kime`at nimna`at le-gamrei," "almost impossible to accept." For, as I have noted, Maimonides could not possibly have included these laws as a separate unit in the *Book of Knowledge*. To briefly repeat: In his Introduction to the *Mishneh Torah* Maimonides characterizes the units found in the *Book of Knowledge* as containing commandments "that are the fundamental principles of the religion of Moses and that a person must know at the very outset." But, for reasons I explain in the text, the laws of conversion—the same obviously holds true for the laws of circumcision—cannot be characterized as "fundamental principles of the religion of Moses and that a person must know at the very outset." It follows that neither on its own belongs in the *Book of Knowledge*, and the only way these two sets of laws could be included in the book would be if they were internally connected to one of the primary topics of the units constituting that book. Whether persuaded by my argument to this effect in my lecture or for other reasons, Soloveitchik wisely modified his suggestion, and just as he in his first two suggestions seeks to "piggyback" the laws of conversion onto the "Laws of the Foundations of the Torah" and the "Laws of Idolatry," respectively, so in his third suggestion he seeks to "piggyback" the laws of conversion and circumcision together onto the "Laws of Repentance." However, as I argue in the body of this essay, this suggestion raises its own set of difficulties. (In truth, if Maimonides wished to combine conversion and circumcision as an independent unit, rather than piggybacking circumcision onto conversion and placing them both in the *Book of Knowledge*, he would have had to keep circumcision in the *Book of Love* and piggyback conversion onto it. I think Maimonides' own solution was preferable by far.)

may be viewed as a type of repentance from sin and error to righteousness and truth. But the pagan could just as easily "repent" of his sin and error by becoming a *ger toshav*. There is no need for him to become a Jew. Here, again, the particularist nature of conversion comes to the fore.

We finally arrive at Soloveitchik's claim that Maimonides' "ending of the *Book of Knowledge* with conversion and circumcision [is] especially appealing, as he could have melded various sections of that book into a memorable ending that linked up the coming *Book of Love* (*Ahavah*). He could have joined conversion and circumcision with his famous remarks about Abraham's long quest for the true God in 'Laws of Idolatry' and fused them with his ending of 'Laws of Repentance''' ('Teshuvah') and the timeless words he wrote to Obadiah the proselyte in approximately this fashion:" There follows Soloveitchik's hypothetical "memorable ending."

Indeed, Soloveitchik skillfully and eloquently melds together various phrases from Maimonides' writings, but in doing so he distorts Maimonides' portrait of Abraham, joins together motifs that Maimonides carefully keeps apart, substitutes a particularistic context for a universalistic one, and, finally, creates an "imaginary" ending that has Maimonides looking forward to the coming *Book of Love*, as opposed to Maimonides' "real" ending, which more than looking forward to the *Book of Love*, very deliberately and emphatically looks *back* to the very beginning of the *Book Knowledge*, namely, the first four chapters of the "Laws of the Foundations of the Torah."

It is time to take a closer look at Soloveitchik's hypothetical "memorable ending."

> על פי הדעה וההכרה תהיה האהבה, אם מעט מעט ואם הרבה הרבה. ומי ששטט בדעתו כמו אותו איתן עד שהכיר את בוראו ונכספה נפשו לאהוב את ה', ורדף אחריו והלך בדרך הקודש עד שנכנס תחת כנפי השכינה, הרי הוא מבניו של אברהם אבינו, שבבריתו נכנס, שנאמר אב המון גויים נתתיך, ועליו אמר הכתוב, זרע אברהם אוהבי.

> According to the understanding and recognition will be the love. If [the former is] little, [so will the latter be] little; if [the former is] great, [so will the latter be] great. And he whose mind began to reflect about the world as did that titan [Abraham] until he came to recognize his creator and his soul longed for the love of God, and he pursued Him and went in the path of holiness until he came under the wings of the *Shekhinah*, he is indeed a son of Abraham our father, for he [the searcher-convert] has entered into his [i.e. Abraham's] covenant, for it is written [Gen. 17:4] "thou shalt be the father of

many nations;" and about him the verse was said [Isaiah [Isa.41:8], "[he is] of the seed of Abraham who did love Me."

As we have seen, the reference to Abraham's covenant is entirely out of place here. Moreover, as we have also seen, Abraham is the father not just of converts, but of "all those who profess the unity of God's Name," and, indeed, as we have seen, in his codification of the laws of conversion Maimonides does not even mention Abraham. But more. Abraham in the last and concluding chapter of the "Laws of Repentance" is not just the teacher of monotheism, of "the unity of God's Name," as he is in the "Laws of Idolatry" and in the Letter to Obadiah the Proselyte; rather, as I have already indicated, he serves as the exemplar of that rare individual who loves God based on the knowledge he has attained and who worships God out of that love, who "performs what is true because it is true" (10:2), that is, for the sake of God Who is the truth (*Laws of the Foundations of the Torah* 1:3-4). Abraham's love of God, based as it was on his knowledge of the sciences, was on such an exalted level that, as Maimonides states, even most Sages cannot attain it. The convert, for Maimonides, is no doubt a very admirable person, whom we are command to love (*Laws of Moral Dispositions* 6:4), but, given Abraham's lofty rank, for Soloveitchik to have Maimonides describe the convert as one who loves God in the same manner as Abraham did, and for him to further have Maimonides state in that connection that the convert "[is] of the seed of Abraham who did love Me," is to fail to appreciate Maimonides' exalted and philosophically oriented portrait of Abraham. Has the convert mastered the natural and divine sciences?! Has he reached a level beyond that of even most native-born Jewish sages?! Indeed, it should be noted that Maimonides is careful not to cite the verse "[he is] of the seed of Abraham who did love Me," but just to state that God referred to Abraham as "he who did love Me" (*ohavi*). Maimonides in this context evidently does not wish to speak of the "seed of Abraham." In sum, just as any mention of the covenant would be out of place in the conclusion of the "Laws of Repentance," so would any mention of the convert.

But let us turn from Soloveitchik's hypothetical ending to Maimonides' actual ending, and readers may determine for themselves which of the two is the more "memorable." I am following here, for reasons that will become clear in a moment, Maimonides' paragraphing as found in the Oxford Manuscript.

י דבר ידוע וברור שאין אהבת הקדוש ברוך הוא נקשרת בליבו של אדם, עד שישגה בה תמיד כראוי ויעזוב כל שבעולם חוץ ממנה כמו שציווה ואמר "בכל לבבך ובכל נפשך" (דברים ו,ה; דברים י,יב; דברים ל,ו): אלא בדעה שיידעהו. ועל פי הדעה--על פי האהבה--אם מעט מעט, ואם הרבה הרבה.

יא לפיכך צריך האדם לייחד עצמו להבין ולהשכיל בחכמות ותבונות המודיעין לו את קונו כפי כוח שיש באדם להבין ולהשיג, כמו שביארנו בהלכות יסודי התורה.

It is a well-known and clear matter that the love of God will not become attached within a person's heart until he becomes obsessed with it at all times as is fitting, leaving all things in the world except for this. As [Scripture] commands and states: "with all your heart and all your soul" (Deut. 6:5), [that is to say,] with the knowledge with which he knows Him. And according to knowledge will be the love. If [the former is] little, [so will the latter be] little; if [the former is] great, [so will the latter be] great.

Therefore a person must devote himself to understand and conceive the sciences and concepts that make his Maker known to him in accordance with the ability that he possesses to understand and comprehend as we explained in *Hilkhot Yesodei Ha-Torah*.

The first paragraph—the penultimate one in the *Book of Knowledge*—with its interweaving of knowledge and love both sums up the gist of that book and, at the same time, looks forward to the *Book of Love*. And the pathos and passion of this paragraph are, indeed, memorable.

But, then, lest we forget exactly what is involved in attaining the knowledge of God, Maimonides shifts keys. The tone is no longer one of passionate exhortation, but one of austere, almost dispassionate intellectualism. In the last paragraph, there is no mention of the love of God, though, of course, it is implied; all the emphasis is on the overriding need to study the sciences necessary to obtain the knowledge of God.[47] And the very last five words of the "Laws of Repentance," that is to say the very last five words of the *Book of Knowledge*— "כמו שביארנו בהלכות יסודי התורה"—bring the reader back to the book's beginning, to the first four chapters of the "Laws of the Foundations of the Torah," which outline both the divine science and the natural science and stress that it is only through studying these sciences that one can attain the love of God. And this knowledge of God, flowing from the knowledge of these sciences, is universal in nature, just as the sciences themselves are universal in nature. In sum, both in the first four chapters of the "Laws of the Foundations of the Torah" and in the last chapter of the "Laws of Repentance," that

---

47 Note, as well, the progression of *Guide 3:51–54*, the *Guide*'s famous last four chapters. Chapters 51 and 52 are devoted to the love and fear of God, both as outgrowths of the knowledge of God. Then in Chapters 53 and 54 Maimonides drops all reference to either the love or the fear of God, focusing entirely on man's achieving his ultimate goal of intellectual perfection culminating in the knowledge of God.

is to say both in the beginning and end of the *Book of Knowledge*, the knowledge of God that constitutes the main theme of the book and gives it its name is placed in a universal context.

The *Book of Knowledge* thus forms a circle, its end pointing back to its beginning, just as the *Mishneh Torah* as a whole forms a circle, Maimonides' declaration at the end of its very last chapter, Chapter 12 of the "Laws of Kings and Wars," that in the days of the King Messiah "the occupation of the entire world will be only to know God... each person in accordance with his ability" (12:5), pointing back to his declaration at the beginning of its very first chapter, Chapter 1 of the "Laws of the Foundations of the Torah," that "the foundation of foundations and pillar of the sciences is to know that there is a first existent and He brought all existents into existence, and all the existents from heaven to earth and what is between them exist only on account of the truth of His existence" (1:1). Note especially that it is the theme of the knowledge of God that links both the beginning and end of the *Book of Knowledge* and the beginning and end of the *Mishneh Torah* as a whole. Note also that the end of the very last chapter of the "Laws of Kings and Wars" is linked to the end of the very last chapter of the "Laws of Repentance," inasmuch as both refer to a person's knowledge of God "in accordance with his ability."[48]

If there are any lessons to be drawn, then, from my comparison between Soloveitchik's hypothetical ending of the "Laws of Repentance" and Maimonides' actual one, it is, first, that we must give Maimonides credit for knowing *exactly* what he was doing in ending the "Laws of Repentance" as he did, and, second, that we rewrite the *Mishneh Torah* at our peril. In his recent essay, "*Mishneh Torah*: Polemic and Art," Soloveitchik writes "*Mishneh Torah* is that rarest of things—a book of law… that is at the same time, a work of art."[49] Maimonides' ending of the "Laws of Repentance" is a work of art; Soloveitchik's substitute ending, while very fine from a literary point of view, is a pastiche.

To sum up, then, the relative merits of the "Laws of Forbidden Sexual Relations" in the *Book of Holiness* or one of the units in the *Book of Knowledge* suggested by Soloveitchik as the "appropriate locus" of the laws of conversion: I believe I have shown that there is a deep connection between the laws of conversion and the "Laws of Forbidden Sexual Relations,"

---

48 Note, as well, how the conclusions of both the "Laws of Repentance" and the "Laws of Forbidden Sexual Relations" cite Prov. 5:19; and how the end of the "Laws of Repentance" and the end of the *Guide* resemble each other not only in their stressing the central importance of the knowledge of God, but in their both referring back in literally their very last words to earlier passages elaborating on this point.

49 "*Mishneh Torah*: Polemic and Art," p. 387.

scanted by Soloveitchik, and similarly believe I have shown that while the links drawn by Soloveitchik between the laws of conversion and the "Laws of the Foundations of the Torah," the "Laws of Idolatry," and the "Laws of Repentance" cannot be ruled out entirely, they are much weaker than he suggests. Two things, however, I believe, are certain. First and positively, in light of the connection Maimonides draws in the Introduction to the *Mishneh Torah* between the holiness of abstinence and the holiness of Israel, the laws of conversion fit very well into the primary theme of the *Book of Holiness*. Second and negatively, since, in Maimonides' view, an integral part of the essence of conversion is entry into the covenant, and since Maimonides very deliberately chooses not to mention either Israel's covenant with God or Abraham's covenant with God in the *Book of Knowledge*, *none* of the units in that Book is an appropriate locus for the laws of conversion.

***

We return to the beginning. Soloveitchik began his essay by declaring that we must combine modern Maimonidean scholarship's concern with the *Mishneh Torah*'s "principles of ... arrangement and organization" with the traditional rabbinic approach to its study, which, "without fear or favoritism, questions whatever in the work appears to be problematic." But I would add that if this essay has shown anything it is that we can answer Soloveitchik's penetrating and fruitful questions regarding the *Mishneh Torah*'s "principles of ... arrangement and organization" only by combining the traditional rabbinic emphasis on the close and careful legal analysis of Maimonides' individual rulings and the internal legal connections between them with modern Maimonidean scholarship's emphasis on analyzing the *Mishneh Torah*'s multifaceted nature and its historical context, on the importance of a close and careful reading of Maimonides' introductions to his various works, particularly the Introduction to the *Mishneh Torah*, on both carefully integrating the *Mishneh Torah*'s treatment of key issues with their treatment in Maimonides' other works, where called for, and carefully differentiating between these treatments, where called for, on, more broadly, examining the complex relationship between law and philosophy in Maimonides' works in general and the *Mishneh Torah* in particular,[50] and,

---

50 One particularly striking example of such interaction with respect to both Maimonides' views regarding circumcision and the universal significance of Abraham may be noted. In the *Guide* 3:49, when speaking about circumcision, Maimonides states: "Circumcision is a covenant made by Abraham with a view to the belief in the unity of God.... This covenant imposes the obligation to believe in the unity of God." Note here the wide-ranging scope of this obligation. It

finally, on exploring the *Mishneh Torah*'s compositional history and the light that Maimonides' surviving drafts might shed on it. Soloveitchik's ringing declaration, "Maimonides is in no need of our praise; we are in need of understanding him" (367), should serve as a prod and challenge to us all.[51] ↪

---

would appear to follow that since, for Maimonides, Muslims, as we have seen, "profess God's unity in a proper and flawless manner," they too, in some manner, should be brought into the covenant of circumcision. This might help explain Maimonides' famously controversial ruling in *Laws of Kings and Wars* 10:4: "The Sages said that the children of Keturah, who are the seed of Abraham who followed upon Ishmael and Isaac, are obligated with respect to [the commandment of] circumcision. And since today the children of Ishmael have intermingled *(nit'arvu!)* with the children of Keturah, all are obligated with respect to [the commandment of] circumcision on the eighth day. But they are not killed for [failing to perform] it." Note how Maimonides in two easy steps arrives at the conclusion that the Ishmaelites, that is, the Arabs who "profess God's unity in a proper and flawless manner," are obligated with respect to the commandment of circumcision on the eighth day. First he interprets the rabbinic statement (*Sanhedrin* 59b) that "the children of Keturah are included in [the commandment of] circumcision" as referring to the descendants of Keturah for all generations, as opposed to the interpretation of Rashi ad loc., supported by most commentators, that it refers only to the six sons of Keturah. Second, he argues that factually, "today the children of Ishmael have intermingled with the children of Keturah." The conclusion that "all are obligated with respect to [the commandment of] circumcision on the eighth day" automatically follows. In this way Abraham's covenant of circumcision truly is "a covenant made …with a view to the belief in the unity of God."

51 I would like to thank the editor of *Ḥakirah*, R. Asher Benzion Buchman, for his close reading of my typescript and many learned and incisive suggestions that contributed greatly to improving this article.

Pikuach Nefesh for a Ger Toshav

By: ASHER BENZION BUCHMAN

Ramban — The *Mitzvah* of Saving the Life of a *Ger Toshav*

In Rabbi Charles Ber Chavel's brief biography of Ramban, he quotes Rabbi Yitzchok Kanfantun's words about studying Ramban. "One is to exercise utmost care in studying the *chiddushim* of Ramban, as all his words are carefully chosen with precise measure and intent, not a syllable in them being redundant."[1] In his introduction to *Ramban Al HaTorah* he quotes Ri Be'rav as saying that they would "sit *shivah neki'im* over every word of Ramban."[2] Ramban's idiom of expression is so succinct and so dense with meaning, that he is often misinterpreted. Even *Rishonim* sometimes misinterpret his intent.[3]

In his *Hasagos L'Sefer HaMitzvos,* Ramban documents a new *mitzvah* that he feels Rambam had left out, the *mitzvah* of saving the life of a *ger toshav.* Based on his reading of this brief passage, Rav Don Plotzki in his *sefer Chemdas Yisrael*[4] says that "it appears" that Ramban believes that it is permitted to violate Shabbos to save the life of a *ger toshav.* He then proceeds to point out how difficult this position is.[5] The only *Rishon* to cite this Ramban is Tashbetz in his *Zohar HaRakia*[6] and his language there, though not conclusive, leans towards this interpretation and has been a factor in leading many latter-day scholars to understand Ramban in this

---

1 *Ramban, His Life and His Teachings*, p. 30, from Kanfantun's *Darchei HaTalmud.*

2 In a subsequent edition he says he was no longer able to find the quote.

3 See, for example, the Tur's understanding of Ramban's position about when the *meshichah* of the *Mishkan* was done, at the end of *Parashas Pekudei,* where the Tur himself realizes that what he attributes to Ramban is difficult. Rabbi Chavel provides the explanation that is undoubtedly correct.

4 See *Kuntres Ner Mitzvah* 52, p. 27. Rav Plotzki is better known by the title of his classic work, *Kli Chemdah.*

5 In his edition of *Sefer HaMitzvos*, Rabbi Chavel refers his reader to Rav Plotzki's discussion on the topic. See also his note on *Ramban Al HaTorah* to *Vayikra* 25:35.

6 *Azharah* 39.

Asher Benzion Buchman is the author of *Encountering the Creator: Divine Providence and Prayer in the Works of Rambam* (Targum, 2004) and *Rambam and Redemption* (Targum, 2005). He is the editor-in-chief of *Ḥakirah.*

way. There is not necessarily contemporary halachic relevance to this opinion, since halachic consensus is to permit *chillul Shabbos* for all gentiles on the grounds that it is dangerous (סכנת נפשות) for the Jewish community to allow any gentile to die when a Jew might have been able to save him.[7]

Rav Plotzki attempts to identify Ramban's source for what he considers a radical *shittah*, and concludes again with how difficult it would be to make such a derivation. In fact, Ramban did not hold this opinion and in this very passage tells us the exact opposite, that *chillul Shabbos* is not allowed for a *ger toshav*. It is necessary to read Ramban line by line to understand what he actually said. Since the issue is important, Ramban's *shittah* is sometimes misquoted, and an understanding of his *shittah* sheds light on Rambam's position as well, it is worthwhile going through this process of analysis. In addition, this is a good example for demonstrating the validity of the warnings of Rabbi Yitzchok Kanfantun and Ri Be'rav.

The full text of Ramban is as follows:

> **מצוה טז** - שנצטוינו **להחיות** גר תושב להציל לו מרעתו שאם היה טובע בנהר או נפל עליו הגל שבכל כחנו נטרח בהצלתו ואם היה חולה נתעסק ברפואתו **וכל שכן מאחינו ישראל או גר צדק** שאנו מחוייבים לו בכל אלה **והוא בהם פקוח נפש שדוחה שבת** והוא אמרו ית' (פ' בהר) וכי ימוך אחיך ומטה ידו עמך והחזקת בו גר ותושב וחי עמך. ומאמרם בתלמוד (פסחי' כא ב, ע"ז כ א, חולין קיד ב) גר אתה מצווה עליו להחיותו גוי אין אתה מצווה עליו להחיותו. והמצוה הזו מנאה בעל ההלכות (אות מט) החיאת האח. והרב כלל אותה עם הצדקה במצות קצ"ה מפסוק פתוח תפתח את ידך (פ' ראה טו). והם שתים מצות באמת: **(השגות הרמב"ן לספר המצוות לרמב"ם שכחת העשין)**

מצוה טז—*שנצטוינו להחיות גר תושב.*

Mitzvah 16[8]—We are commanded to preserve the life of a *ger toshav*

Ramban believed that Rambam had left out the *mitzvah* in the Torah that requires us "להחיות גר תושב", literally, "to give life to the *ger toshav*." The Talmud often speaks of this *mitzvah* להחיותו, as Ramban will note later, but in his estimation it never gives the verse in the Torah that mandates this law.[9] He surmises it is from the verse והחזקת בו גר ותושב וחי עמך (ויקרא כה:לה). This providing of the Torah verse is Ramban's own *chiddush* (novel interpretation) and he does not here or anywhere else say this is stated in

---

7 See *She'eilos U'Teshuvos Chasam Sofer, Yoreh Deah siman* 131; *Igros Moshe, Orach Chaim* 4:79.

8 Ramban lists the *mitzvos* that he believes Rambam mistakenly left out of the *Taryag Mitzvos*.

9 As we will see later, Rambam does believe the Talmud gives the source of the law.

the *Sifra.*[10] I emphasize this point, since some have claimed that this *shittah* they attribute to Ramban is actually an explicit *Sifra* and hence attribute even more authority to it.[11] The *Sifra* never says this and Ramban does not say that it does.[12]

> **להציל לו מרעתו שאם היה טובע בנהר או נפל עליו הגל שבכל כחנו נטרח בהצלתו ואם היה חולה נתעסק ברפואתו.**
>
> To save him from evil that befalls him, that if he was drowning in the river or a landslide fell upon him, we should devote our full energy to try to save him, and if he were sick, we should involve ourselves in curing him.

This definition of the *mitzvah* להחיותו — "to save him" — differs from the standard interpretation of this *mitzvah* — which is "to support him," a reading that fits most Talmudic contexts.[13] Even when the term is used in the *Gemara*[14] with regard to the obligation towards a foundling who is of uncertain heritage, Ramban[15] says that while Rashi (and Rambam) understood that the meaning is to save the life of such a child, the explanation he prefers is that it refers to support.[16] It would seem that at the time of his writing of the *Hagahos l'Sefer HaMitzvos*[17] he interprets the term as Rashi had in that context, with the *mitzvah* of להחיותו being to save from imminent death. Nevertheless, "support" would be mandated as well, as this, too, saves one from death by starvation and the requirement to "involve ourselves in curing him" would be included as well.

> **וכל שכן מאחינו ישראל או גר צדק שאנו מחוייבים לו בכל אלה.**
>
> And certainly with regard to our Israelite brother or a righteous convert, we are commanded in all this.

---

10 Those who have studied *Ramban Al HaTorah* know that it is not unusual for him to provide verses and his own *limudim* for halachic opinions expressed by *Chazal* and even to state *l'halachah* a new position that is not spelled out explicitly in *Chazal* based on what he considers *pshuto shel mikra.* See, for example, his *limud* on אשר יחרם מן האדם.

11 See *teshuvah* of Rav Nachum Rabinovitch in *Melumdei Milchamah* pp. 146–149.

12 We will deal with the *Sifra* later. He mentions it neither here nor in his commentary on the Torah.

13 See *Hilchos Melachim* 10:12.

14 *Bava Metzia* 84b.

15 His explanation is given in *Toras HaAdam* pp. 34–35 of *Kisvei Ramban,* Vol. 1.

16 ומסתברא כרבינו הגדול ז"ל, דלהחיותו **לאו פקוח נפש** הוא אלא לפרנסו כאחד מעניי ישראל, דכל רוב גוים אינו מצווה עליו בצדקה כעניי ישראל.

17 Ramban says that he found it late in his life. See his introduction to his *Hagahos.*

This term "כל שכן" is puzzling, if one does not understand the context of Ramban's words. The verse he is about to bring includes אחיך וגר (צדק) explicitly, as well as a גר תושב, and if it is the *mitzvah* of *pikuach nefesh* that is being learned from this verse which includes all three types of people, then why did Ramban start by saying it is a *mitzvah* towards a *ger toshav*, and why speak of a *kal v'chomer* to apply it to Jews, since Jews are explicit in the *passuk* and the application to Jews is the most primary and deserves the most emphasis? It is precisely because Ramban is adding the *mitzvah* of להחיותו that is novel and directed specifically towards a *ger toshav* that he expresses himself in this way. Towards a Jew, there are other *mitzvos* that require a Jew to save the life of his brother, and Rambam counts two prohibitions *(lavin)*: לא תעמוד על דם רעיך; לא תחס עינך and the positive command (*aseh*) of וקצתה את כפה.[18] With regard to the aspect of support, the obligation towards a Jew is mandated by the *mitzvah* of *tzedakah* which is broader and requires providing all the needs (די מחסרו) of one's brother.[19] However, the reason this *mitzvah* needs to be counted independently is because it is more general in that it includes the obligation to save the life of a *ger toshav,* and thus he begins by saying this is the *mitzvah* that is stated in the Torah to include *ger toshav*, and of course it applies to Jews and converts as well.

והוא בהם פקוח נפש שדוחה שבת.

And with regard to them it is *pikuach nefesh* that pushes aside Shabbos.

The errant readings of this phrase are a result of not heeding the warnings of Ri Be'rav and Rabbi Yitzchok Kanfantun and hence ignoring the words "והוא בהם"— which means "and with regard to **them**,"[20] i.e., אחיך הישראלי and גר צדק , there is the element/concept of *pikuach nefesh* that dictates pushing Shabbos aside. At this point we again reference Ramban in *Toras HaAdam.* In TB *Yuma* 84b, Rav says that the foundling in a town where the majority are Aramim should be treated as a non-Jew and thus there is no obligation "להחיותו", while Shmuel argues, saying "ולענין פקוח הגל אינו כן". Ramban writes as follows:

---

18 See *Hilchos Rotze'ach* 1:14. It is possible that Ramban does not apply the *aseh* of וקצתה את כפה to all acts of saving a person from death and therefore sees וחי עמך as the only *aseh* for *pikuach nefesh*, but there is no reason to believe this.

19 In *Toras HaAdam* (which will be discussed further on) the explanation of the term "להחיותו" that he prefers is identical with *tzedakah.*

20 In fact, the probable correct reading is והיא בהם, with והיא referring to the *mitzvah*, which is feminine.

חזינן השתא דרב פליג עליה דשמואל ואזיל בפקוח נפש בתר רובא, דהשתא להחיותו דאיכא פקוח נפש ולית ביה עבירה דמצוה בעי רב מחצה על מחצה, הא רוב גוים גוי הוא ואין עליו להחיותו, לגבי פקוח גל בשבת דאיכא איסור סקילה לא כ"ש.

We see now that Rav argues on Shmuel and with regard to *pikuach nefesh* goes after the majority, and thus with regard to להחיותו (sustaining life), which is an issue of *pikuach nefesh* and there is no [issue of] sin involved in the performance of the *mitzvah*, he requires that it be half and half (i.e., at least half Jews in the town) and if it is a majority of gentiles we [assume the foundling] is a gentile, to whom there is no requirement להחיותו, thus certainly with regard to uncovering the pile (*pikuach hagal*) which carries the prohibition of stoning [he does not permit].

Ramban here refers to two types of פקוח נפש. When Rav refers to להחיותו he is speaking of the type of *pikuach nefesh* which is done during the weekday and he says that even this need not be done[21] when the majority are Aramim, whereas when Shmuel speaks of לפקח את הגל, he is speaking of the *pikuach nefesh* for which *chillul Shabbos* is required.[22] The words of Ramban here in the *Sefer HaMitzvos* become clear. For the *ger toshav* the *mitzvah* is להחיותו but for the *Yisrael* and *ger tzedek* he changes the term to *pikuach nefesh,* which is associated more closely with *chillul Shabbos.* In fact, however, the term *pikuach nefesh* is used for this concept even when done on a weekday, as Ramban makes clear in the above passage from *Toras HaAdam.* The Talmud in *Yuma* (85a) asks מנין לפקוח נפש שדוחה את השבת — "How do I know that *pikuach nefesh* pushes aside the Shabbos?" i.e., the term פקוח נפש refers to the concept of saving a life whether it be on Shabbos or not, and the *Gemara* seeks the source for applying it even to performing work on Shabbos.

והוא אמרו ית' (פ' בהר) וכי ימוך אחיך ומטה ידו עמך והחזקת בו גר ותושב וחי עמך.

And this is what the Blessed One says in [the verse] "Should your brother be weakened and his hand turn with you, you should strengthen him, as a *ger* or *toshav*, he should live with you."

We must understand that this verse is being brought by Ramban to

21 Perhaps "**should not** be done" because the Aramim are clearly not *gerei toshav.*

22 I do not quote every line of the Ramban, but the fuller context makes this reading clearer and the serious reader should study the entire Ramban.

teach the independent *mitzvah* requiring saving a life and says nothing about whether one can and should do so even on Shabbos. The *Gemara*[23] suggests many *limudim* (derivations of a Biblical nature) to answer the question of how we know that this *mitzvah* can include *chillul Shabbos*. The *Gemara* concludes that the most comprehensive answer is from the verse וחי בהם, which is interpreted to mean that *mitzvos* are given to Israel to live by, and not to die by — thus if it would cause one's death they are suspended. On the verse וּשְׁמַרְתֶּם אֶת-חֻקֹּתַי וְאֶת-מִשְׁפָּטַי, אֲשֶׁר יַעֲשֶׂה אֹתָם הָאָדָם וָחַי בָּהֶם, Ramban (*Al HaTorah, Vayikra* 18:5) quotes the Talmud in saying this is the source for permitting *chillul Shabbos* for *pikuach nefesh*.[24] The *limud* from this verse would most probably not apply to a *ger toshav* as it is addressed to the Jewish people, meaning that we should not perform *mitzvos* at the expense of our lives.[25] The term האדם is used and the Rabbis say, "You (Israel) are called *Adam* and the nations of the world are not called *Adam*."[26]

Elsewhere[27] Ramban quotes the *limud* חלל שבת אחת כדי לקיים שבתות הרבה — "Violate one Shabbos so that many Shabbosos will be fulfilled," in order to argue that even for an unborn child we are *mechallel Shabbos*. Though this is not the final source in the discussion in TB *Yuma*, nevertheless the *Gemara* uses it in TB *Shabbos* 151b to illustrate the logic behind why we are *mechallel Shabbos* for a one-day-old baby and not for the honor of the dead body of King David.[28] Ramban extends this logic even to the unborn and paraphrases it saying שמא ישמור שבתות הרבה "perhaps he will fulfill many Shabbosos," and thus the logic should apply even though there is no presumption (חזקה) that the child will live. The TB *Yuma* expressed its preference for the *limud* from וחי בהם because it teaches that action should be taken even for cases of uncertain *pikuach nefesh* (ספק

---

23 *Yuma* 84ab.

24 I explain this since some mistakenly have written that the *mitzvah* of *pikuach nefesh* intrinsically includes *chillul Shabbos* and that from the verse וחי עמך itself we would learn that there can be *chillul Shabbos* and struggle to understand why this verse is never brought by the Talmud.

25 Another special *limud* is necessary to teach that for *Kiddush Hashem* one does sacrifice his life.

26 *Bava Metzia* 114b (see Oz V'hadar text). Another *girsah* is "and the idol-worshippers are not called *Adam*." And in general there is room to dispute this and we will return to this later.

27 *Toras HaAdam*, p. 29.

28 תניא רשב"ג אומר תינוק בן יומו חי מחללין עליו את השבת דוד מלך ישראל מת אין מחללין עליו את השבת תינוק בן יומו חי מחללין עליו את השבת אמרה תורה חלל עליו שבת אחד כדי שישמור שבתות הרבה דוד מלך ישראל מת אין מחללין עליו כיון שמת אדם בטל מן המצות.

פקוח נפש),[29] but it seems that Ramban felt that once we add the *limud* from וחי בהם we continue to apply the logic and limitation of כדי שישמור שבתות הרבה. Thus we understand why Ramban in the *Sefer HaMitzvos* says "והוא[30] בהם" and does not allow *chillul Shabbos* for a *ger toshav.*

> ומאמרם בתלמוד (פסחי' כא ב, ע"ז כ א, חולין קיד ב) גר אתה מצווה עליו להחיותו גוי אין אתה מצווה עליו להחיותו.
>
> The Talmud refers to [this *mitzvah*] with the statement, "You are commanded '*lehachayoso*' to a *ger*, and you are not commanded '*lehachayoso*' to a gentile."

This *Gemara* is the only source in *Chazal* that Ramban quotes with regard to this *mitzvah*, and since there the Talmud does not sufficiently provide a Biblical source for this law, Ramban provides it to us himself. As noted above, some have claimed[31] the source for Ramban is the *Sifra* on וחי עמך. In fact, Ramban did not consider the *Sifra*'s *limud* on the verse וחי עמך relevant, or else he would have quoted it. The relevant *parashah* reads as follows:

> **לה** וְכִי-יָמוּךְ אָחִיךָ, וּמָטָה יָדוֹ עִמָּךְ--וְהֶחֱזַקְתָּ בּוֹ, **גֵּר וְתוֹשָׁב וָחַי עִמָּךְ**. **לו** אַל-תִּקַּח מֵאִתּוֹ נֶשֶׁךְ וְתַרְבִּית, וְיָרֵאתָ מֵאֱלֹקֶיךָ; **וְחֵי אָחִיךָ, עִמָּךְ**. **לז** אֶת-כַּסְפְּךָ--לֹא-תִתֵּן לוֹ, בְּנֶשֶׁךְ; וּבְמַרְבִּית, לֹא-תִתֵּן אָכְלֶךָ.
>
> **35** And if your brother be waxen poor, and his means fail with you; then you shall uphold him: as a stranger and a settler shall he live with you… **36** Take no interest of him or increase; but fear your G-d; that your brother may live with you.

The *Sifra* reads as follows:

> גר, זה גר צדק, תושב זה גר אוכל נבילו' וחי עמך, חייך קודמים לחייו. ... (ג) וחי אחיך עמך, זו דרש בן פטורא שנים שהיו הולכים במדבר ואין ביד אחד אלא קיתון של מים אם שותהו אחד מגיע ליישוב ואם שותים אותו שנים שניהם מתים, דרש בן פטורא ישתו שתיהם וימותו שנאמר וחי אחיך עמך, אמר לו ר"ע וחי אחיך עמך חייך קודמים לחיי חבירך. (ספרא בהר פרשה ה)
>
> "*Ger*" refers to a *ger tzedek*. "*Toshav*" refers to a *ger* who eats *nevelos* (animals who were not slaughtered). "Shall he live with you" [implies] that your life comes before his life…. (3) "That your brother may live with you," this was expounded by Ben Petura [to apply to] two who are walking in the desert and one has only one

---

29 See *Rashi, ibid.*, for the *limud.*

30 With regard to a ישראל and גר צדק alone.

31 *Chemdas Yisrael* and Rabbi Rabinovitch among others.

flask of water. If he drinks it then one person will reach civilization, and if both drink from it they will both die. Ben Petura expounded that both should drink and die since it says, "that your brother may live with you." Rebbe Akiva said to him, "that your brother may live with you" [implies] that your life comes before the life of your friend.

The first line of the *Sifra* is proposed as Ramban's source because it says that וחי עמך applies to a *ger toshav.* But let us look closely at the entirety of the *Sifra.* In the first part of the *Sifra* it says that one's life takes precedence over that of a *ger tzedek* and *ger toshav.* It is not intended to teach that one must save the life of the *ger toshav,* although in fact it seems to be assumed.[32] In the latter part it tells of Ben Petura's opinion that one should share his final rations with a fellow traveler and survive or die together with him based on the latter phrase וחי אחיך עמך, while Rebbe Akiva learns from the same וחי אחיך עמך that one should give precedence to his own life. The first part of the *Sifra* would seem to be made superfluous by the latter part, as according to Rebbe Akiva one's life takes precedence even over the life of his fellow Jew, and in fact GRA says it is not authentic and deletes it. Malbim, however, provides an explanation. Since Ben Petura is to later claim based on וחי אחיך עמך that one must share his last rations with his brother Jew, thus the *Sifra* sets up his claim by first clarifying that he did not say this with regard to a *ger toshav.*[33]

32 Some refer to Rabbenu Hillel as quoting the *Sifra* as saying that one can be *mechallel Shabbos* for a *ger toshav.* They are incorrect. Rabbenu Hillel in his commentary on the *Sifra* writes that since the *Sifra* says that one's own life takes precedence over another, then we can infer that there must be a *mitzvah* to sustain the life of the other. But still this *mikra* would not necessarily be the source of this *mitzvah*, and in fact according to Malbim's reading below, this inference is not valid. In any event, even if such a *mitzvah* exists, it is the *mitzvah* of להחיותו which does not include *chillul Shabbos.* Nor does Rabbenu Hillel ever quote the words of the *Sifra* that say we are talking about a *ger toshav* and we do not know if he applies it to a *ger toshav.*

33 ואח"כ מבאר שיש הבדל אם הוא גר ותושב אז וחי עמך. (לכן לא כתוב וחי אחיך כי מדבר בגר תושב) אבל בישראל אל תקח מאתו נשך ותרבית וחי אחיך עמך. וע"כ עמ"ש וחי עמך פי' בספרא חייך קודמין. ועל וחי אחיך עמך מביא דרשת בן פטורא. שזה רק בישראל אבל בגר תושב גם בן פטורא מודה לר"ע. According to Rashi's reading it would mean that even with a *ger tzedek* one's own life should take precedence. See also the *Chemdas Yisrael* who states that it is not plausible that Ben Petura could consider equal rationing with a *ger toshav* as in saving life it is an explicit *mishnah* in *Huriyos* that there are rules for precedence even amongst Jews.

והמצוה הזו מנאה בעל ההלכות (אות מט) החיאת האח.

> This *mitzvah* is counted by *Baal Halachos Gedolos* with the words "Supporting the Life of a Brother."

Ramban was heartened in his introducing of this *mitzvah* by the fact that *B'Hag* seems to count it. However, the formulation of *B'Hag* differs in that he centers the *mitzvah* around "your brother the Jew," but Ramban assumes from the fact that he uses the term החיאת that it refers to להחיותו and includes the *ger toshav* as well and is based on the *mikra* of וחי עמך.[34]

והרב כלל אותה עם הצדקה במצות קצ"ה מפסוק פתוח תפתח את ידך (פ' ראה טו). והם שתים מצות באמת.

> Rambam included this *mitzvah* with *tzedakah* in *mitzvah* 195 and bases it on the verse, "Open your hands [to the poor]," but they are in fact two different *mitzvos.*

This evaluation of Ramban is not based on the assumption that Rambam would be compelled to catalog the *mitzvah* detailed in the *Sifra*, as we have shown there is no such *mitzvah* in the *Sifra*. Rather, Ramban is motivated by two points: First, since the Talmud speaks of the *mitzvah* of להחיות גר תושב Rambam must count it somewhere. Secondly, Rambam quotes the verses וחי עמך and וחי אחיך עמך in the *Sefer HaMitzvos* as alternate *pesukim*[35] that command us to give *tzedakah,* and thus Ramban assumed that Rambam subsumed להחיותו of *ger toshav* under this *mitzvah.*

According to this understanding, he probably felt that Rambam considered the *mitzvah* of להחיותו as being predominantly to support the *ger toshav* and thus in line with *tzedakah.* In this he is undoubtedly correct. However, Rambam in fact records the obligation of להחיותו, not in the laws of *tzedakah* but in *Hilchos Melachim* (10:16).

וכן ייראה לי שנוהגין עם גרי תושב בדרך ארץ וגמילות חסדים כישראל, שהרי אנו מצווין להחיותו, שנאמר "לגר אשר בשעריך תיתננה ואכלה" (דברים יד,כא). וזה שאמרו חכמים, אין כופלין להן שלום--בגויים, לא בגר תושב. אפילו הגויים--ציוו חכמים לבקר חוליהם, ולקבור מתיהם עם מתי ישראל, ולפרנס ענייהם בכלל עניי ישראל, מפני דרכי שלום: הרי נאמר "טוב ה', לכול; ורחמיו,

---

34 In fact this assumption would seem difficult since *B'Hag* speaks only of אח – unless he assumes that the term אחיך can apply to a *ger toshav* as well along the lines of the famous *shittah* of Meiri. Saying this would be especially difficult in this *parashah* that also details the prohibition of *ribbis* which only applies to אחיך even according to Meiri, not to a *ger toshav.*

35 The primary verse is פתח תפתח את ידך.

על כל מעשיו" (תהילים קמה,ט), ונאמר "דרכיה, דרכי נועם; וכל נתיבותיה, שלום" (משלי ג,יז).

> Similarly, it appears to me that in regard to respect and honor and also, in regard to charity, a resident alien is to be treated as a Jew for behold, we are commanded to sustain them, as Deuteronomy 14:21 states: "You may not eat any animal that has not been properly slaughtered... give it to the resident alien in your gates that he may eat it." Though our Sages counseled against repeating a greeting to them, that statement applies to idolaters and not resident aliens. However, our Sages commanded us to visit the gentiles when ill, to bury their dead in addition to the Jewish dead, and support their poor in addition to the Jewish poor for the sake of peace. Behold, Psalms 145:9 states: "God is good to all and His mercies extend over all His works" and Proverbs 3:17 states: "The Torah's ways are pleasant ways and all its paths are peace."

The Talmud consistently brings the verse תתננה ואכלה — "give it to him that he might eat," which encourages giving the *nevelah* as a gift to a *ger toshav,* to prove that there is an obligation to see to it that the *ger toshav* is cared for and this is the proof Rambam gives to the existence of such a *mitzvah.* Ramban continued to seek a verse and a specific *mitzvah* that is a direct command to perform such acts and he found it in וחי עמך and thus added a *mitzvah* based on this verse. Rambam too must have a *mitzvah* that obligates us in these acts of kindness to the *ger toshav,* but there is no indication that he considers it part of the Torah *mitzvah* of *tzedakah* as in *Hilchos Matnos Aniyim* (7:1) he is quite explicit that the *mitzvah* is only to עניי ישראל — "the poor in Israel," as two of the *pesukim* quoted for this *mitzvah* speak of אחיך — "your brother." Though he also quotes וחי עמך , this does not deter him from limiting that *mitzvah* to *Yisrael.* From how he quotes this verse in several places, it seems he understood גר ותושב וחי עמך as Onkelos did, to mean that your brother should "reside and settle and live with you" and is unrelated to *ger toshav.* (Ramban *Al Hatorah* quotes this view as well.)[36]

---

36 However in one place, in some manuscripts he does relate the obligation to this *mikra:*

יב [יא] אסור לישראל ליתן מתנת חינם לגוי, אבל נותן הוא לגר תושב: שנאמר "לגר אשר בשעריך תיתננה ואכלה, או מכור לנוכרי" (דברים יד,כא)--במכירה, ולא בנתינה. אבל לגר תושב--בין במכירה בין בנתינה, מפני שאתה מצווה להחיותו: {שנאמר "גר ותושב וחי עימך" (ויקרא כה,לה), כלומר לא יהיה זה העני פחות מגר תושב שהוא חי עימך.(מתנ"ע ג:יב)}

The *mikra* states that the poor Jew should be no less than a "*ger toshav* who is to live with you" (i.e., be given life by you). From the fact that this addition exists only in some manuscripts, and seems to contradict the way Rambam usually

So what is the source of the commandment להחיותו to a *ger toshav* according to Rambam? From his description of the *mitzvah* שנוהגין עם גרי תושב בדרך ארץ וגמילות חסדים כישראל we can discern that the source is the *mitzvah* of והלכת בדרכיו — "Walking in the ways of G-d" — that dominates *Hilchos Deos*. To act with kindness to others is the quality of G-d that Rambam refers to often. From לגר אשר בשעריך תתננה ואכלה we see that G-d considered him worthy of our concern, and thus we can infer that the general command of how we are to act towards Jews applies to him as well. Note Rambam says יראה לי — "it appears to me," and this equation with treatment of a Jew is his *chiddush*. We will return to this point later.

Let us turn now to Ramban in his commentary on the verses in question, which some claim support the belief that *pikuach nefesh* on Shabbos applies to a *ger toshav*:

> (לה - לז) וטעם וחי אחיך עמך - שיחיה עמך, והיא מצות עשה להחיותו, שממנה נצטוינו על פקוח נפש במצות עשה. ומכאן אמרו (תו"כ פרשה ה ג) וחי אחיך עמך, זו דרש בן פטורא שנים שהיו מהלכין בדרך וביד אחד מהם קיתון של מים, אם שותה הוא מגיע לישוב ואם שניהם שותים שניהם מתים, דרש בן פטורא, מוטב ישתו שניהם וימותו, ולא יראה אחד במיתתו של חבירו, עד שבא רבי עקיבא ולמד, וחי אחיך עמך, חייך קודמים לחיי חבירך. וחזר ואמר וחי אחיך עמך, לחזק ולהזהיר:[37] (רמב"ן ויקרא פרשת בהר פרק כה)

The meaning of וחי אחיך עמך is that he should live with you and this is the positive command of להחיותו based on which we are commanded in פקוח נפש as a positive command. And from this they said (*Sifra*) וחי אחיך עמך, was expounded by Ben Petura that when two were walking on the road and one had in his hand a flask of water, should he drink he will reach civilization and if both drink they will both die, Ben Petura expounded that it is better that both drink and die rather than one see the death of his friend. Until Rebbe Akiva came and learned וחי אחיך עמך, your life comes before the life of your friend. It then repeats and says וחי אחיך עמך to strengthen and warn.

---

deduces this law, it would seem it is a scribal addition, or more likely from an earlier draft, at which time his position was closer to Ramban. In any event, the verse is not used as the source for the *mitzvah* of להחיותו but merely serves as an indication that there is such a *mitzvah*, and we still require a command of the *mitzvah* itself.

37 ומדרשו (ב"מ סב א) אהדר ליה רבית דליחיי עמך, צוה בהחזרת רבית קצוצה, כענין שאמר בגזל (לעיל ה כג) והשיב את הגזילה אשר גזל. ואונקלוס עשה "גר ותושב וחי עמך" הכל מן המצוה, ידור ויתותב ויחי עמך, אבל על דעת רבותינו בגמרא (ב"מ עא א), והחזקת בו ובגר ותושב, וחי כל אחד מהם עמך. (Ramban, concluding words.)

The text above was taken from the Bar Ilan CD. According to this text, Ramban is expounding on the verse וחי אחיך עמך, and if such is the case, he has at this point in time decided that *pikuach nefesh* is learned from the verse limited to Jews. Rabbi Chavel changed the *girsah* of the *kisvei yad,* in alignment with the text of the Tur, to claim that Ramban is commenting on וחי עמך. He says the original text caused לערבוב גדול בדברי רבינו — "great confusion in the words of our Rabbi." And indeed it does seem from several things that Ramban says afterwards that he is referring to וחי עמך, but even this emendation does not free us from "confusion" in the words of Ramban. *Chemdas Yisrael* is puzzled, that it seems Ramban understands Ben Petura to be expounding on the verse וחי עמך with וחי אחיך עמך to "strengthen the issue," which runs counter to our text of the *Sifra.*[38] Something is amiss in the text of Ramban. In any event we note how Ramban quotes Ben Petura from the *Sifra* and makes no mention of it with regard to this verse being a source for *pikuach nefesh.* And, as we have explained, even if he learns *pikuach nefesh* from וחי עמך, this does not imply that the obligation of *chillul Shabbos* comes along with it. On the contrary, his equation of the term להחיותו with פקוח נפש implies that he is speaking of what he refers to in *Toras HaAdam* as *pikuach nefesh* that has no violation of a *mitzvah* in it (אסור מצוה).[39]

Tosafos—אשר יעשה האדם וחי בהם

It is because of the *limud* of שבתות הרבה that Rav Don Plotzki finds it difficult to believe that *chillul Shabbos* is permitted for a *ger toshav.* To this he adds what he considers a logical argument (סברא), that sinning for the welfare of another person —חטא בשביל שיזכה חברך — would only apply to a חבר, i.e., a fellow Jew. Nevertheless, neither of these objections are really insurmountable. Since the TB *Yuma* concludes that וחי בהם is the final source for *chillul Shabbos,* perhaps it applies to *gerei toshav* as well. Perhaps even the concept of שבתות הרבה is stated inexactly and is what we refer to as לאו דוקא and really it refers to one who will do many *mitzvos.* Perhaps one should sin to save a *ger toshav* to whom there is an obligation

---

38 Also it runs against other Talmudic principles since we have laws of precedence of even men over women when life must be saved.

39 Of course, Meiri is often quoted as allowing *chillul Shabbos* for modern gentiles who are not idolaters. Those who believe that he was not sincere in this position and that censorship was involved in some way with this position are generally discounted. But Rabbi Dovid Zvi Hillman's essay on this in *Tzefunot*, I, 1 (1988) is worth reading.

of להחיותו.[40] Are we certain that other[41] *Rishonim* agree that *chillul Shabbos* should not be done for a *ger toshav*?[42]

The TB *Sanhedrin* (59a) learns that a gentile who learns Torah is comparable to the *Kohen Gadol* from the verse אשר יעשה האדם וחי בהם. According to this reading, the Torah teaches that all mankind gains spirituality (חיות) from the Torah. Thus we might argue that this verse includes a *ger toshav* (or even other religious and learned gentiles) and thus in the *limud* of וחי בהם ולא שימות בהם, it should also apply to the life of a *ger toshav.*

But this does not necessarily follow. It would perhaps teach that the gentile himself should violate the seven Noahide laws to save his own or another Noahide's life but it does not necessarily mean that a Jew can violate the Shabbos to save the life of the *ger toshav*. And in fact, *Tosafos* (*Sanhedrin* 74b s.v. *Ben Noach)* is clear that we must view the verse וחי בהם as directed to Jews and it directs the Jew to put his life before other *mitzvos,* and he thus argues that there is no clear source to explain why a gentile need not give up his life rather than violate any of his seven *mitzvos.* Nevertheless the Talmud concludes that the *ger toshav* is not commanded in *kiddush Hashem,* and thus it certainly follows that he can violate all *mitzvos* to save his life — but according to *Tosafos* the *limud* of וחי בהם that teaches that Shabbos can be violated to save a life, only applies to a Jewish life.

Rambam — For Us Who Keep the Shabbos, We Are *Mechallel* It

Both in *Hilchos Shabbos* (*perek* 2) and in *Hilchos Yesodei HaTorah* (*perek* 5), Rambam brings וחי בהם as the source for violating Shabbos or any Torah law when there is danger to life. In *Hilchos Shabbos* he writes:

> ואסור להתמהמה בחילול שבת, לחולה שיש בו סכנה, שנאמר "אשר יעשה אותם האדם וחי בהם" (ויקרא יח,ה), ולא שימות בהם. הא למדת, שאין משפטי התורה נקמה בעולם, אלא רחמים וחסד ושלום בעולם. ואלו המינים שאומרים שזה חילול

---

40 Perhaps we say הותרה on פקוח נפש and in fact no sin is being done.

41 Of course, our text of the Meiri requires that the life of non-Jews who are not idolaters be saved, even if they are not *gerei toshav,* but some argue about whether he wrote this under duress or if perhaps the manuscript that survived was tampered with. This issue requires further investigation.

42 The Talmud talks about the case of one Jew among many gentiles creating a *safek,* but perhaps this is only when the gentiles are idol worshippers, or at least to the exclusion of *gerei toshav.* Rambam uses the term גוים but perhaps *gerei toshav* are different.

ואסור, עליהן הכתוב אומר "וגם אני נתתי להם, חוקים לא טובים; ומשפטים--לא יחיו, בהם" (יחזקאל כ,כה). (הלכות שבת, פרק ב)

It is forbidden to hesitate before transgressing the Sabbath [laws] on behalf of a person who is dangerously ill, as [reflected in the interpretation in the phrase of Leviticus 18:5,] "which a person shall perform to live through them," as "['to live through them'] and not to die through them." This teaches that the judgments of the Torah do not [bring] vengeance to the world, but rather bring mercy, kindness and peace to the world. Concerning those non-believers who say that [administering such treatment] constitutes a violation of the Sabbath and is forbidden, one may apply the verse [Ezekiel 20:25]: "[As punishment,] I gave them harmful laws and judgments through which they cannot live."

Rambam here explicates the *drashah* of וחי בהם. The *mitzvos* are given to us to help us live — to make life more pleasant, and the laws are חסד ושלום — "kindness and peace." Thus we understand that if an interpretation of them leads to cruelty and death then we have misinterpreted. It is this *limud* that *Chazal* found most convincing. Above, we quoted that Rambam tells us we must treat the *ger toshav* with חסד and even other *goyim* with שלום. It is certainly possible to understand these words of Rambam as suggesting that one can violate Shabbos to save the life of a *ger toshav* and perhaps even other gentiles.

While in *Hilchos Mamrim* (2:4) Rambam makes use of the concept of שבתות הרבה:

כשם שהרופא חותך ידו או רגלו של זה, כדי שיחיה כולו: כך בית דין מורין בזמן מן הזמנים לעבור על מקצת מצוות לפי שעה, כדי שיתקיימו כולן--כדרך שאמרו חכמים הראשונים, חלל עליו שבת אחת כדי שישמור שבתות הרבה.

Just like a doctor may amputate a person's hand or foot so that the person as a whole will live; so, too, at times, the court may rule to temporarily violate some of the commandments so that they will later all be kept. In this vein, the Sages of the previous generations said: "Desecrate one Sabbath for a person's sake so that he will keep many Sabbaths."

Nevertheless, the source for our *halachah* remains וחי בהם, and this is because the *Gemara* feels it is more inclusive — including *safek* (possible) as well as certain danger, and thus one could argue that perhaps it includes gentiles as well as Jews.[43]

Still, it is assumed that Rambam would not allow *chillul Shabbos* for a *ger toshav* because he seems to make a clear statement to this effect.

> אין מיילדין את הגויה בשבת, ואפילו בשכר; ואין חוששין לאיבה, ואף על פי שאין שם חילול. אבל מיילדין את בת גר תושב, מפני שאנו מצווין להחיותו; ואין מחללין עליה את השבת. (הל' שבת ב:יב)

> We should not help an idolatress give birth on the Sabbath, even if payment is offered. We do not worry about the possibility of ill-feelings being aroused. [This applies even when] there is no violation [of the Sabbath laws] involved. [In contrast,] one may offer assistance to a daughter of a *ger toshav* who gives birth, since we are commanded to secure his well-being. We may not, however, violate the Sabbath laws on her behalf.

It is, however, possible to claim that Rambam only forbids *chillul Shabbos* for birthing the daughter of a *ger toshav* and not for other cases of *pikuach nefesh*. In the previous *halachah* and subsequent *halachos* he writes that a woman about to give birth or who has just given birth is considered in a state of סכנת נפשות — "life-threatening danger," but following the Talmud he instructs that when a needed object can be carried with a שינוי —"some form of change" — it should be done so, so that the level of *chillul Shabbos* be reduced. The commentaries assume he means that anything that can be done with a שינוי should be done so. And *Maggid Mishneh* writes that this only applies to the case of a woman about to give birth, and not other life-threatening illnesses because the birth process is not considered a full סכנת נפשות. If this is true, then we cannot infer from this *halachah* that *chillul Shabbos* is not permitted for a *ger toshav* in a case of a full סכנת נפשות. What is appealing about this reading of Rambam is that

---

43 Nor does Rambam's language here in *Hilchos Mamrim* necessarily imply that *Chazal* limited דחית שבת — "pushing aside Shabbos" — to the life of Jews and could be interpreted to suggest that this phrase can be used to justify saving the life of a *ger toshav* as well. He explains here that the sound logic of amputating an organ to save a life is echoed by *Chazal's* directive to violate a Shabbos so that a life that will fulfill many Shabbosos will be saved. This logic could just as well apply to violating a Shabbos so that the life of a *ger toshav* who will perform many *mitzvos* can be saved. For the analogy to be similar to that of amputating a limb we must say that that which is cut off is not identical to a multiplicity of that which will be preserved. While that which is cut off is a Shabbos, the preservation is of a life full of all the *mitzvos*. The *Gemara* in *Shabbos* 151b in fact concludes that we are not *mechallel Shabbos* for King David since the dead is פטור מכל המצוות.

it answers why he mentions the *halachah* of *ger toshav* only here, in relation to a woman about to give birth, and not when first stating the principle of *pikuach nefesh*.[44] On the other hand, *Maggid Mishneh*'s understanding that Rambam would require שינוי in every aspect of treating a birthing mother is suspect, since Rambam only states it for carrying, and assuming that a birthing mother is not סכנת נפשות is a hard position to defend and not generally accepted.[45]

There is another way of understanding why Rambam makes this statement at this point that would be consistent with the standard interpretation of his position that *chillul Shabbos* is never allowed for a *ger toshav*. Let us look at the *gemara* that the entire *halachah* is based on. (*Avodah Zarah* 26a):

> ת"ר בת ישראל לא תיילד את העובדת כוכבים מפני שמילדת בן לעבודת כוכבים. ורמינהו יהודית מילדת עובדת כוכבים בשכר אבל לא בחנם אמר רב יוסף בשכר שרי משום איבה סבר רב יוסף למימר אולודי עובדת כוכבים בשבתא בשכר שרי משום איבה א"ל אביי יכלה למימר לה דידן דמינטרי שבתא מחללינן עלייהו דידכו דלא מינטרי שבתא לא מחללינן.

> An Israelite woman should not act as midwife to a heathen woman, because she would be delivering a child for idolatry: The following was cited in contradiction: A Jewish woman may act as midwife to a heathen woman for payment but not gratuitously! Answered Rav Yosef: [With] payment it is permitted to prevent ill feeling (איבה). Rav Yosef had in mind to say that even on Shabbos it is permitted to act as a midwife to a heathen for payment, so as to avoid ill feeling. He was, however, told by Abaye that the Jewish woman could offer the excuse "only for our own who keep the Sabbath may we waive it, but we may not waive it for you who do not keep the Sabbath."

Though there is a prohibition to birth the child of an idolater, it is permitted to do so for pay to avoid hatred - איבה. Rambam quotes this law in *Hilchos Avodah Zarah* (9:16). Rav Yosef wished to infer from this that the birthing can be done on Shabbos as well, to avoid this hatred. Abaye responds that he cannot since on Shabbos one can give an excuse that will nullify this hatred. This is the source for the Rambam in *Hilchos Shabbos* that we quoted above. Abaye is interpreted to mean that since one has an excuse, thus no איבה will occur and thus we cannot permit,

---

44 In addition, the source for this *halachah* is not readily available, and it would seem that Rambam specifically wishes to make this point by a birthing mother.

45 He supports it by saying "only one in a thousand die in childbirth" which does not conform to the situation in most of history.

otherwise איבה would be grounds for permitting *chillul Shabbos.*

Rishonim say[46] that clearly the process of birthing cannot be a case of *chillul Shabbos d'Oraisa* for if so, how could Rav Yosef entertain the possibility of permitting it just because of איבה and why did Abaye only object because there was an excuse? The *Rishonim* are split[47] as to whether the issue was permitting Rabbinic prohibitions or merely to permit birthing on Shabbos in a case where not even Rabbinic prohibitions exist. According to this latter position, Abaye said that even though there is not even a Rabbinic Shabbos prohibition involved in this case, since now there is an excuse, we therefore cannot permit birthing a child for idolatry. The excuse is a trick, as the gentile will not know that there is no *chillul Shabbos* involved in this birthing.

We must note, of course, that were this not an excuse but the truth, then Rav Yosef's statement דידכו דמנטר שבת מחללינן, דידהו דלא מינטר שבת לא מחללינן — "For us who keep Shabbos, we are *mechallel* it, for you who do not keep Shabbos we cannot be *mechallel* it," is the explicit statement we have been looking for. There can only be *chillul Shabbos* for Jews. Moreover, there are indications that Rambam did not interpret the *sugya* in the manner these *Rishonim* did. Strangely, he does not mention the excuse of "you who do not keep Shabbos," nor even the fact that the Jewish midwife would be able to give an excuse, and should give it! Is this not crucial to understanding why birthing is not permitted? Also, he states that it is not permitted "even without *chillul*,"[48] implying that we needed to be told as well that with *chillul* it is not permitted. And of course, as we raised above, if the general law is that there cannot be *chillul Shabbos* for a *ger toshav*, why bring it here and in this context? In addition, we do not know the source of the *halachah* and if it is merely to be assumed that there cannot be *chillul Shabbos* for a *ger toshav* in general, what need is there to make this statement here — why would I think to allow it?

The *halachah* is awkward, unless we interpret as follows: איבה is a reason, closely related to סכנת נפשות, for permitting *chillul Shabbos.* Rav Yosef wanted to extend the principle, to treat איבה as full *pikuach nefesh,* and thus permit *chillul Shabbos.* Abaye said that the danger is not great enough to warrant more than allowing the prohibition of birthing a son to be raised for idolatry, and not even sufficient to permit a Rabbinic violation. Thus, Rambam explains that whether the necessary *chillul Shabbos* required for birthing is only the minor Rabbinic prohibition against birthing on Shabbos, or actual *chillul Shabbos d'Oraisa* is necessary,

---

46 See *Tosafos* and Talmidei Rabbenu Yonah, *ibid.*

47 See above note.

48 Rather than saying ואע"פ we would expect him to say אע"פ.

we cannot permit. The excuse that Abaye produces is a truth, and not meant as an excuse and the essence of his objection is that the danger that arises from refusal is not strong enough a danger to be considered *pikuach nefesh* and that is the upshot from Rambam's statement. Whereas in *Hilchos Avodah Zarah* we learned that the danger produced by איבה is sufficient to permit Rabbinic prohibitions related to *avodah zarah*, איבה is not sufficient to permit any level of *chillul Shabbos.* Rambam does not quote Abaye's reason, for it was a reason he gave in his time and place. There could be other arguments as to why this does not rise to the level of *pikuach nefesh,* and in different times and places different arguments may be relevant. Rambam does not want to limit the *halachah* to this argument.

Thus, in fact, Abaye's explanation is an explicit statement of the principle that for a *ger toshav* there can be no *chillul Shabbos* and hence this is the source for the last part of the *halachah.* First Rambam explains that out of this level of fear, we cannot suspend the prohibitions of Shabbos, and then that while out of the obligation of להחיותו we suspend the Rabbinic prohibition of birthing, we cannot suspend the Torah prohibition. Indeed, the obligation להחיותו and to show kindness — גמילת חסדים — to a *ger toshav* does merit the application to them of וחי בהם and birthing without *chillul Shabbos d'Oraisa* is permitted, but still the argument of R. Shimeon B. Menasia also carries weight and we can only go so far as *chillul Shabbos d'Oraisa* for a brother who shares our dedication to all the principles of the Torah.

Rashba — *Pikuach Nefesh* for Jews

Rav Aryeh Leib Braude[49] notes that on the *mishnah* (*Shabbos* 128b) מילדין את האשה ... ומחללין עליה את השבת, Rashba is explicit that מילדין is itself *chillul Shabbos d'Oraisa* as the *gemara* there clearly implies[50] and thus it is likely to assume that Rashba, as well as Rambam, assumes that Rav Yosef, in wishing to permit birthing, meant to allow *chillul Shabbos* because of איבה. This accords with how we interpreted Rambam,[51] that the danger of gentile hatred is so great that it constitutes *pikuach nefesh.* Rav Braude goes on to explain that this is the source for why there was a *takanah* of the *Vaad Arba haAratzos* to permit Jewish doctors to treat gentile patients on Shabbos. While in the time of the Talmud, Abaye was able to state that

49 בית אב"י או"ח סי' י.

50 ומחללין עליה את השבת לאסוקי מאי.

51 Similarly as with Rambam.

gentiles would understand and accept that a Jew could only violate the Holy Shabbos to save the life of a fellow Jew, in modern times such a claim would lead to such hatred that Jewish life would become even cheaper than it is now.[52]

Chasam Sofer[53] decided that a Jewish doctor must treat gentiles because of *pikuach nefesh* for the Jewish community. According to Rav Braude, this claim is rooted in the *Gemara* itself and our understanding of Rambam is that he also understood the *Gemara* this way. These supportive sources to his ruling are important, because one cannot reasonably claim that any possibility of danger (חשש) constitutes sufficient doubt to be considered ספק פקוח נפש. Rambam and other *Rishonim*, based on *Yuma* 84b, differentiate between different types of ספק and in some cases we do not allow *safek pikuach nefesh* on Shabbos.[54], [55] But the explicit *gemara* that only forbids it because the gentile world will accept the importance of Shabbos turns this source into an explicit מתיר (source for permitting) in today's times. ☙

52 This seems to be what Rav Moshe Feinstein is referring to as well in *Igros Moshe* 4:79, דלא מתקבל במדינתינו הדיחוים שאמר אביי.

53 *Shu"T Chasam Sofer, Yoreh Deah* 131.

54 See the *Toras HaAdam, ibid.*, where he assumes these *Rishonim* do not *pasken* like Shmuel and hold הולכין בפקוח נפש אחר הרוב and while Ramban disagrees he still has criteria that are limiting to some extent.

55 Thus *Mishnah Berurah* 330:8 did not permit for what he did not consider sufficient danger. The printers of my version seemed to disagree and add a note that the Chofetz Chaim is talking about doctors in idol-worshipping lands such as India.

The Intersection of Halakhah and Science in Medical Ethics: The Approach of Rabbi Eliezer Waldenberg

By: **ALAN JOTKOWITZ**

Introduction

The relationship between halakhah and scientific advancement is a complex one. Halakhah was developed in the context of ancient and medieval scientific knowledge and this certainly had an impact on rulings in many areas of the law. The question then arises how halakhah should be affected when modern science disproves the scientific foundation on which the law is based. Various approaches have been suggested to this dilemma. One can simply deny the validity of modern scientific knowledge and maintain that the scientific theories of the ancient Talmudic sages are based on divine revelation and therefore there is no question. Another possible approach is to maintain that both the sages and modern scientists are correct, the contradictions being due to a change in the natural world over time. The approach then begs the question whether the law should also change in response to these changes in the physical world. A third approach is to accept that the sages made mistakes not due to any fault of their own but because they were limited by the scientific knowledge of their time. This position maintains that notwithstanding the spiritual uniqueness of the Talmudic sages, they had no special insight into the scientific workings of the natural world. This essay will demonstrate that over the course of his long and distinguished rabbinical career, Rabbi Eliezer Waldenberg had a consistent approach to this dilemma.

R. Waldenberg was one of the most prolific halakhic decisors of the last century and had special expertise in questions at the intersection of medicine and halakhah. In answering these queries, R. Waldenberg developed a distinct approach that gained much prominence in the halakhic discourse on these important issues. He dealt with all the modern dilem-

---

Professor Alan Jotkowitz is Director of the Jakobovits Center for Jewish Medical Ethics and Associate Director for Academic Affairs Medical School for International Health and Medicine, Ben-Gurion University of the Negev and a Senior Physician at Soroka University Medical Center, both in Beer-Sheva, Israel.

mas in medical ethics, including but not limited to end-of-life-care, abortions, artificial reproduction, triage, confidentiality, definition of death and organ transplantation. He also wrote extensively on the questions of ritual such as circumcision and Shabbat observance that relate to medicine. Despite these achievements there has been relatively little written on his impressive corpus. Professor Rabbi Avraham Steinberg did the initial work in collecting most of his responsa relating to medical ethics in one volume, and this essay will attempt to continue that work by discussing his opinions in greater detail and comparing and contrasting them with opinions of other decisors.

R. Waldenberg was born in Jerusalem in 1915 and spent his whole life in the city learning and serving as a Rabbi in a variety of official and semi-official positions.[1]

He studied with the ultra-orthodox former Chief Rabbi of Jerusalem Tzvi Pesach Frank and with Chief Rabbi of Israel Isaac Halevi Herzog. He was a member of the Supreme Rabbinical Court in Jerusalem and the unofficial Rabbi of Shaare Zedek Medical Center for decades. He had no formal secular education and very little exposure to modern western culture. In addition to being an authority on medical ethics, he was an acknowledged expert on all aspects of Jewish law. His masterpiece is the 21-volume set of responsa called Tzitz Eliezer in which are answered questions on practically every field of Jewish law. He also wrote a multivolume series called *Hilkhot Medinah* on the relationship of Jewish law to modern governance, a topic that it became necessary to address with the birth of the State of Israel. He died in Jerusalem in November 2006.

Definition of Death and Organ Transplantation

R. Waldenberg wrote extensively on how halakhah defines death and his position remained remarkably consistent over decades. The classic Talmudic source for defining death is the gemara in *Yoma* 85a: "If a building collapses on Shabbat and someone may be trapped in the rubble, one must desecrate the Shabbat to try to save the victim. If one finds him

1 Adapted from Avraham Steinberg, "Rabbi Eliezer Yehudah Waldenberg," *Pioneers in Jewish Medical Ethics,* edited by Fred Rosner (Northvale, NJ: Aronson, 1997). For a summary of R. Waldenberg's responses on medical ethics see Avraham Steinberg, *The Laws of Physicians and Medicine according to the Tzitz Eliezer* (Jerusalem: Mossad HaRav Kook, 1978) [Hebrew]; RD Strous, E. Shenkelowsky, "The world of medicine encounters the world of halakha—the great medical halakhist and Israel Prize awardee Rabbi Eliezer Waldenberg (1915–2006)," *Ha-Refuah*, vol. 147, 2008, pp. 85–8, 92 [Hebrew].

alive, one extricates him and tries to save his life. If he is found dead, one leaves him there until the end of Shabbat. How far does one dig to determine whether he is alive or dead? Up to the nose. An additional view is up to the heart. The main sign of life is in the nose, as it is written, "All in whose nostrils is the breath of the spirit of life." Based on the gemara in *Yoma* and a responsum of the Ḥatam Sofer, R. Waldenberg maintains that "death is determined by the cessation of respiration."[2] But R. Waldenberg also accepts the explanation of the Ḥakham Tzvi that absence of respiration is a sign of lack of heart function. In the words of the Ḥakham Tzvi, "everything depends on the heart."[3] This assertion is apparently based on the ancient understanding that the heart was primarily a respiratory organ and its function was to distribute air throughout the body, an understanding that persisted until William Harvey elucidated the circulatory system in the 1600s. The Ḥakham Tzvi brings a number of proofs for this position with which R. Waldenberg concurs:

1. Rashi in *Yoma,* explaining how far one has to check to ascertain if a person buried under rubble is still alive, states that "one says until the heart to see if he is alive because his **soul** beats there, and another says until the nose because sometimes there is no sign of life in the heart but it is recognizable in the nose."[4] Apparently, Rashi feels that life is dependent on heart function, and even according to the opinion that one checks until the nose, that is only if there is no sign of detectable heart function.
2. The Ḥakham Tzvi cites an argument between ancient Greek philosophers whether the source of locomotion is the heart or the brain, and asserts that we follow Rambam, who agrees with Aristotle that the source of movement is the heart.[5] R. Waldenberg himself follows in this direction and quotes Rabbenu Saadiah Gaon, who feels that the soul resides in the heart, and the Zohar, which asserts that "it is impossible for all the limbs of the body to live even one minute without the heart."[6]

---

2 Responsa, *Tzitz Eliezer*, Vol. 10, 25:4.

3 Responsa, *Ḥakham Tzvi*, 77. See E. Reichman, "The Halachic Definition of Death in Light of Medical History," *The Torah U'Madda Journal,* vol. 4, 1993, pp. 148–74 for a discussion of the erroneous circulatory physiology on which the Ḥakham Tzvi based his ruling.

4 Rashi, *Yoma* 85a., s.v. *ad ḥotmo.*

5 Responsa, *Ḥakham Tzvi*, 77.

6 Responsa, *Tzitz Eliezer*, Vol. 10, 25:4:7.

R. Waldenberg was also aware of the modern brainstem definition of death (referred to in the medical literature as the Harvard criteria) and was adamantly opposed to it. But R. Feinstein's last responsum on the issue, written in 1985 one year before he died, explicitly accepts the Harvard criteria: "The definition (of death) called the Harvard criteria is considered as if the patient is decapitated because the brain has already been destroyed. And even if the heart is able to beat for a few days, all the time the patient has no ability to breathe independently he is considered dead."[7]

R. Waldenberg quotes the Ḥatam Sofer that lack of respiration "is a principle that is the accepted definition from the time when we became a holy nation and all the forces in the world will not move us from the place of our holy Torah."[8] Following in the footsteps of the Ḥatam Sofer, R. Waldenberg did not accept that modern medicine could change the medical principles that the ancient Rabbis maintained were true. Therefore advances in neuroscience, which have shown that respiratory function is controlled by the brainstem, would have little impact on his halakhic decision making.[9] In this context he quotes a responsum of the Rivash, who maintains that we do not follow contemporary science if it conflicts with Rabbinical tradition in determining if an animal or person is a *treifah* (doomed to die within thirty days): "We rely on our Rabbis and even if they say right is left because they received the truth and the explanation of the commandment man from man until…And we will not believe the Greek or Muslim wise men who only speak based on their own reasoning."[10] According to this perspective, not only do the laws of the Torah represent the ultimate truth but so do the scientific principles espoused by the Rabbis. Once Rambam decided the source of life resides in the heart, modern science can do little to change this viewpoint. It is not clear why the medieval medical opinion of Rambam should be eternally binding. Rambam himself was apparently relying not only on Torah wisdom but also on the medicine of his time as he understood it. Why then shouldn't modern authorities be allowed to incorporate contemporary medical knowledge into their halakhic rulings? As we will see in other contexts as well, R. Waldenberg adhered to this perspective on the relationship between the Torah and modern science.[11]

---

7 Responsa, *Iggerot Moshe, Yoreh De'ah,* IV:54.

8 Responsa, *Ḥatam Sofer, Yoreh De'ah*, 338.

9 Responsa, *Tzitz Eliezer*, Vol. 10, 25:4:6.

10 Responsa, *Rivash*, 447.

11 For example, Rabbi Waldenberg does not feel that one can use modern scientific tests (e.g., blood typing or DNA testing) to establish paternity in halakhah.

In his last responsum on defining death, written in 1995 when heart transplantation had become commonplace around the world, R. Waldenberg writes, "I was astounded to read in your letter that it has been suggested that I revoked my ruling prohibiting heart transplants or other organ transplants in critically ill patients form donors whose heart still beats but whose brain including the brainstem no longer functions, which is called brain death. I want to emphasize clearly that I have not changed my mind and I strongly forbid it on the basis of halakhah."[12]

R. Waldenberg accepts the principle based on Ramban in *Torat Ha-Adam* that a physician may perform a dangerous operation in order to save the life of a patient.[13] Ramban maintains that a fundamental component of the dispensation given to a physician to heal is the knowledge that he may harm patients with his treatments. But the principle of Ramban might not apply to our situation, because Ramban stated his principle only when the physician is convinced that this intervention is appropriate, but there is always the chance that the patient will have an unanticipated reaction to the medication or the physician will make a mistake in judgment, as opposed to the present situation where even from the onset the physician recognizes the great risk involved.[14] R. Waldenberg is alluding to the different reasons for adverse outcomes recognized in the medical literature.[15] Notwithstanding this distinction, based on the gemara in *Avodah Zarah* 27b he allows one to take a risk in order to attempt a cure. The gemara states: "If a patient will possibly live and possibly die if not treated, he may not be treated by a pagan doctor. But if he will surely die if not treated, he can be treated. Can this be? He still has momentary life that is put in danger by receiving treatment form the pagan doctor. We are not concerned about momentary life." Rashi comments that even if it is definite that the pagan doctor will kill the Jew, one is allowed to take the risk because without going to the doctor one will surely die.[16] The gemara brings support for this assertion from the story in Kings II: 7 where the army of Aram laid siege to a Jewish town suffering from starvation. Four Jewish lepers decided to surrender to the enemy based on the reasoning that if they stay near the city they will surely die of starvation so what do they have to lose by giving themselves up. The question for R. Waldenberg is whether the physician is allowed to attempt a cure that may harm

---

12 Responsa, *Tzitz Eliezer*, Vol. 21, 28.

13 Ramban, *Torat Ha-Adam.*

14 Responsa, *Tzitz Eliezer*, Vol. 10, 25:5:5.

15 Responsa, *Tzitz Eliezer*, Vol. 10, 25:5:5.

16 Rashi, *Avodah Zarah* 27b, s.v. *safek ḥai safek met.*

the patient. For R. Feinstein the discussion centers on whether the patient may take the risk. This is consistent with their general view on patient autonomy. R. Waldenberg feels a patient has little or no autonomy in medical decision making,[17] while R. Feinstein attaches much more weight to patient preferences.

Regarding heart transplantation, R. Waldenberg:

1. Agreeing with R. Feinstein, maintains that there has to be at least a 50% chance that the patient will live from the operation.[18]
2. If the patient does not receive the operation he will die soon, but if there is a chance that he can live for years without the operation, it should not be done. With better survival after transplantation and better prognostic tools, these two objections are potentially surmountable.
3. It is possible that heart transplantation does not fall under the dispensation given for a doctor to heal for two reasons. Firstly, the sages were not aware of this operation and secondly, one is not allowed to obtain the heart for the transplantation.[19] Regarding the first contention it is difficult to understand why if the sages were unaware of the operation this should affect the dispensation given to a physician to heal. If that is true then almost all of modern medicine should be halakhically problematic. This position might be easier to understand if one accepts R. Waldenberg's preference for Rabbinic medicine over modern medicine alluded to previously. Regarding the second contention, other decisors have addressed the question whether one is allowed to accept a donor heart from a patient not considered halakhically dead.[20]

R. Waldenberg quotes authorities who raise the possibility that only a non-Jewish physician is allowed to perform a risky operation because the case of the gemara in *Avodah Zarah* is concerned with a Jewish patient being cared for by a non-Jewish physician.[21] It is difficult to understand why there should be a difference between a non-Jewish and a Jewish doctor in this regard, and R. Feinstein rejects this contention. He points out that the case in *Avodah Zarah* may be about a non-Jewish physician pre-

17 See for example Responsa, *Tzitz Eliezer*, Vol. 18, 62.

18 Responsa, *Tzitz Eliezer*, Vol. 10, 25:5:5.

19 Responsa, *Tzitz Eliezer*, Vol. 10, 25:5:5.

20 Aharon Soloveichik, "Determining the Time of Death," *The Journal of Halacha and Contemporary Society,* vol. 17, 1989, pp. 41–8.

21 Responsa, *Tzitz Eliezer*, Vol. 4, 13:6, quoting the Responsa, *Bnei Tzion*, 11.

scribing a medicine to the Jewish patient, so that, when the patient swallows the medicine, he is a full participant in the act and even so it is allowed. We see that a Jewish patient can act to save himself and therefore we should also allow a Jewish physician to act to save others.[22]

Abortion

R. Waldenberg also wrote extensively on the issue of abortion in halakhah. His opinions on abortion helped solve many difficult personal and family dilemmas but subjected him to criticism from many parts of the rabbinic world. R. Waldenberg felt strongly that the fetus is not considered a "person," and based his position on Rashi's understanding of the gemara in *Sanhedrin.*

The mishnah in *Oholot* 7:6 states: "A women who is having difficulty giving birth, one may dismember the infant in the womb and remove it limb by limb because her life comes before the fetus's life. If most of the fetus[23] has emerged, one does not touch it because one does not put aside one life for another." The gemara in *Sanhedrin* 72b quotes Rav Huna: "A child *rodef* [the halakhic name for a person trying to kill another person] may be killed. He must [then] maintain that a child or adult rodef does not need to receive a warning before he is killed [because a child cannot receive or understand a proper legal warning]. Rav Ḥisda challenged Rav Huna [from the mishna in *Oholot*]: If most of the fetus's head has emerged one does not touch it, because one does not put aside one life for another. But why [not kill it], the baby is a *rodef.* [The gemara responds:] It is different here [in the case of *Oholot*] because the mother is being pursued from heaven [this is not a classic case of *rodef* because the mother's life is threatened by the natural phenomenon of childbirth]." Rashi comments: "all the time that the fetus has not been born he is not a **nefesh** [person] and you can kill him to save the mother, but when his head has been born one may not touch him because it is as if he has been born and one does not put aside one person for another."[24] Rav Waldenberg feels it is clear from Rashi that before birth the fetus is not considered a person and that is why abortion is not considered murder by a Jew.[25]

R. Feinstein disagreed with him and even attacked him in one of his responsa:

---

22 Responsa, *Iggerot Moshe, Yoreh De'ah*, III:36.

23 There are different versions of the text of the mishnah whether the case is of most of the body or most of the head being born.

24 Rashi Sanhedrin 72b. s.v. *yotza rosho.*

25 Responsa, *Tzitz Eliezer*, Vol. 9, 51:3:1:3.

"I was shocked when I saw the responsum of a certain sage [R. Waldenberg] in Israel who permitted abortions in fetuses greater than three months who according to the tests of doctors had Tay-Sachs disease … and one should not err and rely on the responsum of this sage."[26]

R. Feinstein bases his opinion on the Talmud in Sanhedrin 57b, which cites the opinion of Rabbi Yishmael that a non-Jew who aborts a fetus is liable and sentenced to death. Rambam (*Hilkhot Melakhim* 9:4) codifies the law as follows: "A non-Jew who kills a person, even a fetus in its mother's womb, is sentenced to death." R. Feinstein deduces from this law that abortion performed by a non-Jew is a form of murder punishable by death. There is no parallel formulation in the Talmud or Maimonides regarding the law if a Jew performs an abortion. Regarding this point R. Feinstein cites the tosafot who, based on the principle "there is nothing prohibited to a non-Jew that is permitted to a Jew," assert that "even though a Jew is exempt (not punished for abortion) it is not allowed."[27] From this comment of tosafot, R. Feinstein assumes that the prohibition is equivalent for a non-Jew and a Jew.[28] Abortion is a form of murder; the only difference is that a Jew is exempt from punishment. One can challenge this assertion of R. Feinstein's in three ways.

1. R. Waldenberg cites another opinion in Sanhedrin against Rabbi Yishmael's contention that a non-Jew is liable for abortion.[29] The weakness of this argument is there no record of any subsequent decisor explicitly accepting this opinion.
2. R. Waldenberg argues that not everyone accepts the principle "there is nothing prohibited to a non-Jew that is permitted to a Jew."[30]
3. This assertion of R. Feinstein is valid only if you accept that the principle "there is nothing prohibited to a non-Jew that is permitted to a

---

26 Responsa, *Iggerot Moshe, Ḥoshen Mishpat,* Part 2, 69:3.

27 Tosafot, *Sanhedrin* 59a, s.v. *lekha.* As will be discussed further, the law that a non-Jew is liable for aborting a fetus can be understood in one of two ways: 1. a fetus is considered a person and therefore one is liable for its murder as for any other person, or 2. a fetus is not a person but a non-Jew is also liable for aborting a potential life. It is easier to understand that a Jew would not be liable for aborting a fetus according to the second explanation. The text of Rambam (*Hilkhot Melakhim* 9:3) may be more consistent with the first explanation.

28 Responsa, *Iggerot Moshe, Ḥoshen Mishpat,* Part 2, 69:1.

29 Responsa, *Tzitz Eliezer,* Vol. 14, 100.

30 Responsa, *Tzitz Eliezer,* Vol. 9, 51:3:2:2. For example, the *Ḥatam Sofer* (*Yoreh De'ah,* 19) maintains that this is the position of Rambam (*Hilkhot Melakhim* 9:13) based on his ruling that a Jew can eat an animal while it is still twitching but a non-Jew cannot.

Jew" creates an equivalent prohibition: If abortion is considered murder for a non-Jew then it must also be murder for a Jew. But R. Feinstein himself cites others who see in the principle not an equivalent prohibition but a more general lower-level edict. If so, tosafot's use of the principle may not support his contention that abortion is murder.[31]

Based on a responsum of Rabbi Yaakov Emden, R. Waldenberg maintained that an abortion could be performed solely for maternal need (even if it is not life threatening), in particular in the case of a pregnancy resulting from illicit relations.[32]

The development of new technologies in the twentieth century raised new halakhic issues relating to abortion. Physicians now can diagnose severe genetic conditions such as Tay-Sachs disease *in utero*, and the question arises whether to permit elective abortions in such cases. R. Feinstein was strongly opposed, but R. Waldenberg ruled differently. In a case of a fetus with known Tay-Sachs, he writes:

"Is there a greater case of pain and suffering than what will be caused to the mother in giving birth to this child, which everyone says will suffer and surely die within a few years? … And add to this the pain and suffering that the child will experience. And therefore, if there is a situation where the halakhah permits abortion for reasons of pain and suffering and great need, then this should be a classic case for allowing it. And it makes no difference whether the suffering is physical or emotional, because in many instances emotional suffering is greater than physical suffering."[33]

The main focus here is on the needs of the mother, be they physical or psychological. On these grounds, he allows a late-term abortion, in the seventh month of pregnancy, for a fetus with Tay-Sachs.

R. Waldenberg was subsequently asked about the permissibility of abortion for a fetus with Down Syndrome—a much more complex question, because of the varied prognosis of such children and the differing ability of families to cope with them. He was reluctant to give a general dispensation, but instead told the couple to talk to their own rabbi, who would be better able to ascertain their ability to raise the child. He noted,

---

31 Responsa, *Iggerot Moshe, Ḥoshen Mishpat*, Part 2, 69:1. For example, Tosafot in *Ḥullin* 33a s.v. *eḥad* maintain that a Jew is not liable for the prohibition of eating flesh from a live non-kosher animal, because in any case a Jew is not allowed to eat a non-kosher animal even when it is dead.

32 Responsa, *Tzitz Eliezer*, Vol. 9, 51:3.

33 Ibid., Vol. 13, 102:1.

however, that there is room to permit abortion in selected cases, because the birth of a child with Down Syndrome has the potential "to destroy the psychological well-being of the wife and husband and also to put them at risk for a serious or not-serious illness and also to destroy their way of life."[34]

R. Waldenberg's permissive approach is based partly on the opinion of the medieval decisor R. Yair Ḥaim Bacharach, who views the prohibition of abortion as an extension of the prohibition of masturbation. For R. Waldenberg, this makes abortion much less of a halakhic problem, since women are not forbidden to "waste seed." For this reason, R. Waldenberg suggests it is optimal for the procedure to be performed by a woman doctor.[35]

It is clear that R. Waldenberg's relatively liberal position on abortion is not based on a woman's right to choose. In other contexts, as we will see, he has written forcefully that a person does not have the right to decide what will happen to their body because all life belongs to God. Regarding terminal care, for example, he maintains that the physician is required to do everything in his power to compel the patient to extend his life.[36] Ronald Dworkin has written that one could oppose abortion because one believes "that human life has an intrinsic, innate value; that human life is sacred just in itself; and that the sacred nature of a human life begins even before the creature whose life it is has movement or sensation or interests or rights of its own. According to this claim, abortion is wrong in principle because it disregards and insults the intrinsic value, the sacred character, of any stage or form of human life."[37] He labels this the *detached* objection because it does not depend on any particular rights or interests, as opposed to the *derivative* position, which maintains that fetuses share the basic rights and interests of all humans, including the right not to be killed. Rabbi Waldenberg's position is best understood from a *detached* perspective, and hence his difficulty in formulating a precise legal reason for his reluctance to approve the procedure himself, besides an obvious discomfort with ending a potential life prematurely.

His permissive stance on abortion in halakhah seems unaffected by the emergence of new technologies such as prenatal ultrasound, which enables one to see clearly the developing fetus and to which we owe the increasing success in treating premature infants. One might expect this

---

34 Ibid., Vol. 14, 101:2.

35 Responsa, *Tzitz Eliezer*, Vol. 9, 51:3:3:2.

36 Responsa, *Tzitz Eliezer*, Vol. 5, Ramat Raḥel, 28.

37 Ronald Dworkin, "Life's Dominion: An Argument About Abortion, Euthanasia, and Individual Freedom" (New York: Vintage Books, 1994).

success to work against abortion in the fetal stage. In fact, third-trimester abortions are illegal in many countries. But this point does not seem to affect R. Waldenberg's position that halakhic decisors do not have to consider technological advancements.

End-of-life Care

R. Waldenberg in his book *Ramat Raḥel*[38] addresses the questions 1. whether one is allowed or even required to do everything in one's power to extend the life of a *gosses* (a dying patient),[39] and 2. whether you are allowed to desecrate the Shabbat in order to do so. It is interesting that he connects these two questions but as we shall see for him they are interdependent. In answering the second question he begins by examining why one may desecrate the Shabbat to save a life. The Talmud in Shabbat 151a gives a reason when the life is that of a day-old infant: so that it will be able to observe many more *Shabbatot.* From this reason it is not clear that saving a life takes preference over Shabbat observance. Perhaps one may not violate the Shabbat to save a *gosses* who may not live for more *Shabbatot.* Based on this reasoning R. Waldenberg quotes the *Ohr HaḤayyim* who claims that one is not allowed to save a non-Shabbat observer because the potential for further Shabbat observance doesn't apply. R. Waldenberg rejects this line of reasoning for two reasons. 1. It's not just the potential for further Shabbat observance that allows one to violate the Shabbat to save a life, but the potential to do any mitzvah, and in our case for example, the *gosses* may repent in his last hours of life 2. But in reality R. Waldenberg rejects this whole line of thinking and based on the Talmud in *Yoma* 85b claims that the dispensation given to save a life on the Shabbat has nothing to do with future mitzvah observance but is based

---

38 Responsa, *Tzitz Eliezer*, Vol. 5, Ramat Raḥel, 28. Ramat Raḥel is not a collection of classic responsa but R. Waldenberg's commentary on sections of the *Arukh Ha-Shulḥan.* Other responsa of his relating to end-of-life care deal with real-life cases while others are more theoretical. R. Feinstein's responsa are also a combination of real and theoretical cases. It would be interesting to see if the form of the question has any impact on the response. Rabbi Moshe David Tendler ("Introduction," in *Responsa of R. Feinstein*, New York: Ktav, 1996) has previously pointed out that at times R. Feinstein just responds with a brief discussion and the practical answer to the question, and at other times with a detailed analysis of the relevant sources and his understanding of them. In this case it appears that R. Feinstein is using the question as a springboard for a detailed presentation of his opinion on the manner.

39 There is much confusion and uncertainty nowadays on how to define a *gosses.* The standard halakhic definition is one who is expected to live less than three days.

on the principle of you should live by them and not die by them. Not based on any utilitarian decision making, saving a life simply takes precedence over Shabbat observance. If that is the case, it should also apply to a *gosses* who as the mishnah in *Semaḥot*[40] tells us is considered alive for all purposes. He brings proof for this principle from the Talmud in *Yoma* 85a, which says that you are allowed dig out from the rubble on Shabbat even someone who will live for only a short period (*ḥayei sha'ah*),[41] and this halakhah is quoted by Rambam[42] and the *Shulḥan Arukh*.[43]

R. Waldenberg then claims that if one is allowed to desecrate the Shabbat for a *gosses* then it follows that is one is required to do everything humanely possible to extend the life of a terminal patient in every situation, even if they are suffering.[44] According to R. Waldenberg, the reason for this requirement to extend life in every situation is that every moment of life is valuable, for there are people who justify their entire existence with a thought of repentance at the end of life.[45] In addition, suffering has the potential to erase one's culpability from sin.[46] He brings further proof that a life of suffering is preferable to death from the case of the Sotah (a women found guilty of adultery who in ancient times was given a potion to drink that either caused her to die immediately or if she was worthy after a delay of a few years), whose life is extended in pain if she merits it, as opposed to dying immediately.[47] Rambam quotes the halakhah as follows: "A *sotah* who has merit of learning Torah, even if she is not obligated in it does not die immediately …but suffers greatly for a year or two or

---

40 *Semaḥot* 1:1.

41 There is no clear halakhic definition of a *ḥayei sha'ah*. Some consider it to be someone who will die within 12 months, while others think it is closer to a gosses. For a full discussion of the precise definition of a *ḥayei sha'ah* see Avraham Steinberg, "Terminally Ill," *Encyclopedia of Jewish Medical Ethics* (Jerusalem: Feldheim, 2003).

42 Maimonides' Shabbat, 2:18, Rav Waldenberg.

43 *Shulḥan Arukh, Oraḥ Hayyim* 329:4.

44 He explicitly says that as much pain medicine should be given as necessary even if the medicine has the potential to shorten life as long as that is not the purpose of giving the medication. The reason that one is allowed to give the pain medication even if it has the potential to shorten life is based on Ramban in *Torat Ha-Adam* that part of the permission given to doctors to practice medicine is that they are allowed to give medications that also have the potential to harm.

45 Responsa, *Tzitz Eliezer,* Vol. 5, Ramat Raḥel, 28.

46 Responsa, *Tzitz Eliezer,* Vol. 9, 47.

47 Responsa, *Tzitz Eliezer,* Vol. 14, 80.

three according to her merit and dies with a swollen abdomen and with her limbs falling off."[48]

What happens if the patient does not want his life extended? Do we listen to him? R. Waldenberg cites Rav Yaakov Emden[49] who discusses a case of a patient who prefers to die rather than live in suffering and requires the doctor to amputate a limb even against his own will because it is not his decision to make. R. Waldenberg explains Rav Emden's opinion based on the principle that a person's soul belongs not to him but to God.[50] He says in similar situations that it is not the patient's or the family's decision to make whether to extend life but the physician is required to do everything in his power to compel the patient to extend his life.[51]

He brings halakhic proof that a person does not have ownership over their body and hence does not have decision-making capacity from the halakhah that one is not allowed to injure oneself,[52] and the law that a relative is not allowed to accept *kofer* (monetary restitution) from a murderer because in the words of Rambam "the soul of the deceased does not belong to the redeemer but to God."[53]

R. Waldenberg maintains that the normative obligation requiring a physician to heal the sick is all-encompassing and applies to all patients at all times even in the midst of great suffering.[54] He has harsh words for physicians who "wrap themselves in the cloak of mercy" and actively end a patient's life, and he is also concerned about the slippery slope if we allow physician-assisted suicide.[55]

R. Waldenberg also addresses the practical implications of his ruling. He was opposed to the practice common among physicians of stopping chemotherapy, radiation and even antibiotics in patients with metastatic cancer in whom there was no hope for a cure.[56] R. Waldenberg's insistence on full treatment for all patients obliquely addresses the issue of medical futility. Many bioethics believe that if a patient requests a treatment that has no potential to extend life in a meaningful way or improve their quality of life then the physician and society is not required to offer

---

48 Maimonides, *Sotah* 3:20.

49 Rabbi Jacob Emden, *Mor u-Ketzi'ah, Oraḥ Ḥayyim* 328.

50 Responsa, *Tzitz Eliezer*, Vol. 18, 62.

51 Responsa, *Tzitz Eliezer*, Vol. 18, 62.

52 Maimonides, *Ḥovel u-Mazik* 5:1, *Shulḥan Arukh, Ḥoshen Mishpat*, 420:31.

53 Maimonides, *Rotzeaḥ* 1:4.

54 Responsa, *Tzitz Eliezer*, Vol. 14:80.

55 Responsa, *Tzitz Eliezer*, Vol. 5, Ramat Raḥel #29.

56 Responsa, *Tzitz Eliezer*, Vol. 14:80.

or provide it.[57] Apparently, R. Waldenberg would advocate for any treatment in any patient that could extend life even for a short period.

To summarize R. Waldenberg's approach to the terminally ill patient:

1. The halakhic justification for his position that one must extend life at all times is based on the comparison with Shabbat. If you are allowed to violate Shabbat in order to extend the life of a *gosses* than you must be required to do so. The first assumption is almost universally accepted, but the extension to all situations is open to debate. Just because you are allowed to desecrate the Shabbat for a *gosses* doesn't necessarily mean you are required to extend his life in all circumstances.[58]
2. R. Waldenberg's position that essentially a person has no autonomy in his medical decision making and can be compelled to accept treatment is also open to debate. One can accept his theological claim that a person's body doesn't belong to him but still accept the idea that in certain instances God gave man a certain degree of control over his body. It is a far cry from decreeing that man is not allowed to harm himself to maintaining that man must always choose a life of suffering over death.
3. R. Waldenberg maintains based on Talmudic sources that a life of suffering is always preferable to death. As we will see there are other sources that suggest otherwise. His acceptance of suffering is based on the proposition that any time living is beneficial for one has the potential to do mitzvoth during that time, and that suffering has the potential to erases ones culpability for past actions.
4. R. Waldenberg claims that in order to fulfill his normative obligation to heal, a physician must always work to extend life and in no circumstances may hasten death.

Taken as a sum total, R. Waldenberg's positions are a strident critique of Western bioethics. Modern secular bioethics are primarily based on the principle of unlimited personal autonomy and a deep concern with quality of life. In addition, many ethicists feel that at a certain point a physician is

---

57 Albert R Jonsen, "Forgoing life support: The quality of life," *Bioethics Beyond the Headlines: Who lives? Who dies? Who decides?* (Lanham, MD: Rowman and Littlefield, 2005).

58 This might depend on the well-known question of whether *pikuaḥ nefesh* on Shabbat is *hutra* or *dukhuya* (for example see *Teshuvot Ha-Rashba* I:689). If it is *dukhuya* it might be easier to accept Rav Waldenberg's claim, but even in that case I still think it is debatable.

no longer morally obligated to work to extend life but his therapeutic interventions should be used to ease the dying process.[59] This is the ethical underpinning of the hospice and palliative care movement, which has gained great acceptance in the Western world. Whether the physician should have an active or passive role in easing the dying process is open to great moral and legal debate in the modern world. R. Waldenberg is obviously opposed to any such role for a physician and stridently upholds the position that every minute of life in this world has infinite value. In addition, the fact that the question of how one cares for the terminally ill patient might be different in the modern environment due to the development of new technologies that can extend life in even the most dire of circumstances does not seem to be an issue for R. Waldenberg.

Artificial Reproduction and Surrogate motherhood

R. Waldenberg has argued forcefully against the use of artificial insemination using a donor's semen (AID) and is even hesitant to permit it using the husband's sperm (AIH). In his own words:

This whole question of using AI is an abomination to the tents of Jacob and there is no greater desecration of the family in the tents of Israel. This [AI] destroys all the principles of **purity and sanctity** in the life of a Jewish family which has distinguished us from the time we became a nation. It also breaks the chain between sons and fathers ... and who are those who donate their sperm for this purpose in order to receive money. They are the lowest of the low and what kind of children can come from this seed. And the seed of the father is what creates the brain in the fetus. ... the *Sefer Ha-Ḥinukh* teaches us that the nature of the father is hidden in the child. And how can the holy children of Israel think we can build from these seeds and not see that it will bring destruction upon the family. ... and when we are speaking about the sperm of a non-Jew all words are extraneous to describe the disgust and the horror of the act and the great spiritual destruction it will bring into the house of Israel and the individual homes.[60]

R. Waldenberg also raises the possibility that AID would be considered a form of adultery.[61] He postulates that there are two components to the prohibition of adultery: 1. Forbidden sexual relations even without ejaculation and 2. the placement of another man's sperm into the women's

59 Baruch A. Brody and H. Tristram Englehardt, "Hospice Care," *Bioethics: Readings and Cases* (Englewood Cliffs: Prentice-Hall, 1987).

60 *Arukh Ha-Shulḥan, Even Haezer*, 23:1.

61 Responsa, *Tzitz Eliezer*, Vol. 9, 51;4:1,3.

vagina even without intercourse. He brings proof for this idea from Ramban,[62] who infers from the use of the word "seed" in the text of the verse in Leviticus 18, 20 which prohibits adultery ("Thou shall not lie carnally with thy neighbor's wife for seed") that the reason for the prohibition of adultery is that there should be no confusion who the father of the child is. If that is the reason it should also apply to AID. He also quotes the *Sefer Ha-Ḥinukh*[63] who says the reason for the prohibition of adultery is that people should know who their father is.

On a halakhic level he claims that it is possible that the position of Rabbenu Peretz by a *ben niddah* [a child who was conceived while the mother was ritually impure] would not be applicable to the case of AI. Rabbenu Peretz writes, "a woman in *niddah* can lie on her husband's sheets; however she should be careful about lying on the sheets on which another man lay for the fear that she may become pregnant. And why shouldn't we be afraid that she might become pregnant from her husband's semen and the child will be the son of a *niddah*. And he answered because there were no illicit relations the child is completely legitimate and even if she became pregnant that way from another man we see that Ben Sira [who according to the aggada was the son of the prophet's Jeremiah's daughter who became pregnant in a bathhouse from the sperm of her own father] was completely legitimate. But we are concerned about the semen of another man because it might happen that the child will marry his father's sister (unknowingly)."[64] In the case of lying on the sheets there was no conscious action by the woman to try to get pregnant; in the case of AI there was a conscious act by the woman's donor and doctor to impregnate her and in this case maybe Rabbenu Peretz would consider it adultery.[65] Rav Waldenberg admits this contention is tenuous because Rabbenu Peretz himself says that the reason for his ruling was that there was no "illicit relations." But he quotes another medieval authority, Rabbi Shlomo of London,[66] who writes, "A woman should not wash on the day of her immersion in the bath that her husband washed in because she might become pregnant and the child will be a *ben niddah*." Apparently, Rabbi Shlomo considers a child born from a bathhouse conception problematic. Furthermore, he quotes the *Shiltei Gibborim* in tractate *Shevuot*:[67] "I found that it was asked of Rabbi Meir [the Maharam of

---

62 *Ramban al ha-Torah*, Leviticus 18,20.

63 *Sefer HaḤinukh, Mitzvah* 35.

64 Quoted in *Taz, Yoreh De'ah*, 195;7.

65 Responsa, *Tzitz Eliezer,* Vol. 9, 51;4:1,8.

66 Quoted in the *Birḥai Yosef, Even ha-Ezer,* 1:14.

67 *Shiltei Hagibborim*, Talmud Babli, *Shevuot*, beginning of the second chapter.

Rottenburg], Why aren't we careful that a women should not lie on her husband's sheets because maybe she will become pregnant and the child will be a *ben niddah*, like we don't let a women lie on the sheets of another man because of the concern that she might become pregnant with the semen left on the sheets like Ben-Sira. And he answered that because the child of a *niddah* is legitimate in every sense [not considered a mamzer] we are not concerned." Implicit in his answer is that Rabbi Meir accepted the contention that the child is a *ben niddah* and in the case of semen from another man that the child is a mamzer. Remarkably, R. Waldenberg suggests that this responsum of Rabbi Meir is the same responsum of Rabbenu Peretz that is quoted above and the name was mistakenly changed from Rabbi Meir to Rabbenu Peretz along with the real meaning of the responsum, which should be that the child is considered a *ben niddah*. We therefore cannot determine halakhah from this possibly distorted opinion of Rabbenu Peretz.[68]

Regarding the legend of Ben Sira which implies that there is no concern of *mamzerot* after a bathhouse conception, R. Waldenberg doubts the veracity of the legend and cites Ramban quoted by the Ḥatam Sofer[69] who maintains that one does not have to believe in the truth of stories not found in the Talmud or Midrash and certainly cannot learn halakhah from them. In conclusion, he feels that a child born from AID is a *safek* [possible] mamzer [bastard] and the husband should divorce the wife.[70] It is worth noting that in an earlier responsum, R. Waldenberg was less forceful in his conclusions and maintained that the "woman is not forbidden to her husband because there were no illicit relations."[71]

R. Feinstein was aware of R. Waldenberg's proof from Ramban in Leviticus and objects to it for a number of reasons:[72]

---

68 Responsa, *Tzitz Eliezer,* Vol. 9, 51;4:1,8. It is not the intent of this paper to evaluate the correctness of Rav Waldenberg's assertion regarding the validity of the text, rather I think it shows the length he is willing to go to support his thesis. For a further discussion on the text in question see Green, J. *Assia* vol. 5. 1986, pp. 112–24.

69 Responsa, *Ḥatam Sofer, Oraḥ Ḥayyim,* 16.

70 Responsa, *Tzitz Eliezer,* Vol. 9, 51;4:1,8. In another responsum (*Tzitz Eliezer,* Vol. 13, 97) he quotes the Responsa, *Minḥat Yitzḥak*, Part 4, 5:14: "Is it possible to doubt that the fact that the women is lying naked before the physician with her genitals uncovered and he repeats the procedure over and over again injecting the sperm until it is absorbed that this is illicit behavior?" The implication of this approach is that the actual procedure of AI is akin to adultery. It is not clear to what extent R. Waldenberg agrees with this notion.

71 Responsa, *Tzitz Eliezer,* Vol. 3, 27.

72 Responsa, *Iggerot Moshe, Even ha-Ezer,* Part 2, 11.

1. He cites the Ibn Ezra[73] who rejects the interpretation of Ramban and explains that the use of the word "seed" teaches that adultery is forbidden even for the purpose of procreation.
2. R. Feinstein himself interprets that the use of the word "seed," based on a rabbinical teaching, is to exclude liability if the relations were with a dead man.
3. The concern about not knowing who the father is is only a rabbinic edict and therefore could not be the reason for the Torah prohibition.
4. The Ramban himself in the same piece stresses that relations with a married women even without ejaculation is equally punishable so the concern about lineage could not be the reason for the prohibition.

R. Waldenberg's primary concern is the effect that AID will have on the family. Even though illicit sexual relations did not occur, he considers AID a form of adultery and encourages the husband to divorce his adulterous spouse. In addition, he is concerned about the lineage of the child and the influence of the donor father on the spiritual development of the child. In his world view, knowledge of one's predecessors is of crucial import.

R. Waldenberg's harsh words are partly directed at R. Feinstein, who permits AID using a non-Jewish donor. R. Feinstein responds to another contemporary who also criticized his ruling:

> It appears from your letter that I would be insulted by your rebuke, but on the contrary I am satisfied that there are spiritual people that are not afraid or embarrassed to give rebuke. But in truth there is nothing in what I wrote and instructed that will cause any desecration of the sanctity of Israel but it is the eternal truth from our Rabbis, the *Rishonim.* And your objection comes from philosophies based on external knowledge that influence even very wise people to understand the mitzvoth of the Torah based on this alien knowledge … but I am not like that and all my philosophies come only from knowledge of the Torah without any outside influences … . And any reasons that come from external knowledge or explanations that come from the heart are worthless even if they are more stringent and are thought to increase the purity and sanctity of Israel.[74]

R. Waldenberg responds to R. Feinstein's arguments by stating, "How awful is the thought that someone would entertain the possibility that it is permissible to cause mixture with non-Jews through AI. My feelings on

---

73 *Ibn Ezra al Ha-Torah,* Leviticus, 18,20.

74 Responsa, *Iggerot Moshe, Even ha-Ezer,* Part 2, 11.

this are as clear as daylight and are not from external sources or come from the heart but from a holy place, the core of Jewish law, and from the great knowledge of the obligation placed upon us to be a kingdom of priests and a holy nation. This true philosophy comes from the living Torah."[75]

R. Waldenberg holds that a child born of in vitro fertilization has no legal mother (even if the same woman is the egg donor and birth mother) and prohibits the procedure.[76] He advances this theory based on his contention that parenthood is established only through natural sexual relations between a man and woman and not through the manipulations of a "third power." In order to be recognized as a mother, the woman must have fertilization take place inside her body. R. Bleich has already pointed out the lack of halakhic precedent for these ideas.[77] I agree that using conventional halakhic methodology there does not seem to be much room for R. Waldenberg's opinion, but it appears to me that he is using another more controversial methodology. The primary reason for his opposition is theological in nature. He quotes approvingly the words of the *Arukh Ha-Shulḥan* [late 19th century legal decisor] who comments that "a person who was created in the image of God should understand that (sexual) desire that was created in him is not for the purpose of the desire because this is illogical…..it was only created for the purpose of populating the world. ….Because if God did not create this desire no person would have relations because of the disgust associated with it."[78] In R. Waldenberg's thought the only reason for sexual relations is propagation of the species. The Catholic Church also had great reservations about permitting all forms of artificial reproduction because they believe there is no substitute for natural fertilization. The prominent Protestant theologian Paul Ramsey was also bothered by the separation of the sexual act from conception.[79] R. Waldenberg further writes:

---

75 Responsa, *Tzitz Eliezer,* Vol. 9, 51;4:5,2.

76 Responsa, *Tzitz Eliezer,* part 15, 45.

77 J. David Bleich, "In vitro fertilization: questions of maternal identity and conversion," *Jewish law and the new reproductive technologies,* ed. Emanuel Feldman and Joel B. Wolowelsky, (Hoboken: Ktav, 1997), pp. 47-8.

78 *Arukh Ha-Shulḥan, Even ha-Ezer,* 23:1. For further discussion on this topic see Alan Jotkowitz, "The Role of Theology in Contemporary Jewish Ethical Decision-Making: The Case of Artificial Insemination," *Journal of Contemporary Religion,* vol. 28, 2013, pp. 141–53.

79 Paul Ramsey, "Moral and Religious Implications of Genetic Control," *On Moral Medicine: Theological Perspectives in Medical Ethics,* ed. Stephen E. Lammers and Allen Verhey (Grand Rapids: William B. Eerdmans, 1988).

The future of the process of artificial reproduction is to create a "laboratory child" which means that the pregnancy and birth will all occur outside the body of the woman in the laboratory. And there is also a plan to create a human clone……and this will cause destruction and loss of the human spirit and will rule in all problems of conception and it will turn into a science without any humanity. Many scientists have already expressed their deep fears about this future…that will create a new being without free choice and without familial relationships and this will also create fear and confusion among many regular people. And therefore what have we accomplished with the creation of these new beings that do not fulfill the obligation to procreate found in the holy Torah and only cause complicated problems that are bound to set the human race back a thousand degrees.[80]

R. Waldenberg is essentially identifying with the concerns of the bioconservative stream of modern bioethics, which is hesitant to accept new technologies that upset the natural order. For example, expressing similar sentiments as R. Waldenberg, the prominent bioethicist Leon Kass has written:

1. "Man is defined partly by his origins and his lineage; to be bound up with his parents, siblings, ancestors, and descendants is part of what we mean by human. By tampering with and confounding these origins and linkages, we are involved in nothing less than creating a new conception of what it means to be human."
2. "The new procedures for making babies all involve a new partner: the scientist-physician. The obstetrician is no longer just the midwife, but also the sower of seed. Even in the treatment of intramarital infertility, the scientist-physician who employs in vitro-fertilization and laboratory culture of human embryos has acquired far greater power over human life than his collogue who simply repairs the obstructed oviduct. He presides over many creations in many patients."
3. How and why dehumanizing? Because human procreation is not simply an activity of our rational will… Is there possibly some wisdom in the mystery of nature that joins the pleasure of sex, the inarticulate longing for union, the communication of love, and the deep and partly articulate desire for children in the very activity by which we continue the chain of human existence? Is biological parenthood a built-in device selected to promote the adequate caring for posterity? Before we embark on new modes of reproduction, we should

80 *Responsa, Tzitz Eliezer*, part 15, 45.

consider the meaning of the union of sex, love, and procreation, and the meaning and the consequences of its cleavage."[81]

Another example of this conservative tendency is R. Waldenberg's opposition to plastic surgery because he feels that it does not fall under the general dispensation which is learnt from the verse "he shall surely be healed," which gives a physician permission to heal. He continues, "one should know and believe that there is no creator like God and he created each person in a unique way and one should not add or detract from this creation."[82] This concern of the doctor playing the role of creator does not enter at all into the thinking of R. Feinstein, who permits cosmetic surgery.

Methodological issues

Newman has written that that halakhists make moral judgments by using a three-step process:

1. they identify precedents from the Rabbinic literature
2. they adduce principles from these texts
3. they apply these principles to new cases[83]

a process Ellenson has labeled halakhic formalism.[84]

While there is debate among scholars of halakhah on the relative weight of formalism versus values-driven *psak* in halakhic decision making, it is probably true that no authority exclusively uses one of the methodologies. But certain tendencies can be appreciated. Rami Reiner in a review of Rabbi Elyashiv's decision making makes the argument that especially in his later opinions he was very formulistic as opposed to some of his contemporaries[85] and I have argued that Rabbi Haim David Halevi following in the footsteps of his teacher Rabbi Uziel took very seriously

---

81 Leon R. Kass, *Toward a More Natural Science* (New York: The Free Press, 1985).

82 *Responsa, Tzitz Eliezer,* 11:41.

83 Louis E. Newman, "Woodchoppers and Respirators: The Problem of Interpretation in Contemporary Jewish Ethics," *Modern Judaism,* vol. 10, 1990, pp. 17–42.

84 David H. Ellenson, "How to Draw Guidance from Heritage: Jewish Approaches to Mortal Choices," *A Time to be Born and a Time to Die*, ed. Barry Kogan (New York: Aldine de Gruyter, 1990), pp. 219–32.

85 Avraham (Rami) Reiner, "R' Yosef Shalom Elyashiv as a Halachic Decisor," *Modern Judaism,* vol. 33. 2013, pp. 260–300.

meta-halakhic values in his decision making.[86] Others have argued that Rabbi Shlomo Zalman Auerbach was similarly inclined.[87] I do not think that Rabbi Waldenberg fits nicely into one of these categories. On the one hand his position on end-of-life care appears very formulistic while his position on abortion seems driven by a concern for the suffering of the baby and mother. In addition, his distaste for all new forms of artificial reproduction seems to be based on a specific value system.

Walter Wurzberger has written on the role of intuition in halakhic decision making. He praises the halakhah for making "space for the input of individuality and subjectivity on religiously significant issues."[88] He maintains that halakhic intuitions are necessary to provide normative guidance in many instances that do not fall under explicit rules (like many cases in modern bioethics) and to resolve situations of conflicting moral principles. He is aware of the difficulties that this very subjective system relying on individual idiosyncrasies could theoretically face but is confident that "the residual influence or exposure to halakhic categories of thought makes itself felt in areas where the law itself cannot be applied."[89]

Newman has thoughtfully written on the difficulty of doing modern bioethics from a Jewish perspective as in many instances there is a paucity of ancient sources from which to build a response.[90] For example how does one formulate a Jewish response to the ethical dilemma of reproductive cloning when the ancient and medieval authorities never even dreamed of the possibility? In response to these dilemmas modern authorities have taken different approaches. For example in his responsum on end-of-life care, R. Feinstein bases his answer on a Talmudic narrative and other authorities use the midrash of Leah and Rachel switching fetuses to help determine parenthood in surrogacy. R. Waldenberg in a sense denies the question, there is nothing new because the sages knew everything. And if the sages did not discuss it his "intuition" is not to allow it, as we have seen in his responsum dealing with transplantation

---

86 Alan Jotkowitz, "Gentleness and Patience in the Medical Ethics Decision Making of Rabbis Benzion Uziel and Haim David Halevy," *Modern Judaism,* vol. 29, 2009.

87 Amir Moshiach, "Rabbi Shlomo Zalman Auerbach's Halakhic Philosophy in a Dynamic Era of Socio-technological Transformation" (Ramat Gan: Bar Ilan University, 2013).

88 Walter S. Wurtzberger, *Ethics of Responsibility* (Philadelphia: JPS, 1994).

89 Ibid.

90 Lewis E. Newman, "Woodchoppers and Respirators: The Problem of Interpretation in Contemporary Jewish Ethics," *Modern Judaism,* vol. 10. 1990, pp. 17–42.

and artificial reproduction. This approach is based on a specific world view in which all wisdom is contained in the Torah and there is no notion of scientific progress. He believes that the Talmud's scientific principles based on revealed wisdom are infallible. R. Waldenberg is skeptical of modern science and comments that medical knowledge is constantly changing, casting doubts on its veracity.[91] In contrast he believes in the absolute truth of the wisdom of the Talmudic sages even regarding scientific matters. This is reflected in his acceptance of the Rivash's explanation of the eternal truth of the *treifah* halakhot and his adoption of this conservative position when opposing a redefinition of death. Lurking behind this attitude of R. Waldenberg's is more than just skepticism towards science but it reflects a certain theological position on the nature of halakhah. R. Feinstein recognizes the gradual progression of scientific knowledge and comments that the Talmudic definition of a human *treifah* changes according to the medical knowledge of the time.[92]

This understanding can help explain his vigorous opposition to artificial insemination from a non-Jew, because the Talmud maintains that the "father supplies the semen, the white substance, out of which are formed the child's bones, the sinews, the nails, the brain and the white of the eye" (*Nidda*, 30a). It is inconceivable according to R. Waldenberg that the infant's "brain" should come from a non-Jew. As we have seen, R. Waldenberg permitted even third trimester abortions in some instances and was not at all concerned with such modern medical terms as viability or the ability to see the growing fetus with ultrasound. Since these concepts were unknown to the sages they were irrelevant to him. It is worth noting that at times even R. Feinstein who did not shy away from the use of modern science in developing his halakhic positions used similar reasoning to discount the halakhic importance of microorganisms or electrocardiographic evidence of heart function.[93] This attitude towards modern science can also be seen in two other positions of R. Waldenberg. A child born with female external genitalia is halakhically considered a female even if his genetic phenotype is male.[94] The fact that the child has a Y chromosome is irrelevant to R. Waldenberg because the Talmud was concerned only with external appearance, not genetic makeup. He goes as far as to suggest that a woman who undergoes a sex change operation becomes halakhically a man as reflected in the external genitalia (and vice

91 Responsa, *Tzitz Eliezer,* Vol. 13, 104.

92 Responsa, *Iggerot Moshe, Yoreh De'ah* III:36.

93 Responsa, *Iggerot Moshe, Ḥoshen Mishpat,* vol. 2:73:4.

94 Responsa, *Tzitz Eliezer,* Vol. 11, 78.

versa) and does not need a bill of divorce from her spouse because a man cannot be married to another man.[95]

Nowhere is this attitude demonstrated more conclusively than in a response he gave to the question whether blood typing has any validity in halakhah.[96] The exact query was whether one can use blood to exclude paternity, a fact that modern science takes for granted. Relying on the above-quoted form the Talmud in *Niddah* that the mother provides the red part of the child, which includes the skin, muscles, hair and the black of the eye, R. Waldenberg concludes that obviously the red part of the child includes the blood and therefore all the child's blood comes from the mother. Therefore blood typing is irrelevant when it comes to paternity determination. R. Waldenberg continues, "and there is no contradiction between the scientific test and the words of our sages because even if we accept the scientific fact that the father's blood type is not consistent with the child's, this does not mean that he is not the father because we know that the blood does not come from the father."[97]

He further writes "that it sometimes occurs that a person's blood type can change, because when a person receives a transfusion doesn't his blood type change, and this is perhaps the reason that sometimes the child's blood type is not consistent with his mother's."[98]

He also makes the point that "we see in many circumstances that what science thinks is true today after a while changes and that is because of the new advances and discoveries. And the view of the great poskim is that we do not adjudicate halakhah based on the opinions of physicians and this is clearly different from when we accept the opinions of physicians based on x rays or on what they see."[99]

In order to explain Rabbi Waldenberg's thinking, one can invoke Rabbi Soloveitchik's conception of an autonomous halakhic universe as described in *Halakhic Man*: "Halakhah has a fixed a priori relationship to the whole of reality in all of its fine and detailed particulars. Halakhic man orients himself to the entire cosmos and tries to understand it by utilizing an ideal world which he bears in his haklakhic consciousness. All halakhic concepts are a priori, and it is through them that halakhic man looks at the world… And when many halakhic concepts do not correspond with the phenomenon of the real world, halakhic man is not distressed. His

---

95 Responsa, *Tzitz Eliezer,* Vol. 10, 25.

96 Responsa, *Tzitz Eliezer,* Vol. 13, 104.

97 Ibid.

98 Ibid.

99 Ibid.

deepest desire is not the realization of the Halakhah but rather the ideal construction which was given to him at Sinai, and this ideal construction exists forever...the foundations of foundations and the pillar of halakhic thought is not the practical ruling but the determination of the theoretic Halakhah."[100]

But as Rabbi Soloveitchik himself notes, he was more concerned with developing a model for the theoretical understanding of halakhah than with explaining how practical halakhic decision making should operate.

Rabbi Waldenberg's approach has Kabbalistic overtones in explaining the nature of Torah and its relationship to the world. As we have seen, he was not averse to quoting the Zohar in explaining that "it is impossible for all the limbs of the body to live even one minute without the heart,"[101] and as Danny Lasker has pointed out, his opposition to artificial insemination is also indebted to a Kabbalistic understanding of human procreation.[102]

This essay has attempted to demonstrate that over the course of a lifetime of work, R. Waldenberg developed a distinct halakhic approach to bioethical dilemmas characterized by an "intuitive" bioconservative mindset combined with an understanding that all wisdom, including scientific knowledge, is to be found in the revealed Torah. ☙

---

100 Joseph B. Soloveitchik, *Halakhic Man* (Philadelphia: JPS, 1983), pp. 23-4.

101 Responsa, *Tzitz Eliezer,* Vol. 10, 25:4:7.

102 Daniel Lasker, "Kabbalah, Halakhah, and Modern Medicine: The Case of Artificial Insemination," *Modern Judaism,* vol. 8, 1988, pp. 1–14.

A Controversy in the Amsterdam Community in 1650: Can a Ger Tzedek be Appointed Parnass?

By: JEREMY I. PFEFFER

There are few more contentious issues in public affairs than the selection of appointees to positions of power and authority, and never is it more divisive than when the candidate is an outsider. One such incident occurred in the Amsterdam Jewish community in or about the year 1650. The office to be filled was that of *parnass* (lay head of the community) and the eligibility of the leading candidate, an otherwise impeccable nominee, was challenged at the meeting of the membership convened to confirm his appointment on the grounds that he was a *Ger* (proselyte) and hence prohibited by the Torah from occupying a position of coercive authority over the community.

> From amongst your brethren shall you set a king over you; you may not place a foreigner over you, [one] who is not your brother.[1]

On the face of it, the objection was well founded. In the *Mishneh Torah*, Rambam had formulated the *Halakhah* as follows:

> A king should not be appointed from amongst the *gerim* [מקהל גרים], even after a number of generations, until his mother is an Israelite, as it says: *You may not place a foreigner over you, who is not your brother.* This applies not to the monarchy alone, but to all positions of authority within Israel…All appointments you make shall be none other than *from amongst your brethren.*[2]

---

1 *Devarim* 17:15.

2 *Mishneh Torah, Hilkhot Melakhim,* 1:4.

Jeremy I. Pfeffer is a retired physics teacher at the Rehovot campus of the Hebrew University of Jerusalem. His published writings include co-authored University-level textbooks on Modern Physics in both English and Hebrew; two works on the Book of Job, a history of the London Bet Din from 1805 to 1855, with emphasis on its dealings with the Jewish convicts transported to Australia, and researches into medieval Hebrew manuscripts.

Thus, it would appear that *gerim*, as a class, are excluded from holding office in a Jewish community. This ruling was an issue of concern for the Amsterdam community, many of whose members were *Anussim* who had begun arriving in the newly independent Northern Dutch Provinces after 1593. Most of the males were uncircumcised when they arrived and would have had to undergo *giur*, the all-pervading surveillance of the Inquisition having made circumcision in Iberia impossible.[3]

The candidate was the son of an *Anuss* (*Cristiano Nuevo*, *Converso* or *Marrano*) and a Christian woman, and as such he was not a Jew from birth. His father had died and he had made his way from Iberia to Amsterdam where he underwent *giur* and properly became a Jew.[4] He had become a respected member of the community, a "brother" Jew, but did this make him a "brother" in the sense required for an appointment to a position of coercive authority?[5]

Unsure how to act in the matter without slighting the said *ger* or going against Rambam's ruling, the Amsterdam Jewish community appealed for outside guidance. The replies they received from two rabbinical scholars have recently come to light; they were discovered in the Hebrew codex Ms. 199 of Christ Church Library, Oxford.[6] The first of these scholars

---

3 The flow of *Anussim* and their offspring into Holland continued well into the seventeenth century and, as often occurs in immigrant societies, tensions had begun to surface between the earlier and later arrivals. Notwithstanding, as loyal supporters of the House of Orange, they prospered in their new home by dint of their skills and hard work.

4 Non-Jews are not 'converted' to Judaism; they become Jews (or Hebrews or Israelites). Becoming a Jew involves more than just changing one's religious affiliation. To be a Jew means to belong to the nation of Israel (עם ישראל), and when a gentile becomes a Jew, he joins that nation. By Jewish law, however, the only way of joining the nation of Israel is by acceptance of the *Torah* of Israel (תורת ישראל), and it is this that gives the process its religious connotations.

5 The word "brother" or a declension of it [...(י)אח] occurs some 250 times in the Torah, its definition and import depending in each instance on the particular context.

6 Pfeffer, Jeremy I., Authorship in a Hebrew Codex…MS 199: Tracing Two Lost Works by Delmedigo, *Christ Church Library Newsletter*, Volume 6, Issue3; <http://www.chch.ox.ac.uk/sites/default/files/Newsletter%20Tri10.pdf>. Pfeffer, Jeremy I., "From Eisenstadt to Oxford: The Provenance of MS 199 in the Hebrew Collection of Christ Church Library," *Christ Church Library Newsletter*, Volume 9, Issues 1–3. <http://www.chch.ox.ac.uk/sites/default/files/Christ%20Church%20Library%20Newsletter-Vol%209_0.pdf>.

was the polymath R. Joseph Solomon Delmedigo (1591–1655), also known as *YaShaR* of Candia (Heraklion, Crete);[7] the second was his pupil, R. Issachar Ber Jeiteless of Prague (d. 1685).[8]

***

Delmedigo summarizes the details of the affair in the opening paragraphs of his reply.

> A man of the seed of Israel, one of the *Anussim* in Portugal, profaned himself with a gentile woman who bore him a son; the man subsequently died. The lad remained with his mother until he grew up and learned wisdom, and 'the spirit of the Lord began to stir in him'...And he chose well and did not follow the ways of her idolatry and went in search of the Lord. And he came to Holland...and became a Jew...And it was on the day the leaders of the community were assembled...and they proposed to appoint him *parnass* and head of the community or *gabai* [treasurer] of the community chest for the redemption of prisoners, and [one of those present] objected...calling out "he is disqualified by the Torah [from holding the positions]"...but many stood up for him...and supported the righteous *Ger.*

This introduction also goes into some detail about the background and general circumstances of the *Anussim* and Jews of Amsterdam. Who

---

The inclusion of Issachar Ber's short *responsum* in a codex whose principal content is two works by Delmedigo is explained by the fact that he was a pupil of Delmedigo. We learn this from an inscription on the title page of a copy of David Ibn Yachya's book *Lashon Limudim* (Constantinople: Eliezer Soncino, 1542) that came up for auction in January 2013 at Kestenbaum & Co. New York (Auction No. 57: Lot 120). The inscription states that the volume was given to Issachar-Ber Jeiteless by his teacher Joseph Solomon Delmedigo.

7 A scion of a distinguished Ashkenazi family of rabbis and physicians that had settled in Crete during the fourteenth century. He was a student of Galileo in Padua where he studied medicine, and is credited with being the first Jewish Copernican. After spending much of his life on the move, Delmedigo ended his days in Prague where his tombstone still stands in the old Jewish Cemetery.

8 The first recorded mention of a person named Jeiteless (Geidels) is of a certain Moses ben Simon, who was listed as a house owner in Prague in 1615. His son Yehuda Leib (d. 1666) was *gabbai* of the Prague *hevra kaddisha* (Jewish Burial Society) for 30 years and also of the Altneuschul. His son, R. Issachar Ber, the author of the said *responsum*, was a leader of the Prague community until his death in 1685.

the questioner was, however, is not stated; Delmedigo just observes that "[the question] was apparently written by a great man, one of the wise men of the Portuguese [Jews]."

Although he was residing in Eisenstadt, Hungary, at the time—the colophon on his reply reads "Written here in the city of iron [Eisenstadt], near the city of Vienna, in the state of Hungary, Wednesday 15th *Menaḥem* (5)411 [August 2, 1651]"—Delmedigo was not unfamiliar with the Jews of Amsterdam. By 1627, or possibly earlier, his travels had brought him to the city where he would stay until 1630 and officiate as the community's *ad hoc* Rabbi. In his mid-thirties when he arrived, he had encountered much antagonism during his wanderings. "Whoever holds his soul dear must remove himself from secular sciences," he was told, "for they are contrary to the true Jewish nature." At once a rabbinical scholar, mystic and mathematical scientist who counted Karaites among his friends, an early proponent of the Copernican heliocentric model (he had been a student of Galileo during his medical studies in Padua) and the first Jew to use logarithms, he could not be other than controversial.[9] And like many such polymath geniuses before and after him, he would end his life a bitter and lonely person. Delmedigo had already composed thirty or more Hebrew books and essays (on astronomy, mathematics, medicine, logic, alchemy, astrology and *Kabbalah*) by the time he arrived in Amsterdam. All were still in manuscript, but despite the appeals of his friends and pupils, he refused to have them printed because, he claimed, they were still unfinished, though it was more likely for fear of denunciation. Notwithstanding, two compilations of his correspondence and essays on a range of scientific and mathematical topics, *Sefer Elim* and *Sefer Ma'ayan Gannim*, were published in Amsterdam by Menasseh ben Israel in 1629, evidently with his agreement.

Though it appears that he dearly hoped for it, he would never be appointed to the position of communal Rabbi (*Av Bet Din*), and in 1630 he left Amsterdam to take up the lesser position of physician to the Jewish community in Frankfurt-on-Main.[10] This was a rebuff that Delmedigo

---

9 For a discussion of the legitimacy of scientific activity amongst Jews in early modern times and the earliest Jewish allusions to Copernicus see: Ruderman, David B., *Jewish Thought and Scientific Discovery in Early Modern Europe* (Yale University Press, 1995); Brown, Jeremy, *New Heavens and a New Earth: The Jewish Reception of Copernican Thought* (Oxford University Press, 2013).

10 Before his authorship of the *responsum* in the Christ Church codex was uncovered, little had been known of Delmedigo's writings or activities after his departure from Amsterdam to take up the position of physician in Frankfurt. All that

would never forget, and the request from the Amsterdam community some twenty years later for guidance in the matter of the *Ger* who was the son of an *Anuss* was an opportunity for him to settle accounts. Accordingly, his reply opens with a dissertation on the importance of כבוד הבריות—Human Dignity or showing consideration for others. So important is this ordinance that the Talmud states "it can supersede a negative injunction (לא תעשה) of the Torah."[11] Delmedigo avers that this is the first lesson that the burghers of the Jewish community in Amsterdam have to learn: the *ger* should not be treated in the same insensitive manner as he had been when he was a stranger (the alternative meaning of the Hebrew word גר) in their midst.

Delmedigo was so agitated by this possibility that he attached a polemic he had composed entitled ספר בתי הנפש (*The Book of the Houses of the Soul*) to the halakhic *responsum* he dispatched to Amsterdam. The work is in part a passionate outpouring against those who are unwelcoming of *gerim* and in part a lyrical paean in their praise. In its introduction he explains that he was driven to write the piece by the grudging manner in which *gerim* were often received by their host communities. The body of the work comprises twenty-two paragraphs, composed and ordered such that their initial letters give the sequence of the Hebrew alphabet, from *Aleph* through *Tav*. In the first nine paragraphs, he berates the Jewish burghers of Amsterdam for their attitude towards the *gerim* amongst them; at one point he even compares their inhospitality to that of the biblical citizens of Sodom. In the next ten paragraphs, written in the first person, it is the son of the *Anuss* who speaks, telling his own story. He recounts how his father had been beguiled by a gentile woman (his mother) and died shortly afterwards; how he himself had come to reject the religion of the land in which he had grown up (Portugal) and escape and make for Amsterdam; his feelings during the circumcision and ritual immersion he had undergone in becoming a Jew; and, finally, his dismay at the unfriendliness of his new coreligionists. Delmedigo reappears in the last three paragraphs and concludes his rebuke with this call: "...[the welcoming of *gerim*], this is charity; this is love, kinship, peace and friendship; this is the solicitude ordained by the Torah in the thirty-six places the text refers to *gerim*."

But this was not all he had to say; he would also show those Jewish burghers what they had missed by not appointing him as their Rabbi. His

---

was known for certain was that he had died some twenty-five years later, in 1855, and was buried in the Prague Jewish cemetery where his grave can still be visited.

11 *TB Shabbat* 81b.

responsum, which he entitled ספר נפש הגר (*The Book of the Soul of the Ger*), takes up eighty-eight of the codex's one hundred and ten pages. It is an academic *tour de force* that goes far beyond the immediate question of the eligibility of this son of an *Anuss* to the position of *parnass*. Exhibiting an encyclopedic knowledge of the traditional sources, Delmedigo examines the halakhic standing of *gerim* over a whole range of issues, including their filial and levirate obligations, inheritance rights and kinships. This is followed by a review of all the biblical and historical precedents of persons who had occupied positions of authority over Israel even though their mothers had been born gentiles, as well as a selection of Talmudic, Midrashic and Kabbalistic tales and homilies regarding *giur* and *gerim*.

In coming to his decision in the present matter, however, Delmedigo does not introduce any controversial halakhic *novella*; he seems to be most concerned with exhibiting the extent of his knowledge rather than its originality. Indeed, he is quite conventional throughout and does not dispute that, halakhically, a *ger* should not be appointed to a position of coercive authority (שררה). Notwithstanding, Delmedigo concludes that this particular *ger,* whose identity he evidently knew, could be appointed to the position of *Parnass* of the community. In justification of this, he cites two extenuations:

1. The *Parnass* in Amsterdam does not exercise sole or absolute authority over the community; his powers are limited and are exercised only in conjunction with others whose eligibility is not in question. Indeed, the Jews of Amsterdam resolved all monetary disputes that arose between them in the civil courts and not before a *Bet Din.*
2. This particular individual is such an exceptional righteous *ger* (גר צדק) that the kinship to his gentile mother, by reason of which he was ineligible for a position of authority, no longer existed: "He has returned to his father's family, to be his heir presumptive, and can be considered a son of Israel."

***

Unlike Delmedigo, his pupil R. Issachar Ber Jeiteless had no personal axe to grind nor did he have any prior connection with the Amsterdam community; he was however no less of a polymath as the inscription on his tombstone in the Prague cemetery testifies (Appendix II). His sole concern was with the specific question of whether a person such as this *Ger Tzedek*, the son of an *Anuss* and a gentile woman, may be appointed to a position of authority. His *responsum* is accordingly concise and to the point and occupies just the last two pages of the codex. Notwithstanding, it is an exemplary piece of halakhic writing.[12]

As is customary, Jeiteless opens his *responsum* by restating the question he will be answering.

> גר צדק בעל תורה ירא אלהי' ועבד לו, זך וישר פעלו, והוא בן ישראל אנוס ואמו נכרית מהו למנותו בשררה על ישראל אם על כיוצא בזה אמרו חז"ל שום תשים עליך מלך (כל משימות שאתה משים יהיו) מקרב אחיך[13] ולא מן הגרים.

And in translation

> A *Ger Tzedek* [righteous convert], learned in Torah, God fearing and His servant, whose deeds are chaste and honest; and he is the son of an Israelite *Anuss* and his mother is a gentile. What is [the legal position] regarding his appointment to a position of coercive authority over Israel? Whether it was with regard to such [persons] that the Talmudic Sages stated: "*You should appoint a king over yourselves* (that all appointments you make, shall be) *from amongst your brethren*[14] and not from the *gerim*."[15]

The question comes down to this: When the Sages decreed that *Gerim* may not be appointed to positions of coercive authority (שררה), did they intend this ruling to apply to *Gerei Tzedek* such as this son of an *Anuss*? Jeiteless contends that they did not. In his opinion, the Sages had considered the issue of the appointment of a *ger* to a position of coercive authority only by reference to what he terms a "*Ger Stam*– גר סתם."

> What we find in the Talmud regarding this matter relates wholly to a *Ger Stam*.

The expression *Ger Stam* does not occur anywhere in the Talmud, however. Jeiteless' use of the term in this context is innovative and requires clarification.

The notion of two classes of *gerim*—*Gerei Tzedek* and *Gerei Stam*—has its origin with Rambam, who differentiated between those whose *giur* had been authorized by a properly constituted *Bet Din* of three learned rabbis or scholars (*dayanim*), and those whose *giur* was by an *ad hoc*, though legitimate, *Bet Din* of three observant but not necessarily learned Jews. *Giurim*

12 A Hebrew transcript of the *responsum* can be found in Appendix I.

13 *TB Yevamot* 45b; *TJ Kiddushin* 4.5.

14 *Devarim* 17:15.

15 *TB Yevamot* 45b; *TB Kiddushin* 76b.

carried out by the latter are valid and confer all the obligations and privileges of being a Jew upon the *ger*, even though his or her motives may not have been altruistic; such a *ger* was called a *Ger Stam* (an ordinary proselyte). By contrast, *gerim* whose motives had been thoroughly investigated by a *Bet Din* of three learned *dayanim* and who were found to be genuinely sincere, were termed *Gerei Tzedek*.[16] But Jeiteless' use of the term *Ger Stam* in the context of coercive authority appears to have a different purpose, namely, to indicate a *ger* with no prior Jewish credentials.

Regarding *gerim* as a class, Jeiteless notes a consensus amongst the *poskim* that they cannot be appointed to any judicial or coercive position in a Jewish community. The only exceptions to this are Rashi's minority opinion regarding their fitness to judge monetary cases, which found no support and was thus set aside, and the rare circumstance of a *Ger* whose mother was an Israelite.

> According to Rashi, [a *ger*] may judge monetary cases[17]... but is unfit for a position of coercive authority[18]... and should not be appointed to any such position if his mother was not an Israelite.[19] But in the opinion of *Ha-Rif* (Isaac Alfasi), Rambam, *Ha-Rosh* (Asher ben

---

16 *Mishneh Torah, Hilkhot Issurey Bi'ah*, 13:15, 17. "For this reason [doubts as to their sincerity], the *Bet Din* did not accept *Gerim* throughout the reigns of David and Solomon. In David's time, [the apprehension was] that they sought to become *Gerim* out of fear, and in Solomon's time that they were motivated by the sovereignty, prosperity, and eminence that Israel enjoyed. [They refrained from accepting such *Gerim* because] a gentile who seeks to become a *Ger* because of the vanities of this world is not a righteous *Ger*. Nevertheless, there were many people who underwent *Giur* in the presence of ordinary persons during the era of David and Solomon...A *Ger* who had not been examined [by a *Bet Din*] and who had not been informed about the *Mitzvot* and the punishment for [failing to observe] them but had circumcised himself and immersed in the presence of three ordinary people is nevertheless a *Ger*. Even if it is discovered that he underwent *Giur* for an ulterior motive, since he circumcised himself and did undergo *Giur*, he has exited the category of gentiles...Even if he subsequently worships false deities, he is like an apostate Jew. [If he] consecrates [marries a woman], the consecration is valid, and it is a *Mitzvah* to return his lost property. For having immersed himself, he has become an Israelite."
For a comprehensive survey of the subject see: אמסלם חיים, ספר *זרע ישראל*, ירושלים (5570), פרק ג, עמ' קסח, קפד, ער, שם.

17 *TB Yevamot* 102a.

18 *TB Yevamot* 45b.

19 *TB Kiddushin* 77a.

> Yeḥiel) and Tosafot, and all the *poskim* who came after them, in particular *Ha-Tur* (Ya'acov ben Asher),[20] a *ger* whose mother was not an Israelite is barred from judging even monetary cases.
> And when [the Talmudic Sages] stated that "all persons are fit to judge monetary cases,"[21] even a *ger*, [what they meant was] a *ger* whose mother was an Israelite;[22] for [Israelite women] are often victims of rape or kidnapping; or that he can sit in judgment on a fellow *ger* even if his mother was not an Israelite. And Rashi's [opinion that a *ger* may judge monetary cases] is set aside by reason of his being in a minority.

The concept of a *ger* whose mother is an Israelite requires clarification. Although the accepted halakhic position today is that the child of an Israelite woman is *ipso facto* an Israelite from birth, irrespective of the circumstances of its conception, this was not always so. There are a number of different legal opinions in the Talmud regarding the difficult question of the status of a child born to an Israelite woman who was impregnated by a gentile: the child may be a *mamzer*, a lawful gentile or a lawful Israelite, and accordingly might or might not have required *Giur* depending on the circumstances.[23]

But what of the appointment of *gerim* to executive positions, such as that of the *parnass* of a community; must they satisfy the same criteria as candidates for judicial posts? Apparently, the answer is yes:

> As regards the leading householders and elite of the community, those who are called *Parnassim* or *Manhigim*, they [have the standing of] a *Bet Din* as stated by *Ha-Mordecai* (Mordecai ben Hillel);[24] therefore, *gerim* whose mothers were not Israelites [cannot be appointed to these positions].

This would appear to settle the matter: the said *ger* was the son of a gentile woman and so could not be appointed *parnass*. But Jeiteless does not give up:

> But as regards the issue currently before us, we do not find any explicit reference to such an instance in the *Gemara*, that is to say, to a person whose father was an Israelite and whose mother was a gentile.

20 *Yoreh De'ah* 269 and *Ḥoshen Mishpat* 7.

21 *Mishnah, Sanhedrin* 4:2.

22 *TB Kiddushin* 76b; *Mishneh Torah, Hilkhot Sanhedrin* 11:11.

23 *TB Yevamot 45a*; *TB Kiddushin* 68a/b; Tosafot, *Yevamot* 16b and 23.

24 Mordecai ben Hillel, *Sefer Ha-Mordekhai*, Riva de Trinato, 1559, p. 63a.

What we actually find is that a father's Israelite status is of major importance in all such matters, as the *Tur* and the *Bet Yosef* state in *Yoreh De'ah* 269 and *Ḥoshen Mishpat* 7. Thus, as regards [the obligation to perform] *Ḥalitzah*,[25] Tosafot and the *Rosh* wrote [in their glosses on] Chapter 12 of *TB Yevamot* that a person's father matters more than his mother, and likewise the *Tur* and the *Bet Yosef* in *Even Ha-Ezer* 169. But this is only if the person's conception was in holiness, such as when an Israelite man marries a *gioret*.[26]

[The person's status] in such an instance is superior to that of one whose mother was an Israelite and father a gentile and whose conception was not in holiness; [for] although the latter is fit to be a judge, he is disqualified from performing *Ḥalitzah* [by reason of his gentile genitor]. But if a person's father is an Israelite and mother a *gioret*, he is eligible to perform *Ḥalitzah* and is also lawful as regards matters of Aaronide descent.

Notwithstanding, instances such as the present case, where the mother is a gentile and the father an Israelite, are not mentioned anywhere, neither in the *Gemara* nor by the *poskim*.

Albeit, it is well known that the son of a gentile woman [and an Israelite] is called her son and is not the son of his Israelite genitor, as it says in *Yevamot*:[27]

"R. Yochanan replied in the name of R. Shimon b. Yohai, when Scripture stated, *For he* [the gentile's son who has married your daughter] *will turn your son* [*or grandson*] *away from following Me.*[28]"

This implies that [by law] the Israelite man has no son by her and even if [the child] subsequently converts [to Judaism] he still bears no filial relationship to his genitor given that [*gerim*] are considered as though newly born.[29] And Rambam wrote in Chapter 5 of *Hilkhot*

---

25 The formal procedure that frees the widow of a childless man to marry whoever she wants when her deceased husband's brother refuses to carry out his levirate obligation of marrying her. Since medieval times and the institution of a prohibition on polygamy, its performance has become obligatory in all circumstances.

26 Paternity is established by the parents' cohabitation which is taken as proof that the man is the father of the woman's children.

27 *TB Yevamot* 23a.

28 *Devarim* 7:3-4. The passage in *TB Yevamot* 23a continues: "[The words] 'your son' [when referring to a child] born of an Israelite woman mean *your son* [or *grandson*]; [the words] 'your son' [when referring to a child] born of a gentile woman mean not 'your son' but *her son*."

29 A *Ger* is regarded as having no relatives: *Giur* is tantamount to a rebirth and breaks all former familial connections. *Gerim* (proselytes) are deemed the children of *Avraham Avinu* (our father Abraham) and as such have no legal affiliation

> *Mamrim*, that should he curse or smite his genitor, he is not indictable for this act; nor is he his heir.[30]

In principle, Jewish Law determines the status of a child by reference to his or her natural (biological) parents, irrespective of whether or not they were legally married at the time of its birth; there is no such thing as an *illegitimate* child or *filius nilius* (nobody's child) in Jewish Law.[31] Even the child of a forbidden union, a *mamzer*, has a legal mother and father with all the concomitant rights and mutual responsibilities. There is, however, one exception to this rule. In Jewish Law, the child of an Israelite man and a gentile woman has no legal father: the child's genitor is not his or her legal father.[32] Even if the child subsequently undergoes *giur*, he or she will still be known not as the Israelite genitor's child but as the child of "our father Abraham."[33] This being so, what weight, if any, can be given to the Israelite father in the case before us?

Furthermore, contrary to those instances in which the father's status carries some weight, albeit only when the mother is a *gioret*, as regards his inheritance rights a *ger* whose father is an Israelite may be even worse off than one who is the son of a gentile genitor and a gentile woman.

> According to Torah Law, a gentile is his father's heir, and even if he undergoes *giur* he remains his heir according to Scribal Law...[34] But the son of an Israelite man and a gentile woman is not [his genitor's

to their biological fathers (genitors). A *Ger*'s patronymic is "...son/daughter of our Father Abraham."

30 A child bears its Israelite genitor's name, together with all the filial rights and obligations that go with it, only if both its conception and birth were "in holiness."

31 In Muslim *Sharia* Law, the child of an unmarried woman has no legal father.

32 The rationale for this is taken from an interpretation of the verse "You shall not marry them, neither give your daughter to their son nor take his daughter for your son; for he will turn your son away from following Me and they will worship other gods; so will the anger of the Lord be kindled against you" (*Devarim* 7:3-4).

33 This exception to the rule that parentage is determined by biology has troubled Jewish scholars and *Poskim* throughout the ages, and it underlies the issue of the status of the said son of an *Anuss*. Notwithstanding, in recognition of the natural affinity of the child and its genitor, various expedients have been adopted over the ages in order to soften its impact. For example, such persons are often referred to as זרע ישראל (*Zera Yisrael* - Seed of Israel).

34 *Tur*, *Ḥoshen Mishpat* 283.

> heir] according to either Torah Law or Scribal Law, even if he undergoes *giur*.[35]

How, asks Jeiteless, did this distinction between the inheritance rights of a *ger* whose genitor is a gentile and those of one whose genitor is an Israelite, to the detriment of the latter, arise in Scribal Law; and secondly, does it have any bearing on the matter at hand?

> But the reasoning behind this [ruling] should be properly examined. [On the one hand] it is right that the gentile woman's son should not inherit his Israelite genitor, seeing that he naturally clings to his mother and will [most likely] worship idols as she does. As Scripture plainly puts it: *For she will turn your son away from following Me*;[36] she will turn him away from being a follower of God. And it is for this reason that he cannot be indicted for abusing his father and does not release [his genitor's widow] from the levirate requirement.[37]
>
> But this [ruling] is wholly a matter of inheritance. The Sages bolstered [the law] so as not to equate the inheritance [rights] of [the son of an Israelite man and a gentile woman] with those of the rest of his brothers [his genitor's lawful sons], even if he undergoes *giur*, lest his [*giur*] be only because he had set his eyes on the money. Besides, this ruling is no more than a rabbinical ordinance (*Takkanah*) like the one introduced by the Talmud Sages which allows a *ger* to inherit from his gentile genitor even though, according to Torah Law, he should not. It was only enacted lest he otherwise return to his previous [gentile] ways. For were he not to inherit [from his gentile genitor] by reason of being a *ger*, he might well return to his gentile ways whereupon he would [ironically] be eligible to inherit from him according to Torah Law.

As regards the *Takkanah* that a *ger* who is the son of a gentile genitor is entitled to an inheritance from him, the Sages reasoned that should he be denied this by the strict application of Torah Law, he might well be persuaded to return to his former gentile ways, whereupon, ironically, he would be entitled to the inheritance by virtue of the same Torah Law; it

---

35 *Hilhkot Naḥlaot* 2:11. "If a person had sons while still a gentile and then converted, he does not have a firstborn with regard to the rights of inheritance. However, if an Israelite fathered a son from a gentile woman then, since [this child] is not considered his son, any son he fathers afterwards from a Jewish woman is considered his firstborn with regard to the laws of inheritance, and receives a double portion [from his father's estate]."

36 *Devarim* 7:4.

37 If the genitor dies without children from his lawful Jewish wife, his brother will still be obliged to marry her.

was in order to remove this temptation that they instituted the ruling. On the other hand, the Torah law that a *ger* is not the heir of his Israelite genitor was not amended for fear that his conversion might be prompted by monetary considerations; had such a *Takkanah* been enacted and he became entitled to an inheritance from his Israelite genitor, the motive for his *giur* might have been just that and not a sincere desire to become a Jew.

> But when he has undergone *giur* and we know that he is following in the ways of his father, it cannot be right for us not to consider him to be his son. For at all events, he has a father, and he is his son as regards the yoke of *Torah* and *Mitzvot*. Accordingly, he should also be eligible for a position of authority (שררה) just like his father and should be designated *from amongst your brethren* seeing that the fear that *he will turn your son away*...has gone.

Jeiteless finds support for his contention that the combination of Israelite paternal descent and *giur* is sufficient for the child of a gentile mother to be appointed to positions of authority in the biblical accounts of the Royals of the kingdoms of Judah and Israel. The first example he cites is the distressing story of Amnon and Tamar.[38] Without going into the salacious details of Tamar's assignation with King David's firstborn son Amnon, it is clear from the biblical text that she was regarded as a royal princess, i.e. as a daughter of King David, in which case their relationship would appear, at first sight, to have been incestuous. The text does not say who her mother was, however. This mystery is resolved by the Talmud, which states that she was the daughter of a *Yefat T'oar*, a gentile woman whom David had ravished in the heat of battle and, as such, not legally Amnon's sister.[39] Presumably, both she and her mother subsequently became *giorot*, but for Jeiteless, the key point is that she was considered a 'Royal of the House of David' even though her mother had been a gentile at the time of her conception; her patrilineal descent was what mattered.

---

38 2 *Samuel* 13.

39 A *Yefat Toar* is a beautiful woman who is ravished by an Israelite solider in the heat of battle and whom he may subsequently legitimately marry (*Devarim* 21:10). According to *TB Sanhedrin* 21a, the soldier who had ravished Tamar's gentile mother was David himself. Since she was conceived when her mother was still a gentile, she was not legally Amnon's sister and so there was no legal impediment to their union.

> "Rabbi Judah said in the name of Rav, Tamar was the daughter of a *Yefat To'ar,*[40] as it is written: *Please speak to the king [David], that he not withhold me from you [Amnon].*[41] Is it conceivable she was the offspring of a legitimate marriage; how could his sister be granted to him [in marriage]?[42]" And furthermore, both he and David called her Amnon's sister and she called him my brother. Absalom also asked her, "Was Amnon your brother with you?"[43] And [the text] also states that [she wore a robe of many colours,] for such was the dress of the king's virgin daughters.[44] It follows that his daughter from a gentile woman was his daughter [i.e., a royal princess].

But what of those biblical kings whose mothers were gentiles; how could they have risen to the throne? It is here that Jeiteless exhibits his most creative thinking. The Talmud had determined that the Torah injunction *nor curse a ruler of your people*[45] applies only to one who "practices the proper usages of your people (עושה מעשה עמך)."[46] Turning this statement around, Jeiteless applies it to the question of who may be appointed king.

> One 'who practices the proper usages of his people' [behaves as an Israelite should] may be *a ruler of your people*, and such a person is even fit to be king.

A gentile who undertakes *giur* may be said to have adopted the "the proper usages [*Mitzvot*] of your people." And so, if the royal sons born to gentile mothers undergo *giur*, they can become kings.

> Behold, Rehoboam [Solomon's son who succeeded him as king] was the son of an Ammonite woman and there is no mention in Scripture that his mother became a *gioret.* And even if [the son] follows his mother's [idolatrous] ways, if he becomes a *ger* he may succeed to the

---

40 A beautiful women ravished by an Israelite solider during battle (*Devarim* 21:10). According to *TB Sanhedrin* 21a, the soldier who had ravished Tamar's gentile mother was David himself. An alternative interpretation given by the *Tosaphists* is that she was the daughter of an already pregnant woman that David married and whom David subsequently adopted as his own.

41 *2 Samuel* 13: 13.

42 *TB Sanhedrin* 21a.

43 *2 Samuel* 13:2, 6–8, 11-12, 20.

44 *2 Samuel* 13:18.

45 *Shemot* 22:27.

46 This proviso occurs in a number of different contexts in the Talmud, not all relating to rulers: *TB Yevamot* 22b; *TB Baba Kama* 94b; *TB Bava Mezi'a* 48b, 62a; *Baba Batra* 4a; *TB Sanhedrin* 85a; *TB Makkot* 8b.

> throne. And the proof for this is from the sons of Aḥab, Aḥaziah and Jehoram, the sons of the accursed Jezebel, daughter of the king of the Zidonians, who caused both her husband and sons to sin, as Scripture testifies.[47]

And what of the many other gentile wives of Solomon and of Samson's wife Delilah? Rambam had asserted that they underwent *giur,* but Jeiteless points out that Scripture gives no hint of this.[48]

> Rambam wrote in Chapter 13 of *Hilkhot Issurei Bi'ah* that Solomon and Samson did not marry gentile women before making them *giorot*, but this does not appear anywhere in the Scriptural text. The *Gemara* likewise says nothing [about his gentile wives] other than that Solomon made Pharoah's daughter a *gioret.*[49]

Jeiteless concludes that a *ger* who is the son of an Israelite genitor can be considered *from amongst your brethren* for the purpose of public appointments, whether or not his gentile mother ever underwent *giur.* He adds that he finds support for this from what Rambam might well have added, but did not add, to his assertion that Solomon made his gentile wives become *giorot.*

> Rambam could have added force to his supposition [that Solomon had made his gentile wives *giorot*] by stating that were this not so, how could Rehoboam have become king? But he [evidently] considered that if a person's father is an Israelite, he is deemed to be *from amongst your brethren* so long as he becomes a *ger.* But if he does not undergo *giur*, even in the case where his mother is an Israelite, since his father was a gentile, he is a gentile and is called his son and not hers.[50]

The notion that one who "practices the proper usages of your people" may be eligible to occupy a position of authority did not originate with

---

47 2 *Kings* 3-8. An early 13th-century work—*Sefer Tannaim Ve-Amoraim*—by R. Yehudah ben Kalonymous of Worms (d. 1217) raised the question of how these two could be considered sons of Ahab in light of the Talmud ruling (*TB Kiddushin* 68b) that the child of gentile woman and an Israelite genitor is called her child and not his.

48 *Mishneh Torah, Issurei Bi'ah*, 13:14.

49 *TB Yevamot* 76a.

50 Jeiteless appears to be implying that Rambam would require the child of a Jewess and a gentile to undergo *Giur.*

Jeiteless. According to Tosafot, before the Rabbinical Sages ruled otherwise, the Torah could be understood to permit a liberated slave or a *ger* to become king so long as he was "your brother in *mitzvot*" (אחיך במצות); the intent of the ruling that the king must be *from amongst your brethren* was only to exclude gentiles.[51] But the Sages amended this and decreed that henceforth a king could be appointed only from "amongst the unequivocal of your brethren" (הברורין שבאחיך), a designation taken to mean only a person whose parents were both Israelites at the time of his birth.[52]

The ruling that only a person who was unequivocally "from amongst your brethren" could be appointed king had an immediate negative impact on the legitimacy of Herod's rule in Jewish eyes. According to the Talmud, his parents were Idumeans and he himself had been a slave in the house of the Hasmoneans.[53] As such, he did not have any true Israelite credentials and like most usurpers and autocrats, he was fearful of his hold on the throne. Whether the Sages' motives for changing the law were political and directed against him or not, Herod thought they were and reacted by ordering the slaughter of those who had instituted the change. According to the account in the Talmud, one Baba ben Buta, who was a confidant of Herod and whose advice he valued, was spared. In what might be described as a confessional exchange, ben Buta told Herod that the slaughter he had ordered was unwarranted; he had nothing to fear from the Sages since they were traditionally supportive of whoever was in power. Whereupon, to make amends, Herod was persuaded to undertake the construction of a new and finer Temple building.[54]

The change in law initiated by the Sages would also affect Herod's grandson Agrippa I (10BCE – 44CE), the son Aristobulus IV and his cousin Berenice.[55] Agrippa had been brought up and educated in Rome,

---

51 Tosafot *Bava Batra* 3b. "Tosafot and other Rishonim explained that were it not for the Sages' elucidation, the Torah text could be construed to mean that although a person who is not an Israelite may not be appointed king, anyone who 'belongs with the Mitzvot' (שייך במצוות) was fit to be king." (Adin Steinsaltz, *in situ*).

52 Tosafot *Sotah* 41b. Subsequently this rule was applied to all positions of communal authority, not just to the king (*TJ Kiddushin* 4:5; *TB Yevamot* 45b).

53 The Talmud states that he had killed all but one of the members of the household, a maiden he wanted to marry, but she subsequently committed suicide by throwing herself off a roof. According to Josephus, she was Mariamne I, the daughter of Alexander, a son of Aristobulus II, and she was put to death by Herod after several years of marriage to him (*TB Bava Batra* 3b).

54 *TB Bava Batra* 4a.

55 The daughter of Herod's sister Salome I.

and his credentials for the post of King of the Jews were no better than his grandfather's. Whilst living in Rome he had assisted in securing the accession of Claudius as emperor when Caligula was assassinated in 41CE, in reward for which he was appointed ruler of Judea and its adjacent territories. Keen to ingratiate himself with his Jewish subjects and establish his legitimacy as their monarch, Agrippa fixed his permanent residence in Jerusalem and ostentatiously observed the ancestral laws. The *Mishnah* relates that he led the public reading from the Torah in the Temple on the festival of *Sukkot* immediately following the conclusion of the seventh year in the *shemittah* cycle,[56] and that his eyes ran with tears when he reached the verse *you may not appoint a foreigner [as king] over you.*[57] Whereupon the Jews present called out to him, "Don't fear, Agrippa, you are our brother, you are our brother!"[58] The Talmud comments on this: "At that moment, the enemies of Israel [a euphemism for Israel itself] incurred extermination, because they flattered Agrippa." Just thirty years later, the second Temple was destroyed.[59]

Taking the Talmud's account of the life of Agrippa as historically correct, Jeiteless cites a gloss from Rambam's *Commentary on the Mishnah* to the effect that he was a *ger* and that this was the reason it had been wrong for the people to flatter him and acclaim the legitimacy of his rule by calling him a brother.

> And in his *Commentary on the Mishnah*, Chapter 7 of *TB Sotah*: *Parshat HaMelekh*, Rambam wrote the following: "Agrippa was from the category of *Gerim* [מקהל גרים] and did not have an Israelite mother;[60]

56 *Devarim* 31:10–13.

57 *Devarim* 17:15.

58 *Mishnah Tractate Sotah* 7:8; *TB Sotah* 41a.

59 A King Agrippa appears in a number of stories in the Talmud, but whether the events described relate to Agrippa I, his son Agrippa II or some combination of the two is a matter of scholarly debate. For a discussion of this issue see: Schwartz, Daniel R., *Agrippa I: The Last King of Judea*, J.C.B. Mohr (Paul Siebeck), (Tűbingen, 1990), pp. 157–171.

60 According to Rashi (*TB Sotah* 41b), however, his mother was an Israelite and it was because he was a slave that he could not be king. In their discussion of Rashi's glosses, Tosafot differentiate between the criteria for appointing a person to a regular position of authority and that for appointing him as king. Whereas for the former it is sufficient if the candidate's mother is an Israelite, for him to be appointed king both parents must be Israelites. Only Agrippa's mother was an Israelite and so he did not fully satisfy this requirement. But that by itself would not have justified such a severe punishment. But by proclaiming,

> and he was not *from amongst your brothers*; and therefore Israel was punished for proclaiming, 'You are our brother!'"

Jeitless notes that Tosafot and Rashi offer other reasons that Agrippa could not be king, namely, that his father had been a gentile or that he had been a slave.[61]

> Besides, his father was a gentile or a slave as Tosafot state in their glosses on Chapter 4 of *TB Yevamot*[62] and Rashi likewise in his glosses on Chapter 7 of *TB Sotah*[63] and in *TB Kiddushin*.[64]

Rambam's proscription of Agrippa in his *Commentary on the Mishnah* on the grounds that he was a *Ger*, was in line with his ruling in *Hilkhot Melakhim*[65] prohibiting the appointment of a king from the category of *gerim* (מקהל גרים).

> A king should not be appointed from amongst the *gerim* even after a number of generations, until his mother is an Israelite, as [Scripture] says: *You may not place a foreigner over you, who is not your brother*.[66]

But for Jeiteless' purposes, it was not what Rambam said in either his *Commentary on the Mishnah* or the *Mishneh Torah* that was important, but what he did not say.

> And take note, he [Rambam] did not state that the son of an Israelite man and a gentile woman may not be appointed, which [the case of] Rehoboam proves.[67]
> And with regard to the rider [Rambam added], 'until his mother…': if even his mother is said to be sufficient [to qualify him to be appointed king], how much more so his father, for when he follows

---

'You are our brother!' they sought to flatter him though they knew he was ineligible. That was very wrong; they should have remained silent.

61 The Talmud considered Herod's slave status to have been passed on to all of his descendants (*TB Kiddushin* 70b).

62 *Tos. Yevamot* 45b.

63 *TB Sotah* 41b.

64 *TB Kiddushin* 70b.

65 *Mishneh Torah, Hilkhot Melakhim* 1:4.

66 *Devarim* 17:15.

67 The legality of Rehoboam's ascent to the Davidic throne is no small matter. Upon it depends the legitimacy of the ensuing succession of the House of David down to that of the Messiah.

the fitting usages of his father, he is not called her son but his son.[68]

But is there any support in *Halakhah* for the argument that the ineligibility to a position of authority, by reason of affinity to his gentile mother, can be negated by that to his Israelite father? Jeiteless suggests that there is by reference to the *Halakhah* regarding the prohibition on slaughtering an animal and its young on the same day.

> And the Torah spoke in the way the world does, [namely] that a child clings to its mother, for she encourages it with her words. And as [the Talmud] states in the matter of *it and its young* [the prohibition to slaughter an animal and its progeny on the same day],[69] that this means 'it and its mother,' for it is to the females that [the offspring] instinctively cling.[70] And out of concern that this same instinct may also exist towards males, [the same-day slaughter of the young] and its father is also prohibited, if it is known for certain that he is its father, as the *Tur* states in *Yore De'ah* 16.
> And it is likewise in the laws of the nations, for they call the son of a concubine/mistress 'a natural son,' and a true son born in wedlock is called 'a legitimate son.' But it cannot be denied that the former is his natural son and, should he take his place, he will be the heir to his authority though not to his money.[71]

Jeiteless now confidently summarizes his ruling in the matter:

> And when the issues are correctly understood, no scholar or *posek* can dissent from this. And this *Ger Tzedek*, whose father was one of the *Anussim*, should certainly be regarded as his son and has the status of *Zera Yisrael* (זרע ישראל), even though he is not his heir for the reasons given above. But as regards all matters of authority or sitting in judgment, he is a fit person. For [his standing] is above that of one whose mother in an Israelite and father a gentile. And reliance should be put on this principle, for everything else that has been said is irrelevant. And there is no need for Talmudic casuistry, or to cite the *Gemara* and the *poskim*, for the Sages spoke only about a *Ger Stam*

68 This is essentially the same rationale as that brought by Delmedigo in the second of the two reasons he gave as to why the said *Ger* could be appointed to any position the Amsterdam community decided.

69 *Leviticus* 22:28.

70 *TB Ḥullin* 78a. The Torah ordinance is stated in the masculine—אותו ואת בנו—but it was taken to apply to a cow or ewe and her young; whether it also applies to a bull or ram and its young is discussed in the Gemara.

71 Only legitimate offspring are lawful heirs.

from the category of *gerim* [one without any previous Israelite credentials] and a *ger* whose mother was an Israelite.[72]
This is my opinion and I am not bothered should anyone stiffen his neck or be stone-faced in dissent.
These are the words of the frail youngster, Issachar called Ber, the son of R. Yehudah Leib Jeiteless, Dayan.

***

Exactly when the *responsa* of Delmedigo and Issachar Ber were received by the Amsterdam community is not documented. But on November 6th 1651, just three months after the date of the signature to Delmedigo's *responsum* in the Christ Church Library manuscript, the son of an *Anuss*, a *ger* by the name of Moseh Roiz da Costa, was declared by Menasseh ben Israel and David Prado "fit to be appointed to any post the congregation might give him…without exception." The text of the decree makes it clear that this was an exceptional case and would not become a precedent.[73] This rider may have been added by reason of the dissenting opinion of R. Jacob Sasportas who was living in Amsterdam at the time and to whom the following question had been put by the physician Samuel de Mercado:[74] "May a *Ger*, whose mother is not an Israelite, occupy a position of coercive authority over the community?"[75]

Mercado's question was evidently prompted by differences as to the import of R. Josef Karo's gloss on Rambam's ruling in particular regarding the proviso "until his mother is an Israelite."[76] The Hebrew text of Karo's gloss reads as follows:

---

72 In the eighteenth century, the influential authority R. Yehezkel Landau, who resided in Prague from 1755 to 1793, stated that a king's lineage should be questioned only at the start of a dynasty when the monarch is first "appointed." Once the dynasty has been established, a descendant who inherits the throne may do so even if his mother is a Gioret (Noda B-Yehudah, *Ḥoshen Mishpat*, Responsum 1).

73 *Menashe ben Israel and his World*, ed. Y. Kaplan, H. Mechoulan & R.H. Popkin, E.J. Brill, Leiden (1989) p. 58.

74 In the extant annals of the Amsterdam community, Mercado's name is given as Samuel Israel de Mercado or Samuel Jessurun de Mercado. The addition of 'Israel' or 'Jeshurun' usually denotes a returning *Anuss* who had undergone *Giur.*

75 *Sefer Ohel Ya'acov* (Sasportas' *responsa*, edited and prefaced by his son Abraham Sasportas), Amsterdam 1737, *Responsum* 4.

76 In the *Kessef Mishneh* commentary on Rambam's code.

...כל שתשימהו עליך לא יהא אלא מן הברורים שבאחיך ומשמע לי דלרבותא נקט אמו ומכל שכן אם היה אביו מישראל אע"פ שאין אמו מישראל כשר וכן כתבו התוספות בפרק מצות חליצה ובהכי ניחא לי היאך מלך רחבעם דלא הוה אמו מישראל...

And in translation:

> ...All those you appoint over you shall be none other than from the unequivocal of your brethren. And it seems to me that he mentioned his mother by way of an 'optional extra,' seeing that he would anyway be eligible if his father was from Israel even though his mother was not from Israel, as Tosafot wrote in their glosses on *TB Yevamot* 102a.[77] And as for me, this resolves [the question of] how Rehoboam could have been king even though his mother was not from Israel...

The Tosafot cited by R. Josef Karo state that having an Israelite father would suffice for one to be appointed to a position of judicial authority. Drawing on the verse *the King establishes the land with justice*[78]—which places judges and kings on a similar standing—Tosafot's ruling can be taken to apply to the appointment of kings as well.[79] Karo observes that this view explains the accession of Rehoboam, whose mother was the gentile Naamah the Ammonite, to his father's throne without recourse to apologetics such as Rambam's surmise: "One should not think that Samson who saved the Jewish people, and Solomon, King of Israel, who is called 'the friend of God,' married gentile women who did not undergo *giur*."[80]

Sasportas, who is known for his conservatism (he was one of the contemporary rabbis who most vigorously opposed the Sabbatean movement), rejected this understanding of Karo's gloss out of hand: a *Ger* who was the son of an Israelite man and a gentile woman could never be eligible for a position of coercive authority. Drawing on the case of R. Mari bar Raḥel bar Shmuel, who is referred to in the Talmud only by his matronymic, Sasportas argues that only a person whose mother is an Israelite can be called *from amongst your brethren*. The Talmud relates that R. Mari's

---

77 Tosafot held that whereas having an Israelite mother does not of itself make one eligible to judge cases of *Ḥalitzah*, having an Israelite father is of itself sufficient: לענין חליצה עד שיהא אביו ואמו מישראל - פי' באמו לא סגי עד שיהא גם אביו מישראל אבל באביו לחוד סגי...

78 *Proverbs* 29:4.

79 This equivalence between the standing of judges and kings is drawn by Rashi in his glosses on the same page in the Talmud, *TB Yevamot* 102a, as the said ruling of the Tosafot appears.

80 *Mishneh Torah, Issurei Bi'ah*, 13:14.

mother, the daughter of the great Babylonian sage Shmuel, had been impregnated by a gentile Babylonian soldier, and according to the ruling that both parents must be Israelites, he should not have been eligible for any position of authority. Yet the Talmud states that "Raba declared R. Mari bar Raḥel to be a legitimate Israelite and appointed him a supervisor…for if a person's mother is an Israelite he is called *from amongst your brethren*."[81]

Sasportas asserts that Karo's gloss cannot mean that "his father alone being an Israelite [is sufficient for an appointment to a position of authority] and that this is superior to his mother being an Israelite: God forbid!"[82] The candidate's mother must always be an Israelite, making him an Israelite from birth. Rambam's purpose had been only to clarify the situation where the father is an Israelite and the mother a *gioret.* Such a person can still be considered *from amongst your brethren*, his circumstance being superior to that of one whose mother is an Israelite and father a gentile.

The incident in Amsterdam was not unique. At around the same time, an almost identical controversy arose in a Jewish community in the Ottoman Empire, where Iberian Jews had been invited by Sultan Beyazit II after he heard of their expulsion by the Catholic King Ferdinand and Queen Isabella in 1492. The source for this case is the halakhic compendium *Knesset Ha-Gedolah* composed by Rabbi Chaim Benveniste of Izmir (1603–1673).[83]

In this instance too, the matter in dispute was the appointment of a *ger*, the son of a Jewish man and a gentile woman, to the position of *parnass* of a community. Two rabbis had been consulted by the community. One ruled that the said *ger* could be appointed to the position whilst the other ruled he could not. The issue was then brought before R. Benveniste for his ruling and his initial response was to agree with the rabbi who had ruled against the appointment. As he writes in his *Knesset Ha-Gedolah*, however, he had second thoughts in the matter after reading a *responsum* by R. Avraham de Boton (author of the *Leḥem Mishneh*, c. 1560–c. 1605) regarding the judicial status of *Anussim.* After a comprehensive reappraisal of the case, he revised his opinion and concluded that since the position of *parnass* was one of only limited authority, the community being subject to the overriding sovereign rule of the Sultan, the said candidate could be appointed *parnass* if he was acceptable to the community. In essence, this

81 *TB Shabbat* 154a, *TB Kiddushin* 76b, *TB Yevamot* 45b.

82 "כי באביו מישראל לחוד שגי ועדיף טפי מאמו מישראל וחלילה."

83 *כנסת הגדולה*, חושן משפט, הלכות דיינים, סעיף ז.

was the same conclusion Delmedigo had come to in *Sefer Nefesh Ha-Ger* regarding the Amsterdam case.[84]

***

A search of the Stadsarchief in Amsterdam, which holds the annals of the Jewish community, has uncovered additional information about Moseh Roiz da Costa. He was a man of some standing; among the communal positions he had occupied, prior to the fracas over his election as *parnass*, was that of administrator of the *Avodat Ha-Ḥesed* charity established by the Sephardi Community in Amsterdam to provide for needy itinerant Ashkenazi Jews. Subsequently, he was honored as *Ḥatan Bereshit* in 1652 and was elected *parnass* of the *Ḥevra* (Burial Society) in the following year. The payments of his *Promessas* (voluntary contributions) and *Impostas* (assessed fees) for the years from 1650 to 1660 also appear in the community accounts.

The extant early records of the Spanish and Portuguese community in London provide further information that may well relate to his descendants. The small London community was made up almost entirely of immigrants from Amsterdam, and in 1664 it drew up its first set of regulations known as *Ascamot*. One of the seventeen signatories to this founding charter was a certain Abraham Roiz da Costa.[85] When these *Ascamot* were amended in 1677, following changes in the community's circumstances, the signature of Abraham Roiz da Costa appears on the new charter. Thirdly, the tombstones of an Abraham Roiz da Costa (d.16(7)9) and a Yitzḥak Roiz da Costa (d.1679) were amongst those identified by the Royal Commission on Historical Monuments of England survey (1930), in the "burial Ground of the Sephardi Jews in Stepney… founded in the middle of the 17th century."

Although no documents have been uncovered proving that Moseh, Abraham and Yitzḥak Roiz da Costa were related, considering the small size of the Amsterdam and London Sephardi communities at the time—the former numbered only about 2000 souls and the latter no more than a few hundred—and the uniqueness of their family names, the probability of more than one family called Roiz da Costa is low. ☙

---

84 Sasportas had rejected the notion that the *Ger* could be appointed to be *Parnass* since the *Parnass* does not exercise sole authority over the Amsterdam community and has no power to enforce his decisions.

85 Gaster, Moses, *History of the Ancient Synagogue of the Spanish and Portuguese Jews – The Cathedral Synagogue of the Jews in England Situate in Bevis Marks* (London, 1901), p.11.

Appendix I
Transcript of the *Responsum* of R. Issachar Ber Jeiteless: Ms. 199. Christ Church Library, Oxford.

שאלה: גר צדק בעל תורה ירא אלהי' ועבד לו, זך וישר פעלו, והוא בן ישראל אנוס ואמו נכרית מהו למנותו בשררה על ישראל אם על כיוצא בזה אמרו חז"ל שום תשים עליך מלך (כל משימות שאתה משים יהיו) מקרב אחיך ולא מן הגרים.

תשובה: מה שמצינו בתלמוד בענין זה כלו אמור בגר סתם.
ולרש"י כשר לדון ד"מ [דיני ממונות] כדאי' בפ' מ"ח ופסול לשרר' כדאית' בפ' החולץ ובפ"י יוחסין דנראה התם בהדיא דאין למנותו על שום שררה אם אין אמו מישראל אבל לדעת הרי"ף והרמב"ם והרא"ש והתוס' וכל הפוסקי' הבאים אחריהם ובפרט הטור י"ד סי' רס"ט ובח"מ סי' ז' הגר שאין אמו מישראל אפי' לדון ישראל בד"מ פסול ולא אמרו הכל כשרין לדון ד"מ ואפילו גר אלא בגר שאמו מישראל דשכיחי אנוסות ושבויות או לדון גר חברו אפי' אין אמו מישראל ורש"י בטל במיעוטו.
לגבי ב"ב [בעלי בתים] גדולים וטובי הקהלו' שקוראין פרנסים או מנהיגים הם במקום ב"ד כמ"ש המרדכי הילכך א"א בגרים שאין אמן מישראל.
אבל מענין שאלה זו לא מצאנו בהדיא בגמר' שום דבר ר"ל כשאביו ישראל ואמו נכרית כנ"ד דאטו ברשיעי עסקינין.
איברא שמצאנו שאביו מישראל עדיף לכל מילי כמ"ש הטור והב"י בסי' רס"ט בי"ד [ביורה דעה] ובח"מ [ובחושן משפט] סי' ז' ובענין חליצה כתבו התוס' והרא"ש בפר' מ"ח [מצות חליצה] שעדיף אביו מאמו וכ"כ הטור והבי' בא"ה [באבן העזר] סי' קס"ט.
אבל זה דוקא כשהורתו בקדושה כגון ישראל נשא גיורת דבכי האי גונא עדיף מכשאמו ישראלי' ואביו גוי שהיתה הורתו שלא בקדושה דלדינא הוי כשר ולחליצה פסול.
וכשאביו מישראל ואמו גיורת כשר אפי' לחליצה דהא לענין יחס כהונה הוי נמי כשר.
ברם בנדון דידן שאימו גויה ואביו ישראל לא הזכירו כלל לא הגמ' ולא הפוס'. אמנם בעלמא ידענ' שבן הנכרית קרוי בנה ואינו בן הישראל אביו כמ"ש בפ' כיצד א"א רבי יוחנן בשם רשב"י [רב שמעון בר יוחאי] ומפרש קר' כי יסיר בנך מאחרי והוי כאילו אין לישראל בן ממנה. ואפילו נתגייר הבן אין לו שום יחוס אחר אביו דכקטן שנולד דמי. וכתב הרמב"ם בפר' ה' מהל' ממרים שאינו חייב על קללת ומכת אביו ושאינו יורשו; ובפ' א' מהל' יבום וחליצה כתב שאינו פוטר את אשתו מן היבום וכן אחיו מן הגויה אינו זוקק את אשתו אעפ"י שהיתה לידתו בקדושה כיון שהורתו שלא בקדושה.
ונראה שבן ישראל מהנכרית גרע מבן גוי מגויה אפילו נתגיירו שהרי גוי יורש אביו מד"ת [דברי תורה] ואפי' נתגייר יורש אותו מד"ס [דברי סופרים] כמ"ש הטור בח"מ [חושן משפט] סי' רפ"ג ואילו בן ישראל מהגוי' אינו יורש אותו לא מד"ת ולא מד"ס אפי' נתגייר; וכתב הרמב"ם בפ' ב' מהל' נחלות ז"ל היו לו בני' בגיותו ונתגייר אין לו בכור לנחלה אבל ישראל שהיה לו בן מן הגויה הואיל ואינו קרוי בנו, הבא לו אחריו מהישראלי' בכור לנחלה ונוטל פי שנים.
ברם יש להתבונן בטעם הדבר היטב שהדין נותן שלא יהיה בן הגוי' יורש אביו הישראל שמסתמא כרוך אחר אמו הוא ועובד ע"ז כמוה וכדמפרש טעמה קרא כי יסיר את בנך

מאחרי מסי' אותו מלהיות אחרי ה' ומטעם זה פטור מבזיון אביו ואינו פוטר אשתו מן היבום.

והכל תלוי בירושה ואפילו נתגייר החמירו חכמים שלא להשוותו יורש עם שאר אחיו דשמא הוא מתגייר מפני שנתן עינו בממון. ואין דין זה אלא לתקנה כמו שתקנו חז"ל לגר שיורש אביו הגוי אע"ג שמן התורה אינו יורשו וכדי שלא יחזור לסורו תקנו כך שאם אינו יורש בהיותו גר ישוב לסורו ויהי יורש אותו מן התורה. אבל כשנתגייר ונודע לנו שהולך בדרכי אביו אין הדין נותן שלא נייחסהו אחריו שעכ"פ אב יש לו והוא בנו לעניין עול התורה והמצוות ולפי זה יהיה זוכה גכ"ן לשררה כאביו ומקרב אחיך קרינן ביה שטעמא דכי יסיר את בנך אזל ליה.

ובגמר' דהוריות פ' כ"ג [כהן גדול] אמר ר"י אמר רב תמר בת יפת תואר הית' שנא' דבר נא אל המלך כי לא ימנעני ממך ואי ס"ד [סלקא דעתך] בת נישואין הואי אחתי' מי הוה שרי' ליה ואפי' הכי הוא ודוד קורי' אותה אחות אמנון והיא קורא' לו אחי ואבשלו' גם כן אמר האמנון אחיך. וע' וכתי' כי כן תלבשנה בנות המלך הבתולות אלמא בתו מן הגויה בתו היא מ"מ.

ובעושה מעשה עמך יהיה נשיא בעמך: ואפילו למלוכה בכי האי גוונא כשר שהרי רחבעם היה בן עמונית ולא הוזכר בקר' שנתגיירה אמו. ואפילו הולך אחר דרכי אמו כיון שנתגייר הוא יורש המלכות וראי' מבני אחאב אחזיהו ויהורם בני איזבל בת מלך צידוני' הארורה שהחטיאה בעלה ובניה כמו שהעיד עליה הכתוב.

והרמב"ם כתב בפר' י"ג מהל' א"ב [איסורי ביאה] ששמשון ושלמה לא נשאו נשים נכריות עד שגיורם אבל זה אינו בכתובים וגם בגמ' לא אמרו רק על בת פרעה שגיירה שלמה כדאית בפר' הערל. וה"ל לרמב"ם להחזיק דעתו ולומר דאי לא תימ' הכי היאך מלך רחבעם אלא נראה לו שאם אביו ישראל מקרב אחיך קרינן ליה כל זמן שנתגייר דאי לא נתגייר אפילו אמו ישראלית אם אביו גוי, גוי הוא ובנו קרינן ליה ולא בנה.

ובפר' אלו נאמרים בפי' רמב"ם במשנה פרשת המלך כתב ז"ל אגריפס היה מקהל גרים ולא היה לו אם מישראל ולא היה מקרב אחיך ולפיכך נענשו ישראל שאמרו לו אחינו אתה ואביו גכ"ן היה נכרי או עבד כמ"ש התוס' פ' החולץ וכ"כ רש"י ז"ל בפ' אלו נאמרים ובקדושין.

וכ"כ בפ"א מהל' מלכים אין מעמידין מלך מקהל גרים אפי' אחר כמה דורות עד שתהא אמו מישראל שנ' לא תוכל לתת עליך איש נכרי אשר לא אחיך הוא והנך רואה שלא אמר על בן ישראל מן הנכרי' שאסור למנותו שרחבעם יוכיח.

ומ"ש עד שתהי' אמו אפי' אמו קאמר דסגי וכ"ש אביו שבשעושה מעשה אביו אינו קרוי בנה אלא בנו.

ודברה תורה דרך העולם שהבן כרוך אחר אמו לפי שמשדלתו בדברים וכמ"ש בענין אותו ואת בנו שפי' אותו ואת אמו שנוהג בנקבות שכרוך אחריה ומספק שמא נוהג גם בזכרים אסרו גכ"ן אביו אם ידוע ודאי שהוא אביו כמ"ש הטור י"ד [יורה דעה] סי' ט"ז.

ובדיני האומו' הוא גכ"ן כך שקוראין לבן פלגש בן טבעי ולבן האמתי בנישואין קורין לו בן נימוסי' שא"א להכחיש שהוא בנו לפי הטבע ואם הוא ממלא מקומו יהיה יורש שררתו אבל לא ממונו.

וכשיובנו הדברים על אמתת' אין שום חכם ופוסק חולק ע"ז ובודאי גר צדק הזה שאביו הי' מהאנוסי' הוא נקרא בנו ומזרע ישראל הו' אע"ג שאינו יורש אותו מהטעמי' שאמרנו

ולכל מילי דשררה ודינא כשר הו' דעדיף מכשאמו ישראלי' ואביו גוי. ועל יסוד זה ראוי להשען שזולתו כל הנאמרים הם חוץ מהענין ואין צורך לפלפל להביא גמרו' ופוסקים שלא דברו חכמי' רק על גר סתם מקהל גרי' ועל גר שאמו מישראל.

זה דעתי ואשר יקשה ערפו וישים פניו כחלמיש לחלוק איני חושש לו.

אלה דברי הצעי' החלש יששכר הנקרא בער בהח"ר יאודה ליב ייטליש דיין.

Appendix II
The Inscription on the Tombstone of R. Issachar Ber Jeiteless in the Prague Jewish Cemetery[86]

יום ג' ג' תמוז תמ"ו [25 ביוני 1686] לפ"ק: פ"נ המופלא המפורסם פאר פרנס
וגדול הדור, במותו פנה הזיו וההדר הרב מו"ה בער ייטלס
בן המושלם כהרר ליב ייטלש ז"ל: בני אלם "מלאכים ואראלם
צעקו חוצה ומתאבלין" כל צבא הגלגלים קדר אורם ומר יבכיון,
על פטירת מבחר אנושי בתורה גדול כרב אשי, בעמקי תוספות
ורש"י, דבר הגדול עליו יאתיון, רב החובל בים הפוסקים, ירד וצלל
במעמקים והעלה חכו ממתקים פנתנו (מציון) מסיני ויצאו מציון
"יששכר יודעי לעתים בינה,"[87] בקידוש החודש והתכונה,
כרבן גמליאל ביבנה, שם הישכל חוקי הרעיון, "יתקרי חכם
אסו רבי"[88], בדקדוק הקמחי והתשבי, והוא יקרא אב תופשי
המליצה וחכמי הגיון, טבעו יצא בכל האקלמים על כל
החכמים, והם אלו מדומים כמו הנקודה לגלגל העליון, לו
נהירין שבילין דרקיע, ראשו השמים מגיע, זו בטבע...
דבר ויביע מארז עד האזוב והקיקיון, שקול בהוראה
כשמואל הרואה ששפט בלי הנאון, במתי נפשו באה אתו
במחיצתו כחום חברון

Tuesday 3rd Tammuz 5446 [25th June 1686]: Here lies the wondrous, famous and splendid *parnass* and genius,[89] at whose death radiance and glory were turned off, the Rabbi, Our Teacher, Ber Jeitless son of His Honour the Accomplished Rabbi Leib Jeiteless.
Lost for words,[90] "The messengers and the valiant cried out loud and mourned;"[91] the cosmic host dimmed its light and wept bitterly, at the passing away of the choicest amongst men; as great in Torah as Rav Ashi; in the depths of the Tosafists and Rashi, [every] great issue was brought to him; a ship's captain in the sea of the *poskim*, he delved and dived into the depths and his fishhook brought up sweetmeats.

---

86 No. 1199 in the Transcriptions made by Leopold M. Popper.

87 דברי הימים א יב:לג.

88 בבא מציאה פו/א.

89 Lit. 'greatest of the generation.'

90 Lit. 'the dumb.'

91 *Isaiah* 33:7.

Our corner-stone (is from Zion); from Sinai and out of Zion the [perfection] came forth;[92] "[The children of] Issachar that have an understanding of the passage of time;"[93] the sanctification of the New Moon and astronomy, like Rabban Gamliel in Yavne, where he formulated the laws of the method.

"He shall be called Sage, Rabbi's healer;"[94] on the subject of the grammar of the Kimḥi and the Tishbi, he shall be called the father of those who grapple with rhetoric and of the wise men of logic. It was his nature to go forth in all climes, foremost in all the sciences; though these are just imaginary like the point of the celestial sphere,[95] for him they were clear trails in the sky; his head reached up to the heavens; this in Nature…

He spoke and conversed [with all persons] from the cedar to the hyssop and gourd; comparable in his rulings to Samuel the seer who judged without personal gain; at his soul's pinnacle it came to him, in His presence as in the heat of Hebron.

92 *TB Yoma* 54b.

93 1 *Chronicles* 12:32.

94 *TB Baba Meẓiah* 86a.

95 Ibn Ezra on *Psalms* 119:90: נקודת הארץ היא נקודת הגלגל העליון.

Beyond the Written Word: Some Aspects of Originality in the Responsa of R. Simeon Duran

By: SAMUEL MORELL

I. Introduction

Rabbi Simeon ben Tzemah Duran (1361–1444) grew up on the island of Majorca, then under the sovereignty of Aragon. He was born into an aristocratic family, connected through his paternal grandmother to Gersonides.[1] He married into another aristocratic family. His father-in-law, R. Jonah de Maistre, a recognized scholar, was a direct descendant of Naḥmanides. R. Jonah lived in Teruel, in Aragon, and Duran lived there for a certain amount of time and studied with him, before moving back to Majorca. Duran's education was wide indeed. In addition to his mastery of rabbinic studies, he mastered philosophy, mathematics and astronomy in his early years in Majorca.[2]

In the wake of the anti-Jewish riots and forced conversions of 1391, Duran, at the age of thirty, fled to Algiers, along with many other coreligionists in Majorca. The coastal cities of Algeria became populated by refugees from Aragon, among them a number of rabbis. The most important of these was Rabbi Isaac bar Sheshet Perfet, known by his acronym, Rivash (1326–1408). Rivash was a prime student of R. Nissim

---

1 Duran's great grandfather was both a first cousin of Gersonides and his brother-in-law.

2 On Duran see I. Epstein, *The Responsa of Rabbi Simon B. Zemah Duran as a Source of the History of the Jews of North Africa* (Ktav: New York, n.d., first published in 1930); *Sefer ha-Tashbetz*, Mekhon Yerushalayim edition, v. 1 (1998), Introduction, Rabbi Yoel Katan (in Hebrew). Regarding Duran's philosophical writings, see the recent dissertation of Seth Kadish, published in PDF format: <https://sites.google.com/site/kadish67/avraham-avinu>.

Samuel Morell (PhD JTSA) is an Associate Professor Emeritus in the Department of Judaic Studies at Binghamton University. He has published two books, on the halakhic methodologies of R. Yitzhak ben Lev and of R. David ben Zimra (Radbaz), articles on halakhic methodology and related issues, articles on the Geonic work *Halakhot Pesuqot*, and numerous book reviews and review essays.

Gerondi (c.1290–1376), the most important halakhic authority in Catalonia, and in Aragon in general. Rivash served as rabbi in Saragossa, and then in Valencia. It was in Valencia that he was caught up in the cataclysmic events of 1391. About two years later, Rivash showed up in Algiers, and was recognized as the leading rabbinic authority there. Rivash ultimately became the chief rabbi of Algiers.[3]

The relations between Rivash and Duran were complex. They were completely different personalities. Whereas Duran had wide knowledge of philosophy and science, Rivash was a master solely of rabbinic studies.[4] Duran, who was thirty-five years younger than Rivash, was assertive and self-assured, whereas Rivash was a gentleman. Duran took issue with Rivash's rulings on a number of instances. In a later period, after the death of Rivash, he apologized for the disrespect he exhibited toward Rivash on one occasion, and attributed it to the brashness of youth.[5] But in many other ways Duran respected Rivash.[6] Rivash, for his part, respected the learning of Duran, even while disagreeing with him. He consulted Duran orally on occasion, and sometimes changed his mind as a result. Rivash appointed Duran to become a member of his rabbinic court. At the end of his life, Rivash indicated that Duran should succeed him. The position of chief rabbi of Algiers was subsequently passed down from Duran to his descendants for a number of generations.

There are a number of significant legal cases that both Rivash and Duran dealt with, and that each recorded in his respective responsa. In these cases, the responsa were edited by the authors themselves for publication. This allows for the ability to see Duran through the perspective of an alternative approach. I have also included some instances in which elements of Duran's methodology, as described in this study, are reflected in Rivash's responsa as well.

Duran named his collection of responsa *Tashbetz*, an acronym of "Teshuvot (Responsa) of Simeon Ben Tzemah." Duran's original *Tashbetz* consisted of three volumes. Subsequently, Duran's descendants added their own work to it as a fourth volume. The *Tashbetz* did not appear in print until the mid-18th century. In this study I used the new edition of

---

3 On Rivash see A. M. Hershman, *Rabbi Isaac ben Sheshet Perfet and his Times* (New York, 1943).

4 He was, however, familiar with philosophy, at least on a popular level. See Hershman, p. 89.

5 *Tashbetz*, 1:58, opening lines, at the end of his presentation of the case.

6 See Epstein, pp. 18–26.

the *Tashbetz* by Mekhon Yerushalayim (1998–2013), which utilizes manuscripts and supplies notes.[7] References to specific pages, notes and paragraphs refer to this edition. The Mekhon Yerushalayim edition also added a fifth volume, which included manuscript material of earlier, unedited versions of some of the responsa, some responsa of Duran that were not included by him in the *Tashbetz*, and responsa by his contemporaries that had never been published.

The translations are my own unless otherwise indicated. My additions to the Hebrew wording, designed to make the passage clearer for the English reader, are indicated by brackets.

Phrases in bold type indicate my emphasis.

II. Circumstantial Evidence

[1] <u>A Drowning at Sea</u> (*Tashbetz* 1:73–84; Rivash 155, 181–183)

The following case is a good window into the originality of Duran's approach to legal decisions. An incident that took place in Algiers in the year 1406 or 1407[8] resulted in a ruling by Duran, which led to a controversy between him and other halakhic authorities, most significantly Rivash. A summary of the events is as follows:[9]

> A ship from Bejaia, a town on the Algerian coast about 150 miles east of Algiers, was on its way to Algiers. Two Jews were on board. As they approached the coast of Algiers, a Christian ship bent on piracy was spotted bearing down on them. The crew jumped into the sea and swam toward shore. The two Jews jumped in as well. One of them quickly realized that he was not a strong enough swimmer to reach the shore, and returned to the ship. Miraculously, a sudden wave pushed it away from the attackers and toward the shore as the pirating ship approached, and he escaped. He later testified that after he returned to the ship he saw the other Jew floundering, in a way that indicated that he didn't know how to swim, but then lost sight of him. When he arrived ashore, he immediately climbed to a view that overlooked the sea, and noticed a body floating head down in the water.

7 The original three *Tashbetz* volumes were prepared by Rabbi Yoel Katan. His notes are superb, as is his lengthy and comprehensive introduction to the man and his work.

8 Hershman, p. 225.

9 All the testimony regarding the events presented below are from *Tashbetz* 1:74.

In addition to the testimony of the Jew who escaped, there was a good deal of technically inadmissible evidence suggesting that the other Jew had indeed drowned at sea. In order to appreciate the weight of this evidence, I will summarize it.

1. On the day of the event, some of the crew members entered the city gates. It was a Sabbath, and a number of Jews were leisurely standing around there. The crew members mentioned the missing Jew to them by name, and indicated that he drowned while trying to swim ashore.
2. It subsequently became known that there indeed were only two Jews on the ship.
3. The attackers subsequently docked at a Christian port, and related how they almost looted a Muslim ship, but everyone escaped, except one Jew who drowned.
4. A Muslim, who had been a prisoner on the Christian ship during the event, later escaped, and reported to Jews that the Christians on the ship were unsuccessful in taking any captives from the Muslim ship, either Muslim or Jew. This would rule out the possibility that the missing Jew was alive as a captive.
5. Another piece of evidence supported this conclusion. Subsequent to the escape of the ship from the Christian pirates, the latter encountered another Muslim ship, also on its way from Bejaia to Algiers. This ship they successfully looted. All aboard were taken captive, including a number of Jews. They subsequently docked at Majorca. Jews who had been in Majorca at the time testified in Algiers that they questioned the Jewish captives, and they knew nothing of a Jewish captive from an earlier attack.

Legal certification of the death of a missing person is a central issue in halakhic discourse. The classic context of this discourse is the situation of *'iggun*, the case of a woman whose husband is missing and believed to be dead. Such a woman may not remarry until her husband's death is certified by a rabbinic court. As we shall see, our case is unusual, because nowhere in the entire extended discussion between Duran and his challengers is there any mention of *'iggun*. It appears that there was no wife. The question before us has to do with a different issue entirely, as we shall see shortly. Nevertheless, the legal categories developed for the issue of *'iggun* lie in the background, and it is necessary for our purposes to understand the basics of the rabbinic approach to certifying a missing husband's death.

The attitude governing these rules is complex. Fundamentally, the standards of proof for the identification of a corpse, for the purpose of enabling his wife's remarriage, are very high. After all, if a mistake is made, and the husband who is presumed dead shows up after the woman has remarried, she would be guilty of "adultery," and the rabbinic court that gave her permission to remarry would be complicit. One example of these standards is that the major features of the face must be visible for an identification. Another example is the one before us. It is known as "falling into water without an end," that is, a body of water whose boundaries are not visible in their entirety. The Talmud refuses to recognize such a person as dead, because of the exaggerated fear that the victim might have emerged from the water in a spot that was not visible to the observer. Certainly, any circumstantial evidence would be unacceptable. Nevertheless, in spite of this extreme fear of even improbable error, there is a contradictory tendency toward leniency, out of concern for the wife in a situation in which the death is presumed but not legally proven. The Talmud expresses the sentiment that everything possible should be done to interpret the law such as to enable the wife's remarriage. The specific examples cited by the Talmud involve a relaxation of the rules of evidence. An important example of this is the acceptance of the testimony of only a single witness, instead of the normally required two. Even the incidental report of a non-Jew, "speaking in innocence" (i.e., in casual conversation and not as an official witness in court), is accepted.

The case before us has to do with the issue of inheritance. The man who did not make it to the shore at Algiers had, before he embarked at Bejaia, entrusted his assets to someone during his absence. This trustee now faced the question whether he should release these apparently considerable assets to the man's heir in Algiers. Duran supported the legal certification of the missing man's death. Everyone else on record opposed it.

It is possible to reconstruct the chronology of this extended correspondence, and it would be helpful to do so to get a sense of the extent of the opposition to Duran's ruling.

1. The hearing of evidence by a rabbinic court in Algiers. It appears that this was the court presided over by Duran.[10]
2. Objections from other rabbinic authorities, compelling Duran to respond.[11]

---

10 *Tashbetz*, 1:73, end of opening paragraph.

11 *Tashbetz*, 1:73, opening paragraph.

3. Duran's detailed justification of his ruling.[12]
4. A critique of Duran's justification by R. Moshe Gabbai, the rabbi of Hunein,[13] and the brother of Duran's mother-in-law.[14]
5. Duran's response, rejecting R. Moshe Gabbai's critique (4 above).[15]
6. R. Moshe Gabbai's response, rejecting Duran's response to him (5 above).[16]
7. Duran's second response to R. Moshe Gabbai.[17]
8. R. Shem Tov ha-Levi of Hunein's critique of Duran's decision, which he sent to Rivash for his opinion.[18]
9. Rivash's response to R. Shem Tov ha-Levi, in which he agrees with the latter's criticism and adds some of his own.[19]
10. R. Moshe Gabbai's solicitation of Rivash's reaction to Duran's rejection of his (Gabbai's) argument against Duran's decision (5 and 7 above).[20]
11. Rivash's response to R. Moshe Gabbai, supporting his argument against Duran.[21]

This apparently universal opposition to the certification of the victim's death,[22] in the face of what would seem to a layman to be overwhelming evidence in favor of it, in fact bespeaks the traditionally accepted legal approach to the issue. That approach draws on the only body of settled law that deals with this issue, that is, the laws governing *'iggun*. Circumstantial evidence is not acceptable. The one witness to the floating body saw it with its head down, the face not visible, and that only from a considerable distance. The one area in which the law of *'iggun* would favor

---

12 *Tashbetz*, 1:73–82.

13 *Tashbetz*, 1:83, Heading.

14 *Tashbetz*, 1:152, third paragraph from the beginning. For a bit more about R. Moshe Gabbai, see Hershman, p. 176.

15 *Tashbetz*, 1:83.

16 *Tashbetz*, 1:84, Heading.

17 *Tashbetz*, 1:84.

18 Heading and opening sentence of Rivash 155.

19 Heading and opening sentence of Rivash 155.

20 Rivash 181, heading and opening sentence. R. Moshe ben Gabbai's query to Rivash, summarizing Duran's argument but without his own rebuttal, was published from manuscript in the Mekhon Yerushalayim edition of the *Tashbetz*, 5:45.

21 Rivash 181–183.

22 In addition to the above, see also the responsum of Yeshu'a ha-Levi Provencal, published from manuscript in the Mekhon Yerushalayim edition of the *Tashbetz*, 5:199.

the certification of death is the acceptance of testimony from a single witness. But this is a case of inheritance, not of a wife's remarriage. Maimonides writes:

> Heirs do not inherit until they bring clear proof that their bequeather has died. But if they [merely] heard that he had died, or if there were non-Jews speaking in innocence [indicating his death], even though they allow his wife to remarry on the basis of their word, and she can [even] collect her marriage settlement [from the estate], the heirs do not inherit on the basis of their word.[23]

"Clear proof" is not defined by Maimonides in this immediate paragraph. However, in the sequel he writes:

If one drowned in water that has no end, and **witnesses** came [and testified] that he drowned in their sight, and the memory of him was lost, even though his wife is not permitted to remarry *ab initio*, the heirs inherit on the basis of **their** testimony. So too, if **witnesses** came [and testified] that **they** saw him fall into a den of lions or tigers,... [he lists a few similar scenarios of strong circumstantial evidence]—in all these situations and others like them, and [if] subsequently the memory of him was lost, they [the heirs] inherit on the basis of **their** testimony, even though his wife is not permitted to marry. For I maintain that they [the Rabbis] were stringent in these cases only because of the prohibition of *karet* ["being cut off" from one's people, the biblical punishment for adultery]. But in matters if civil law, if **witnesses** testified to situations where there was a presumption of death, and **they** testified that they actually saw these things, and later the memory of him was lost, and it was heard that he died, they [the heirs] inherit on [the basis of] **their** testimony.[24]

The implication is that Maimonides' phrase "clear proof" means two witnesses.[25] An explicit requirement of two witnesses, precisely in the situation under discussion, is found in the early ge'onic work *Halakhot Gedolot* (ninth century): "If one fell into water without an end, on the basis of two witnesses, it is [considered] certain that he died with regard to civil matters [and] his heirs take possession of his property; [but] with regard to his wife, the Sages were strict [and he is not considered dead] until they [the witnesses] report the description of his forehead and his nose, and his other physical attributes."[26]

---

23 *Laws of Inheritance*, chap. 7, par. 1. See also par. 10.

24 Ibid., par. 3.

25 See also *Ketubbot* 107a bottom, Rav Papa; *Yevamot* 117a top, Mishna, and Rashi ad loc.

26 *Halakhot Gedolot, Yibbum ve-Ḥalitza*

Duran's lengthy and detailed justification of his ruling was made necessary by the severe critique leveled against it by his peers, as he himself explains. It extends from *Tashbetz* 1:73 through 1:82, and continues through two subsequent responses to the objections of R. Moshe Gabbai, 1:83 and 1:84. It is a tour de force of out-of-the-box legal interpretation. Duran's rhetoric betrays his conviction that everyone knows that the man is dead.[27] He bases this conclusion on the overwhelming weight of the circumstantial evidence summarized above, along with the surviving Jew's testimony of his distant sighting of a corpse head down in the water, which itself is little better than circumstantial evidence for the purpose of identification. From Duran's perspective, this body of evidence, taken in totality, is compelling. The man's death is obvious to all. He sees the halakhic objections as technical obstacles, which have to be overcome in a technical way. That entails original interpretation of the relevant legal sources.

Circumstantial evidence in halakhic jurisprudence was the subject of a doctoral dissertation at the Hebrew University by Chaim Shlomo Ḥeifetz.[28] The following discussion of circumstantial evidence prior to Duran draws heavily on Ḥeifetz's study. Ḥeifetz collected various references in the Talmud to the application of judicial discretion in determining the truth, including within that category the reliance on circumstantial evidence in civil cases.

In the Talmud these cases were each treated *ad hoc*, without any attempt to bring them together into a single conceptual category. It appears that the first to do so is Hai ben Sherira Ga'on (d. 1038), who speaks with reference to himself and his father:[29]

> Our [i.e., my] opinion, and that of my father and teacher: It is known that in civil law one should always go according to the assessment [of the situation], and [one should] always look carefully into the actuality of the matter, ensuring that there be no trickery and evildoing. Rather [one should] go according to the truth of the matter, and bring the facts to light, and rule according to the truth.[30]

---

27 The most explicit example is *Tashbetz*, 1:77, p. 168, col. 2, cited below at the end of this article.

28 Shelomo Ḥayyim Ḥeifetz, *Re'ayot Nesibatiyot ba-Mishpat ha-Ivri* [Circumstantial Evidence in Jewish Law], diss. 1974. The following discussion of circumstantial evidence prior to Duran draws heavily on Ḥeifetz's study.

29 Ḥeifetz, however, does not interpret Hai's statement as the expression of a general principle.

30 *Tashbetz*, 1:80. *Ittur, matnat shekhiv mera'*, ed. Meir Yonah, 58 col. 4, 59 col. 1.

This general approach of arriving at the truth, *contra* restricting the ruling to the literal rules of evidence and procedure, is in evidence in a responsum of Alfasi, in the 11th century,[31] and by Rashba [R. Solomon ben-Adret], in the 13th.[32]

A far-reaching advance in the reliance on circumstantial evidence and its role in judicial discretion finds its expression in the responsa of Rabbenu Asher ben Yeḥiel (acronym: Rosh, c. 1250–1327).[33]

Rabbenu Asher saw the role of the judge as assuring the maintenance of justice, defined as what is moral, rather than what is technically legal.[34] He had no patience for legal loopholes that allowed for injustice in the face of convincing circumstantial evidence. If there were talmudic rulings to the contrary, he would reinterpret them in a way that allowed for what he believed was a just ruling.[35] What Rabbenu Asher did not do is propose a broad theoretical basis that would integrate his approach with the mainstream legal conventions of the Talmud. Where he does cite a talmudic rule in these cases, they have an *ad hoc* character to them.[36]

---

31 Cited by Ḥeifetz 33-35 (= Harkavi, no. 456, p. 238, tr. into Hebrew, p. 322).

32 Responsa, v. 1 no. 1146, and others. See Ḥeifetz, 69–76. See also Maimonides, *Mishneh Torah, Laws of the Sanhedrin*, chap. 24, par. 1, which recognizes the broad judicial discretion of a judge to rule on the basis of his own understanding of the truth, and par. 2, which limits such discretion now that judges are "not properly learned and lacking in wisdom." But Maimonides' ruling does not seem to reflect actual court practice in this matter. Rashba does not cite him in this regard.

33 Rabbenu Asher was born and educated in Germany. He migrated to Spain, and in 1305 he became the rabbi of Toledo. All of Rabbenu Asher's responsa that are in our possession were written in Spain, but his learning derived from Germany. His conception of the role of judicial discretion had its roots in the approach of his teacher, R. Meir ben Barukh (Maharam Rottenberg). Ḥeifetz, 134-135 on R. Meir ben Barukh; 88 on Rabbeu Asher.

34 The discussion that follows is informed by Ḥeifetz's section on Rabbenu Asher, pp. 79–96.

35 See Ḥeifetz, p. 85, fn. 94.

36 According to Ḥeifetz, Rabbenu Asher based his approach on three talmudic principles. One of these is *hora'at sha'ah*, an *ad hoc* extralegal ruling. A second is *yedi'a be-lo' re'iya*, "testimony derived from knowing without seeing," see Shevu'ot 33b bottom, a phrase used only once, in reference to a very specific circumstance. The third is *din merummeh*, also of an *ad hoc* nature. *Din merummeh* is the conviction of a judge that the ruling that would be dictated by the evidence is false.

Duran, in his entire extended discussion, cites Rabbenu Asher only once in reference to circumstantial evidence, and then only briefly, almost as a passing reference.[37] Nevertheless, it would seem that in the present case Duran was influenced very much by Rabbenu Asher. He too relies heavily on the collective weight of circumstantial evidence. But unlike Rabbenu Asher, Duran, besieged by opposition, seeks to anchor his position in the bedrock of mainstream *halakha*. This he does by an original radical redefinition of "two witnesses." It is this redefinition to which Rivash, R. Yom Tov ha-Levi and R. Moshe Gabbai all raise objection.[38]

The requirement of two witnesses in civil cases was derived by the Talmud from a midrashic interpretation of Deuteronomy 19:15, and it was considered a biblical law. Duran, in the face of this fact, lays out the following argument. Why, he asks, is the testimony of two witnesses probative? Because, he answers, there is a legal presumption that witnesses testify truthfully. So why isn't a single witness sufficient? Because even though there is a presumption that the witness is testifying truthfully, there nevertheless remains some degree of possibility that a specific witness might be lying. The requirement of a second witness serves to guard against that rare occurrence. But, argues Duran, when there is another factor supporting the testimony of a single witness, such as convincing circumstantial evidence, then that extra support for the testimony serves the role of a second witness.[39] Duran argues that a single witness, whose

---

37 *Tashbetz*, 1:80, fn. 34.

38 Rivash, 155; *Tashbetz*, 1:83-84.

39 Some other examples of a supporting factor to which Duran refers in this regard include: (1) The casual conversation of non-Jews. This is accepted by the Talmud too in establishing a man's death in order to allow his wife to remarry, but the reference there is to first-hand knowledge of the death. Duran extends it here to circumstantial evidence, and to civil law in general. (2) A similar acceptance of casual conversation from Jews who are disqualified from testifying. In this case they would not be relied upon to release a widow from *'iggun*, because as Jews, who are presumed to be aware of the implications, they are suspect of simulating "speaking in innocence." (3) The presumption that a witness would not lie in a situation in which the lie is likely to be found out, as is the case here if he is really alive. This consideration derives from Maimonides, who mentions it three times in the *Mishneh Torah* in connection with the testimony of one witness, though not in matters of civil law. The one which is closest to our case is that of a woman who returns from abroad and asserts that her husband died. The Talmud accepts her assertion. Maimonides supplies the reason, that she would not lie in a situation in which she is likely to be found out.

testimony is supported by other convincing factors, is considered **by biblical law** to be the equivalent of two witnesses. When Duran is challenged by his opponents with authoritative sources which specifically mention the need for two witnesses, among them most notably Maimonides,[40] he simply insists that the legal term "two witnesses" connotes also a single witness supported by other convincing factors. This, of course, implies that Maimonides and others (e.g., the ninth-century author of *Halakhot Gedolot*) understood the term "two witnesses" the way he did, and that they expected their readers to understand it that way as well. This is one example of Duran's use of a forced interpretation, a byproduct of his need to arrive at a ruling which for him was obviously just.

III. Functional Interpretation

In the case above, Duran interpreted "two witnesses" in a non-literal way, which he believed was true to the function of two witnesses, namely, to arrive at the truth. Duran's interpretive methodology in this regard, which ignores the traditional literal understanding of a law and defines it instead in terms of its function (henceforth: "functional interpretation"), is in stark contrast to that of Rivash and the others who disagreed with him in this case.[41] Duran's penchant for a functional interpretation of the law is attested in a number of other responsa.

[2] <u>Honoring the Dead</u> (*Tashbetz* 1: 22; Rivash 116)

In this instance, too, Duran and Rivash stood on opposite sides.

The case involves the intersection of two laws. One is the obligation to cease from certain activities defined as "work" on those holidays that the Bible describes as "holy convocations." These include the first and last days of the pilgrimage festivals. In the Diaspora, the practice arose of adding a second holy-convocation day at both the beginning and the end

---

40 *Laws of Inheritance*, chap. 7, par. 3, cited above.

41 In Case [4] below, Rivash, again in accord with the prevalent view, adopts a narrow literal interpretation. In another responsum, written in the early years of his career as a community rabbi, he responded to a question about a *get ḥalitza*, in which one of the letters of the date was accidentally omitted. Rivash insisted on an extremely literal interpretation, thereby disqualifying the document (Rivash 382 and 385). He sent his responsum to his mentor, R. Nissim Gerondi. In his answer (no. 78 of the latter's responsa, ed. Feldman), R. Nissim set him straight. See also Feldman's introduction, p. 22. However, Cases [6] and [7] below adduce instances in which Rivash does indeed utilize functional interpretation.

of the festival. But the prohibition of work on the added second day was considered to have the status of rabbinic, rather than biblical, authority, and had a lower degree of sanctity, allowing for some leniencies in special situations.

The other law is the obligation of the kinsmen of a deceased to see to his proper burial at the earliest possibility. Such a burial entails the engagement in activities that are prohibited on days of "holy convocation." The Talmud drew a distinction in this regard between the first holy-convocation day and the second, rabbinically ordained, holy-convocation day: "If one dies on the first holy-convocation day, he should be dealt with by non-Jews; on the second holy-convocation day, he should be dealt with by Jews."[42] The extent to which Jews may engage in prohibited work on the second holy-convocation day is formulated in the pithy ruling in the Talmud by Rav Ashi: "The second holy-convocation day, with regard to the burial of a deceased, has been set by the Rabbis as a weekday."[43]

Here is the account of the events presented in the Responsa of Rivash:

> It happened that a Jew died in the evening during the Ten Days of Penitence,[44] eight days distant from a Jewish settlement. It became known to his relatives that Arabs placed him in a cave in his clothing, and closed the opening to the cave. But he was not buried, because there is no Jew in that entire region. This was on the eve of Sukkot.[45]

The event occurred in Mostaganem. The rabbinic authority there, Rabbi Abraham bar Natan, instructed the relatives to set out on the second holy-convocation day, when a deceased should be dealt with by Jews. And this includes travel to where the deceased is, there to give him a proper burial.[46]

The propriety of that ruling was subsequently challenged by the rabbi of Oran, Rabbi Amram ben Marwam, who sent his brief to Rivash for his opinion.[47] Rivash rejects some of R. Amram's peripheral arguments, but otherwise finds in favor of R. Amram's opinion, that the relatives should have been instructed to wait until after the entire festival before they set

---

42 BT *Shabbat* 139b; BT *Bezah* 22a.

43 *Bezah* 6a.

44 The ten days beginning with Rosh ha-Shana. The crucial events occurred on Sukkot, which begins two weeks after Rosh ha-Shana.

45 In the more abbreviated version of the circumstances in *Tashbetz*, it states that he died on the eve of Sukkot.

46 *Tashbetz*, 1:22, heading and first paragraph.

47 Rivash, 116. This is part of a lengthy sequence of queries that Rabbi Amram sent to Rivash. The first, where the correspondent is identified, is #102.

out.[48] Except for those arguments of R. Amram that Rivash rejects, his response addresses and develops just one that had been raised by R. Amram. One should remember, though, that in general the queries that introduce responsa were formulated by the responder, or selectively abridged by him. Having himself edited the text of the query, and having found in favor of R. Amram's stringent position, Rivash, it is fair to assume, accepted those points that were raised by R. Amram and that he himself did not explicitly reject. He simply felt no need for further elaboration in his own response to R. Amram.

I'll begin with the one that he addresses specifically. The festivals of Passover and Sukkot extend seven and eight days respectively (*sans* the added "second day" on each end). The first and the last of these days are "holy convocations," in which all the activities that define "work" are prohibited. On the intermediate days, necessary "work" is permitted; the Talmud defines which activities those are. With regard to dealing with a burial during the intermediate days, the Talmud appears to indicate a concern lest some of the activities entailed be misunderstood by observers who are unaware of their purpose, and mistakenly believe that those activities are generally permitted on the intermediate days. Rivash applies an *a fortiori* argument, that if this is true for the intermediate days, it is certainly true for the second holy-convocation day:

> Certainly in the case under discussion, which [involves] a holy-convocation day before the intermediate days, [and] in which the body[49] is several days distant from them so that they won't arrive until after the [entire] festival, one should prohibit [the travel] because of the fear lest people say, "They are traveling for their own business, for a matter that is not obligatory."

However, from the immediate sequel it is clear that Rivash's position is informed by a broader issue. He proceeds to cite a contrary opinion of Naḥmanides, who permitted the accompanying of the deceased to his burial on the second holy-convocation day even beyond the town's environs, where one is normally not permitted to stray on the Sabbath or on days of holy convocation.[50] To this Rivash counters:

48 "Entire festival" appears to be Rivash's intention. He writes in his opening line: "Surely, they should not [have been allowed] to go beyond the town's environs (*ha-teḥum*) for the purpose of burying a deceased who is not present, and who could not be reached until after the entire festival (*ha-mo'ed*).

49 *Ha-met,* translated above as "deceased."

50 *Torat ha-Bayit*, ed. Cheval p. 114.

> But in the case under discussion, in which they are not [actually] accompanying the body, it appears certain that it is forbidden to violate the second holy-convocation day by travel outside the town's environs.

Why does this "appear certain"? Naḥmanides had made his point with reference to a funeral procession. Rivash interprets him in a very narrow, literal way, as being limited only to a funeral procession accompanying the body, but excluding travel that is necessary in order to reach the deceased. But a funeral procession is the usual circumstance in which this issue is encountered, and it is possible that Naḥmanides used it as an example of the principle in general. Rivash does not justify in argument this narrow literal reading, he just asserts it. It appears to be an arbitrary interpretation in order to counter the challenge that Naḥmanides' ruling presents to his own position. But what motivated Rivash to take the stand that he does to begin with?

It seems to me that the answer lies with the closing sentence of R. Amram's query. Since the query as a whole was edited by Rivash, and this passage was not challenged by Rivash in his own responsum, it is fair to accept that it represented Rivash's own position. The sentence refers to *kevod ha-beriyot*, the respect given to human beings, here specifically in their death. The entire subject of the burial of the dead comes under the rubric of *kevod ha-beriyot.* The query, after presenting the reasons to disallow travel on the second holy-convocation day, concludes:

> And the reason that *kevod ha-beriyot* does not apply, is because the body is not present among us.

A similar sentiment occurs earlier in the query. R. Amram asserts that the leniencies allowed on the second holy-convocation day apply only if the burial will take place that same day. He explains:

> What would these [kinsmen] achieve in their violation of the sanctity of a holy-convocation day, given that they will [in any case] not be able to bury the body on the same day?

In other words, the obligation of *kevod ha-beriyot*, manifest in the act of burying the dead, an obligation that mandates prohibited work on the second holy-convocation day, is defined only by the act of burial itself. It does not extend to preliminary activities unless they culminate in a burial the same day. Rivash apparently shared that position. And they were not alone in this opinion. The rabbi who originally issued the permissive ruling, R. Abraham ben Natan of Mostaganem, after being challenged by R. Amram and unsure of his ground, sent a query to Duran, asking for his opinion on the matter. The query, edited by Duran, closes with the following sentence:

> And you wrote that you permitted it only because you were told that the very same day it would be possible for them to reach him and to bury him.

Duran, after presenting the "fifth argument" for the disallowance of travel in the case at hand (cited immediately below), paraphrases it this way: "You have already [in your query] apologized for this, because the one who asked you the question misled you by telling you that there was enough time in the day to go [there] and bury him."

So it appears that this view of *kevod ha-beriyot* as it relates to the burial of the dead, namely, that it applies only to the physical burial itself, was in fact a consensus opinion.

Duran tells us that R. Abraham ben Natan's detailed legal argument did not reach him. He did, however, have access to R. Amram's counter-argument, and responds to it point by point. Duran organizes his rebuttal by listing five arguments cited for disallowing the relatives to set out beyond the town's environs on the second holy-convocation day, and rejecting each in turn. The responsum is rhetorically arranged, beginning with those arguments that are easiest to dispose of, and leading up to the more serious ones. The one that concerns us here is the last one:

> The fifth argument: That the body was [a distance of] four or five days' travel beyond the town, and what would they be able to accomplish [even by] traveling quickly?[51]

Duran proceeds to challenge the entire consensus that *kevod ha-beriyot* as it relates to the burial of the dead is limited to the physical burial of the body, and its prerequisite activities on the day of the burial:

> Since we say that "the second holy-convocation day, with regard to the burial of a deceased, has been set by the Rabbis as a weekday," we make no distinction between a burial that very day and a burial the following day, as long as the acts performed on the [second] holy-convocation day enable a sooner burial. For after all, as long as the body lingers it becomes uglier [i.e., it deteriorates more] ... and one who rushes to care for it so as to hasten its burial performs a *mitzva*. The second holy-convocation day does not stand in the way

51 Following the text of the *Abridged Tashbetz*, a work widely known long before the publication of the original responsa. The text before us appears to be corrupted. See fn. 40 in the Mekhon Yerushalayim edition.

> of the obligation to bury the body, since it "has been set by the Rabbis as a weekday."[52]

That is to say, *kevod ha-beriyot*, the respect given to human beings by giving them a proper burial, is to be interpreted broadly, in consonance with its functional interpretation. This was in opposition to a literal interpretation of "burial," which had been the consensus.

[3] Entrenched Religious Practice vs. Talmudic Law: Case One (*Tashbetz* 1: 22; Rivash 116)

Early in the same responsum, in Duran's response to "the first argument," there is another example of his use of functional interpretation of halakhic rules. It is used to justify a widely established custom that appears to be in contradiction to a talmudic ruling.

Duran paraphrases Rabbi Amram's argument thus:

> It says in [the Talmud] Chapter "One may suspend,"[53] that neither Jews nor non-Jews may care for the deceased, neither on the first holy-convocation day nor on the second. And the reason [for this stringent ruling] was explained, because they [the people of Bashkar, who asked this question] were not learned in Torah. And we are not learned in Torah.

The talmudic ruling, cited from Tractate Shabbat, is contrary to the accepted *halakha* governing burial on holy-festival days, which allows for such burial. The Talmud explains it as an *ad hoc* stringency, lest those who are unlearned in Torah, seeing that these activities are permitted, mistakenly believe that they are generally permitted on holy-convocation days. Rabbi Amram's argument is based on the theory of the decline of generations. Jews today are generally considered to be "not learned in Torah," and the restrictive ruling should apply to them. The source in the Talmud refers to both the first and second holy-day convocation days, but the situation under discussion is restricted to the second day only. Both sides of this dispute treat the issue as referring to the second day.

---

52 In the sequel he takes issue with Rabbenu Asher, who, following Rashi, prohibited the beginning of the digging of a grave on the second holy-convention day, which will be completed that night at the conclusion of the day. After referencing Rabbenu Asher's ruling, he writes: "But I wrote what appears to me [to be the truth]," i.e., that for the reasons stated above it is permitted.

53 BT *Shabbat* 139a-b.

Duran begins as follows, addressing himself to R. Abraham bar Natan of Mostaganem, who had permitted the relatives to begin their traveling on the second holy-convocation day:

> And I say, that this argument of his [R. Amram's] is not an argument that can challenge you. Go and see how people act,[54] and Jewish practice is Torah.[55] We have not seen in our generations anyone who is concerned about this, and one who permits [something] on the basis of entrenched religious practice [henceforth: *minhag*] should not be scolded at all.

Duran does not deny the theoretical legitimacy of the restrictive ruling, and he does not deny that Jews in his generation are to be categorized as "not learned in Torah." "One who permits on the basis of *minhag* should not be scolded," but that formulation still does not give such permission total theoretical legitimacy. He avers, however, that to the extent possible, it is the rabbinic scholar's job to interpret the *halakha* to accord with *minhag*, thus to truly legitimate it:

> But what is proper for every rabbinic scholar to do in such a case is to fix it so that the *minhag* accords with the *halakha*.

Since the rabbinic scholar has no effective control over accepted popular religious practice, Duran means that the *halakha* should be interpreted so as to accord with the *minhag*.[56] And indeed, he proceeds to propose a number of ways to do this, and it is one of these that is our concern here.

---

54 BT *Berakhot* 45a and parallels.

55 *U-minhagan shel yisrael torah hi.* This derives ultimately from the Palestinian Talmud, *ha-minhag mevatel et ha-halakha*, PT Yevamot 12:1, Ven. 12c; PT *Bava* Meẓi'a 7:1, Ven. 11b. The phrase (with variants) as it appears here is evidenced in early Ashkenazic sources, see Ta-Shma, *Minhag Ashkenaz ha-Kadmon*, p. 38, n.33. The second source cited above, from PT Bava Meẓi'a, is limited in scope, because it refers to the right of contract in civil law, which in any case is recognized in talmudic jurisprudence. It is that source of limited scope that is cited by Alfasi, Bava Meẓi'a ch. 7, no. 495, 52a in the current pagination, thus entrenching it in Sephardi *halakha*. Duran, however, applies it here to religious law, giving it a wider applicability. See another explicit example of this principle in religious law, *Tashbeẓ* 1:125, concluding sentence.

56 There is a close parallel to this in *Tashbeẓ* 1:50, in which, as here, he accepts the pure halakhic position *de jure*, but in practice finds a way to reinterpret the *halakha* to bring it into accord with the *minhag*; see especially the paragraph beginning on p. 112b and continuing on p. 113a. This approach to *minhag* had long been standard halakhic practice in Ashkenaz from its earliest days. See Ta-Shma, op. cit., p. 28 bot., 29 top. In Case [4] below there is an example of Rivash's reaction

Referencing only the second holy-convocation day, he points out that in the specific issue at hand, the factor of being "not learned in Torah" works, in (his) contemporary times, in the opposite direction from that implied by the Talmud. The second holy-convocation day was originally adopted before the adoption of a permanent calendar. Without such a calendar, the day on which the new month began was determined by the rabbinic leadership in Palestine by the sighting of the new moon, and it could vary by one day. Since the day of the festival was determined by the day the month began, Jewish communities beyond the reach of notification from the Palestinian center celebrated a second holy-convocation day to cover that uncertainty. Under such conditions, Duran explains, unlearned Jews, knowing from the Bible that only one such day was ordained, could easily become skeptical of the second day. Today, however, the second holy-festival day is so ingrained in religious practice, that unlearned Jews mistakenly think that it has the same biblical authority as the first. Their ignorance leads them to be more stringent than they need be on the second day, not less.

Unlike Duran's definition of *kevod ha-beriyot* later in the responsum in his response to "the fifth argument" in Case [2], his response to "the first argument" here is somewhat peripheral to his "bottom line." R. Amram's argument is that "they are not learned in Torah," and the Talmud sees that as a cause for stringency. Duran begins with the admission that he is attempting to adjust the *halakha* to the realities of *minhag*, and such a procedure invites forced interpretation. He brings a number of proofs for leniency, and he does not indicate any greater weight to this halakhic adjustment than the others he presents. Nevertheless, it is a legitimate example of his interpreting the *halakha* in light of its functional purpose rather than its literal reading.

[4] Entrenched Religious Practice vs. Talmudic Law: Case Two (*Tashbetz* 1:28; Rivash 35)

The *halakha* mandates that a woman immerse herself in a ritual pool (*miqveh*) after her menstrual period before having intercourse with her husband. Every part of her external body must be exposed to the water. In order to ensure that no foreign agent on her body block access to the

to a *minhag* he believes to be halakhically untenable, which is more typical of Sephardic halakhic decisions. See also Rivash's explicit statement in Rivash 146, which responds to the same question as *Tashbetz*, 1:50; see especially the last paragraph on p. 151.

water of the *miqveh*, she must thoroughly wash her body and her hair before entering the *miqveh*. The talmudic sage Rava states that the use of a hair-scrubbing agent, which the Talmud refers to as *neter*, may not be used for this purpose, because it detaches the hair.[57] The reason was understood to be that unattached hairs may entwine themselves with growing hair, thereby blocking the water's direct access to it.

It was common practice among women in Majorca to prepare for entering the *miqveh* by washing their hair with a scrubbing agent, called in the Romance vernacular *qalida*. The same vernacular term was used to translate the biblical word *neter* in Jeremiah 2:22, where it clearly refers to a body cleansing agent. The identification of *qalida* with *neter*, along with the Talmud's prohibition of the use of *neter* before entering the *miqveh*, led Rivash to object strongly to its use.

Rivash's statement comes as an addendum to a responsum on another subject entirely, sent in response to a query by the same R. Amram, the rabbi of Oran, whom we have met before. The query regarded a detail in the procedure for reading the Torah. It involved a *minhag* that Rivash himself believed to be contrary to *halakha*, but that he had no power to change. In an addendum, Rivash warns R. Amram about the insurmountable difficulties of changing a halakhically questionable *minhag*. He tells him of his previous experience in such an endeavor that regarded a different matter, an attempt to change women's practice of using *qalida* in preparation for immersion:

> When I saw that the women obey [rulings] to be lenient, [a leniency] that is not proper for them in this matter, I backed away, so that they not say that I am casting an aspersion on a *minhag* regarding their immersion. But[58] regarding my own household,[59] with[60] my female relatives who listen to me and pay attention, I gave them orders to act properly. And thus I put into practice what the Sages, of blessed memory, said: "Just as it is a proper thing [*mitzva*] to say something that will be listened to, so it is a proper thing to refrain from saying something that will not be listened to. Rabbi Abba said: It is an obligation [*hova*]."[61]

It appears that the use of *qalida* before immersion was specific to Majorca. Rivash, who had lived in Catalonia, Aragon and Valencia, writes,

---

57 *Niddah* 66a-b.

58 Literally, "and."

59 Literally, house, perhaps meaning his wife. The Talmud mentions the use of "my house" in the sense of "my wife."

60 Literally, "and with."

61 *Yevamot* 65b.

"In our land [the women] had the practice of scrubbing their hair only with hot water."

The lenient ruling that women obey, to which Rivash objects, is that of Duran, which we find in his responsum to the same R. Amram. Rivash tells of having heard of Duran's position from the women of his household, who asked him about it when he instructed them otherwise. In Rivash's responsum, cited below, his reference to Duran's argument omits the latter's major point (see below), leading to the strong probability that he had not seen Duran's responsum to R. Amram, but only heard about it. That R. Amram sent this very question to Duran suggests that he did so in reaction to Rivash's inclusion of his stringent ruling regarding *qalida*, inserted as an aside in his response to R. Amram's original query, which dealt with an unconnected *minhag*.

Duran begins by concisely summarizing the objection to *qalida*, which was commonly identified with the prohibited *neter*. He proceeds as follows:

> Now, let's see. What did women [originally] rely on to scrub their hair with this *neter*? After all, the simple reading of the law prohibits it! [Surely], in a matter in which school children do not err, one cannot put the blame on error for such a widespread *minhag*!

Here we are, back to the position Duran presented in Case [3], when confronted by a dissonance between common practice and halakhic ruling: "What is proper for every rabbinic scholar to do in such a case is to fix it so that the *minhag* accords with the *halakha*," i.e., to interpret the *halakha* to accord with the *minhag*. Duran "fixes it" by means of the following syllogism:

1) The reason that Rava, in the Talmud, gave for prohibiting *neter* was that it detaches the hair.
2) *Qalida* does not detach the hair, but makes it wavy.
3) Ergo, *qalida*, and the *neter* that Rava prohibits, are not the same product. (Or, he suggests alternatively, there are two different meanings to the word *neter*.)

This amounts to a functional interpretation of the *halakha*. The definition of the prohibited *neter* is determined by what it does. It is instructive to compare this with Rivash's presentation. As we saw above, Rivash had objected to the Majorcan practice, which was new to him:

> When I was informed of the practice of these [Majorcan] women, I ordered the *ḥazan* [here denoting a certain communal official] to tell his wife to privately warn the women coming to immerse to refrain from this practice. But this was hard for them to do. And some of Rabbi Duran's female relatives asked him about this, and he said that

> on the contrary, there is no [proper preparation for] immersion without *qalida*, because it cleans the head very well. And the meaning of *neter* is not *qalida*.... And when I heard [about it], I said that it is well known that the *la'az* [Romance vernacular] of *neter* is *qalida* according to all the Bible teachers. Also the Ga'on Sa'adia, in his commentary, translated "*neter*"[62] [into Arabic] as *tfl*,[63] which is *qalida*.[64]

The argument appears convincing. Sa'adia established the tradition of identifying biblical *neter* with Arabic *tfl*. The identification of the biblical *neter*, which is used for washing, with the talmudic *neter*, used for washing but disallowed for pre-immersion hair cleansing, is extremely plausible. The *qalida* used in Majorca for hair scrubbing, and identified with *tfl*, was imported, we are told, from Valencia.[65] Valencia had a bilingual history of Arabic and Romance, and it is not unlikely that the term *qalida* was applied from the beginning of Christian settlement there to the product called in Arabic *tfl*. It appears likely that Duran's functional interpretation of *qalida* as something other than *neter* is original.

It is worth noting that Duran's argument, that *qalida* cannot be the same as the talmudic *neter* because *qalida* does not detach the hair, whereas the *neter* prohibited by the Talmud does, is based on empirical evidence. This is an example of the use of empirical evidence to challenge the authority of traditional understandings. By way of comparison, elsewhere Rivash expresses a sharply negative view of such a procedure. The halakhic context to which the responsum relates is different,[66] and the immediate example he brings to make his point is one that Duran would hardly challenge.[67] But the tone of his statement speaks for itself:

> We may not deal with the laws of our Torah and its commandments on the basis of the scholars of nature and medicine. For if we accept

62 Jeremiah 2:21: "Though you wash with *neter*..."

63 Wehr Cowan, p. 562, col. 2: *tufaal* – potter's clay; argil; clay, loam.

64 Rabbi Yoel Katan, who edited the Mekhon Yerushalayim edition of *Tashbetz*, writes *ad loc* in n. 14: "From this [we learn] that Sa'adia composed a commentary to Jeremiah, though I haven't located as of now evidence for this elsewhere."

65 *Tashbetz*, 1:28, after the notation for footnote 136.

66 The determination of whether a child was born at full term.

67 The physiology of animals presumed by the Talmud, which governs the laws of *kashrut*. Rivash follows in the sequel with other examples dealing with the science of human reproduction.

their words, there would be no Torah from Heaven, God forbid! For so they laid down in their false proofs.[68]

In an addendum to this section I will adduce two other instances in which Duran has recourse to empirical evidence.

[5] The Widow's *Ketubba* and her Daughter's Inheritance (*Tashbetz* 2:150)

A wife does not inherit from her husband. In lieu of inheritance, at the time of marriage her husband undertakes a specific financial obligation to his wife, which takes effect at the dissolution of the marriage, either by death or by divorce. This obligation is called a *ketubba* (literally: "a written document"), and the husband's real property is held in lien for payment of the *ketubba*. The value of the *ketubba* was flexible, and reflected the socio-economic status of the parties concerned.[69] For her part, the wife brought into the marriage a dowry, consisting of valuable clothing, jewelry and home furnishings, referred to by the Talmud as "the assets of her paternal property."[70] In its broader sense, the term *ketubba* is applied to the dowry as well. The wife's dowry also reverts to her at the dissolution of the marriage, and her husband cannot alienate it without her permission. If the wife predeceased her husband, his *ketubba* debt is cancelled, and her dowry reverts to his outright possession.

As is the case with any creditor with a lien, a wife can sell her *ketubba* to a third party. However, this would be at a discounted rate, since, if the wife predeceases her husband, the husband's obligation to her lapses. The third-party purchaser of such a *ketubba* is betting that the wife will outlive her husband.

In addition to the sum specified in the *ketubba*, a number of other obligations bind the husband or his heirs. These are considered part and

---

68 Rivash 447. See, however, Rivash 349, which deals with the status of wine in caskets, the boards of which were glued together with prohibited fat (*ḥelev*). Rivash presents an argument for stringency, specifically rejecting a possible argument for leniency drawn from preceding authorities. He then continues with the following addendum: "I afterwards saw that everyone acts [leniently] in this matter. **And they showed me clearly that the fat never mixes at all with the wine**.... So I said, [citing BT *Pesaḥim* 66a]: 'Let the Jews be [in maintaining their questionable practice]. Though they are not prophets, they are sons of prophets.' Since it is the nature of wine not to adhere to fat, there is not even any [physical] contact here..." Given his own argument for stringency, the arguments he now presents for leniency are grudging, a way to accommodate a practice he disagrees with but can't prevent. The empirical proof he cites must be seen in that light.

69 This is not true of the Askenazic *ketubba*, which was set at a fixed value.

70 BT *Yevamot* 66b, translation Soncino.

parcel of the *ketubba*, even though they are not included in its written text. These are called "*ketubba* stipulations."

One *ketubba* stipulation gives the widow the right to be supported by the heirs in the style to which she was accustomed, as long as she chooses to continue living in her late husband's residence, or until she collects her *ketubba* or indicates her desire to remarry. A corollary to this right is that if she seizes moveable property from the estate after the death of her husband, and claims that she is doing so to insure her future support, she may keep the property for that purpose.

Another *ketubba* stipulation, referred to below, is called "the *ketubba* of male children." When a man died, he was inherited by his sons, or his daughters if there were no sons. If a man had more than one wife, either together or in succession, according to the law of the Torah all his sons divide the inheritance equally.[71] If the man outlived his wives, their dowries became part of his estate. That meant that the dowries of his wives were divided equally among his heirs. If one wife had brought a large dowry and had few sons, and the other had brought a small dowry and had many, the children of the second would be inheriting, to some extent, the dowry of the first, "the assets of her paternal property." In order to prevent this, there was a *ketubba* stipulation, that the sons of each wife should first take from the estate their mother's dowry before the remainder of the inheritance was divided equally among the sons of all the wives.

The question posed to Duran was as follows:

> You asked: A woman forwent [the right to] her *ketubba* in favor of her husband, in order [to enable him] to increase her daughter's dowry, because she sought her daughter's welfare, and was ashamed [of the small dowry] in the eyes of her daughter's in-laws. She was [subsequently] widowed, and the property [of her deceased husband] was inherited by her daughter, since he had no son. The wife [however] seized them [the items that constituted the dowry] for [satisfaction of] her *ketubba*. What is the law concerning this? Does the daughter take all of the property as the heir of her father and the widow take nothing, since she forwent her right [to the *ketubba* obligation]? Or does the widow take them by right of her *ketubba*, and her forgoing [of the *ketubba*] be voided?

The Talmud discusses the situation of wife selling her *ketubba* to her husband:

---

71 Except for a firstborn who gets a second portion. See Deut. 21:17.

> Rava said: It is obvious to me, that if she sells her *ketubba* to others, she maintains her [right to the] "*ketubba* of male children." Why? Because she was forced [to do so] by [the need for] funds. It is also obvious to me, that if she forgoes her *ketubba* to her husband, she does not maintain her [right to the] "*ketubba* of male children." Why? [Because, after all,] she forwent it. Rava [then] posed the question: If she sells her *ketubba* to her husband, is it like one who sells it to others, or like one who forgoes it to her husband? [Having posed the question,] he then made plain [the answer]: One who sells her *ketubba* to her husband is as one who sells to others.[72]

If one applies this talmudic ruling to the case at hand, it would seem that in this case the widow has no right to her *ketubba*. She forwent, rather than sold, her *ketubba* to her husband. One who sold her *ketubba* to her husband maintains her right to the *ketubba* after her husband's death, but one who forwent it does not. Duran, however, applies a functional interpretation to the law. After paraphrasing the ruling in the Talmud, he continues:

> In the case at hand, the law concerning this woman is, without any doubt, like the law of one who sold [her *ketubba*], because the reason [in both circumstances] is one and the same. Just as in the case of selling we say that she does not lose her *ketubba* because "she was forced [to sell] by [the need for] funds," so it is with this woman. It is not the law that she should lose her *ketubba* rights, because "she was forced [to do so] by [the need for] funds." She wanted to contribute to the dowry of her daughter above what her husband was willing to give. And since this is the law, even though this woman undoubtedly forfeited her *ketubba* because she gave it to her daughter, she [nevertheless] did not lose [her rights to] the other *ketubba* stipulations. And it is a *ketubba* stipulation that she be supported from her husband's estate.

That is, in this specific case, "forfeiting" must be defined legally as "selling." Here we do not have the advantage of an opinion of Rivash with which to compare it. But it is clearly an example of interpreting the talmudic law from the perspective of its function, and a rejection of its literal reading.

---

72 BT *Ketubbot* 53a.

[6] The Reluctant Levir (Rivash 159; *Tashbetz* 1:100)

In all the cases discussed above, Duran's use of a functional and/or non-literal interpretation shifted the ruling to a more lenient result than the literal interpretation would have yielded. It is possible to suggest, therefore, that Duran tended to utilize this method specifically in instances in which it would have an effect on the final outcome, not just for its own sake. This possibility is strengthened by the case to be presented now. It involves the law of levirate marriage.

The law of levirate marriage is found in Deuteronomy 25:5–10. The description presented here is based on the Talmud's interpretation thereof, which differs in important ways from the plain sense of the biblical passage. If a man dies without child, his brother (the levir) has an obligation to marry his widow. A widow in such a position, whose late husband has a brother but no children, is called a *yevama*. If the brother chooses not to marry his *yevama*, an alternative is offered. This involves a ceremony that includes the *yevama*'s removal of the levir's shoe. This ceremony is referred to as *ḥalitza* (literally: "removal"; in this context: "shoe removal"). There is no doubt that in the biblical description *ḥalitza* is presented as an act that is meant to shame the levir for not fulfilling his obligation. Nevertheless, the Talmud records a dispute as to whether levirate marriage or *ḥalitza* is the preferable choice. The Sephardic tradition accepted the view that levirate marriage was preferable. If there was more than one brother, the eldest was approached to fulfill the levirate obligation.[73] If he refuses, the choice goes down the age ladder.[74] If none accepts to marry the *yevama*, then the eldest is approached to submit to a *ḥalitza*. If he refuses, he is compelled to do so. A *yevama* whose condition is not yet resolved by either levirate marriage or *ḥalitza* is called "bound to a levir." She is an "anchored" woman, that is, a woman who, in her present condition, may not remarry. But in a case in which two brothers are married to two sisters, so that marrying the *yevama* would result in incest,[75] the law of levirate marriage does not apply.

This is Rivash's presentation of the query from Rabbi Amram of Oran, whom we have met before:[76]

---

73 This is based on a forced midrashic interpretation of Deut. 25:6, "the first son that she bears." The "she" is understood as the mother of the deceased, rather than as his wife.

74 Mishna *Yevamot* 4:5; BT *Yevamot* 39a.

75 Lev. 18:18.

76 In Case 2.

> You were also in doubt about a *yevama* whose husband left her with[77] three brothers. She was forbidden to the eldest, because he was married to her sister. The remaining two brothers quarreled. The older one rushed to take a stringent oath,[78] that he will neither marry her nor submit to *ḥalitza*.[79] The other one said, "The obligation [*mitzva*] falls upon you, because you are the older.... Are we to compel the older one to either marry her or submit to *ḥalitza*, even though he vowed [not to do so]? Or is there a way for him [the older brother] to avoid it since he took a vow to neither marry nor perform *ḥalitza*, so that we now compel the younger brother to either release her by *ḥalitza* or marry her?

The basic law is that an oath to violate a biblical commandment is *ipso facto* invalid.[80] We learn from Duran's account that Rivash discussed this with him. Rivash had questioned whether perhaps, for a technical reason that need not concern us here, the older brother's oath in this specific case was an exception to this rule, and was in fact valid. Were that to be so, the levir could not be compelled to submit to *ḥalitza* in violation of his oath, which he was commanded by biblical law to uphold. Rivash, in his responsum, raises this position as a hypothesis, and then proceeds to reject it, apparently as a result of his earlier oral conversation with Duran. Accordingly, Rivash rules that the older brother's oath is invalid, and he is to be compelled to submit to *ḥalitza*. Duran's responsum was written to Rivash as a follow-up to their oral discussion. It is an expanded analysis of the case in all its aspects. His conclusion coincides with that of Rivash, that the levir, the older brother, cannot escape *ḥalitza*.

The passage in Rivash's responsum that is relevant to this discussion comes after he had already proven that the oath was indeed invalid, and the brother should be compelled to submit to *ḥalitza*. It appears as an addendum at the end of the responsum:

> There is yet another reason [for the oath to be null and void]. Since he is bound by the obligation to either perform levirate marriage or submit to *ḥalitza*, this oath that the levir undertook constitutes an infliction of injury [upon the widow, in violation of the biblical pro-

---

77 Literally: "who fell to."

78 Literally: "leapt and swore." The idiom connotes an impulsive or sudden act.

79 Duran suggests that the brother included *ḥalitza* in the oath out of ignorance of its true legal meaning, mistakenly thinking that it was part of levirate marriage.

80 Mishna *Shevu'ot* 3:8, BT 29a.

> hibition of injuring another], insofar as it prohibits her from marrying. And an oath[81] to do injury to others and to deprive them of their rights is not valid, as is mentioned [in the Talmud] in the aforementioned chapter.[82] Even though they said there: "What constitutes doing injury to others? 'I will strike so-and-so and split his head,'" this was not meant literally. The same is true if he said: "I will rob or plunder him." And there is no greater [cause of] sorrow than "anchoring" the widow.

Rivash applies here a functional interpretation to the phrase "I will strike so-and-so and split his head." Rather than restricting it to its literal boundaries, he expands it to include broader forms of deep distress. The example of an oath to rob someone was drawn from Maimonides' Code.[83] But Rivash extends it further, to an oath to apply non-tangible forms of extreme distress. It is of interest that Rivash introduces this argument, which reflects a deep emotional response, as an addendum. The body of the responsum is reserved for formal legal analysis.[84]

Surprisingly in light of what we have seen, Duran takes issue with Rivash's functional interpretation. Duran agrees with Rivash that the levir can be compelled to submit to *ḥalitza*, because his oath to the contrary was invalid, as Duran argues in great detail. But he rejects Rivash's broad definition of "injury":

> But this is not [a case of] vowing to do injury to others [which would nullify the oath], because we have not found any prohibition in the Torah of "anchoring" a *yevama*. "Doing injury to others" includes only what the Torah prohibits, such as "I will strike so-and-so and

---

81 Literally: "An oath of expression," i.e., an oath to do something or not to do it.

82 BT *Shevu'ot* 27a.

83 Laws of Vows, chap. 5, par. 16.

84 Rivash's use of an addendum to expose his deep inner motivation in arriving at a decision after he had argued the case on technical halakhic grounds is dramatically evident in responsa 266-267. The case concerns a powerful unscrupulous individual, whose proposal of marriage to a woman is rejected. After her betrothal to another, he concocts a case with false witnesses, to prove that he had actually betrothed her earlier. Responsum 266 is an unusually lengthy responsum. In the first part he presents arguments that would seem to support his own position of rejecting the evidence of prior betrothal, and then dismisses each one in turn on halakhic grounds. Then he presents the arguments that indeed lead to freeing the woman from the claim of prior betrothal. He does all this slowly and methodically, without any indication of emotion. Responsum 267 is an addendum. In it he pours his heart out over the shameless villainy of the affair, and the degeneration of the society that allows it to happen.

> split his head" which is mentioned in the Talmud, or robbing or informing on someone, which Maimonides mentioned [in this connection]. But not something like this.

Duran rejects the inclusion of severe mental or emotional harm as part of the definition of "an oath to inflict injury" for purposes of compelling *ḥalitza*.[85] One cannot, of course, say this for certain, but given Duran's penchant for utilizing functional interpretation, it is tempting to suggest that if the decision would have depended on it, he might have himself adopted Rivash's broadened definition of "injury."

[7] The Legal Guardian (Rivash 489)

In the preceding example, Rivash's expansion of the legal definition of "doing injury" appears as an addendum to his responsum. Its omission would not have changed the decision in any way. It is not infrequent for the authors of responsa to include arguments that do not emanate directly from the objective reading of the law, but are necessary for the decision that the responder believes to be the just and moral one in the case at hand. Here Rivash's argument, based on the prohibition of mental anguish, is not such a case; the ruling would have been the same without it. Nor is it an example of a make-weight argument (Hebrew: *senif*), an additional argument commonly used to strengthen the force of the decision, but one that would not be convincing on its own.[86] From the passion evidenced by Rivash's words cited above, "there is no greater [cause of] sorrow than 'anchoring' the widow," it is clear that his broad definition of "doing injury" was intended as one that was fully valid in its own right. It was meant as a definition that could serve by itself to determine the ruling in a future case where it might be relevant. Its inclusion here is a reflection of what Rivash believed to be the proper reading of the law.

Another instance of this pattern in the responsa of Rivash is the following. The case involves a widow with minor children. These children are the heirs of their late father's estate, and the Court had assigned a

---

85 Rivash's position, that in spite of the Talmud's examples, mental distress is equivalent to physical distress, can be seen as a meta-halakhic stance based on primary principles, in this case stemming from basic morality. There is a similar phenomenon in Rivash 175, where the primary principle is the teaching of Torah to children. There too, Duran, in *Tashbetz*, 1:64, rejects Rivash's decision on the basis of a straightforward reading of the Talmud.

86 For a discussion of *senifim*, see my volume, *Precedent and Judicial Discretion: the Case of Joseph ibn Lev*, Chapter 7.

guardian to take care of their financial affairs and to represent their interests. Such an undertaking entails time and effort, without compensation. The Court cannot compel an individual to take this upon oneself, so its choice of a guardian is limited to one who is willing to undertake it. The Tosefta, a component of talmudic literature but not part of the Talmud itself, speaks to the issue of a guardian of this type who accepted the task, but subsequently sought to withdraw from it:

> Guardians, until they have taken possession of the assets of the orphans, may withdraw. Once they have taken possession of the assets of the orphans, they cannot withdraw.[87]

In the present case, the guardian had not yet taken physical possession of the assets. He did, however, engage in two acts on behalf of the orphans. The first, in order of presentation in the responsum, is that he represented them in court on a few occasions. The second is that he allowed the widow to collect on a debt that the estate owed her. The question is whether these activities on behalf of the orphans qualify as "taking possession of the assets," and thereby prevent the guardian from withdrawing from his position.

The guardian's role in allowing the widow's collection of the debt is a strong case for classifying the guardian as having "taken possession of the assets," even though the assets did not physically pass through his hands. Rivash points out that if a guardian sold land from the estate, even though he did not take physical possession of the land, his sale of the land nevertheless counts as his having taken possession, and allowing the widow to collect on a debt is no different. Rivash could easily have ruled on that basis alone that the guardian cannot withdraw. But he opts to argue first the weaker case, namely, that the act of representing the orphans in court in itself disqualifies him from withdrawing.

After some preliminaries that do not add up to a compelling argument, Rivash states his position explicitly, and justifies it by an original reinterpretation of the sense of the Tosefta. After paraphrasing the Tosefta, that guardians can withdraw "as long as they have not taken possession of the assets," he continues:

> But it appears that if they began to function in their appointment as guardians [in any way] they cannot withdraw... And that which the Tosefta states, "took possession of the assets," comes to teach us something special,[88] that the reception of assets is [in itself] a beginning [of the guardianship], even though they did yet engage in any

87 *Tosefta, Bava Batra* 8:3; 8:12 ed. Lieberman.

88 *Revuta*, Jastrow: "something remarkable."

> other guardianship activity. And so, if one appeared before a court of law several times as a guardian and argued on their behalf, this would constitute a beginning [of the guardianship], and he is now obligated to complete [his role as such].

Rivash is aware of the weakness of his argument. He begins his transition to the second, more convincing, act of guardianship, the allowance of the widow's collection of her debt from the estate, the following way:

> And even if one say that we require actual possession of the assets, **like the plain sense of the Tosefta**, in this case, of a guardian who allowed the widow's collection of the debt, there is no greater [example of] taking possession of assets than this.

So it appears that Rivash has no firm basis in the sources to rule as he does with regard to the guardian who had represented the orphans in court. He is fully aware that his interpretation of the Tosefta is original. A guardian, having begun his work, cannot withdraw from it. The Tosefta, the only source that defines what a guardian's "beginning his work" means, says that it means "taking possession of the assets." But as Rivash sees it, this is simply a ready example of a guardian's beginning his work, and does not exclude other activities on behalf of his charges. In the current instance, "beginning his work" happens to be representing the orphans in court. What Rivash has done here is apply a functional interpretation of the law. It wasn't necessary for him to do so in this case. He does so because he believes it is correct, and even if it isn't necessary to resort to it in the case at hand, he apparently wanted to establish it as a precedent. This is exactly parallel to the case of the reluctant levir. There, too, Rivash did not need to apply a broad functional interpretation of "injury" in order to establish the ruling that he believed to be just, but he nevertheless did so. Duran, however, who, as we have seen, utilized that approach in a number of cases in which it changed the decision, took issue with Rivash who used it on principle, without needing it to arrive at a desired conclusion.[89]

[89] It is instructive to compare these responsa with two of Rivash's early ones, Responsum 382 and its follow-up, Responsum 385, composed about two years after he began his rabbinic career in Saragossa (cf. Hershman, p. 234). See above, n. 41.

Addendum on Empirical Evidence

In Case [4] above, we saw Duran's use of empirical evidence. Following are two other cases in which empirical evidence is referenced. But unlike in Case [4], both of them fall short of determining his ruling on the basis of this factor alone.

[8] The Overloaded Ass (*Tashbetz* 3:106)

Barley is lighter in weight than wheat. The Mishna discusses the liability of one who hires an ass to transport wheat but uses it instead to transport barley, when in the end there was damage to the ass. The passage is not entirely clear, and there is discussion of its meaning in the Talmud.[90] In the *Mishneh Torah*, Maimonides presents the decisive view as follows:

> If a man hired from another an animal for carrying 200 pounds of wheat but made it carry 200 pounds of barley instead, and the animal died, he is liable because bulkiness makes carrying more difficult, and barley is bulkier.[91]

The Mishna states, in the reading accepted as law, "Volume is hard for bearing."[92] This is understood to mean that once the weight is the same, any additional volume beyond that is more difficult for the beast to bear.

The question posed to Duran is a simple one:

If one hires an ass to transport ten measures of wheat, and he transported eleven measures of barley, and [the ass] died on route, [is he liable].

Duran answers briefly that the issue of more volume comes into play only once the weight is the same. In this case, the weight of eleven measures of barley is less than ten measures of wheat. After pointing out the obvious, that lessening the weight does not make the hirer liable, he continues as follows:

> And even if it were of equal weight, the early authorities[93] wondered how the addition of volume [alone] could be [considered] an addition [to the difficulty of bearing the load]. **But experience proves that this is so, as workers of the land have told me.**

It appears that Duran was troubled by the principle underlying this law, namely, that an increase in volume, without any additional increase in weight, "is hard for bearing." Common sense would indicate that

---

90 BT *Bava Meẓi'a* 80a.

91 *Laws of Hiring*, chap. 4, par. 4. Trans. Yale Judaica Series.

92 The reading supported by Rava.

93 The generally thorough notes in the Mekhon Yerushalyim edition do not identify who they are.

weight alone determines the difficulty in bearing a load. He tells us that he sought out workers of the land to supply him with empirical evidence regarding this issue. Contrary to his expectations, they corroborated the counterintuitive principle enunciated in the Mishna.

[9] Two Kinds of Raisins (*Tashbetz* 1:57; Rivash 9)

The festive meal on the eve of sabbaths and festivals is preceded by a liturgical declaration of the sanctity of the day, called *kiddush*, which is accompanied by a glass of wine. The same question about this, which emanated from Oran, was posed to both Rivash and Duran.

This is the query as it appears in the *Tashbetz*:

> You asked: What is the law [as to whether it is permitted] to recite the *kiddush* for the [holy] day with raisin wine. And you said that there is one [rabbi] among you who ruled that it is forbidden.

The issue of raisin wine is raised in the Talmud, where it is clearly decided that it may be used for *kiddush*.[94] Both Rivash and Duran, therefore, try to understand how anyone could have ruled to prohibit it. In this context, Duran quotes Maimonides. Maimonides here uses the term *devash*, which refers to the sweet liquid of ripe fruit.[95] He writes:

> Wine that has the smell of vinegar but tastes like wine – one may recite *kiddush* with it. The same is true for ... raisin wine, one can recite *kiddush* with it. This is true as long as the raisins have [sufficient] moisture, so that, when treaded, they exude *devash*.[96]

The wording implies that there are two kinds of raisins, those that exude *devash*, and those that do not. Duran suggests that Maimonides construed the term *devash* narrowly. According to him, liquid from raisins that, because of their poor quality, would not be referred to as *devash*, would not qualify for the purpose of *kiddush*. This would exclude raisins as they were produced in North Africa.[97] This, says Duran, is a misunderstanding.

---

94 BT *Bava Batra* 97b.

95 *Devash* refers also to bee's honey, which is its only meaning in Modern Hebrew.

96 Laws of the Sabbath, chap. 29, par. 17.

97 Rivash zeroes in on this aspect of the issue. He cites Alfasi, *Pesaḥim* no. 779, 22b in the current pagination. After quoting the Talmud to the effect that raisin wine is permissible for *kiddush*, Alfasi continues: "But the Great Ones [the *ge'onim*] say that not all raisins are permissible for the purpose of reciting *kiddush*, only those that are like the ones that dried [literally: "withered"] on the vine, and are not [totally] dried out." Rivash suggests that those who objected to North African

The dichotomy is between those raisins that, though dried, have some moisture, and those raisins that are so old that their natural moisture is completely gone. There may be some liquid that can be extracted from these raisins as well, but it is not a product of the original liquid of the fruit. It is what the Talmud calls *qiyuha*, an acidulous liquid,[98] which the Talmud explicitly distinguishes from wine and other kinds of fruit juice on a number of occasions with the dismissive expression "mere *qiyuha*."[99]

None of this would be relevant to the purpose of this study, were it not for an argument based on empirical evidence that Duran introduces at this point, almost as an aside:

> And it is apparent to the eyes that it [i.e., the raisin wine in use] is not mere *qiyuha*, because it ages and increases its strength with its aging. And if it were *qiyuha*, it would not maintain [its character]. So it is certainly not *qiyuha*, and it is [true] grape wine.

The case could have been made without this passage, as indicated by the rest of the responsum, and by Rivash's responsum, which comes to the same decision without this argument. But Duran felt the need, apparently, to introduce an empirical proof.

IV. Redefining the Law

[10] "He's Not my Son!" (*Tashbetz* 2:19; Rivash 41)

I have defined "functional interpretation" as interpretation based on the original intent of the law, in contrast to its being based on the law's specific wording. The example before us now does not fit that exact definition. But it has an affinity to functional interpretation in the sense that, like it, it exhibits a more rational process of decision making, rather than a more mechanical/literal approach to it, and consequently yields an original legal ruling by Duran.

Deuteronomy 21:15–17 refers to a law of inheritance, in which a man's firstborn inherits a double portion. The passage describes a man who has two wives, one whom he loves and the other whom he spurns, though his firstborn is the son of the latter. The Torah tells us that the father does not have the right to ignore the firstborn's priority, and bequeath the double portion to a son of the wife he loves:

---

raisin wine mistakenly took the example of drying on the vine as restrictive, excluding other ways of drying them that were used in North Africa.

98 Translation ArtScroll.

99 The occurrence most relevant to our purpose is at BT *Bava Batra* 97a.

> He shall acknowledge the firstborn, the son of the spurned one, by giving him a double portion of all that he has.[100]

The Talmud understands the phrase "He shall acknowledge the firstborn" to mean that the father has the unilateral right to establish the son's identity as the firstborn.[101] A corollary of this is that if there are older siblings, the father has the right to declare them illegitimate.[102] This, of course, runs counter to the accepted rules of evidence, and is understood as a unique right conferred upon the father by the Torah.

This issue is cited by both Rivash and Duran in the course of their respective responsa. Each of them responds to a different case, but both cases deal with the question of an unwed mother's identification of the father. The case to which Duran responded arose after Rivash had died. Duran was aware of Rivash's earlier responsum, and tells us that he disputed it with him orally at the time. Both cases concern an unmarried pregnant woman, who identified the father, who in turn denied the entire affair. In talmudic law, illegitimacy has no bearing on matters of civil law. Once the father acknowledges his child, or is proved in court to be the father, he is obligated to support his child. Most likely, this is the core of both cases.

The circumstances in the case before Rivash, as paraphrased by him from the original query, are unusually detailed, and present the woman as irrational, conniving and untrustworthy. It is not surprising that Rivash rejects the woman's claim. One of the arguments Rivash presents is based on the law cited above, that in a marital situation a father has the right to declare that a child of his is in fact not his. Rivash argues that if this is true in a marital situation, it is certainly so in a non-marital situation. The alleged father has the right, derived from the Torah, to deny his paternity.

Unlike Rivash's responsum, in which the query is given in lengthy and vivid detail, Duran's later responsum provides very little detail, and it is not possible to reconstruct the details from the responsum. Duran rejects a number of Rivash's arguments in the earlier case, among them the one based on the father's right to declare his child to be illegitimate. In doing so, he offers various narrow interpretations of that law, which would preclude the defendant from escaping liability in the case at hand. The first of these is of interest to us. Duran does not deny that the Torah allows a father to declare his child to be illegitimate, contrary to the established rules of evidence. But he limits it to a rational claim on the father's part. He can do so, says Duran, only if he maintains that he did not have sexual

---

100 Deut. 21:17, based on RSV.

101 BT *Bava Batra* 127b.

102 *Qiddushin* 78b. The *halakha* follows R. Yehuda.

relations with his wife for a length of time that precluded his paternity. In other words, the special dispensation that the Torah gives the father suspends the normal rules of evidence in favor of the father's word. But the father's word must be based on a rational argument. As far as I can determine, it appears that Duran's interpretation of this law is original. Maimonides, for instance, describes the law as follows:

> If the father said, "This is not my son," **or** if her husband was abroad, then he [the child] is [legally] presumed to be illegitimate.[103]

The declaration "This is not my son," and the circumstance of being abroad for a period that precluded his paternity, are two independent instances in which the child is considered illegitimate. Duran, however, rolls the two into one. The father has the right to declare "this is not my son," but **only** when the situation makes his certainty of that claim feasible. In effect, Duran redefines the law that allows a father to declare his presumed son illegitimate, by restricting it only to a situation in which he could know that with certainty. Duran's redefinition of a law, in order to bring it into accord with the decision he is advocating, is attested in a few other cases.

[11] Honoring the Dead Revisited (*Tashbetz* 1: 22; Rivash 116)

Case [2] dealt with a Jew who had died among non-Jews, a week's travel from a Jewish settlement. The local rabbi permitted his relatives to set out on the second holy-convocation day of Sukkot, for the purpose of burying him. He was challenged on this decision, and turned to Duran, who supported, and substantially broadened, the lenient decision. One of the arguments for stringency, not cited above, is relevant here. Duran presents it as "the third argument" for stringency. According to the accepted law, activities that are permitted on the second holy-convocation day for purposes of burial must be done in private, and not in the public eye, as was the case here.[104] Duran presents a number of reasons that this consideration is not relevant in the case at hand. Among them is the following:

> I further say, that even according to the position of one who is strict [and rejects the arguments previously offered for leniency], one cannot challenge you on this matter. For they prohibited [burial activities] in public only where it was possible to do so in private, **or** [in a case] of delaying it for one day, such that it [the corpse] would not deteriorate so much as a result of such a delay. But in a case like this, one should permit it even in public.

103 Laws of Forbidden Intercourse, chap. 15, par. 19.

104 *Tur, Oraḥ Ḥayyim*, no. 526

Duran offers here two reasons for justifying public activity in preparation for a burial. The second, introduced with the conjunction "or," is presented as if it were a variant of the first. In fact, it is an independent reason, not connected to the former. He follows with a prooftext from the Talmud, but in fact it supports the first reason only. It is the second reason, however, that is at the heart of Duran's argument. As we have seen above in Case [2], Duran asserts that it is the minimizing of the corpse's continuing decay to the extent possible that defines the respect given to human beings in their death, not just the burial itself. This in itself has nothing to do with the requirement of private activity, the topic of "the third argument." He introduces it here surreptitiously, and, without any source,[105] redefines the law requiring private activity in burial preparation to apply only to a one-day delay.

[12] The *Mamzer* of Uncertain Status (*Tashbetz* 3:327)

Deuteronomy 23:3 states: "A *mamzer* may not enter into the congregation of the Lord." The *halakha* defines a *mamzer* (fem: *mamzeret*; m. pl: *mamzerim*) as one whose birth resulted from an act of adultery or incest. It defines not being able to "enter into the congregation of the Lord" as a prohibition to marry within the Jewish fold, except with another *mamzer*. This prohibition is qualified by the Talmud:

> "A *mamzer* may not enter into the congregation of the Lord" – A *mamzer* of certain status may not enter. But a *mamzer* of uncertain status may enter.[106]

If there is uncertainty whether or not one is a *mamzer*, then the restriction of marriage does not apply in biblical law.

Levirate marriage is considered a religious obligation in the Sephardic halakhic tradition, but it applies only when a man dies without living children. Otherwise it is a violation of incest for a man to marry his brother's wife, even after his brother's death. There is no middle ground between the obligation of the levir to marry his sister-in-law when her husband had no living children at the moment of his death, and the prohibition of incest that is incurred if he marries her when he had a living child at that moment. In cases of doubt whether or not there was a living child at the moment of the husband's death, there can be no levirate marriage, and the wife must undergo *ḥalitza* to be able to remarry. If a child was born live, but lacking signs of vitality, and in fact does not survive thirty days,

105 In addition to Duran's own silence, the usually thorough notes in the Mekhon Yerushlayim edition do not cite any references.

106 BT *Qiddushin* 73a.

then he is considered a stillborn, and the widow is a candidate for levirate marriage.

Toward the end of his life Duran was involved in a controversy regarding a levirate marriage.[107] The incident took place in the city of Taza, in Morocco, on the route between Fez and Tlemcen, in Algeria. A man died without children, leaving a brother and a pregnant wife. The baby was born sickly and malformed, with signs that the midwives believed to be fatal, and indeed the baby died a few days later. The Talmud lists specific physical signs that define a child born live as a stillborn, but those in the present case were not among them.[108] Yet both the widow and the levir wanted to undergo levirate marriage. Furthermore, the levir was from a powerful family with considerable clout.

The case produced an extended correspondence, because the rabbi of Tlemcen, R. Ephraim Alneqawa, allowed the levirate marriage, while Duran, in Algiers, opposed it vehemently.[109] Most of the legal issues in this extended conflict do not concern us now. Suffice it to say that with the backing of Alneqawa, and the political power of the levir's family, the levirate marriage was allowed to go forth. Duran declared that any children born should be declared *mamzerim*. The family fought back, soliciting the backing of the rabbi of Soria, in Castile.[110]

We do not have the original argument of the rabbi of Soria, but it can be reconstructed from Duran's response. He based himself on the talmudic ruling, that the restrictive biblical law of the *mamzer* does not apply if there is an element of uncertainty with regard to his status. In the present case, the uncertainty derives not from the facts, but from conflicting legal opinions. The law, deriving from the Talmud, is that if the baby, born live, yawns suddenly and dies, it is considered a stillbirth in a case of levirate marriage. On the other hand, if it falls from a roof or is eaten by a lion during the thirty days, it is considered a live birth.But there was an unresolved controversy over a baby who took sick after birth and died during the thirty days.[111] In light of this controversy, the rabbi of Soria

107 The issue extends over several responsa: 3:242, 257, 285, 286, and 327. The latter, the one we are concerned with, is the last responsum in the three original volumes of the *Tashbetz*. The details of this case are summarized and analyzed by Noah Aminoah, *Rabbi Joseph Sasportas and his Responsa* (in Hebrew), Tel Aviv, 1994, pp. 90–93. The description that follows draws from this work.

108 BT *Yevamot* 80b. The issue of signs of vitality relates to premature births. But in practice, there was rarely certainty in this regard.

109 A responsum by Alneqawa to Duran defending his position is published from manuscript in the Mekhon Yerushalayim edition of the *Tashbetz*, 5:47.

110 Aminoah identifies him as Joseph Albo, author of *Sefer ha-Iqqarim*.

111 BT *Shabbat* 136a.

argued that the most that could be said about children subsequently born through this union was that their status as *mamzerim* was uncertain. They would not be *mamzerim* by biblical law, and therefore there should be no formal declaration declaring them as such.

Duran counters this argument by redefining the ruling of the Talmud regarding the status of an uncertain *mamzer*:

> Even so, one may not permit them to "enter into the congregation" on the grounds that we say, "A *mamzer* of uncertain status was not prohibited by the Torah." For this was said regarding one whose only flaw was in our knowledge [of the facts], because we don't know whether he is legitimate or a *mamzer*, such as in the case of ... [he lists cases of children of uncertain provenance]. For then he could say, "I am legitimate, and I should not have to worry about your lack of knowledge." But one who has fallen into an uncertain status because of a flaw is within him, like the case at hand, in which he was born through possible incest – regarding such a one we do not say, "The Torah prohibited only a *mamzer* of certain status."

The reason it is "possible incest" is because the law is in doubt as to whether the child who died is considered a stillborn, which would permit the levirate marriage, or whether it is considered a live birth, which would exempt the widow from a levirate marriage and make the union with her brother-in-law incestuous. Duran distinguishes between doubt of the facts and doubt of the law. But this distinction is original.[112] Duran redefines the law in order to bring it into accordance with his intended ruling.

[13] A Drowning at Sea Revisited (*Tashbetz* 1:77, **[1]**; *Tashbetz* 2:19, **[8]**)

Another example of this technique takes us back to the case with which we began, "A Drowning at Sea." In that situation there was only one witness. Duran had no doubt at all that the man who had tried to swim to shore was dead. His main thrust was finding a way to justify reliance on a single witness in a civil litigation. He does so by supplementing the testimony of a single witness with other corroboratory evidence, and arguing that this would be sufficient, as part of the legal definition of "two witnesses." In the course of doing so, he cites a passage in the Talmud regarding the rules of procedure in civil cases. Although the burden of proof is on the plaintiff, there are certain situations in which the plaintiff's evi-

112 The editor in the Mekhon Yerushalayim edition refers to two rabbinic authors "who discuss the great innovation (*hiddush*) of our Rabbi [i.e., Duran] here."

dence falls short of being probative, yet the defendant is nevertheless required to take an oath to acquit himself of the plaintiff's claim.[113] But there are instances in which the defendant cannot take the oath. An obvious example is a case in which he has a proven record of swearing falsely. In such cases, the oath is transferred to the plaintiff, who can then collect on the basis of his own oath. The Talmud relates that the talmudic sage Rava was trying a case in which a female defendant was required to take such an oath. Rava's wife, the daughter of Rabbi Ḥisda, told him that she happens to know that this woman was untrustworthy. On the basis of that informal information, Rava transferred the oath to the plaintiff. Subsequently another case arose, and Rava's student, the later sage, Rabbi Papa, was present. He whispered to Rava that he happens to know that the note of indebtedness being presented had in fact already been paid. Rava told him that unless he has a second witness to testify with him, his testimony is not acceptable. When Rabbi Papa asked why his testimony was less reliable than that of his wife, Rava answered, "I have complete faith in the word of Rabbi Ḥisda's daughter. I do not have complete faith in you."[114] Maimonides ruled that although this rule of procedure is accepted in theory, nowadays courts do not have the authority to decide cases on the subjective basis of "I have complete faith in him."[115] Maimonides' ruling, which limited the range of acceptable evidence, militated against Duran's purposes. He confronts the challenge as follows:

> And even though great rabbinic authorities have said that a judge does not have the right to say, "I have complete faith in him," ... that [ruling] refers to a situation in which no one but that [specific] judge has faith that this testimony is true. But in a situation in which the entire world has faith that this testimony that he testifies is true, we properly act according to it.[116]

In this manner Duran creates a new legal category for actionable testimony, namely, a wide popular conviction that a certain testimony is true, even though the supporting evidence by itself is legally unacceptable. Duran, without precedent, redefines the parameters of a law in order to reach a decision that he believes is just.

---

113 Mishna *Shevu'ot*; BT *Shevu'ot* 44b.

114 BT *Ketubbot* 85a.

115 *Laws of the Sanhedrin*, chap. 24, par. 1-2.

116 *Tashbetz*, 1:77, p. 168, col. 2.

Summary

This study has traced a number of ways in which Duran's originality is manifest in his responsa. We began with his daring redefinition of the biblical requirement of "two witnesses," which allowed him to bring under the umbrella of the law what he saw as the correct and proper ruling, clearly reflecting the facts on the ground. He did this by applying the function of two witnesses to other kinds of testimony of equivalent certainty. I called this "functional interpretation," and we saw a number of other examples in which he Duran utilizes this technique. Redefining the law to arrive at a ruling that he felt was the correct one for the case at hand is also evident in a number of other cases. In one of our examples of Duran's use of functional interpretation, that interpretation drew on empirical evidence. Two other cases were presented in which Duran relates to empirical evidence, thus indicating that empirical evidence played a role in Duran's judicial mentality. These are all examples of Duran's going beyond the literal word of the codified law as it had been traditionally understood. **☙**

Mourning the Ḥurban in a Rebuilt Jerusalem: Qeria, a Case Study

By: SHIMSHON HaKOHEN NADEL

The Talmud (*Mo'ed Qatan* 26a) instructs one to rend his garment (*qeria*) upon seeing the Cities of Judah, Jerusalem, and the site of the Holy Temple (*Maqom ha-Miqdash*) in a state of destruction (*ḥurban)*:

> One who sees the Cities of Judah in their destruction says, 'Your holy cities have become a wilderness,' and rends. [One who sees] Jerusalem in its destruction says, 'Zion has become a wilderness; Jerusalem a wasteland,' and rends. [One who sees] the Holy Temple in its destruction says, 'The Temple of Your holiness and our splendor, where our fathers praised You, has become a fiery conflagration, and all that we desired has become a ruin,' and rends.[1]

But today Jerusalem is not laid in ruin. With over 500,000 Jewish residents, Jerusalem is teeming with life, her skies lined with new buildings, as the city continues to grow by leaps and bounds. Observers cannot help but feel they are witnessing before their very eyes the fruition of Zechariah's prophecy, "Old men and women will once again sit in the streets of Jerusalem… and boys and girls will play in her streets" (Zech. 8:4-5).

In fact, following the miraculous birth of the State of Israel, and the dramatic reclamation of Jerusalem and the Temple Mount, the question of *qeria* for the *Ḥurban* became the subject of much discussion and debate. Later, following the Oslo Accords and the Disengagement, scholars would debate the status of territories under the administration of the Palestinian Authority, and whether or not *qeria* is warranted.

At the heart of the controversy is the question of how *ḥurban* is defined, and how the political reality impacts on the *halakha*.

---

1 Cf. *Yerushalmi Mo'ed Qatan* 3:7; *Semaḥot* 9:19. See also Rambam, *Hilkhot Ta'aniot* 5:16; Rambam, *Hilkhot Eivel* 9:2; *Tur, Orah Ḥayyim* 561 and *Yoreh De'ah* 340; *Shulḥan Arukh, Oraḥ Ḥayyim* 561:1–5 and *Yoreh De'ah*, 340:38.

Rabbi Shimshon HaKohen Nadel lives and teaches in Jerusalem.

Ḥurban

In his work on the laws and geography of the Land of Israel, *Kaftor va-Feraḥ,* Ishtori ha-Parḥi defines *ḥurban* as the absence of Jewish settlement.[2] Should an area be settled, one would be exempt from rending his garment. *Beit Yosef* at first accepts this definition, but concludes instead by defining *ḥurban* as subjugation under foreign rule.[3] It is Jewish Sovereignty that determines whether an area is considered to be in a state of *ḥurban,* and whether one must rend his garment. Most authorities accept this latter definition of *ḥurban.*[4]

Cities of Judah

Cities in the Biblical portion of the Tribe of Judah, as opposed to other Israeli cities, were designated for this practice. *Baḥ* explains that the Cities of Judah have a greater importance than other cities in Israel.[5] *Levush* writes that it is due to their proximity to Jerusalem, which makes them unique.[6] Some suggest they possess a greater level of sanctity than other cities.[7] But according to *Pe'at ha-Shulḥan,* the Cities of Judah share a unique status as the seat of the monarchy.[8] Their destruction represents the destruction of *Malkhut Yisrael,* reinforcing that it is indeed sovereignty, or the lack thereof, that defines *ḥurban.*

Historically, rending one's garment for the Cities of Judah, and even for Jerusalem, fell out of practice.[9] Rabbi Yeḥiel Mikhel Tukachinsky of-

---

2 *Kaftor va-Feraḥ*, Chap. 6.

3 *Oraḥ Ḥayyim* 561, s.v. *haro'eh.*

4 See *Baḥ, Oraḥ Ḥayyim* 561, s.v. *haro'eh*; *Magen Avraham* and *Taz, Oraḥ Ḥayyim* 561:1; *Pe'at ha-Shulḥan, Hilkhot Erets Yisrael* 3:1; *Mishnah Berurah, Oraḥ Ḥayyim* 561:2; *Kaf ha-Ḥayyim, Oraḥ Ḥayyim* 561:4. But see Rabbi Yehudah Herzl Henkin, *Bnei Banim,* Vol. 2, no. 24, where he writes that in addition to sovereignty, a city must also be settled to exempt one from *qeria.*

5 *Oraḥ Ḥayyim*, 561, s.v. *haro'eh.* See also *Mishnah Berurah, Oraḥ Ḥayyim* 561:1.

6 *Oraḥ Ḥayyim* 561:1.

7 See Rabbi Moshe Nahum Shapira, *Har ha-Qodesh* (Jerusalem, 1992), pp. 1-2; Rabbi Shlomo Goren, *Meishiv Milḥamah* (Jerusalem: ha-Idra Rabbah, 1996), Vol. 3, pp. 339-340. This would also appear to be the position of Ramban. See Rabbi Yaakov Zisberg, *Naḥalat Ya'akov* (Har Berakha, 2005), Vol. 2, p. 579.

8 See *Pe'at ha-Shulḥan, Hilkhot Erets Yisrael* 3:1 and *Beit Yisrael,* ad loc.

9 See *Teshuvot ha-Radvaz,* Vol. 2, no. 646; *Birkei Yosef, Oraḥ Ḥayyim* 561:2; *Sha'arei Teshuvah, Oraḥ Ḥayyim* 561:5. See also *Mishneh Halakhot,* Vol. 6, no. 110; *Divrei Yoel, Oraḥ Ḥayyim,* no. 30:6; *Divrei Yetsiv, Oraḥ Ḥayyim,* no. 89; *Halikhot Shlomo al*

fers two defenses for the laxity in observance: Firstly, he writes, the identity and exact location of the ancient Cities of Judah is not clear today.[10] (There is, for example, a doubt regarding the status of Hebron, which was a City of Refuge.[11]) Secondly, most of those traveling to the Land of Israel would disembark in one of the port cities, like Jaffa or Haifa, and then travel to Jerusalem before visiting the Cities of Judah. Once one has already performed *qeria* for Jerusalem, he is exempt from rending a second time for the Cities of Judah.[12]

Following the founding of the State of Israel, a number of authorities ruled that one is no longer obligated to rend his garment when seeing the Cities of Judah.[13] Some, however, questioned whether a secular State, not governed by Jewish Law, should be considered a Jewish Sovereignty.[14] This controversy would remain dormant for another nineteen years, as Judea was captured and remained under Jordanian control until June 1967.

Hilkhot Tefilah (Jerusalem: Yeshivat Halikhot Shlomo, 2000), p. 288, fn. 116; *Iggerot Moshe, Oraḥ Ḥayyim*, Vol. 5, no. 37:3; *Teshuvot ve-Hanhagot*, Vol. 4, no. 131; *Mo'adim u-Zemanim*, vol. 7, no. 257. *Ir ha-Qodesh ve-ha-Miqdash* (Jerusalem, 1969), vol. 3, p. 215.

10 *Sefer Erets Yisrael* (Jerusalem, 1966), p. 68; *Ir ha-Qodesh ve-ha-Miqdash*, Vol. 3, p. 215.

11 *Birkei Yosef, Oraḥ Ḥayyim* 561:1; *Sha'arei Teshuvah, Oraḥ Ḥayyim* 561:1; *Kaf ha-Ḥayyim, Oraḥ Ḥayyim* 561:3. See also Rabbi Betsalel ha-Kohen, *Reishit Bikkurim*, Vol. 1, no. 9; Rabbi Hershel Schachter, *B'ikvei ha-Tson*, (Brooklyn, NY: Flatbush Beth Hamedrosh, 1997) pp. 105-106; Rabbi Seraya Deblitzky, *Kuntres Aḥar Kotleinu* (Bnei Beraq, 1967), p. 9; Rabbi Betsalel Zolty, *Mishnat Yavets, Oraḥ Ḥayyim* (Jerusalem, 1984), no. 48.

12 *Ir ha-Qodesh ve-ha-Miqdash*, Vol. 3, p. 215, based on *Shulḥan Arukh, Oraḥ Ḥayyim* 561:3. Cf. *Sefer Erets Yisrael*, p. 68.

13 See, for example, Rabbi Reuven Katz, *Sha'ar Reuven* (Jerusalem, 1952), p. 32; Rabbi Shlomo Yosef Zevin, *ha-Mo'adim ba-Halakha* (Jerusalem, 1983), Vol. 2, p. 442.

14 *Divrei Yoel, Oraḥ Ḥayyim*, no. 30:6; *Shevet ha-Levi*, Vol. 7, no. 78; *Be'er Moshe*, Vol. 7, *Dinei Bnei Erets Yisrael ve-Ḥutz la-Aretz*, no. 561; Rabbi Menahem Mendel Schneersohn, *Teshuvot u-Bi'urim be-Shulḥan Arukh* (Brooklyn, NY: Kehot, 1987), p. 213; Idem, *Sha'arei Halakha u-Minhag*, (Jerusalem: Heikhal Menahem, 1993), vol. 2, p. 186; Rabbi Seraya Deblitzky, *Zikhron Betsalel* (Bnei Beraq, 1977), p. 144. See also the story cited in *Pri Megadim, Eishel Avraham* 561:1. But see Rabbi Hershel Schachter, *Be-Ikvei ha-Tson*, p. 106, fn. 10, where he notes that even during the First Temple period, many Kings of Israel were idolaters and yet Israel still maintained its status as "*Malkhut Yisrael.*" See also Rabbi Ovadiah Yosef, *Ḥazon Ovadiah, Arbah Ta'aniot* (Jerusalem, 2007), p. 438, note 4, and Rabbi Moshe Nahum Shapira, *Har ha-Qodesh*, pp. 325-326, fn. 1.

After the Six Day War, many authorities ruled it no longer necessary to perform *qeria* upon seeing the Cities of Judah, as they now were under Jewish Sovereignty.[15] Rabbi Moshe Feinstein wrote:

> Because of the kindnesses of Hashem, the Nations do not rule over the Cities of Judah and Jerusalem, and additionally they are settled, it is a great reason not to rend. Even though the Redemption has not come through the King Messiah, and we still fear the Nations, [one should] not rend [his garment].[16]

Jerusalem

In addition to the Cities of Judah, many authorities ruled that one is no longer obligated to rend his garment upon encountering Jerusalem, following the events of June 1967.[17] Rabbi Shlomo Zalman Auerbach, however, felt that since Jerusalem contains within it gentile houses of worship, gentile graves, and gentile culture, it is still to be considered in a state of *ḥurban*, thereby warranting *qeria*.[18]

Additionally, some extend the requirement to rend for the *Maqom ha-Miqdash* to the city of Jerusalem.[19] Rabbi Seraya Deblitzky rules that since the Holy Temple is not standing, Jerusalem is to be considered in a state of *ḥurban*, and one should be stringent and rend his garment upon seeing

---

15 See *Iggerot Moshe, Oraḥ Ḥayyim*, Vol. 4, no. 70:11, and *Oraḥ Ḥayyim,* Vol. 5, no. 37:1; *Minḥat Shlomo*, vol. 1, no. 73; Rabbi Eliezer Waldenberg in *Ha-Pardes, Tishrei,* 5728, p. 12, and *Shevat*, 5728, p. 15; Rabbi Seraya Deblitzky*, Zikhron Betsalel*, p. 142-143; Rabbi Shlomo Yosef Zevin, *Ha-Moadim ba-Halakha,* Vol. 2, p. 442; Rabbi Haim David ha-Levi, *Meqor Ḥayyim ha-Shalem* (Jerusalem, 1986), Vol. 2, p. 207; Rabbi Ovadiah Yosef, *Ḥazon Ovadiah*, *Arbah Ta'aniot*, p. 437; Rabbi Moshe Shternbuch, *Mo'adim u-Zemanim*, Vol. 5, no. 348, note 2.

16 *Iggerot Moshe, Oraḥ Ḥayyim,* Vol. 5, no. 37:1.

17 See *Iggerot Moshe, Oraḥ Ḥayyim,* Vol. 4, no. 70:11, and *Oraḥ Ḥayyim,* Vol. 5, no. 37:1; Rabbi Eliezer Waldenberg in *Hapardes*, *Tishrei,* 5728, p. 12, and *Shevat*, 5728, p. 15; Rabbi Ephraim Greenblatt, *Rivevot Ephraim, Oraḥ Ḥayyim,* Vol. 3, no. 384; Rabbi Shlomo Goren, *Meishiv Milḥamah*, Vol. 3, pp. 329-330; Idem, *Torat ha-Medinah* (Jerusalem: Ha-Idra Rabbah, 1996), p. 105; Rabbi Ovadiah Hedaya, *Yaskil Avdi*, Vol. 8, *Oraḥ Ḥayyim*, no. 43; Rabbi Haim David ha-Levi, *Meqor Ḥayyim ha-Shalem*, Vol. 2, p. 207; Rabbi Ovadiah Yosef, *Ḥazon Ovadiah*, *Arbah Ta'aniot*, p. 437.

18 *Minḥat Shlomo*, Vol. 1, no. 73. See also the position of Rabbi Dovid Jungreis, cited in Rabbi Avraham Horowitz, *Orḥot Rabbeinu* (Bnei Beraq, 1991), p. 318, concerning the influence of the United States on the State of Israel and Jerusalem.

19 See Rabbi Yaakov Ariel's comprehensive discussion in his *Be-Ohaloh Shel Torah*, Vol. 2, no. 76.

the Old City.[20] Similarly, Rabbi Yosef Dov Soloveitchik explained that since Jerusalem shares some of the sanctity of the Holy Temple itself, one should rend his garment when seeing Jerusalem, just as he would at the *Maqom ha-Miqdash*.[21] Nevertheless, Rabbi Hershel Schachter explains that the custom is *not* to rend for Jerusalem, as we follow the lenient opinion in matters of mourning (*halakha ke-divrei ha-meikil be-eivel*).[22]

Maqom ha-Miqdash

Motta Gur's famous battle cry, "*Har ha-Bayit be-yadeinu*—the Temple Mount is in our hands," is forever etched into our collective consciousness. The imagery and sounds of those fateful days in 1967 still resonate with us, today. The question, however, arose whether to rend or not when visiting the Temple Mount, as suddenly the *Makom ha-Miqdash* was under Jewish Sovereignty.

In a moving description, Rabbi Mordekhai Fogelman, who served as Rabbi of Qiryat Motskin and was a member of the council of the Chief Rabbinate, captured the scene in a responsum:

> On the 7th of *Sivan* 5727, following a conference of rabbis at Heikhal Shlomo in Jerusalem, I visited the liberated Western Wall together with a number of rabbis. Whoever did not see the joy at the Kotel, has not seen joy in all his days. Thousands flocked to the Kotel and their faces shone with joy and delight. They prayed with fervor and joy and thanksgiving to Hashem. Among those celebrating, there were many who had rent their garments…
>
> When I saw this, I turned to those with me and said, 'Now, after the victory against our enemies… and after the liberation of the Old City of Jerusalem, and with it the *Maqom ha-Miqdash* and the Western

---

20 *Zikhron Betsalel*, p. 144. See also his *Kuntres Aḥar Kotleinu* pp. 9-10, and his article "*Be-Inyan Ḥiyyuv Qeria al Yerushalayim be-Sha'ah she-Hi Taḥat Shilton Yehudi*," *Ha-Ne'eman* 35 (*Tishrei-Heshvan*, 5728), pp. 18–22.

21 Rabbi Herschel Schachter, *Be-Ikvei ha-Tson*, pp. 107-108; Idem, "*Be-Din Qeria al Arei Yehudah be-Ḥurbenan be-Zeman ha-Zeh*," *Torah she-Ba'al Peh* 22 (1981), pp. 182-183. See also Idem, *Nefesh ha-Rav* (Brooklyn, NY: Flatbush Beth Hamedrosh, 1994), p. 79. Similarly, Rabbi Soloveitchik objected to changes made to the liturgy of the *Naḥem* prayer, as Jerusalem today is still considered in ruins without the Holy Temple standing. See *Nefesh ha-Rav*, ibid., and the Orthodox Union's *Mesorah* 7 (Elul, 5752), p. 19.

22 *Be-Ikvei ha-Tson*, pp. 107-108. See also the position of Rabbi Moshe Shternbuch in *Mo'adim u-Zemanim*, Vol. 5, no. 348, fn. 2, and *Teshuvot ve-Hanhagot*, Vol. 4, no. 131.

Wall, we should no longer rend when visiting—rather, we should recite the Blessing of *Sheheḥiyanu, be-Shem u-Malkhut…*'[23]

Rabbi Fogelman continues and justifies his ruling, arguing that Jewish Sovereignty obviates the need to rend, and that *qeria* is an expression of mourning—inappropriate considering the great salvation Hashem has provided for the Jewish Nation.[24]

Rabbi Tsvi Yehudah Kook issued a similar ruling in the Religious Zionist newspaper *Ha-Tsofeh*,[25] as did Rabbi Shlomo Goren.[26] However, the initial euphoria of those days in June would ultimately give way to a starker reality. Rabbi Goren would later retract his ruling when it became clear that the Temple Mount was not under true Jewish Sovereignty, as administration over the site was given to the Islamic Waqf.[27] Rabbi Ovadia Hedayah ruled that had true sovereignty been achieved, one would still rend his garment out of mourning, as entrance to the area is prohibited without proper purification by the ashes of the Red Heifer, with the coming of the Messiah.[28] Rabbi Ḥayyim David ha-Levi wrote that while in theory one need not rend when seeing the Temple Mount, the matter awaits a formal decision by the Chief Rabbinate.[29]

Today too, one may question whether there exists Jewish Sovereignty over the Temple Mount, as Jewish groups attempting to visit areas permitted by Jewish Law are regularly harassed by Muslims worshippers and at times forbidden to visit the site by Israeli police.

But questions of sovereignty and control aside, many authorities rule that one is indeed obligated to rend his garment upon seeing the *Maqom ha-Miqdash* today, as the Holy Temple is not standing, and therefore in a state of *ḥurban*.[30] As mentioned above, it is *Beit Yosef*'s definition of *ḥurban* as a lack of Jewish Sovereignty that becomes adopted by later authorities.

---

23 *Beit Mordekhai*, Vol. 1, no. 33.

24 Ibid. See also his article in *Ha-Tsofeh*, 22 *Sivan*, 5727.

25 *Ha-Tsofeh*, 13 *Tammuz*, 5727. On the position of Rabbi Kook, see also Rabbi Eliezer Melamed, *Peninei Halakha be-Inyanei ha-Am ve-ha-Arets* (2005), p. 198, fn. 2.

26 *Ha-Tsofeh,* 13 *Av*, 5727.

27 *Meishiv Milḥamah*, Vol. 3, p. 333. Cf. *Torat ha-Medinah*, p. 108.

28 *Yaskil Avdi*, Vol. 8, *Oraḥ Ḥayyim*, no. 25, 43. Cf. Idem, "*B'she'eilat ha-Shtaḥim she-Shuḥr'ru al Yedei Yisrael be-Milḥemet Sheshet ha-Yamim*," *Noam* 11 (1968), pp. 178-179.

29 *Meqor Ḥayyim ha-Shalem*, Vol. 2, pp. 207–209.

30 *Iggerot Moshe, Oraḥ Ḥayyim,* Vol. 5, no. 37. Cf. *Iggerot Moshe, Oraḥ Ḥayyim,* Vol. 4, no. 70:11. See also *Be-Ikvei ha-Tson*, p. 106, and Nefesh ha-Rav, p. 79; Rabbi Ḥayyim David ha-Levi, *Meqor Ḥayyim ha-Shalem,* pp. 207–209; Rabbi Ovadiah Yosef, *Ḥazon Ovadiah, Arbah Ta'aniot*, p. 438.

However, upon careful inspection of the text itself, *Beit Yosef* defines *ḥurban* vis-*à*-vis the Cities of Judah, and not explicitly the *Maqom ha-Miqdash*. In addition, while the Beraitta (*Mo'ed Qatan* 26a) instructs one to rend upon seeing the site where the Temple stood (*Makom ha-Miqdash*), the Talmud (ad loc.) instructs "[one who sees] the Holy Temple in its destruction" to rend, suggesting that it is indeed the state of the Holy Temple itself that is the determining factor, and not control over the site.

Post-Oslo

Following the Six Day War, Rabbi Shlomo Goren questioned if the Cities of Judah can indeed be considered under Jewish Sovereignty, as the State of Israel never formally annexed Judea and Samaria, instead implementing Israeli Civil Administration.[31] He concluded that even though Israeli Law is not imposed, Israel's military rule suffices as governance in this regard.[32]

But since the implementation of the Oslo Accords, the status of these cities has changed. Cities in the West Bank designated as Area 'A,' Bethlehem for example, are under the full administrative authority of the Palestinian Authority. Even entry is prohibited to Israeli citizens. A number of contemporary authorities, among them Rabbi Hershel Schachter,[33] Rabbi Mordekhai Eliyahu,[34] Rabbi Avigdor Nebenzahl and Rabbi Dov Lior,[35] have therefore ruled that since these cities are not currently under Jewish Sovereignty, one must rend his garment upon seeing them.

Rabbi Eliyahu Bakshi-Doron writes that while Bethlehem is not currently under Jewish Sovereignty, the custom is not to perform *qeria* today as generally one passes through Jerusalem first, and *qeria* for Jerusalem exempts one from rending for the other Cities of Judah.[36] In addition, he expresses concern for the prohibition of destroying property unnecessarily.[37]

---

31 *Meishiv Milḥamah*, Vol. 3, pp. 330–332. Cf. *Torat ha-Medinah*, pp. 105–107.

32 Ibid.

33 Rabbi Chaim Jachter, *Gray Matter 2* (Brooklyn, NY: Yashar Books, 2006), p. 71.

34 See Rabbi Mordechai Friedfertig, *Qum Hithalekh ba-Arets* (Ma'aleh Adumim, 2008), p. 78.

35 See the letters of Rabbis Nebenzahl and Lior published in Rabbi Yaakov Zisberg, *Naḥalat Ya'akov*, Vol. 2, pp. 598-599.

36 *Binyan Av*, Vol. 4, no. 30, based on *Shulḥan Arukh, Oraḥ Ḥayyim* 561:3. See also *Ir ha-Qodesh ve-ha-Miqdash*, Vol. 3, p. 215; *Sefer Erets Yisrael*, p. 68.

37 *Binyan Av*, ibid. Concerning *qeria* and the prohibition of destroying property, see *Pitḥei Teshuvah, Yoreh De'ah* 340:1.

While Area 'A' is under the Palestinian Authority's administration, the Israeli Defense Forces can enter when necessary to carry out military operations. Rabbi Shlomo Aviner makes a distinction between "autonomy," and "sovereignty," and suggests that while the Palestinian Authority may have autonomy, they do not have sovereignty in the form of Statehood. Therefore, according to Rabbi Aviner, one is not obligated to rend his garment, but may do so if he wishes.[38] Similarly, Rabbi Aharon Lichtenstein rules that, while one is not obligated to rend his garment for those Cities of Judah in Area 'A,' he may do so as an expression of pain and anguish.[39]

The Disengagement

In August of 2005, the State of Israel unilaterally withdrew from the Gaza Strip, dismantling a bloc of seventeen Jewish settlements in Gush Qatif, and evicting some 8,600 Israeli citizens from their homes. In addition, four settlements in Northern Samaria were also dismantled. During this turbulent time, contemporary authorities discussed the obligation to rend one's garment.

The most glaring objection to *qeria* for Gush Katif is that this territory is not part of the Biblical inheritance of the Tribe of Judah.[40] But according to some authorities, the Gaza Strip is indeed part of the Biblical portion of Judah.[41] Additionally, some question the intent of the Beraitta (*Mo'ed Qatan* 26a) when it refers to the "Cities of Judah." Rabbi Shlomo Goren[42] and Rabbi Moshe Nahum Shapira[43] suggest that the intent of the Beraitta is the Kingdom of Judah (i.e., the Southern Kingdom that began

---

38 *Qum Hithalekh ba-Arets*, pp. 78-79.

39 Ibid., p. 78.

40 See Rabbi Avraham Danziger, *Sha'arei Tsedek, Sha'ar Mishpat ha-Arets, Ḥokhmat Adam* 11:7, where he explicitly refers to the "portion of Judah," suggesting that this law applies only in the Biblical portion of the Tribe of Judah.

41 See *Kaftor va-Feraḥ*, Chap. 7, 11. See also Pinhas Raz, "*Ḥiyyuv Qeria al Pinui Yishuvei Gush Qatif*," *Beit Hillel* 22 (Adar II, 5765), pp. 47-48.

42 *Meishiv Milḥamah* (Jerusalem: Ha-Idrah Rabbah, 1994) Vol. 2, no. 141, p. 333. But see Idem, *Meishiv Milḥamah*, Vol. 3, pp. 333–340, where Rabbi Goren concludes that today one need rend only for the Cities of Judah, as they enjoy a greater sanctity than the rest of the Cities of Israel.

43 *Har ha-Qodesh*, pp. 1-2.

following the Civil War described in the Book of Kings). In fact, Maharsha[44] and Rabbi Yaakov Emden[45] assume that the author of the Beraitta, writing after the destruction of the Second Temple, includes all areas settled during the Second Commonwealth when he writes "Cities of Judah," as it was the Tribes of Judah and Benjamin who ascended from Babylonia to settle the Land.[46] Both of these suggestions encompass a much larger territory, and include the Gaza Strip.

In addition, there exists a minority opinion that suggests that the requirement of *qeria* applies to *all* Israeli cities in a state of *ḥurban*.[47] In fact, the verse cited by the Talmud as the proof text for rending for the Cities of Judah mentions cities in Northern Israel, suggesting that people had already rent their garments in those cities: "Men came from Shekhem, from Shiloh, and from Shomron, eighty men with shaven beards and rent garments…" (Jer. 41:5). Many, however, explain that the men described in the verse originated from those Northern cities, but rent their garments later, upon reaching the Cities of Judah and hearing of the destruction of the Temple.[48]

Based on the above, some authorities encouraged rending one's garment during the Disengagement.[49]

But even if Gush Qatif is not part of the "Cities of Judah," *qeria* may still have been warranted. For while the Beraitta (*Mo'ed Qatan* 26a) obligates *qeria* for Cities of Judah and Jerusalem, it also obligates *qeria* upon hearing tragic news (*shemu'ot ra'ot*). Indeed many, including soldiers, rent their garments out of anguish during the Disengagement itself, with the endorsement of leading authorities. Rabbi Shlomo Aviner ruled that even

---

44 *Mo'ed Qatan* 26a.

45 *Mor u-Q'tsia, Oraḥ Ḥayyim* 561.

46 But see Rabbi Yehosef Schwartz, *Divrei Yosef*, Vol. 3, p. 31, and Rabbi Mordekhai Gimpel as cited in *Iggerot le-Reiyah* (Jerusalem, 1986), p. 257, where a distinction is made between the "Portion of Judah," and the "Land of Judah."

47 This opinion is attributed to Tosafot. See Rabbi Moshe ibn Ḥaviv, *Qol Gadol*, Vol. 1, no. 51; Rabbi Betsalel ha-Kohen, *Reishit Bikkurim*, Vol. 1, no. 9; Rabbi Yehudah Herzl Henkin, *B'nei Banim*, Vol. 2, no. 24. This too would appear to be the position of *Tur*, *Oraḥ Ḥayyim* 561. But see *Baḥ* and *Beit Yosef*, ad loc., and compare with *Tur*, *Yoreh De'ah* 340. See also *Mor u-Q'tsia, Oraḥ Ḥayyim* 561; Maharsha to *Mo'ed Qatan* 26a; *Ḥatam Sofer*, *Yoreh De'ah*, no. 234.

48 See *Kaftor va-Feraḥ*, Chap. 6; *Beit Yosef* and *Baḥ*, *Oraḥ Ḥayyim* 561. See also Rashi and Radak to Jer. 41:5.

49 See Pinhas Raz, "*Ḥiyyuv Qeria al Pinui Yishuvei Gush Qatif*," and the approbations of Rabbis Zalman Nehemiah Goldberg and Meir Mazuz, ad loc.

one seeing the images on television should rend his garment and recite the blessing of *Dayan ha-Emet* with the Divine Name.[50]

Following the Disengagement, however, Rabbi Dov Lior and others ruled that there is no longer an obligation to rend when seeing the remnants of the uprooted communities of Gush Qatif.[51]

Conclusion

Over the last half-century, attitudes towards the obligation of *qeria* have changed based on the changing political landscape. Rending one's garment for the *Ḥurban* today expresses a dialectical tension: After 2,000 years we have returned to the Land of Israel and Jerusalem, but still mourn the absence of the Holy Temple. We recognize how far we have come, and yet how far we still are. We live during confusing and challenging times, but also during exciting times. We live at a unique moment in history. By observing these customs of mourning, may we merit to see the fulfillment of the Talmudic dictum: "All who mourn for Jerusalem will merit to see her in her joy" (*Ta'anit* 30b; *Bava Batra* 60b). ☙

50 *Itturei Kohanim* 254 (Heshvan, 5766), p. 19.

51 See *Qum Hithalekh ba-Arets*, p. 80.

Acknowledging a Miracle with a Berachah: Can It Be Done in the Kidron Valley in Jerusalem?

By: **ARI Z. ZIVOTOFSKY**

Introduction

A Jew should see the "hand of G-d" in the natural world. In order to assist in that goal, *Chazal* have formulated appropriate blessings to be recited upon such sightings as the ocean, a rainbow, mountains or an elephant.[1] How much more so should G-d be recognized in His supernatural manifestations! Thus, *Chazal* instituted blessings to be said at sites where a national or personal miracle occurred.[2,3] These are rare indeed and are

---

1 See Ari Z. Zivotofsky, "Praising God at the Zoo," *The Journal of Halacha and Contemporary Society*, LXII (Fall 2011):43–54 and Ari Zvi Zivotofsky, "*Birkas Meshaneh Habriyos b'Gan HaChayos*," *Tchumin* 32 (5772) 431–434.

2 The obligation for this *berachah* is derived from the *berachah* recited by Jethro (Exodus 18:10). See Maharsha and Pnei Yehoshua who discuss the fact that Jethro did not mention *Shem u'Malchus*. In general, the *berachah* is only recited at the site of the miracle and Jethro was neither in Egypt nor at the Red Sea when he recited the *berachah*. *Meiri* (*Berachos* 54) and *Shittah Mekubetzes* explain that it is also recited when one sees the masses who were saved (cf *Rema* 218 and *Shaar HaTziyun* 218:18) as was the case with Jethro. Iyun Yaakov suggests that because the Clouds of Glory flattened the mountains, Jethro was actually able to see Egypt. Maharsha suggests that the manna, miraculous well, and clouds of glory were a continuation of the Exodus miracles and it was upon seeing them that he recited the *berachah* on the entire process. *Gilyonei Hashas* (*Shabbos* 31b) says that because all the traveling was by direct command of G-d, it is all like one location. *Imrei Emes* (*Likutim*, p. 38) says that Moshe showed Jethro a continuation of the miracle, like photographs, and it was as if he saw the place and was thus able to recite the *berachah*. (This would indicate that seeing a picture of a place where a miracle occurred warrants a *berachah* and yet no one seems to suggest that in practice.) See *Harchev Davar* to *Haamek Davar* on Exodus 18:10 for the difference in the philosophy and scriptural sources for the *berachos* on natural good vs. on an open miracle.

Ari Zivotofsky, a professor of neuroscience at Bar Ilan University, is a tour guide in Ir David and has a Master's degree in Jewish history. He writes widely on Jewish traditions and communities. Many of his articles can be found at <http://halachicadventures.com>.

mostly associated with the Biblical period, and the locations of most of the miracles of national salvation are no longer accurately known. An example of G-d personally intervening on the battlefield on behalf of the Jewish nation for which the location might be known was the destruction of Sancheriv's Assyrian army in its attempt to capture Jerusalem during the reign of the righteous King Hezekiah in 701 BCE. In this article we will explore the nature of the *berachah* said at the site of a miracle, the applicability of that *berachah* to the miracle wrought in Hezekiah's time, and whether the location is identifiable with enough certitude to permit or possibly even require that the *berachah* be recited.

Berachah at the Site of a Miracle

The ninth chapter of *Mishnah Berachos* opens with: "A person who sees a place where a miracle was done for Israel says, '*Baruch she'asah nissim l'avoseinu bamakom hazeh* — Blessed are You Who did miracles for our ancestors in this place." The *Gemara* (*Berachos* 54a) specifies that this *berachah* is for a national miracle, whereas for a personal miracle the beneficiary (and his descendants and students) recite a modified version. The *Mishnah* does not detail which national miracles require the recitation of the *berachah*, so the *Gemara* (*Berachos* 54a) cites a *braisa* that lists some examples: "Our Rabbis taught: If one sees the place of the crossing of the Red Sea,[4] or of the crossing of the Jordan River, or of the crossing of the streams of Arnon, or the stones of Elgavish in the descent of Beis Choron, or the stone which Og king of Bashan wanted to throw on the Israelites,[5] or the stone on which Moshe sat when Joshua fought with Amalek, or Lot's wife, or the wall of Jericho which sank into the ground, for all of these he should give thanksgiving and praise to the Omnipresent."

---

3 The Rambam (*Moreh Nevuchim* 3:50) suggests that the reason Joshua barred the rebuilding of Jericho was to preserve the sunken walls and offer people a chance to personally see the result of the miracle. Regarding Joshua's ban, see: Ari Zivotofsky, "Jericho in Halakha and Hashkafa," *Tradition* 29:3, 21–39, Spring, 1995.

4 For this translation see "Legal-ease: What's the Truth about … the Translation of Yam Suf?" *Jewish Action*, Spring 5770/2010 (Volume 70, no. 3), pp. 62–65.

5 The inclusion of these two seems to indicate that the *Gemara* accepts the *Aggadeta* about these events as literal accounts of historical events and not as some sort of parable, a very difficult position.

This seems like a relatively straightforward passage and the earlier codifiers[6] simply quoted it without modification or comment. For example, the Rambam (*Hilchos Berachos* 10:9) ruled that: "A person who sees a place where miracles were performed for the Jewish people, such as the Red Sea or the crossings of the Jordan, should recite the blessing: 'Blessed are You, G-d, our Lord, King of the universe, Who wrought miracles for our ancestors in this place.' This blessing is recited wherever miracles were performed for many people. In contrast, in a place where a miracle was performed for an individual, that individual, his son, and his grandson should recite the blessing: 'Blessed are You, G-d, our Lord, King of the universe, Who wrought a miracle for me in this place' or '...Who wrought a miracle for my ancestors in this place.' A person who sees the den of lions [into which Daniel was thrown] or the fiery furnace into which Chananiah, Misha'el, and Azariah were thrown should recite the blessing: 'Blessed are You, G-d, our Lord, King of the universe, Who wrought miracles for the righteous in this place."

The Shulchan Aruch (*OC* 218:1) similarly rules directly from the *Mishnah* and *Gemara* that upon seeing the location of a national miracle one recites the appropriate *berachah*, and presents a list of such locations. Presumably to emphasize that the list is illustrative and not exhaustive, it is preceded by: "for example." There is no indication of any hesitation or limitation, and it would seem to follow that any location at which a national miracle occurred generates an obligation to recite the *berachah*.

The Shulchan Aruch stresses that this *berachah*, as well as all *birchos hare'iyah*, are said with *Shem* and *Malchus*.[7] *Biur Halachah* observes that as a *birkas hare'iyah*, it is recited only when one is at the location of the miracle and can see the site.[8] After leaving the site one may not pronounce the *berachah* unless he returns after a 30-day interval.

---

6 Strangely, some of the later codifiers left out the entire category of a *berachah* on national miracles and only included the *berachah* on personal miracles. See e.g. *Kitzur Shulchan Aruch* (Ganzfried) 60:8; *Chayei Adam* 65:4–5; Ben Ish Chai, *Shana Alef*, *Ekev*:11.

7 This was debated regarding all *birchos re'iyah* (see *Beis Yosef OC* 218). The Rambam, Tosafos, Ri, Rosh, Rashba, Rabenu Yonah all agree that they are "true *berachos*" that require *Shem* and *Malchus*. The Ra'avad (see *Hasagot haRa'avad*, Rif p. 44a) disagreed. The Meiri (*Berachos* 54) explains the Ra'avad's position and *Birkei Yosef* (218:1) tries to find support for it. See *Kaf HaChayim* 218:5 and *Yechaveh Da'as* 2:27, first footnote.

8 See *Shu"t B'Tzel HaChochmah* 2:16 that it is sufficient to see the site clearly even if not standing at that location. And it can even be seen through a window or binoculars.

This *berachah* is not often recited nowadays. The precise location of most of the sites listed in the *braisa* are unknown. After all, where exactly are the crossing places of the streams of Arnon or the stones of Elgavish? We certainly have no idea what happened to the stone that Og wanted to throw or to the rock upon which Moshe sat. Some might argue that the *berachah* can be recited at Tel Yericho[9] or on the banks of the Jordan just opposite Jericho. But these are not commonly visited locations. Are there other possible sites at which a miraculous national salvation occurred, as implied by the open lists of the Rambam and Shulchan Aruch?[10] This raises the titillating question about reciting a *berachah* when looking out from Ir David at the Kidron Valley and the slopes of the Mount of Olives,

---

9 This site is well known and has been extensively excavated. See, e.g., Kathleen Kenyon, *Excavations at Jericho*, London: British School of Archaeology in Jerusalem, 1960–1983; *Archaeological heritage in the Jericho Oasis: a systematic catalogue of archaeological sites for the sake of their protection and cultural valorization*, edited by Lorenzo Nigro, Maura Sala, Hamdan Taha, Rome, 2011; Margaret Wheeler, *Walls of Jericho*, London: Arrow Books, 1959; Bryant G. Wood, "Did the Israelites conquer Jericho? A new look at the archaeological evidence," *Biblical Archaeology Review* 16, 2 (1990) 44–59.
However, following the Oslo Peace Accords, Israeli citizens are in general barred from visiting the site.

10 I have found no discussion in the halachic literature about saying a *berachah* at Har Tavor. Yet its location is known and the fact that Devorah sang a *shirah* indicates an open miracle occurred. The story is recounted in Judges 4 and retold in Devorah's song in Judges 5 where it is implied (see 4:15) that the miracle was G-d causing the Kishon to overflow (5:21). Josephus (*Antiquities* 5:5:4) relates that a cold, windy hailstorm incapacitated Sisera's army but did not bother the Jews as it came at their backs. The possible reasons for the total lack of mention in the halachic literature are either that it was obvious that a *berachah* should be recited or, alternatively, a *berachah* is recited only for a super-natural miracle while this one occurred via natural means. The latter is difficult in that Judges 4:15, 5:20–21 and Psalms 83:10 makes it sound awfully like direct Divine intervention. Furthermore, the *Mishnah Berurah* (219:31), commenting on the *Shulchan Aruch*'s discussion of *Birkas HaGomel* for miracles such as being saved from being trampled by a bull, suggests that rather than *HaGomel*, the beneficiary should recite "He Who performed a miracle for me" at the location. Clearly, the *Mishnah Berurah* does not require a supernatural miracle for this *berachah*. Why should the national miracle at Mt. Tabor be any less significant? However, the Shulchan Aruch himself (218:9) seems to require a supernatural miracle for a *berachah* on an individual miracle and based on this Rav Moshe Feinstein (*Sefer Mesores Moshe*, 2013, page 55) ruled exactly opposite the *Mishnah Berurah* and said that following being saved from a car accident, *HaGomel* was preferable to the *berachah* on a miracle.

the area where (possibly) Sancheriv's army was miraculously decimated in one awesome night.[11]

The Miracle of Sancheriv's Defeat

In 722 BCE, the Assyrian army captured the Northern Kingdom's capital city of Shomron and exiled its inhabitants, known today as the "10 lost tribes." Assyria would obviously not be content with just one of the two Jewish kingdoms, and soon headed south to Judah. At the time, Achaz and his son Hezekiah ruled together and the southern kingdom of Yehudah was a tax-paying vassal state of the more powerful Assyria. In approximately 715 BCE, Achaz died and Hezekiah began his righteous rule (II Kings 18:5) with sweeping religious reforms that included removing idol worship from Jerusalem. In addition, he modified the political allegiances, refusing to continue paying tribute to Assyria and forming an alliance with Egypt (Isaiah 30–31). Sancheriv, the relatively new Assyrian king, did not take kindly to this affront and in 701 BCE attacked Judah, destroying many of the cities,[12] and advanced on Jerusalem (II Kings 18:13–16). The story of the ensuing siege and salvation is recorded in Isaiah, II Kings, and II Chronicles.

Biblical and archeological evidence indicate that Hezekiah engaged in defensive tactics to protect the city's water source and to defend the city. Possibly among the most significant projects was the digging of the ½ kilometer (1200 *amah*) tunnel (known today as Hezekiah's Tunnel or the Siloam Tunnel) to divert the water from the Gichon Spring to the south of the city. In addition, while his great-grandfather Uzziah had started refortifying the city (II Chronicles 26:9; 27:3), he continued the fortification of the city walls including building a new wall, of which the "Broad Wall" in today's Jewish Quarter is a section (II Chronicles 32:1–6).

Isaiah decried the reliance on Egypt and the fortifying of the city (Isaiah 22:1–14), but Hezekiah also engaged in religious preparation, reminding the people that G-d is on their side (II Chronicles 32:7–8). The Talmud (*Sanhedrin* 94b) credited Hezekiah with having made enormous

---

11 According to tradition this occurred on the first night of Pesach (see *Rashi*, II Kings 20:1; *Tosafos Yom Tov*, *Megillah* 3:5). In the *Seder piyut* "*Va'yehi b'chatzi halailah*" the stanza "*ya'atz mecharef*" refers to the defeat of Sancheriv, as do the stanzas "*sorfu mi'shmanei pool*" and "*od hayom b'Nov*" in the *piyut* "*V'amartem zevach Pesach*." Because of this miracle, the *Haftarah* for the eighth day of Pesach in *chu"l* and also read by some on Yom Ha'atzma'ut is "*od hayom b'Nov*" (Isaiah 10:32–12:6) (*Levush OC* 490:9).

12 See פאוסט, אברהם. מסע סנחריב להר יהודה וירושלים : מבט חדש. חידושים בחקר ירושלים יד (תשסט) 89-106, 2008.

efforts to spread knowledge of the Torah throughout the land, saying that "he stuck a sword over the entrance of the study hall announcing that anyone who did not occupy himself with the Torah would be pierced by the sword." And it seemed to work. *Chazal* state that during this period a check from Dan to Beersheba could not find a single *am ha'aretz*, and a search from Gevat to Antipras did not find a single young boy or girl, man or woman who was not expert in the laws of ritual impurity (*Sanhedrin* 94b). It is this dedication to Torah study, according to the Talmud, which led to Sancheriv's defeat.

There are varying accounts of what took place. According to II Kings 18:13–16, Hezekiah agreed to pay a huge sum in exchange for an Assyrian withdrawal. In order to pay the 300 talents of silver and 30 talents of gold, he emptied the Temple and royal treasuries and even stripped the gold from the doors of the Temple. Nonetheless, at some point Sancheriv marched on Jerusalem with a large army and laid siege. And then, in what can only be described as an overt miracle, the siege simply ended.

The Taylor Prism and Sennacherib Prism, discovered in the 19th century, are clay prisms inscribed with the annals of Sancheriv. Such texts generally boast of the king's successful military campaigns and indeed these texts, dated from 690 BCE, record that Sennacherib destroyed 46 Judean cities and trapped Hezekiah in Jerusalem "like a caged bird." It then continues with the Assyrian king returning to Assyria. There is no mention of Jerusalem capitulating or what happened to the "caged bird," suggesting that Hezekiah escaped defeat. Josephus (first century CE; *Antiquities* 10:1:5) reports that G-d sent a pestilential distemper on the Assyrian army on the first night of the siege that killed 185,000 soldiers. The Egyptian version of the Assyrian defeat is recorded by Herodotus (c.484 BCE – c.425 BCE). This account relates that the Assyrians were camped at Pelusium in Egypt and during the night a huge number of field mice "attacked" the Assyrian camp and gnawed their quivers, bows and shield-straps, so as to render them useless. In the morning the panicked Assyrians fled and the Egyptians pursued them, killing a large number.

What does the *Tanach* say? In no less than three places it is reported that Sancheriv laid siege to the Holy City (2 Kings 18:17; 2 Chronicles 32:9; Isaiah 36), and in all three accounts the entire Assyrian army was destroyed in one night by "the angel of the Lord." In II Kings 19:35 it is recorded that 185,000 Assyrian soldiers were killed in that single night.[13] The conclusion of the Talmudic discussion about how G-d struck Sancheriv's army is that He opened the ears of all the soldiers so that they

---

13 This story is memorialized in a popular 1813 poem by Lord Byron, "The Destruction of Sennacherib."

heard the song of the angelic Chayos, and out of sheer rapture at such beauty, their souls flew out and they simply expired (*Sanhedrin* 95b).

Is an Artifact Necessary for a *Berachah* to Be Recited?

It would seem that the site of this miracle certainly warrants a *berachah* and yet it is not mentioned in the context of a *berachah* in the *Gemara* or *tosefta* or any other tannaitic or amoraic sources. However, it seems to be obvious that one should recite a *berachah* at that location. The first one to explicitly mention this is *Tosafos* (*Berachos* 54b *sv avnei*), who initially states that in addition to all the locations mentioned in the *Gemara*, one should make a *berachah* at the site where Sancheriv's army was defeated, but that the *braisa* did not bother to mention it because the place is well known.[14] *Tosafos* then does an abrupt about-face and quotes Rabenu Yehudah's[15] position that only if the miracle is evident by artifacts at the site is the *berachah* recited; otherwise it is only recited by those who experienced the miracle. The site of Sancheriv's defeat, he argues, is not like the examples cited in the *braisa* and thus does not warrant a *berachah*.

Tosafos in these few lines introduced a far-reaching novelty that would seem to have no source. He distinguishes between a site of a miracle and an artifact of a miracle and further distinguishes between national and private miracles. For a *berachah* to be recited commemorating a national miracle, *Tosafos*, in this second position, posits that it is not enough to be at the location but there must be an artifact, while for a personal miracle the location suffices. This requirement of an artifact seems contra the *Mishnah* which states explicitly "one who sees a **location** ...." This requirement also seems to have no basis in the *Gemara*. It is not obvious that the citing of Rabenu Yehudah's dissenting opinion indicates that *Tosafos* is rejecting his initial position. The *Piskei Tosafos* records only that "*kol adam*" say the *berachah* even if there is no artifact and does not record that on a national miracle an artifact is required. The *Meromei HaSadeh* (Netziv; *Berachos* 54a) attempts to find a hint to Rabenu Yehudah's position in the fact that the *Mishnah* includes the word "*bo*" and similarly that the *Shulchan Aruch* includes that word, but in contrast leaves it out in *se'if* 4 when discussing personal miracles. *Nahar Shalom* (Rav Shabtai Vintura, first printed

---

14 It is not clear to me how *Tosafos*, located in France, knew the location and called it well known.

15 This is most likely Rabbi Yehudah Sirlion (d.1224; רבי יהודה בן רבי יצחק מפריז, המכונה גם רבי יהודה שירילאון). See אורבך, אפרים אלימלך, בעלי התוספות : תולדותיהם, חיבוריהם, שיטתם p. 602 who, partially based on this, thinks Rabbi Yehudah Sirlion is the main author of *Tosafos* to *Berachos*.

1775) suggests that Rashi (*sv ha'roeh*), by stating that the site must be similar to those listed in the *Gemara*, is hinting to Rabenu Yehudah's rule. *B'mchilas kvodo*, this seems to be quite a stretch and there does not seem to be any hint that a requirement of an artifact ever occurred to Rashi.

The Rambam (*Berachos* 10:9) simply states "any place in which a public miracle was performed," indicating any place, without the need for an artifact. So too Roka'ach (end of 342) repeats the language of the *Mishnah* and provides the list from the *Gemara* with no indication of a caveat. If there was one, it certainly should be mentioned and it is not.

Despite the novelty and difficulty with Rabenu Yehudah's position, it has found its way into normative *halachah*. The *Mordechai* (*Berachos* 211) quotes *Tosafos* with the opinion of Rabenu Yehudah without comment, seemingly in agreement. The *Magen Avraham* (218:1) quotes *Tosafos* and the *Mordechai* as the accepted opinion that a site must be similar to those listed in that the miracle is recognizable via the location, and that this is as opposed to the Sancheriv miracle near Jerusalem. Regarding that miracle, writes the Magen Avraham, even if one can identify the exact location, because the miracle is not evident from the location because it did not happen in "the ground," no *berachah* is recited. He thus rules not to make a *berachah* at the site of Sancheriv's defeat and this is cited in the *Be'ir Heitev* (218:1).[16] *Kaf HaChayim* (*OC* 218:1) also cites this position, but then also quotes a book, *P'dah es Avraham*, which quotes *Kometz Minchah* that at all of the resting stops mentioned in *Parashas Masei* one must recite this *berachah*. Clearly, there is no physical evidence at these locations.

Aside from the lack of textual support for Rabenu Yehudah's position, there is an obvious challenge from the Talmudic examples as raised by the *Aruch HaShulchan* (*OC* 218:3). The *Aruch HaShulchan* points out that some of the miracles in the Talmudic list can indeed be seen in the artifacts, such as the *avnei Elgavish* or the stones of Moshe and Og. However, the Red Sea and the Jordan River are flowing and it is simply the location where the miracle occurred. This, according to the Aruch HaShulchan, is exactly parallel to the situation with Sancheriv's army. He agrees that the site of Sancheriv's defeat is not similar to *avnei Elgavish* in regard to an

---

16 An alternate reason why not to recite a *berachah* at that site could have been offered. One could argue not to say it because not all of *Klal Yisrael* were rescued; only the remaining tribes, and this is not enough to warrant a *berachah* (*Shulchan Aruch OC* 218:2). This issue is not raised by *Tosafos* or by the others who discuss the topic. Either they understood that those remaining tribes now constitute *Klal Yisrael* (this can have ramifications for the celebration of Yom Ha'atzma'ut) or they felt that the refugees from the north who were exiled in Jerusalem gave this miracle the status of one affecting all of Israel.

artifact, but, he argues, it is certainly similar to the crossing points of the sea and river. He therefore remains perplexed at *Tosafos*'s ruling and at the Magen Avraham for quoting it.

The Mishnah Berurah (218:7) quotes the Magen Avraham and even attempts to answer the Aruch HaShulchan's problem. He explains that at the crossing points when one sees the water flowing it is recognized that the water stopped flowing so that the Jews could cross.[17] However, the miracle of destroying Sancheriv's army had nothing to do with the ground and thus there is no physical indicator of the miracle at the site. But the Chofetz Chaim was clearly bothered by this explanation because in his *Sha'ar HaTziyun* (218:1) he brings two challenges to it. First he notes that Tosafos HaRosh quotes Rabenu Yehudah as the initial position in *Tosafos*, that the *berachah* is said. And furthermore he observes that the *Gemara* gives no indication that there is any difference between national and private miracles in regard to the qualification of the location, and just like for a personal miracle there is no artifact requirement, there should not be for national. He does not like to argue with earlier authorities and thus concludes with "*tzarich iyun*" — there is need to further investigate how to act. However, he is clearly not accepting the Magen Avraham and his position as the final word. The Aruch HaShulchan and the Mishnah Berurah both seem to be leaving room to recite the *berachah* at the site where Sancheriv's army was miraculously defeated. The question that then needs to be answered is: is this location identifiable?

Location of the Destruction of Sancheriv's Army

Is the location of this miracle known? *Tosafos* actually said the location is known! The question is, where was Sancheriv's army located as it besieged[18] Jerusalem? Archeologists have provided rough ideas of the borders of the city at the time of Hezekiah, but nonetheless they cannot be said to be definitively identified. That is, with one exception. The eastern

---

17 Note that in *Biur Halachah* (sv *k'goan*) he seems to agree with the *Kaftor Va'ferach* that the *berachah* is only said at the crossing point. Yet the water there is no different than the water flowing further up- or downstream.

18 This is assuming that the Assyrians had actually imposed a full-fledged siege on Jerusalem. That seems to be the implication of Sancheriv's description of "a caged bird" as well as the plain meaning of II Chronicles 32:10 and possibly II Kings 18:26, 19:32, and Isaiah 37:33. On the other hand, one could read II Chronicles 32:9 as indicating that the bulk of the Assyrian force was in Lachish when it was destroyed. Nonetheless, the bulk of commentators unequivocally understand that the Assyrians laid siege to Jerusalem even if Sancheriv was not personally present.

border of Jerusalem was always the Kidron Valley. The city never developed across the valley, not under the Canaanites, not during any of *Bayis Rishon*, and not during *Bayis Sheni*; in fact, not until about 150 years ago.

In general it would seem that an attacking army that is besieging a city would have one principal camp. Jerusalem has historically been surrounded on three sides by steep valleys. The original city was surrounded by the Kidron Valley and the central or Tyropean Valley, and in the later years of the First Temple period and in the Second Temple period it was surrounded by the Kidron Valley and the Hinnom Valley. A valley is not an ideal location in which to pitch a military camp. Josephus twice (*Jewish War* 5:7:2 [303] and 5:12:2 [504–507]) refers to a location as the "camp of the Assyrians."[19] Clearly, the Assyrian siege left a large psychological mark on the city, such that almost 800 years later the inhabitants had a location that they associated with the site of the Assyrian camp.[20] From Josephus' description it can be deduced that the location was northeast of the besieged city, rather than in the valleys to the east and west. Depending on what the borders of the city looked like, it may have been just northwest of the Temple Mount, in the present-day Old City, or further northwest in the general area of today's Russian compound or municipality building, in either case on the so-called North-west Hill. Another old source that identifies the site of this miraculous demise of Sancheriv's army is the *Targum* on Jeremiah. Near the end of chapter 31, Jeremiah describes the rebuilding of Jerusalem and in delineating the northern boundary, says "and the whole valley of the *pigrim*" which the *Targum Yonasan* says is the plain where the Assyrian troops died. He too identifies the main camp as being north of the city and not in any of the adjacent valleys.[21]

The question of relevance here is whether the fact that the main camp was north of the city precludes the presence of troops to the east on the Mount of Olives or in the Kidron Valley, troops that would have been miraculously killed and generated a requirement to recite a *berachah*? Josephus mentioned Sancheriv's camp in the context of the Roman camps that besieged the city in 70 CE. The Roman army was certainly far larger than Sancheriv's, but it can shed light on where an attacking military might position itself. The Romans under Titus surrounded the city on the north-

19 See "The Camp of the Assyrians in Jerusalem," *IEJ* 29(1979):137–42.

20 It is always possible that the collective memory was faulty. Josephus' identification of Ir David is erroneous. However, there is no reason to suspect error in this instance.

21 See ב"צ לוריא, כיצד תכנן חיזקיהו את מפלתו של סנחריב, בית מקרא ק' ניסן תשמ"ז.

western side with three legions (V Macedonica — Fifth Macedonian Legion; XII Fulminata — Twelfth Legion; and XV Apollinaris — Fifteenth Apollonian Legion) and, importantly, with a fourth legion (the famed X Fretensis — tenth legion) on the Mount of Olives to the east.[22] There are of course differences in the methods used by the two attacking armies: the Romans had superior technology compared to the Assyrians and were capable of hurling large stones considerable distances, and these projectiles indeed caused heavy damage to the ramparts. But this troop placement demonstrates that despite the rough terrain, there is a purpose in stationing troops on the eastern side. If one wants to cordon off and besiege the city, the eastern side cannot be neglected. In one of the earliest battles for Jerusalem, King David fled his son Avshalom's rebellion by going east to the desert.

In preparation for the siege, the Assyrians engaged in quite a bit of psychological warfare (II Kings 18:17–35; Isaiah 36; II Chronicles 32:9–19) and the location chosen for the Assyrian harangue was "by the conduit of the upper pool, which was on the path to the fullers' field" (II Kings 18:17; Isaiah 36:2). This seems to say that at least some of Sancheriv's troops were surrounding Jerusalem,[23] and while their location cannot be identified with certainty, it is certainly not north / northwest of the city where the permanent camp was located. The upper pool in the verse is often identified with the area of the Gichon spring, and hence there were certainly Assyrian troops to the east of the city.

It seems likely that the main Assyrian camp was, as described by Josephus, northwest of the city at a location that is not currently known precisely. But it also seems highly likely that in the siege of the city there were troops stationed on the eastern side, on the Mount of Olives that overlooks the principal water source of the city. It is impossible that a siege could have been successful without troops overlooking the Kidron Valley. The Bible (II Kings 19:35; II Chronicles 32:21) states that on "That night the angel of the Lord went out and smote in the Assyrian camp 185,000. When the people got up the next morning, they were all dead corpses." The verse does not state that the attack was only against the main camp, but rather implies that the entire army, presumably including also those soldiers stationed on the east, were killed.

---

22 Levick, Barbara (1999). *Vespasian*. London: Routledge, pp. 116–119.

23 See, however, *Rashi* to II Kings 19:25 who says the army was in Nov near Jerusalem when they were killed. But see *Sanhedrin* 95a that implies that the army reached and besieged Jerusalem.

Conclusion

The Aruch HaShulchan (*OC* 218:1) points out that in "*Modim*" we thrice daily say that we thank G-d for his daily miracles. There is indeed an imperative in recognizing G-d's role in the hidden miracles of nature. But this does not preclude the importance of also recognizing the overt historical miracles that G-d has done for our nation. This is the basis of many of the holidays when we acknowledge the miracles temporally, in the time of year in which they occurred. The *berachah* of "*she'asah nissim l'avoseinu bamakom hazeh*" provides a means for acknowledging G-d at the spatial location of miracles, and according to the *Gemara* it is an obligatory and not an optional *berachah*.[24] There are today few sites at which we can do this, and it is thus a shame to exclude yet one more. Rather, when visiting the historic, ancient, original Jerusalem one can take the opportunity to recall the miracle that saved the Kingdom of Judah from the same fate that befell the 10 lost tribes.

There is little question that a portion of Sancheriv's army was positioned on the slopes of the Mount of Olives as it drops towards the Kidron Valley and the Gichon Spring, the sole water source of ancient Jerusalem. Standing in Ir David and looking out at those slopes, it is fairly certain that one is gazing upon the ground where Sancheriv's soldiers menacingly stood until the fateful night in which they were miraculously struck down. Furthermore, despite the fact that Magen Avraham cites it, the second opinion in *Tosafos* is difficult to defend and seems to be rejected by the Aruch HaShulchan and the Chofetz Chaim (in *Sha'ar HaTziyun*). These facts together might support one who is inclined to recite a *berachah* at the site.

It is worth noting that *Chazal* harshly criticized Hezekiah for not reciting *shirah* (a song of praise) for his salvation. According to the Talmud, but for the fact that Hezekiah failed to sing a song of praise to G-d for all the miracles performed for him, he would have been Mashiach (*Sanhedrin* 94a). May our *berachah* at the site of his salvation be a repair for Hezekiah's failure and truly usher in Mashiach. ☙

---

24 The *Gemara* says (*Berachos* 54a) "*m'chayvai livruchay*." Rashba (*Berachos* 54a) says that the first time it is obligatory; thereafter (if 30 days have elapsed) it may be recited. An interesting question is whether one who has recited it within the previous 30 days may say it on behalf of someone who is now seeing it for the first time.

The Silk Screen Sefer Torah

By: YISRAEL KLEINHENDLER

Over a decade ago, a new method of writing *Sifrei Torah* using silk screen was introduced. The project was met with fierce resistance and many contemporary rabbis prohibited its use. Much confusion surrounded the topic, and many questions were left unanswered. After a while things quieted down, and not much has been heard since then. The goal of this article is to clarify how a silk screen *Sefer Torah* is produced; discuss the halachic ramifications; explain why it was so strongly opposed; and describe the end result.

1. What Is a Silk Screen *Sefer Torah*?

A silk screen *Sefer Torah* is written using screen printing technology. The process begins by taking kosher *klaf* (parchment paper) that has *sirtut* (lines etched into the *klaf*) in accordance with halachah and placing it on a table or other flat surface. A silk screen frame is then placed above the *klaf,* leaving about a quarter inch between the *klaf* and the screen. The screen covers an entire *yeria* (page). The screen consists of a wooden or metal frame and has a thin mesh sheet stretched over it. The mesh is woven very tightly, leaving millions of tiny holes between the mesh fibers. The holes are so small that ink placed on the screen does not drip through. The screen is covered with a thin coating known as emulsion, blocking the holes and preventing them from being filled with ink. The holes that correspond to the letters that need to be written in the *Sefer Torah* are left open. Every letter in the *Sefer Torah* is represented by hundreds of tiny holes that were not covered over, forming the shape of the letter. There are forty-two lines on every screen just like in any standard *Sefer Torah,* and a clear beautiful font is chosen and meticulously checked for any mistakes.

Ink is then placed on the left side of the screen. The ink used is a bit thicker than the regular ink used in most *Sifrei Torah*. The *sofer* pushes the ink across the screen from left to right with a squeegee filling the holes with ink. At this stage the letters are formed on the screen but no ink drips down onto the *klaf*. The *sofer* then says he is writing *lishmah* (for the sanctity of the *Sefer Torah*), is *mekadesh* (sanctifies) the names of Hashem and pushes the ink from right to left across the screen with a squeegee. As the

---

Yisrael Kleinhendler, a yeshiva student, resides in Lakewood, New Jersey. He has been the *chavrusa* of Rabbi Yitzchak Abadi for the past seven years.

sofer moves the squeegee across the screen, he applies pressure to the squeegee, pressing the screen down onto the *klaf*. As the ink is being pushed across the screen, the ink is forced through the tiny holes and pushed directly onto the *klaf* below. The letters are written directly by the *koach* (effort) of the *sofer* pushing the ink onto the *klaf*. The entire *yeria* is written instantly (*toch kedey dibur*). The final product is a *Sefer Torah* written in a beautiful *ksav* (font).[1]

2. What is the Point in Making Them?

A number of benefits are achieved by writing silk screen *Sifrei Torah*:

1. The *Shulchan Aruch* (Y"D 270:1) writes that there is a positive commandment for every Jew to write a *Sefer Torah*. The *Tur* (ibid.) writes that if he wrote [the *Sefer Torah*] or even edited one letter it is as if he received it on Mt. Sinai. The *Beis Yosef* explains: 'If he wrote it'—He himself or hired a *sofer* to write it and worked hard so that it should be written correctly, it is as if he received it on Mt. Sinai, etc.
   The *Rosh* (*Hilchos Sefer Torah* 1, see *Beis Yosef* Y"D 270) explains that the main purpose of the commandment of writing a *Sefer Torah* is to learn from it. (Not to store it in *shul*.) This means that even if the local community or *shul* does not need another *Sefer Torah*, it is a mitzvah to write one and use it for learning. (Many people are *maavir sidrah* from their personal *Sefer Torah*.)
2. Many *shuls*, especially in places like hospitals and hotels or small settlements, have non-kosher *Sifrei Torah*. This is especially common with old *Sifrei Torah*. They continue to be used and lead to *berachos* recited in vain.
3. Unfortunately there are many non-God-fearing *soferim* who are unscrupulous and don't follow the halachos properly, leading to non-kosher *Sifrei Torah* being sold to unsuspecting buyers.

---

1 I wish to acknowledge the role played by Rabbi Yosef Tesler in developing the silk screen *Sefer Torah* process. With Rabbi Yitzchak Abadi's urging and guidance, Rabbi Tesler spent ten years researching, developing and perfecting the silk screen process. He worked closely with Rabbi Abadi, and consulted with other senior *poskim* and *sofrim* to ensure that the process was in strict compliance with all halachic requirements.
Rabbi Yosef Tesler studied at Beth Medrash Govoha in Lakewood, NJ and received *semichah* from the *Rosh Yeshiva,* Rabbi Shneur Kotler. He then joined Rabbi Yitzchak Abadi's halachah *kollel* where he received *shimush* in the practical application of *psak halachah.*

Silk screen *Sifrei Torah* offer an opportunity for people to purchase beautiful kosher *Sifrei Torah* written by a God-fearing *sofer*, for a fraction of the price of a handwritten *Sefer Torah*. With high cost as the main obstacle to buying a *Sefer Torah*, silk screen *Sifrei Torah* offer an affordable solution and do not compromise on either quality or beauty. With silk screen, many more people would be able to fulfill the mitzvah of writing their own *Sefer Torah*, and many *shuls* would be saved from the sin of blessing and reading from invalid *Sifrei Torah*.

3. The Halachah

There are many laws that pertain to the writing of a *Sefer Torah*, some of which are quite complex. We will summarize some of the basic laws and then see if screen printing a *Sefer Torah* meets the necessary requirements. Since we are looking to replace the traditional handwritten *ksivah* (writing) with a new method of *ksivah*, we will be focusing primarily on the halachos of *ksivah,* not on what kind of *klaf* must be used, how the *sirtut* is done, what kind of ink to use, how the letters should be shaped, how to position the letters on the *klaf*, and what to do if a mistake is made, since there are no differences to these areas in the silk screen process.

- A *Sefer Torah* must be written with the right hand [of right-handed *soferim*] (*Shulchan Aruch,* Y"D 271:7).
- Some say that the *Sefer Torah* should be written with a reed quill and not with a feather quill (*Rama* 271:7).
- When the *sofer* begins to write he must say, "I am writing this sefer with the intention of sanctifying the *Sefer Torah*" (*Shulchan Aruch* 274:1).
- The *sofer* must copy every letter from another *sefer* and may not write by heart (*Shulchan Aruch* 274:2).
- The *sofer* must say every word out loud before he writes (*Shulchan Aruch* 274:2).
- Every time the name of Hashem is written, the *sofer* must say, "I am writing with the intention of sanctifying the name of Hashem" (*Shulchan Aruch* 276:2).
- If some ink falls on a letter to the point where the letter cannot be recognized, it does not help to scrape away the extra ink to restore the proper form of the letter. This is known as *chak tochos* (performing an action to something other than the letter itself in order to achieve the proper form of the letter). For example, scraping away the edge of a *dalet* to turn it into a *reish* (*Shulchan Aruch* O"CH 32:17).

- Tefillin and mezuzos must be written in order and if one letter was left out, the *sofer* may not go back and correct it (*Shulchan Aruch* O"CH 32:23, Y"D 288:3).

Now that we have enumerated some of the basic laws of writing a *Sefer Torah*, we can begin to analyze the silk screen *Sefer Torah* process and see if it is in compliance with halachah. We will also cover other halachic concerns, in addition to those mentioned in the *Shulchan Aruch,* that have been brought up by various halachic authorities over the years.

It is important, however, to first mention the "printing press *Sefer Torah*" that was discussed by the rabbis over 400 years ago. The question arose whether or not a printed *Sefer Torah* is kosher. This process, of course, is referring not to today's automatic printers, but to the manual printing press where the letters were pressed onto the *klaf* by hand. Metal letters were placed upside down in the necessary order to write a page in the *Sefer Torah.* The letters were then covered with ink and the *klaf* was pressed down onto the letters. Many rabbis permitted it, while many others prohibited it.[2] The main point of discussion was whether the printing press was considered *ksivah* or not. This is of particular interest to us because we are also dealing with whether or not the silk screen process is considered *ksivah.* By reviewing the responsa written by the earlier rabbis, and studying the questions and concerns they had, and the conclusions they drew, we can shed some light on the silk screen project and hopefully learn from them and apply it to our case. We will soon go into further detail.

Below is a summary of the various questions raised regarding the validity of silk screen *Sifrei Torah*, and the answers given by those who determined that it is indeed kosher and acceptable for use.

---

2 Some of the rabbis permitting the printing press *Sefer Torah* include: *Aruch HaShulchan* (Y"D 271:39, E"H 125:37), *Beis Shmuel* (E"H 125:3), *Eirech Hashulchan* (O"CH 691:1), *Knesses Yechezkel* (37), *Magen Avraham* (O"CH 32:57, 284:1), *Maharam Ben Chaviv* (*Get Pashut* E"H 125:15), *Maharshal* (*Yam Shel Shlomo Gittin* chapter 2 23), *Mas'as Binyamin* (99), *Rama Mipano* (93), *Taz* (Y"D 271:8), *Ya'avetz* (*Mor Uktziah* 32, page 24, *Migdal Oz Kuntress Even Bochen Pinah* 2:30). Some of those prohibiting it are: *Bach* (O"CH 691:4), *Birkey Yosef* (O"CH 691), *Bnei Yonah* (Y"D 271), *Chavos Ya'ir* (184), *Maharashdam* (Y"D 184), *Maharsham* (Vol. 3 357), *Rav Moshe Provinsalo* (Vol. 1 73), *Rokeach* (280), *Teshuvah Me'ahavah* (Vol. 1 9, Vol. 2 391), *Zerah Emes* (Y"D Vol. 2 117).

Must a *Sefer Torah* be Written with a Quill?

As mentioned earlier, some halachic authorities maintain that a reed quill must be used. In the silk screen process, a reed quill is not used. Does this affect the validity of the *ksivah*, and is a reed quill the ideal tool to use?

The *Be'er Hagolah* (Y"D end of 271) explains that the reason to use a reed quill over another type of quill is to avoid the problem of *chak tochos*. (With a feather quill one may encounter the problem of *chak tochos* if he has to erase ink because the letters didn't come out nice.) This doesn't apply to screen printing, where the quality of the letters is not compromised by using a squeegee as a *kulmus* (quill). The *Gra* (Y"D 271:23) explains, based on the gemara (*Taanis* 20b), that the reed merited being used as a quill to write *Sifrei Torah*, tefillin and mezuzos because it is soft and one should always be soft… According to both reasons, the use of another kind of *kulmus* does not affect the validity of the *ksivah*. The commentaries including *Shach* (Y"D 271:13) and *Taz* (Y"D 271:8) maintain that the custom is not to follow this *Rama*, and most *soferim* today don't use reed quills. The *Aruch HaShulchan* does not even mention this halachah.

Must Every Letter be Written Individually?

Traditionally, every letter is written individually. Is there a problem writing more than one letter at a time? If not, must the name of Hashem be written one letter at a time?

The gemara (*Yoma* 38b) tells about *Ben Kamtzar* who didn't want to teach others his method of writing. He would hold four quills between his fingers and write four letters at once. *Rashi* on the mishnah (*Yoma* 38a) explains that *Ben Kamtzar* would write the four-letter name of Hashem at once. The rabbis wanted to learn from him how to write this way and he wouldn't teach them. Regarding him it was said, "The names of the wicked shall rot" (*Mishlei* 10:7). We see that more than one letter may be written at once, including the name of Hashem. The *Mas'as Binyamin* (91) says that writing more than one letter at once is preferable and that there is much greater holiness that way.

Must Every Name of Hashem be Sanctified Individually?

Every time the *sofer* writes the name of Hashem he must be *mekadesh* that name. In the case of the silk screen *Sefer Torah*, he writes an entire page in one moment, and writes Hashem's name multiple times with one *kiddush*. Is there a requirement to be *mekadesh* every name individually?

The *sofer* is required to be *mekadesh* the name of Hashem just before he writes it. If he writes all of the names separately, he must be *mekadesh* the name every time he writes one. With silk screen, all the names are written right after he is *mekadesh* them (*toch kedey dibbur*), and the *sofer* knows he is writing many names so he has them all in mind. There is no interruption between his *kiddush* and his *ksivah*. (See *Binas Sofer* 1:1.)

Can the Name of Hashem be Written Together With Other Words?

Assuming that it is acceptable to be *mekadesh* many names at once, may the *sofer* be *mekadesh* the names and then write holy and non-holy names together?

The *Rama* (Y"D 276:2) says that if one sanctifies one of the non-holy names the *Sefer Torah* is kosher. If the *Sefer Torah* is kosher when the *sofer* explicitly sanctifies a non-holy name, surely it is kosher when he has in mind to sanctify only the holy names. The *Binas Sofer* says this clearly (1:1).

Can the *Sefer Torah* be Written Out of Order?

A *Sefer Torah* does not need to be written in order, and if a *sofer* makes a mistake he can go back and correct it at any time (Y"D 279:1). The *Ginas Vradim* (O"CH 2:12), however, says that the name of Hashem must be written in order. Is there any problem with the silk screen Torah being written out of order?

Many halachic authorities disagree with the *Ginas Vradim* (see *Yabia Omer* Vol. 3 Y"D 14:7) and maintain that the names of Hashem need not be written in order. In any event, silk screen *Sifrei Torah* are written from right to left, so all the names of Hashem are indeed written in order.

Is Screen Printing Considered *Ksivah*?

The Torah requires *Sifrei Torah* to be 'written.' Is this process considered *ksivah*, or is it some other method of writing that is not considered *ksivah*?

The gemara (*Gittin* 20a) questions whether a mold that is placed on top of a coin and banged to create a form on the coin is considered *chak tochos* or not. *Rashi* explains the question as follows: Does the mold simply bang in the edges surrounding the form, or does the mold push down the sides of the metal, causing the metal in the center of the coin to be pushed up into the mold? If the latter is true, says *Rashi*, this is *ksivah beyadayim*, writing by hand, which is a good *ksivah*. We see from this Rashi that even when working on the *tochos*—the area surrounding the letters—it is a good *ksivah* as long as something has been done to the letter itself. Certainly in our case where an action is being performed to the *yereichos*, the body of the letter (by pushing the ink through the holes in the form of a letter), it would be considered a good *ksivah.*

Ksivah Ke'derech Ha'kosvim: Is This Considered a 'Normal' Way of Writing?

Rabbeinu Krashkash (see *Ritvah Gittin* 9b) explains that if one tears a paper in the shape of a letter and pours ink on top, according to *Tosafos* (*Gittin 9b*) it is not good because *ksivah* entails writing the normal way, and pouring ink on paper is not the normal way of writing. We see from here that the writing must be done '*derech ksivah.*' How is silk screen considered *derech ksivah*?

Rabbeinu Krashkash is referring to when nothing is done to the body of the letter. Rather, the ink is poured on the entire page and spreads to the torn areas, causing the letters to be written by filling the cracks. This is not *derech ksivah. Rabbeinu Krashkash* continues and explains that if the ink is poured directly into the cracks, this is considered *ksivah.* It is with that type of writing that silk screen has more in common, its process more like pouring ink directly into the cracks than on the entire page. This is because the only way to get the ink onto the *klaf* is by pushing the ink through the holes. If the ink was simply poured on top of the screen, it would never go through to the *klaf* below.

Others wanted to say that to be *derech ksivah*, an action must be performed in the forming of every letter. In our case an action is performed to form every letter. This is the action of forcing the ink through the holes onto the *klaf.* This action does not require shaping the letters with a quill.

We can prove that writing many letters at once is *derech ksivah* even without a quill. The proof comes from the *tzitz.* Worn by the *kohen gadol*, the *tzitz* was a golden plate with the words *Kodesh LaShem* on it as required by the Torah (*Shemos* 39:30). All halachos of *ksivah* apply to writing the *tzitz*, so whatever is kosher for the *tzitz* is kosher for a *Sefer Torah* as well. The *Rambam* (*Kley Hamikdash* 9 2) learns, as explained by the *Mahari Kurkus*, that the process of making the *tzitz* involved placing wax on the front and writing *Kodesh Lashem* in ink on the back. The letters were then banged out with a tool to form the words *Kodesh LaShem* on the front, and the wax helped absorb the shock so the gold wouldn't crack. The *Ra'avad* gives another explanation. He says they used a form with the words *Kodesh LaShem* in relief and pressed it into the back of the *tzitz*, embossing the words on its front. According to both the *Rambam* and the *Ra'avad*, the letters weren't formed with a quill. Additionally, according to the *Ra'avad*, the whole *tzitz* was written at once. We can learn from here that writing in such a fashion is indeed called *derech ksivah.*

The *Rashba* (*Shu"t HaRashba Hamyuchasos L'HaRamban* 122) also mentions the concept of *derech ksivah*. He says that *chak tochos* and *hatafah* (dripping ink to form a letter) are invalid because they are not done *derech ksivah*. We will soon explain that silk screening does not incorporate any kind of *chakikah* or *hatafah*, so there wouldn't be a problem according to the *Rashba*.

Another point has been raised from the *Chasam Sofer* (Vol. 6 *Likutim* 29), who seems to indicate that writing many letters at once is not *derech ksivah*. So too in our case, writing an entire page at once is not *derech ksivah*. But a careful read of the *Chasam Sofer* will show he means the opposite. His reference to writing many letters at once is about the thirteen *Sifrei Torah* that *Moshe Rabbeinu* wrote on the last day of his life. That day was Shabbos. How was it permitted to write on Shabbos? The *Chasam Sofer* explains that *Moshe Rabbeinu* used the name of Hashem to make the *kulmus* write the *Sifrei Torah* (by means of a *shvuah*). This, he says, is not *derech ksivah* and is therefore permitted on Shabbos. The reason that type of writing was not *derech ksivah*, the *Chasam Sofer* is saying, is that it wasn't done by hand. The *kulmus* wrote the *Sifrei Torah* by itself. With silk screen, however, all the writing is done by hand, as we have explained, though many letters are written at once. The *Chasam Sofer* does not say that writing many letters at once is not *derech ksivah*. Furthermore, he is speaking about the *Sifrei Torah* of *Moshe Rabbeinu*. Could anyone imagine that *Moshe Rabbeinu's Sifrei Torah* were not kosher? If anything we have proof from here that writing many letters at once is kosher!

The *Rama Mipano* (38) says that if a *sofer* writes with the quill in his mouth, it is invalid because this is not *derech ksivah* (just as when someone right-handed writes with his left hand it is not considered *derech ksivah*). On the other hand, we know that the writing on the *tzitz* was considered *derech ksivah*, even though the manner of writing was different from classic writing. The difference between the case of the *Rama Mipano* and the *tzitz* is this. It is not normal to write with a quill in the mouth, but the *tzitz* was made incorporating the normal way of embossing. Since this is an accepted method of writing, it is considered *derech ksivah*. Silk screening is also a normal process, a method of writing used today around the world by millions. It is in no way similar to using a strange method of writing such as with the mouth.

Lo Chakak—Letters May Not be Etched

The gemara in *Gittin* (20a) says that the letters must be written and not etched, and explains that the problem of *chakikah* (etching) is because of *chak tochos* (etching out the insides of the letters). The commentaries explain that the prohibition of *chak tochos* is violated by performing an action to the area around the letter, thus creating a letter without having done anything to the letter itself. This is not *ksivah.* So too in our case, no action is being performed to form the letter. Rather, the ink is pushed across the screen and the letters are formed on their own. This should be included in the prohibition of *lo chakak.*

It is true that the *sofer* pushes the ink across the screen and that all of the holes are filled in the process. But at this point the *ksivah* has not yet begun. There is no way for the ink to get onto the *klaf* until the *sofer* pushes down on the screen with the squeegee. He must push the ink through the holes in the screen. The letters are written by the *sofer* pushing the *guf ha'os* (the letter itself) directly onto the *klaf.* In order for there to be a problem of *chak tochos,* an action would have to be done to something other than the *guf ha'os.*

This was the main question raised in regard to the printing press *Sefer Torah.* Some rabbis understood that the *klaf* was first engraved in the shape of the letters and then written with ink, posing a problem of *chakikah.* Others maintained that since the *klaf* was pressed down onto the ink instead of the ink being pressed onto the *klaf,* this was like performing an action to something other than the letter, leading to a problem of *chak tochos.* Yet the majority of the rabbis maintained that it was a good *ksivah.* They claimed that the engraving wasn't needed to write the *Sefer Torah* and was done only by those who were inexperienced and were concerned that without first engraving the *klaf,* some letters wouldn't come out nice. In regard to the claim that pressing the *klaf* is *chak tochos,* they argued that there is no difference between pressing the *klaf* onto the ink or pressing the ink onto the *klaf.* Either way, an action is performed to the letter itself.

In any event, this was with the printing press *Sefer Torah.* But even those who considered that *Sefer Torah* invalid would agree that silk screen *Sifrei Torah* pose no question of *chakikah.* That's because the only thing being done to write the letters is the *sofer* pushing ink onto the *klaf.* There isn't any engraving of the *klaf.* Nor is the *klaf* being moved.

Lo Hamatif—Ink My Not be Dripped

The *Yerushalmi* in *Gittin* (chapter 2, halachah 3) says that the letters may not be dripped. There is a dispute in the gemara as to whether that prohibition refers to dripping dots to form the letter and not connecting them, or even if the dots were later connected. The *Ramban* explains the latter opinion as follows: Even if the dots are connected afterwards, it is invalid because this is not *ksivah*. We see from here that making dots in the shape of a letter is not considered *ksivah*, even if they end up connected to form a full letter. The silk screen is composed of many tiny holes. When the letter is formed it consists of many tiny dots of ink, just like in the *Yerushalmi's* case of dripping ink. The full letter isn't formed until after it is pushed onto the *klaf*.

Although the silk screen does consist of millions of holes, and the ink fills those holes, silk screen is in no way comparable to the *Yerushalmi's* case of dripping ink. In that case the entire letter was not complete at the time it was written, as explained by the *Pnei Moshe* (ibid.). With silk screen, by contrast, the moment the *sofer* pushes the letter onto the *klaf*, the letter is written in its entirety. There are no blank spots in the letter, and the ink does not spread once it is on the *klaf*.

Lo Hashofech—Ink May Not be Poured

The aforementioned *Yerushalmi* states another scenario that would render a *Sefer Torah* invalid: The gemara describes a case where one sends his friend a secret letter written with invisible liquid. The paper appears blank, but a special liquid poured on the paper renders the writing visible. (Something like invisible ink.) This method of writing is invalid because the Torah requires a *Sefer Torah* to be written and not poured. With silk screen, the letters are first formed and then pushed onto the *klaf* below. This is comparable to the *Yerushalmi's* case of writing a letter and then pouring ink on the page in order for the writing to appear. When the ink is pushed down onto the page, the letters have already been written.

The *Yerushalmi* prohibits pouring ink as a method of writing because when the ink is poured nothing is being written. The letters were already written before the ink was poured. This is certainly not considered *ksivah*. But with silk screen, the letters are being written on the *klaf* for the first time as the *sofer* pushes the ink down onto the *klaf*. There was nothing there before. Even if one wishes to explain the *Yerushalmi* to mean that pouring ink is forbidden even if the pouring actually writes the letters, it still would have nothing in common with writing silk screen *Sifrei Torah*. One may argue that pouring ink onto a stencil and lifting the stencil to reveal the letters is a problem because the letters weren't written. They merely ended up in the right form because the stencil had holes and the ink filled those holes. But with silk screen, the ink that is spread on the screen is not part of the *ma'aseh ksivah*. The *ma'aseh ksiva* begins when the ink is pushed through the holes and directly onto the *klaf* in the form of a letter.

Does the *Sofer* Have to Copy From a *Sefer*?

The *sofer* is required to copy what he's writing from a written text (*sefer*). How does he fulfill this requirement when writing a silk screen *Sefer Torah*?

A number of reasons are given for the requirement to copy from a *sefer*. The gemara in *Megillah* 18b says that tefillin and mezuzos can be written by heart because people are fluent in them. The *Rashba* explains that that is because everyone is fluent in them. When writing a *Sefer Torah*, by contrast, many people don't know it well, so it is forbidden even for someone who does know it well (a *gezera* for someone who knows it well since there are others who don't). The *Me'iri* says it's forbidden to write a *Sefer Torah* by heart even for someone who knows it well because he may make a mistake. (The *Me'iri* learns that even a *sofer* fluent in the entire Torah may make a mistake.) Both the *Rashba* and *Me'iri* understand the purpose of copying from a *sefer* is to avoid mistakes. The *Ohr Zaruah* (Vol. 1 *Hilchos Tefillin*, *Siman* 545) gives another reason. He maintains that the reason one may not write a *Sefer Torah* by heart is the prohibition of reading Torah *shebiksav* (the Written Torah) by heart (*temurah* 14b). He applies this reasoning to writing as well. Since not everyone is familiar with the entire Torah, it may not be written by heart. But well-known parts of the Torah, he explains, may be recited by heart. Accordingly, tefillin, mezuzos and other parts of the Torah that are well known by all can be said and written by heart. The *Yerushalmi* (*Megillah* chapter 4, halachah 1) also says it is forbidden to write without copying it from a *sefer*. No reason is given. This implies that it is forbidden even if there is no risk of making a mistake. According to the *Yerushalmi*, there's a written command that STa"M (*Sefer Torah*, Tefillin and Mezuzah) may not be written by heart. The *Yerushalmi* is thus saying there is no reason to differentiate between writing a *Sefer Torah* and writing tefillin and mezuzos. *Talmud Bavli,* which makes a distinction between *Sifrei Torah* and tefillin and mezuzos, disagrees with the *Yerushalmi's* reasoning.

According to the *Rashba* and *Me'iri*, the problem of writing without copying from text is the possibility of making a mistake. According to the *Ohr Zaruah,* the problem is writing something that is not well known to all. With silk screen, there is no chance of making a mistake and writing the wrong word. The reasons of the *Rashba* and *Me'iri* apply only where making a mistake is possible. Since with silk screen there is no room for human error when writing the words, there's no concern of writing by heart, and it would be permissible according to the *Bavli*. According to the *Ohr Zaruah*, anyone who writes this way would be considered fluent, since being unfamiliar with the Torah wouldn't lead to any mistakes. The *Ohr Zaruah* himself says that the problem of saying parts of the Torah by heart is that he may make a mistake. Eliminating that possibility, then, eliminates the prohibition of reading Torah *shebiksav* by heart. The *Yerushalmi* is not of concern either, since the Bavli rules otherwise. There are also other opinions in the *Yerushalmi* that disagree with this reason, so this may not be the conclusion of the *Yerushalmi.*

Must the *Sofer* Read the Words He is Writing?

The *sofer* must read from a *sefer* the words that he is about to write. How can he do this when writing a silk screen *Sefer Torah*?

Rashi (*Menachos* 30a), *Tosafos* (ibid.) and others[3] explain that the reason the *sofer* needs to say the words out loud is to avoid making a mistake while writing. The *Magen Avraham* (O"CH 32:42) points out that when writing tefillin and mezuzos, if the *sofer* is copying from a sefer he does not need to say the words out loud. But when writing a *Sefer Torah* or *megillah,* he must say the words out loud even though he is copying from a *sefer.* He explains that the reason for the leniency by tefillin and mezuzah is that people are fluent in them and we are not as worried about mistakes. According to this reasoning, there is no need to say the words before writing a silk screen *Sefer Torah.* Since we are not worried that the *sofer* writing with silk screen will make a mistake, it is comparable to writing tefillin and mezuzos, which is permitted. The *Bach* (O"CH 32:16), however, gives another reason for this halachah. He says that before the *sofer* writes the words he must say them out loud to transfer the *kedushah* coming out of his mouth onto the letters as he writes them on the *klaf.* According to this, the requirement of saying the words out loud has nothing to do with making mistakes. The overwhelming majority of halachic authorities, including the *Shulchan Aruch* (O"CH 32:31), *Magen Avraham, Gra* (O"CH 32:(29)[31]) and *Graz* (O"CH 32:43), do not rule like the *Bach.* There is a strong question on the *Bach* from the gemara in *Menachos* 30a, which says that *Moshe Rabbeinu* didn't say the last eight verses out loud before he wrote them because it pained him. In *Sefer Yirmiyah* (36), *Baruch* wrote the *Kinnos* without saying them either. If the reason to say out loud is to avoid making a mistake, an exception can be made *beshaas hadchak.* But if the words need to be said in order to be *mekadesh* them, how can exceptions be made in a time of pain? We can conclude that *halachah lema'aseh* is not like the *Bach.*

---

3 *Sma"g essin* 22, *Mordechai, halachos ketanos, perek hakometz, siman* 957.

How Does This Compare to the Printing Press Version?

The earlier halachic authorities discussed writing a *Sefer Torah* using a printing press. How does the silk screen process compare? Are there any issues that the rabbis who were lenient regarding the printing press would find with the silk screen Torah? Are there any improvements that the rabbis who were stringent regarding the printing press would find acceptable with the silk screen Torah?

As mentioned previously, the main issue brought up in regard to the printing press *Sefer Torah* was *chak tochos*. We have already explained that silk screen has nothing to do with *chak tochos* since the ink is pushed directly onto the *klaf*. A number of other issues were raised, some that pertain to us and some that do not. Here are some of the issues that do not pertain to us. The *Maharashdam* was concerned that the *ksav* didn't come out nice, regular paper was used, it wasn't written *lishmah*, and it was done with *chakikah*. Silk screen comes out beautiful, kosher *klaf* is used, everything is written *lishmah*, and there is no *chakikah*. *Rav Moshe Provinsalo* was concerned that even if printing *Sifrei Torah* was done without *chakikah*, since it is similar to *chakikah*, one should not print *Sifrei Torah* so as not to come to doing *chakikah*. Silk screen doesn't come close to *chakikah* and would not be confused with *chakikah*. The *Teshuvah Me'ahavah* was concerned with the upside-down letters and the common occurrence of having to discard invalid pages due to the many errors that were made in the process. Again, neither of these have any application to our process. The *Chavos Ya'ir* said that the printed *Sifrei Torah* were invalid because they were written by non-Jews. This would imply that those written by Jews would be okay.

One can safely assume that the many rabbis who considered printing to be a good *ksivah* would certainly consider silk screen a good *ksivah*. There are no known additional issues with silk screen that have not already been addressed by the halachic authorities who discussed the printing press *Sifrei Torah*. Additionally, it is fair to assume that those who considered printing press *Sifrei Torah* invalid, for reasons that do not apply to us, would also approve silk screen *Sifrei Torah*.

Now let's take a look at the issues brought up by the rabbis that do pertain to us. The *Zerah Emes* was concerned that perhaps *chakikah* is not considered *derech ksivah*. We have already addressed this concern (*chakikah* may not be *derech ksivah* but silk screen is). The *Bnei Yonah* raises several issues not mentioned by any of the other rabbis. One issue is that all the letters are written at once and are not formed individually. The *Mas'as Binyamin* argues with him. Many others agree with the *Mas'as Binyamin*, and tens of rabbis who discussed this topic never mentioned this point of the

Bnei Yonah. We have also brought up some strong questions on the *Bnei Yonah*'s stance. Another issue mentioned by the *Bnei Yonah* is the concern that since there is no need for *sirtut*, it will be forgotten. To answer this, we can point out that *sirtut* is indeed used in the process, and why would anybody assume that it will be forgotten? We will always have handwritten *STa"M* that need *sirtut*, and we will always know about *sirtut*. Besides, as long as silk screen *Sifrei Torah* are made by learned God-fearing *soferim* who know the halachah (as is the case), there's no need to come up with new *gezeiros* (rabbinical decrees). Another point made by the *Bnei Yonah* is the issue of writing by heart without first reading the words. We have discussed this at length. Again it is important that none of the other halachic authorities who discussed printing press *Sifrei Torah*, neither the lenient nor the stringent, were concerned with this problem.

Many of the other points discussed in this article were never even brought up by the earlier rabbis, such as the requirement to use a quill, writing from a sefer, *chadash assur min hatorah* and causing a loss of livelihood to other *soferim*. We must conclude that those halachic authorities felt that these issues were of no concern, and posed no compromise to the kashrus of these *Sifrei Torah*.

Can This Process be Used to Write Tefillin and Mezuzos?

Our above analysis applies to a *Sefer Torah*. Can the silk screen process also be used to write tefillin and mezuzos?

The current silk screen process may not be used to write tefillin and mezuzos. This is because all of the lines are written simultaneously, and tefillin and mezuzos must be written in order. All other *kisvei hakodesh*, however, may be written with silk screen. Currently only *Sifrei Torah* and *Megillos Esther* are available.

4. Non-Halachic Arguments

What If This Will Take Away from the Livelihood of Other *Soferim*?

Even if everything checks out as far as the laws of writing a *Sefer Torah* are concerned, what if everyone starts buying silk screen *Sifrei Torah*? This innovation will put all the *soferim* out of business. How can we take away their livelihood?

First and foremost, as religious Jews we have faith in Hashem that He will provide us sustenance. On Rosh Hashanah it is decided how much money a person will make,[4] and Hashem has no shortage of delivery methods. Anyone who thinks otherwise lacks faith.[5] Furthermore, it is unlikely that selling silk screen *Sifrei Torah* will take away from other *soferim*. People who have the means to purchase handwritten *Sifrei Torah* will continue to do so. Silk screen merely expands the market and offers an opportunity for those who previously didn't consider buying a *Sefer Torah*. As a side point, when they began printing *sefarim* instead of handwriting them, some were worried about taking away the livelihood of the scribes who copied *sefarim*. Today *Baruch Hashem* there is an unlimited number of printed *sefarim*, and every Jewish home and *shul* is filled with them. Imagine if someone had prevented *sefarim* from being printed.

What will stop other people from forging *Sifrei Torah*?

Screen printing is a popular and easy-to-use technology. What will stop other people from printing non-kosher *Sifrei Torah*?

Forging *Sifrei Torah* is nothing new. Anyone who buys a *Sefer Torah* must check out thoroughly from whom and from where to buy. Our case is no different. Anyone buying a silk screen *Sefer Torah* must be sure he is buying it from a God-fearing *sofer*. As an extra measure of security, all of the silk screen *Sifrei Torah* written to date have a security feature built in, and the authenticity can easily be verified.

Is it forbidden to create new methods that were not previously used?

There's a common saying that *"chadash assur min hatorah,"* which basically means that new processes are forbidden. How can we go ahead and create something that has not been done in previous generations?

In reality there is no such rule, and many new ideas have been introduced to *Klal Yisrael* throughout our history. Even ideas that were originally rejected because they were new, and there were rabbis who felt that they would lead to bigger problems, were eventually accepted among *Klal Yisrael*. Especially with an idea that has been backed and supported by respected rabbis and performed by God-fearing Jews, we can expect it to be accepted. Perhaps the greatest example is the tumult that was caused with the invention of machine matzos. Many rabbis were adamantly against it while other were for it. Of course we respect the opinion of every rabbi and the point is not to prove who is right or wrong. The point we wish to make is that at the time, people were busy screaming, *chadash*

---

4 *Beitzah* 16a.

5 See *Chovos Halevavos Sha'ar Habitachon* chapter 4.

assur min hatorah! Look how it turned out. Today a large percentage of *Klal Yisrael* eat machine matzos, and for the most part, those who do not, don't say it is *chametz*. What happened to *chadash assur min hatorah*? In the *STa"M* industry too there have been many changes. Machinery has been introduced to the *klaf*- and tefillin-making processes. Plastic quills, new inks and computer checks have been introduced. All of them began with some resistance by people shouting, *"chadash assur min hatorah*." In the end, however, they were all accepted.

This concludes our basic explanation of the halachic and other aspects of silk screen *Sifrei Torah*. A more comprehensive and detailed responsum can be found on this matter in Rabbi Yitzchak Abadi's *She'elos U'tshuvos Ohr Yitzchak* (volume 1, Y"D 53).[6]

5. What Went On Behind The Scenes?

In the 1970s, things were out of control in the world of *STa"M*. The market was flooded with unfit *soferim* and invalid *STa"M*. Something had to be done. In 1975 the *Vaad Mishmeres STa"M*, a group consisting of Torah scholars and God-fearing Jews, was formed to solve these problems. The *Vaad* claimed that between 1976 and 1980 only ten percent of mezuzos were found to be kosher.[7] The *Vaad* set to work removing unfit and fraudulent *soferim* from the market, and checking and removing invalid *STa"M* from the market. They also developed computer software that could check the validity and verify the authenticity of *STa"M*. They educated the public and tested and certified *soferim*. In short, they created a revolution in the *STa"M* industry and did a tremendous job reducing the circulation of invalid *STa"M*, and unfit *soferim*.

Vaad Mishmeres STa"M came to be recognized globally as the leading authority in *STa"M*. They established strong connections with many prominent figures in various Jewish communities and became a powerful and influential organization. It was recommended that any new *sofer* who wanted to get into the *STa"M* market should be tested and certified by the *Vaad*. It was also recommended that anyone who wanted to sell *STa"M* should have his goods verified as kosher by the *Vaad*. All of this helped create a new standard where anything less than 100% kosher was unacceptable. We have a lot for which to thank them.

Naturally, when news of a new method of *ksivah* started circulating, the *Vaad* was interested in learning more about it. For some, there was concern that if the new method became popular, many *soferim* would lose

---

6 See < http://hebrewbooks.org/pdfpager.aspx?req=1525&pgnum=359>.

7 <http://www.shemayisrael.co.il/orgs/stam/guide2.htm>.

their business. During the course of a subsequent discussion an influential person in the community offered a deal to the group producing the silk screen *Sifrei Torah*. He claimed to be able to secure rabbinic consent and overcome all halachic concerns, but in turn he wished to be made a partner in the business venture. When these offers were declined, some people began posting signs belittling the producers of the silk screen *Sifrei Torah*. When that failed to halt the project, they went to various rabbis and misrepresented the technical aspect of silk screen in order to get the rabbis to publicly oppose the methodology. Esteemed halachic authorities gave their opinion on the matter without first seeing the process, and in some cases it is clear from their response that they didn't understand how the process worked. In all probability they trusted those who misrepresented the process because of their respected positions in the community.

Subsequently the *Vaad*, as well as others, actively attempted to persuade the public that the silk screen process is unfit for use. In some cases, those who argued against it on halachic grounds admitted in private that their real opposition was for non-halachic reasons (see above). A number of articles were published to discredit the process. A pamphlet entitled *Ha'emes Vehashalom Ehavu*[8] countered many of those arguments and exposed many distortions.

Although the silk screen process is endorsed by Rabbi Abadi, one of the world's leading *poskim*, subsequent events demonstrate how political pressure can be more influential in determining halachah than the strength of the halachic arguments. Strong political influence is often required to obtain halachic consent on a particular issue. In the case of silk screen, unfortunately, there were no influential people pushing for its acceptance. Proponents of the silk screen method did attempt to speak with different rabbis and demonstrate the process, but in many cases they were denied entry by the rabbis' assistant.

There were a number of rabbis who permitted the use of silk screen but when asked if they would write a letter of approval, they refused. In one case, the grandson of a rabbi who approved the process said that they couldn't write something against another rabbi who had prohibited it. In another case, the son of a rabbi begged his father not to write a letter of approval, fearing the backlash would take a negative toll on his health. In yet another case, a rabbi was surprised to discover his name signed to a letter forbidding silk screen *Sifrei Torah*—a letter he had never before seen. Once the silk screen method became taboo, nobody wanted to speak out in its support.

---

8 < http://www.scribd.com/doc/268208308/Ha-Emet-Vehashalom-Ehavu>.

After the backlash, most people were reluctant to purchase silk screen *Sifrei Torah*. There were others, however, who had no reservations, especially those who followed the *pesak* of Rabbi Yitzchak Abadi.

Quite a few silk screen *Sifrei Torah* and *megillos* were produced and sold, but the project never took off as intended. The group producing the *Sifrei Torah* decided it would be best to let the dust settle before revisiting the topic. Today a few such *Sifrei Torah* and *megillos* are still available, but the project is on hold and silk screen *Sifrei Torah* are not actively being written at this time. Perhaps one day this will change.[9] ☙

9 A video illustrating the silk screen *Sefer Torah* process is available at: < https://www.youtube.com/watch?v=WvFED55xhv8>.

A Statistical Analysis of the Conjunction of Tishrei: The Sin of ADU

By: SHELDON EPSTEIN, YONAH WILAMOWSKY, BERNARD DICKMAN and MAYER WEISS

Introduction

The start of the month of *Tishrei* (Rosh Hashanah, R"H) in the Jewish Lunar Calendar is related to the time of conjunction[1] of the new moon. In reality, the time between successive conjunctions fluctuates, and averages 29 days, 12 hours, and 793 *Chalakim* (i.e., 44 minutes and 3⅓ seconds).[2] To simplify calendrical calculations, the *Molad* rather than the actual conjunction is used. The *Molad* assumes that the time between successive conjunctions is a constant 29D:12H:793C.[3]

Perhaps the best-known acronym concerning the designation of R"H is לא אדו ראש (*Lo ADU Rosh*), i.e., the 1st of *Tishrei* can never be Sunday, Wednesday or Friday.[4] The almost equally well known reason for this is:

If the 1st day of *Tishrei* were:

---

1 When the earth, moon and sun are approximately in a straight line.

2 For a discussion of this value, see Epstein, Dickman and Wilamowsky, "A 5765 Anomaly," *Tradition*, Vol. 38, No. 3, pp. 40–59, Fall 2004.

3 רמבם הלכות ק"הח ו:ג משיתקבץ הירח והחמה לפי חשבון זה עד שיתקבצו פעם שנייה במהלכם האמצעי תשעה ועשרים יום ושתים עשרה שעות מיום שלשים מתחילת לילו, ושבע מאות שלשה ותשעים חלקים משעת שלוש עשרה וזה הוא הזמן שבין כל מולד ומולד וזה הוא חודשה של לבנה.

4 א for the 1st day of the week, ד for the 4th day of the week, and ו for the 6th.

Sheldon Epstein is a Professor of Quantitative Analysis at Seton Hall University and teaches in the Seton Hall - Yeshivah Gedolah of Marine Park Brooklyn (Rabbi Avraham Zucker, *Rosh HaYeshivah*) ITV Graduate Program.

Yonah Wilamowsky is a Professor of Quantitative Analysis at Seton Hall University.

Bernard Dickman is a Professor of Quantitative Analysis at Hofstra University.

Mayer Weiss is an MBA student at Seton Hall University's Graduate School of Business, located in South Orange, New Jersey.

- Sunday, then Hoshana Rabbah would be on Shabbos and there would be no *aravah* ceremony.
- Wednesday or Friday, then Yom Kippur would be on Friday or Sunday. This would result in consecutive days with severe restrictions on burials and food preparation (ירקא and מתיא).[5]

Rambam offers an entirely different reason for excluding ADU days.[6] He asserts that by allowing one day of the week to be R"H and then alternating successive days of the week in which R"H cannot/can occur, discrepancies between the actual conjunction and the *Molad* are reconciled. Thus, starting with Tuesday as a day on which R"H can occur and alternating successive days of the week in the manner described results in R"H never being on ADU. Rambam, however, does not explain:

- How alternating allowable and not allowable sequential days makes it more likely for the resulting calendar to be more consistent with the actual conjunction,
- Why the alternating routine is started on Tuesday, thus resulting in the elimination of ADU rather than starting it on another day and ending with a totally different combination of allowable and non-allowable days.[7]

Ravad, in a caustic gloss, rejects Rambam's explanation and asks "What sin did ADU commit" that the true conjunction never occurs in

---

5 These reasons are alluded to in *Rosh Hashanah* 20a and *Succah* 43a but not with respect to our fixed calendar system. Ravad enunciates it clearly in *K"H* 7: 7. משום יום ערבה שלא יבוא בשבת ומשום יום הכיפורים שלא יבוא לא בערב שבת ולא במוצאי שבת.

6 ומפני מה אין קובעין בחשבון זה בימי אד"ו--לפי שהחשבון הזה הוא לקיבוץ הירח והשמש בהילוכם האמצעי, לא במקומם האמיתי, כמו שהודענו לפיכך עשו יום קביעה ויום דחייה, כדי לפגוע ביום הקיבוץ האמיתי. כיצד--בשלישי קובעין, ברביעי דוחין, בחמישי קובעין, בשישי דוחין, בשבת קובעין, באחד בשבת דוחין, בשני קובעין (ק"ה ז:ז).
Why is it not established when it falls on ADU? Because these calculations determine the average conjunction of the sun and the moon, not their actual true position, as explained. Therefore, they instituted that one day it could be established and on the following day it would be postponed, in order to achieve the day of the true conjunction. How? Tuesday, we establish; Wednesday, we postpone it; Thursday, we establish; Friday, we postpone; Shabbos we establish; Sunday, we postpone; Monday, we establish.

7 E.g., had we started the alternating system with Sunday being a day on which R"H can occur, the result would be R"H occurring on Sunday, Tuesday, Thursday or Shabbos, but never on Monday, Wednesday or Friday (i.e., BDU).

these days?[8] Dr. Hugo Mandlebaum[9] quotes the *Shulchan Aruch Ha-Asid* (Rabbi Yechiel Michel Epstein) explanation of Rambam as follows:

> As Hashem created the moon, He created it in such a fashion, that one day it travels with true speed, and the day after with a mean speed, and the day after that again with true speed, and so on, day after day...

Mandlebaum's response to this is:

> With all due respect to Rabbi Epstein, one should not invent a *metzi'us* (situation) to fit a desired answer.

In this paper we demonstrate that with respect to the actual lunar conjunctions, the days of ADU can be shown to differ quantitatively from the other days of the week. While we do not offer a reason for the difference, we discuss how this difference may help us better understand Rambam's assertion that the ADU deferrals reconcile the conjunction/*Molad* differences.

Variability of the True Conjunction

For any given month, the actual time between two successive *true* conjunctions in the 20th and 21st centuries ranges between approximately 29 days 6.5 hours, and 29 days 20 hours.[10] A detailed analysis of the trend of the relationship between the *Molad* (calendric conjunction) and true conjunctions is given by Mandlebaum. Based on data from 1943 through 1974, he demonstrates that the differences between these two conjunctions, (i.e., *Molad* — true conjunction), form sinusoidal curve cycles that:

- Vary in length from 13 to 16 months;

---

8 א"א מפני שהמחבר הזה מתפאר בחכמה הזאת והוא בעיניו שהגיע לתכליתה ואני איני מאנשיה כי גם רבותי לא הגיעו אליה ע"כ לא נכנסתי בדבריו לבדוק אחריו אך כשפגעתי בדבר הזה שכתב נפלא בעיני הפלא ופלא ואם יהיה המולד בבגה"ז אל הדרך האמצעי למה לא ידחה למחרתו אל המולד האמיתי ולדבריו אין ראוי לעולם לקובעו ביום מולדו ומה חטא אד"ו שלא יהיה בו המולד לעולם באמיתי ולעולם ידחה ומה זכה בגה"ז שיהיה בו ולא ידחה.

9 Mandlebaum, "The Problem of Molad Tohu", *Proceedings of the Association of Orthodox Jewish Scientists*, 1976, Vol. 3–4, pp. 65–84.

10 MEEUS, *Astronomical Algorithms,* 1991, p. 324. Loewinger, *Parshat Bo, Daf Shvui,* No. 116. For the period 1000 BCE until 4000 CE, it ranged from a low of 29 days, 6 hours and 26 minutes (in 302 BCE) to a high of 29 days, 20 hours and 6 minutes (in 400 BCE). (See <http://snahle.tripod.com/ moon.htm>.)

- Have positive and negative segments;[11]
- Vary significantly in terms of maximum and minimum values; and
- Are not symmetrical, i.e., the absolute value of a cycle maximum can vary significantly from the absolute value of its cycle minimum point.

For the 32 years he analyzed, Mandlebaum offers the 1946 cycle and 1969 cycle (Figure 1) as the two most extreme cycles in terms of the magnitude of the difference between the maximum and minimum points, i.e., 15.7 vs –10.8, and 7.7 vs. –3.9.

Figure 1

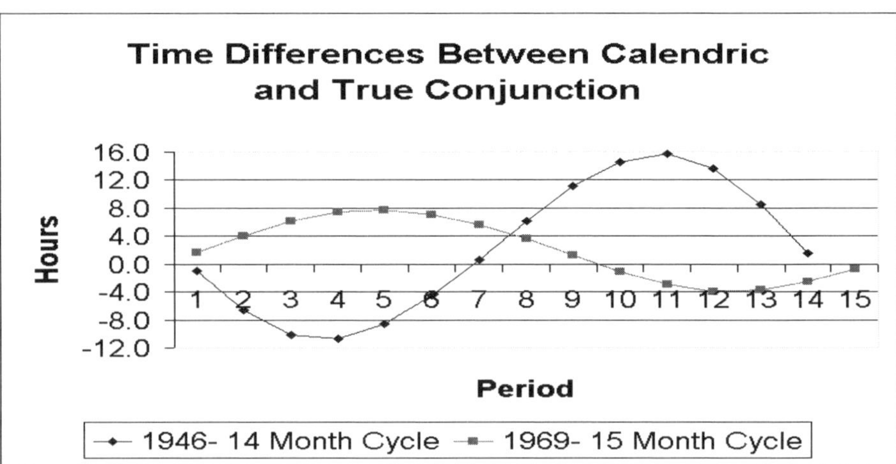

[11] A cycle is a sequence of difference points that begin with the first in a series of positive (or negative) differences and continues through the negative (or positive) differences until it returns once again to a positive (or negative) difference.

Are All Days Created Equal?

Because the *Molad* of a month is based on a calculation that repeatedly adds the same number, it seems intuitively reasonable that it is equally likely that the *Molad* of *Tishrei* would occur in any day of the week (i.e., Uniformly Distributed). However, because of the fluctuation of the inter-conjunction time from month to month, it is by no means obvious how the actual conjunction times are distributed between the days of the week. To test our assumption of the Uniform Distribution of the *Molad* over the days of the week and to see if any pattern is evident in the distribution of the actual conjunction over the days of the week, we initially reviewed the most recent 70 years of data[12] for each set of values. The results are given in Table 1 and pictorially presented in Figure 2.

Table 1
Distribution of the Conjunction[13] and *Molad* 1946–2015

	Conjunction	*Molad*
Sunday	9	9
Monday	11	10
Tuesday	10	11
Wednesday	12	10
Thursday	7	10
Friday	12	10
Shabbos	9	10
Total	70	70

12 The source for the true conjunction time is: US Naval Observatory Website: <http://aa.usno.navy.mil/data/docs/MoonPhase.php>. The data from this site had to be adjusted from: i) Greenwich Mean Time to Jerusalem Standard Time; ii) standard convention of new day starting at midnight to Jewish convention of new day starting at sunset. Note that at *Tishrei* time the sun sets very close to 6 pm.

13 See Appendix 1 for a full listing of the data.

Figure 2
Distribution of the Conjunction and *Molad* 1946–2015

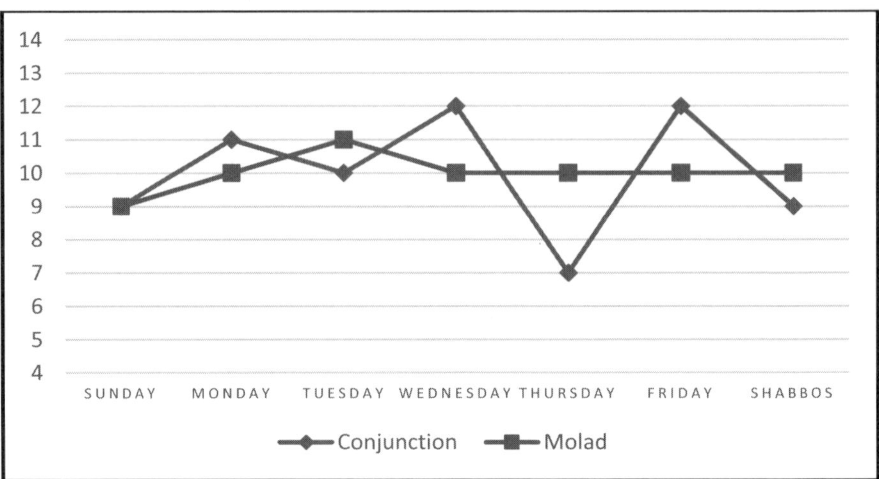

Our assumption about the distribution of the *Molad* over the days of the week is consistent with the data as 5 of the 7 days appear the expected 10 times and the other two days are one more or less than expected (i.e., 9 and 11 respectively). The distribution of the actual conjunction shows considerable variability ranging from a low of 7 for Thursday to a high of 12 for Wednesday and Friday. Although nothing stood out about Sunday (the A of ADU), the DU days of ADU (i.e., Wednesday and Friday) appear disproportionately overrepresented (i.e., 20% more than expected) as they represent only 2/7 (28.6%) of the days of the week but appear 24 times (34.3%) out of the total 70 observations. To see whether this frequency distribution was a localized current phenomenon, we reviewed the conjunction and *Molad* data for a 400 year period,[14] 1700 through 2099. The results are given in the next section.

---

[14] The years to be included in the study were chosen because they are the years for which the True Conjunction data is available on the Naval Observatory website.

Analysis of 400 Years of Conjunction and *Molad* Data[15]

Table 2 summarizes the results of a 400-year review of conjunction and *Molad* data.

Table 2
Distribution of the Conjunction and *Molad* 1700–2099

	Conjunction	*Molad*
Sunday	67	59
Monday	57	55
Tuesday	52	58
Wednesday	67	57
Thursday	44	57
Friday	69	58
Shabbos	44	56
Total	400	400

Table 2 confirms and extends the implications of Table l. The results are dramatically highlighted in Figure 3. With respect to the *Molad,* note the almost flat horizontal line of the graph. Even more strikingly, note how the days of ADU: represent the 3 peak points on the graph; are almost exactly the same; and the graph significantly declines after each of them. These 3 days represent 42.9% of the days of the week but 50.8% (203 out of 400) of the data points (18% more than expected). In general, the distribution of the conjunction among the days of the week appears to be broken into three groups:

Sunday, Wednesday, Friday	—	High Frequency
Monday, Tuesday	—	Intermediate Frequency
Thursday, Shabbos	—	Low Frequency.

For a statistical analysis of these results, see Appendix 2.

15 The raw data is available on line at <www.Hakirah.org/vol19_400Years.xls>. We note that based on Mandlebaum's analysis of the relationship between conjunction and *Molad,* it is possible that the *Molad* occurs the day before the conjunction. However, this occurred only 6 times in the 400 year period, i.e., 1749, 1765, 1872, 1934, 1996 and 2094. While there were many cases of the *Molad* coming before the conjunction, in the overwhelming number of cases they both were on the same day.

Figure 3
Distribution of the Conjunction and *Molad* 1700–2099

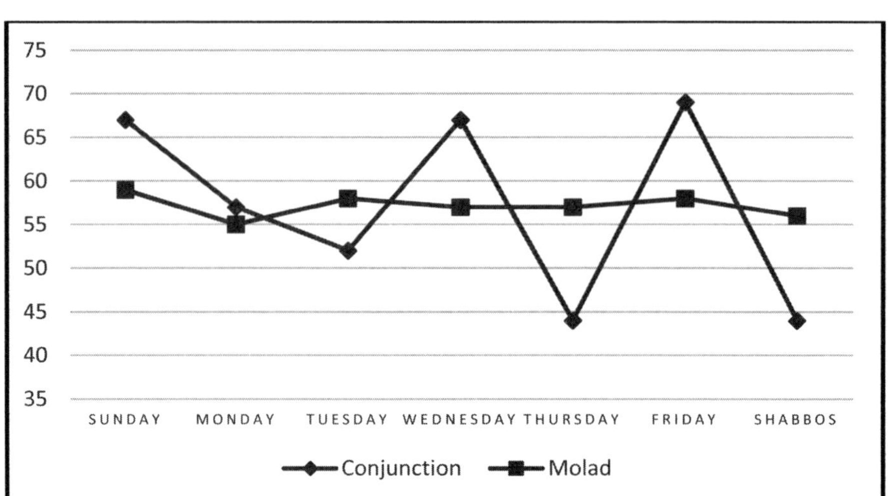

Discussion and Implications

As we said in the Introductory Section, Rambam highlighted the ADU days as being different from the other days but offered no explanation of how or why. Our presentation demonstrates that in fact the *metzi'us* (see Mandlebaum, above) is that Sunday, Wednesday and Friday *are* different than the other days in the week vis-à-vis the actual conjunction. Furthermore, whereas Ravad mocks Rambam for allegedly saying that the true conjunction seldom appears in these days, we have shown that to the contrary it is "more" likely that the conjunction occurs in ADU. The questions that remain are how and why all of these observations justify avoiding declaring R"H on these days. In this final section we will offer some preliminary thoughts.[16]

It is informative in studying our current fixed calendar system to briefly review the "sighting" system (ראיה) which preceded it. Rambam (*K"H* 5:1–3) says that the former system is the preferred one and it was in place from the time of the Exodus until the days of Abaya and Rava when

16 Ultimately whatever we suggest also has to address the other major calendar rule: If the *Molad* occurs on Monday, Tuesday, Thursday or Shabbos

- Before noon: R"H is that day
- After noon: R"H is pushed off to the first day that is not ADU.

We have not yet analyzed the conjunction frequency across the hours of the day.

the Sanhedrin ceased to exist. In the sighting system, the new month begins at the time of the first physical observation of the new moon, with moonrise and moonset occurring in very close proximity to sunset. First sighting is one of several alternate ways of determining the start of a new month in a lunar system. Some societies in the ancient world used last sighting (i.e., the last time the old moon was confirmed, seen) while others used the time of conjunction. Rambam explains, that even when "first sighting" was the system in place, the most sophisticated calculations for the time of the true conjunction were conducted to make sure that the sightings that were reported were possible (Rambam, *K"H* 1:6).[17] Since first visibility never takes place on the day of the conjunction, the day of conjunction could not be Rosh Chodesh or R"H. Thus, even though they knew the exact time of the conjunction they preferred to start the new month up to a day or two later[18] — when the first sighting took place.[19]

ᘓ

---

17 Rabbeinu Bachaya, *Shemos* 12:1 disagrees with Rambam. He cites Rabbeinu Chananel who maintains that calculation was the intended approach and "sighting" began in Tannaic times.
ועניין החודש הזה לכם ראש חדשים אין כונת הכתוב להזהיר אותנו לעבר שנים ולקבוע חדשים על פי ראיית הלבנה כי בקביעות החדשים אין עיקר בתורה לחוש לראית הלבנה אם תראה מוטב ואם לא תראה ביום הקביעות אלא קודם לכן או אחרי כן ליום או יומים אין אנו חוששים כי לא נצטוינו בתורה לקבוע החדשים על פי ראית הלבנה כי אם על פי חשבון וכתב רבינו חננאל ז״ל קביעות החדשים אינו אלא על פי החשבון לא על פי ראית הלבנה והראיה שכל ארבעים שנה שהיו ישראל במדבר היה הענן מכסה אותם ביום ועמוד האש לילה ולא ראו בכלם שמש ביום ולא ירח בלילה והוא שאמר הכתוב (נחמיה ט) ואתה ברחמיך הרבים לא עזבתם במדבר את עמוד הענן לא סר מעליהם יומם להנחותם בהדרך ואת עמוד האש לילה להאיר להם ומהיכן היו קובעים חדשים על פי ראית הלבנה אלא בודאי עקר המצוה בכתוב על פיה חשבון.

18 Rambam K"H 1:3. Loewinger, *Parshat Bo, Daf Shvui*, no. 116, section 2, writes:

> "The first possible sighting, even under exceptionally good conditions, can occur only after about 13 hours (with optical aid) or after 15 hours (unaided vision) from the time of the *true Molad.*"

Thus, "sighting" never takes place on the conjunction day but could occur at sunset at the end of the conjunction day if the conjunction was before 3:00 am (i.e., 15 hours before sunset at 6:00 pm). If the conjunction is after 3:00 am the first sighting occurs at sunset of the day after the conjunction. We have not as yet reviewed the probability of it occurring before or after 3:00 am. See footnote 16.

19 According to Rabbeinu Bachaya's approach it is possible that the beginning of the new month should be determined solely by time of conjunction but since a month cannot begin in the middle of a day, the start of the month is delayed to the day after conjunction so that the entire day, from a lunar perspective, is in this new month.

Appendix 1
Conjunction and *Molad* of Tishrei 5706–5775 (1946–2015)

Year	Conjunction Day	***Molad*** Day	Yea	Conjunction Day	***Molad*** Day
5706	Thursday	Friday	5741	Tuesday	Wednesday
5707	Wednesday	Thursday	5742	Monday	Tuesday
5708	Monday	Monday	5743	Friday	Shabbos
5709	Sunday	Sunday	5744	Wednesday	Wednesday
5710	Thursday	Thursday	5745	Tuesday	Tuesday
5711	Tuesday	Tuesday	5746	Sunday	Sunday
5712	Monday	Monday	5747	Shabbos	Shabbos
5713	Friday	Friday	5748	Wednesday	Wednesday
5714	Tuesday	Tuesday	5749	Sunday	Sunday
5715	Monday	Monday	5750	Shabbos	Shabbos
5716	Friday	Shabbos	5751	Wednesday	Thursday
5717	Wednesday	Wednesday	5752	Sunday	Monday
5718	Tuesday	Tuesday	5753	Shabbos	Sunday
5719	Shabbos	Shabbos	5754	Thursday	Thursday
5720	Friday	Friday	5755	Tuesday	Tuesday
5721	Wednesday	Wednesday	5756	Monday	Sunday
5722	Sunday	Sunday	5757	Friday	Friday
5723	Shabbos	Shabbos	5758	Thursday	Thursday
5724	Wednesday	Wednesday	5759	Monday	Monday
5725	Sunday	Monday	5760	Friday	Friday
5726	Shabbos	Sunday	5761	Thursday	Thursday
5727	Thursday	Thursday	5762	Monday	Tuesday
5728	Wednesday	Wednesday	5763	Shabbos	Shabbos
5729	Sunday	Sunday	5764	Friday	Friday
5730	Friday	Friday	5765	Tuesday	Tuesday
5731	Wednesday	Wednesday	5766	Monday	Monday
5732	Sunday	Monday	5767	Friday	Shabbos
5733	Friday	Friday	5768	Tuesday	Wednesday
5734	Wednesday	Thursday	5769	Monday	Tuesday
5735	Monday	Monday	5770	Shabbos	Shabbos
5736	Shabbos	Shabbos	5771	Wednesday	Thursday
5737	Friday	Friday	5772	Tuesday	Tuesday
5738	Tuesday	Tuesday	5773	Sunday	Sunday
5739	Monday	Monday	5774	Thursday	Thursday
5740	Friday	Friday	5775	Wednesday	Wednesday

Appendix 2
χ^2 (Chi-Square) Test of Significance

The Chi-Squared Goodness of Fit Test is used to determine whether there is a significant difference between the expected frequencies and the observed frequencies in one or more categories. In this case we are starting with the hypothesis that the true conjunction is Uniformly Distributed across the days of the week and testing to see whether the sample is consistent with this assumption. To test this hypothesis we compare the actual data to the expected values based on the hypothesis (i.e., all days being equally likely — thus for 400 trials each day is expected to occur 400/7 times) as follows:

χ^2 (Chi-Square) Test for Uniformity for 1700–2099

	Actual	Expected	$(A\text{-}E)^2/E$
Sunday	67	57.1	1.700357143
Monday	57	57.1	0.000357143
Tuesday	52	57.1	0.462857143
Wednesday	67	57.1	1.700357143
Thursday	44	57.1	3.022857143
Friday	69	57.1	2.460357143
Saturday	44	57.1	3.022857143
Total	400	400	12.37
		p- value	0.054

The bottom row indicates there is less than 6% chance that the data is in fact Uniformly Distributed.

"Our Own Joy is Lessened and Incomplete": The History of an Interpretation of Sixteen Drops of Wine at the Seder

By: ZVI RON

Explaining the custom to remove sixteen drops of wine from the cup as we recite the ten plagues and words associated with them, the *Artscroll Youth Haggadah* writes that "we don't want our cups to be full when we tell about other people's pain."[1] The idea that we remove some wine to show that we cannot fully rejoice when our enemies are destroyed is also found in the *Artscroll Mesorah Series Haggadah*: "Abarbanel, however, explains that we should remove the wine because "You should not rejoice when your enemy falls" (Mishlei 24:17)."[2] This idea does not actually appear in the Abarbanel's commentary to the Haggadah, or in any of his writings. In fact, this explanation for the custom of removing sixteen drops from the cup of wine is a recent innovation. By now it is so entrenched in Haggadot that it is often the only explanation offered. A typical presentation of this idea is, "By spilling a drop of wine from the Pesach cup for each plague, we acknowledge that our own joy is lessened and incomplete, for our redemption had to come by means of the punishment of other human beings. Even though these are just punishments for evil acts, it says, "Do not rejoice at the fall of your enemy" (Proverbs 24:17)."[3] In this article we will trace the development of this interpretation of this cherished Seder-night custom.

---

1 Rabbis Nosson and Yitzchok Zev Scherman, *Artscroll Youth Haggadah* (Brooklyn, NY: Mesorah Publications, 1995), p. 25.

2 R. Joseph Elias, *Artscroll Mesorah Series Haggadah* (Brooklyn, NY: Mesorah Publications, 1977), p. 127.

3 Noam Zion and David Dishon, *The Family Participation Haggadah: A Different Night* (Jerusalem: Shalom Hartman Institute, 1997), p. 101.

Zvi Ron received *semikhah* from the Israeli Rabbanut and his PhD in Jewish Theology from Spertus University. He is an educator living in Neve Daniel, Israel, and the author of *Sefer Katan ve-Gadol* (Rossi Publications, 2006) about the big and small letters in Tanakh.

Origin of the Custom

The earliest reference to this custom, and to an explanation for it, is found in a Pesach sermon of Rabbi Eleazer of Worms (c. 1176–1238), the Rokeach. "For each word a finger [goes] into the cup of wine and they spill out a drop, matching the sword of the Holy One, blessed be He, which has sixteen sides. And the sixteen mentions of plague in Jeremiah. [This custom] teaches us that we will not be injured. Based upon [this] our ancestors created this custom. And sixteen times the word *ḥayyim* [appears in Psalm 119], and sixteen people read the Torah each week,[4] matching the sixteen lambs that are sacrificed in a week. Also, "She is [16 = הי"א] a tree of life to those who grasp her" (Proverbs 3:18). And one should not ridicule the custom of our holy ancestors."[5] This explanation is quoted in *Sefer Amarcal* in the name of the Rokeach, along with a list of rabbis who observed this custom.[6] That the Rokeach emphasized not to make fun of this custom, and that *Sefer Amarcal* brought "an impressive array of names of the German Hasidim"[7] who kept this custom, indicates that it was one of the customs of Chasidei Ashkenaz that were indeed subject to ridicule.[8] The custom is brought in *Sefer Maharil*, quoting the Rokeach and others, where it is explained that the idea is that God should "save us from all these and they should fall upon our enemies."[9] Thus, the sixteen drops are intended to ward off the danger from the sixteen-faced sword of God.[10] The custom is mentioned by R. Moshe Isserles in his comments

4 Seven on Shabbat morning, three Shabbat afternoon, and three each on Monday and Thursday.

5 Simcha Emanuel, editor, *Rabbi Eleazar of Worms: Drasha l'Pesach* (Jerusalem: Mekitzei Nirdamim, 2006), p. 101. Translation based on the one in Joshua Kulp and David Golinkin, *The Schechter Haggadah: Art, History and Commentary* (Jerusalem: Schechter Institute of Jewish Studies, 2009), p. 233.

6 Michael Hager, ed., *Sefer Amarcal al Hilchot Pesach*, siman 30, p. 164 in *Alexander Marx Jubilee Volume – Hebrew Section* (New York: Jewish Theological Seminary, 1950). The author of *Sefer Amarcal* is unknown.

7 Heinrich Guggenheimer, *The Scholar's Haggadah* (Northvale, New Jersey: Jason Aronson, Inc., 1998), p. 302.

8 Avraham Grossman, *The Early Sages of Ashkenaz* (Jerusalem: The Hebrew University Magnes Press, 2001), p. 230, note 105.

9 Shlomo J. Spitzer, editor, *Sefer Maharil* (Jerusalem: Machon Yerushalayim, 1989), pp. 106-107.

10 Joshua Trachtenberg, *Jewish Magic and Superstition* (New York: Athenium, 1984), p. 167; Joshua Kulp and David Golinkin, *The Schechter Haggadah: Art, History and Commentary* (Jerusalem: Schechter Institute of Jewish Studies, 2009), p. 233. In light of this, there may be an additional reason for the custom to use the pinky finger to remove the drops. *Magen Avraham* O.H. 473:28 brings opinions that

on the *Tur* (*Darkei Moshe*, O.H. 473:18) and in his glosses to the *Shulchan Aruch* (O.H. 473:7). In *Darkei Moshe* he quotes the Maharil, and adds that this custom hints to the "the angel in charge of vengeance."

The original explanation can be somewhat difficult to use in the context of a family Seder, as it is based on the idea of the sixteen-sided sword of God and the general symbolism behind the number sixteen, something not widely known or easily related. In the late 19th and early 20th centuries we find a simpler reason offered in popular books of explanations for customs, that the removal of drops of wine from the cup parallels the Egyptians, who were "lessened" with every plague. This explanation is found in the widely read *Sefer Matamim*,[11] *Minhagei Yeshurun*,[12] *Otzar Dinim u'Minhagim*[13] and *Sefer Ta'amei haMinhagim*.[14] *Mishna Berura* explains that the 16 drops represent the first two letters of God's Name (O.H. 473:75). R. Reuven Margaliot, in his 1937 Haggadah commentary *Be'er Miriam*, explains that the removal of drops represents that the plagues are only a small drop from the cups of retribution and punishment that the nations that persecute Israel will drink from in the future.[15] These explanations generally relate the custom to some aspect of vengeance against enemies.[16] They contain no trace of the idea of "incomplete joy" due to the suffering of the Egyptians, and seem diametrically opposed to it.

---

either the index, ring or little finger is used. It is known that the little finger was understood to have apotropaic powers in European folk culture; see A.B. Strachov, "Miscellanea Meterologica Slavica: "Breaking" the Rainbow in Poles'e," *Die Welt der Slaven* vol. 33 (1988), pp. 338-339, where the little finger is used to ward off demonic forces and spells from water and wedding feasts. See also my article, "Pointing to the Torah and Other Hagbaha Customs," *Ḥakirah* vol. 15, Summer 2013, pp. 301–303.

11 Yitzchak Liefitz, *Sefer Matamim* (Warsaw: 1890), p. 56, item 55. Although he seems to reference the *Hagahot haMinhagim* to R. Issac Tirnau's *Sefer Minhagim* as his source, the custom is found there (note 98) but without an explanation. In Haggadot that are more careful about quoting sources, this explanation is cited as being "in the name of *Sefer Minhagim*" rather than actually appearing there. See, Abraham Natan Barnett, *Haggadah Shel Pesach im Likutim Nechemadim* (Jerusalem: 1959), p. 3.

12 Avraham Hershovitz, *Otzar Kol Minhagei Yeshurun* (Vilna: 1899), p. 34, siman 120.

13 J. D. Eisenstein, *Otzar Dinim u'Minhagim* (New York: 1917), p. 282.

14 Abraham Sperling, *Sefer Ta'amei haMinhagim u'Mekorei haDinim* (Lemberg: 1928), p. 66, siman 538.

15 Reuven Margaliot, *Haggadah Shel Pesach – Be'er Miriam, Kehilat Moshe* (Tel Aviv: Margaliot, 1937), p. 40. This explanation is sometimes attributed to the Vilna Gaon, since it may be hinted to in *Biur ha-Gra* O.C. 473:45.

16 Israel Yuval, "Vengeance and Damnation, Blood and Defamation: From Jewish Martyrdom to Blood Libel Accusations," *Zion* vol. 58:1 (1993), p. 38 (Hebrew).

Abbreviated Hallel

The disseminators of the "incomplete joy" explanation generally relate it to a reason given in the midrash for the recital on Sukkot of the full Hallel every day, but on Passover only on the first day, the rest having the abbreviated Hallel. The halachic reason for this, found in the Talmud (B. Arachin 10a, b), is that on Sukkot there are different *Mussaf* sacrifices offered each day, so each day of Sukkot is considered a distinct holiday, whereas on Pesach the same *Mussaf* sacrifice is offered each day. Because of this, on each day of Sukkot the full Hallel is said, but only on the first day of Pesach. Another answer, however, is found in the midrashic literature. The 13th-century work *Shibbolei haLeket* (siman 174), quoted by R. Yosef Caro (*Beit Yosef* O.C. 490:4), brings in the name of *Midrash Harninu*, a midrash collection lost to us today,[17] that Shmuel b. Abba taught that the reason only an abbreviated Hallel is recited after the first day of Pesach is that the Egyptians drowned and "If your enemy falls do not exult" (Proverbs 24:17). This seems to be based on the episode mentioned in the Talmud (B. Megilla 10b, B. Sanhedrin 39b) that when the Egyptians were drowning in Yam Suf, God silenced the angels who wanted to sing, saying that it is not appropriate to do so when His "handiwork is drowning in the sea." It should be noted, however, that the Israelites themselves did sing *Shirat haYam* at this point, and this was not viewed as problematic. Whatever the merits of this particular midrashic explanation for not reciting the full Hallel throughout Pesach,[18] it does not seem to apply to the custom of removing drops of wine from the cup, since that is done on the Seder night when we do in fact recite the full Hallel and do not seem to limit our joy.

---

17 See J.D. Eisenstein, *Ozar Midrashim* (New York: Noble Offset Printers, 1915), p. 137.

18 See the excellent overview of this midrashic explanation by Dr. Avi Zivotofsky in "What's the Truth About…Hallel on Pesach?," *Jewish Action*, volume 60, number 3, Spring 5760/2000. See also the comments of R. Avigdor Nebenzahl, *Yerushalayim be-Moadehah – Pesach* (Jerusalem: Machon Keren Reem, 2005), p. 160. It is worth noting that the idea of displaying mercy toward Egyptian adversaries is also found in the Pseudepigrapha, in *Joseph and Asenath*, a first-century Jewish romance written in Egypt. In the story, when Benjamin is ready to kill Pharaoh's firstborn son, the villain of the story, he is stopped by Levi, who explains, "By no means, brother, will you do this deed, because we are men who worship God, and it does not befit a man who worships God to repay evil for evil nor to trample underfoot a fallen (man) nor to oppress his enemy till death" (29:3). See E.P. Sanders, *Judaism: Practice and Belief 63 BCE – 66 CE* (London: SCM Press, 1994), p. 234.

This explanation for the abbreviated Hallel is also found in some versions of *Pseikta d'Rav Kahana*[19] and in *Yalkut Shimoni* (*Emor*, *remez* 654), but there the midrash begins by asking why the Torah uses the term *simcha*, joy, three times relating to Sukkot but not even once relating to Pesach. Two answers are given. The first is that since judgment is passed on the crops on Pesach and people do not know if their fields will produce crops or not in the coming year, there is incomplete joy on Pesach. The second answer given is "because the Egyptians died." The midrash then says this is also why on Pesach only the abbreviated Hallel is recited after the first day, while on Sukkot a full Hallel is said every day. This expanded version of the midrash is more relevant to the "incomplete joy" explanation. The version in *Shibbolei haLeket* relates only to the abbreviated Hallel, making it irrelevant to the first day of Pesach. In the expanded version, the Torah's omission of the term *simcha* when dealing with Pesach indicates that even on the first day of Pesach there is a lack of joy because of the death of the Egyptians.

English-Language Haggadot

The "incomplete joy" explanation was popularized by being the only one presented in many early English-language Haggadot intended for laypeople. A 1929 English-translation Haggadah published by the Austrian/Hungarian Schlesinger publishing house explains the custom as indicating that "we cannot celebrate the feast of our deliverance full of joy when so many thousands of human beings have perished," and says that "from this cause also, in the last days of Passover, Hallel, the prayer of thanksgiving, is recited only to the half."[20] The Schlesinger's prayer books "were especially popular" throughout the early 1900s.[21] Variations of this Haggadah were continually reprinted and expanded over the years in English-language Haggadot published in Israel after the Schlesinger publishing company moved to Tel Aviv in the late 1930s and changed its name to the Sinai Publishing Company.[22]

---

19 Bernard Mandelbaum, editor, *Pesikta de Rav Kahana* (New York: The Jewish Theological Seminary of America, 1987), p. 458.

20 Joseph Loewy and Joseph Guens, *Service for the First Nights of Passover* (Vienna: Joseph Schlesinger, 1929), p. 20.

21 Kinga Frojimovics, ed., *Jewish Budapest: Monuments, Rites and History* (Budapest: Central European University Press, 1999), p. 179.

22 In some later editions the authors of the notes are not even named. The "Bezalel" Haggadah illustrated by Zeev Raban (Tel Aviv: Sinai, 1965), p. 31, for example, gives this explanation world for word, but no author is listed anywhere

In the 1940s, 50s and 60s this explanation became ubiquitous in American Haggadot.[23] The explanation is presented in the "Introductory Note" by Louis Finkelstein to a 1942 English-translation Haggadah: "The spilling of wine at the mention of the plagues is interpreted as a symbol of regret that the victory had to be purchased by the death of the Egyptians."[24] Finkelstein was "the dominant figure of Conservative Judaism in the twentieth century" and was chancellor of the Jewish Theological Seminary at the time he wrote that introduction.[25] The Haggadah edited by David and Tamar De Sola Pool, first published in 1943 by the National Jewish Welfare Board "for members of the armed forces of the United States," similarly explains that "a drop of wine of rejoicing is diminished from the cup in sign of pity for the suffering Egyptians."[26] This Haggadah, composed by a committee of Orthodox, Conservative and Reform rabbis for Jewish soldiers who were fighting in World War II, addresses the "compatibility of Jewish and American values."[27] The American value

---

in the book. On the history of the Schlesinger publishing company, see Frojimovics, p. 179; Istvan Ormos, "David Kaufmann and His Collection" in Eva Apor, editor, *David Kaufmann Memorial Volume* (Budapest: Library of the Hungarian Academy of Sciences, 2002), p. 140, note 44.

23 Earlier English-translation Haggadot generally either do not explain the reason for the custom, or still give explanations closer to the original one. For example, J.D. Eisenstein's *Hagada: Seder Ritual for Passover Eve* (New York: Hebrew Publishing Company, 1928), p. 18, explains that "we spill out a drop of wine at the mention of each plague to indicate we are immune from the plagues."

24 Maurice Samuel, *Haggadah for Passover* (New York: Hebrew Publishing Company, 1942), p. xvii.

25 Lawrence Hoffman and David Arnow, editors, *My People's Passover Haggadah: Traditional Texts, Modern Commentaries, volume 1* (Woodstock, VT: Jewish Lights Publishing, 2008), p. 83.

26 David and Tamar De Sola Pool, *The Haggadah of Passover* (New York: Jewish Welfare Board, 1943), p. 38. This Haggadah contains essentially no commentary and this explanation was written as part of the instructions before reciting the ten plagues. This Haggadah was republished throughout the 1940s and 1950s.

27 Joel Gereboff, "One Nation, with Liberty and Haggadahs for All," in Jack Kugelmass, editor, *Key Texts in American Jewish Culture* (New Jersey: Rutgers University Press, 2003), p. 285. Translated Haggadot often dealt with the changing sensibilities of their intended readership. See for example A.A. Green, *The Revised Hagada* (London: George Routledge and Sons, 1897), p. 3, where the author explains that he did not translate "nine months of pregnancy" in the song *Echad Mi Yodea* and instead "substituted the nine Jewish festivals as more in consonance with our modern ideas of what is adapted for the perusal of children."

here is "the liberal ethic, believing that all people are essentially good," so that punishing the Egyptians "seems so vindictive and vengeful."[28]

The Haggadah edited by Philip Birnbaum for the Hebrew Publishing Company in 1953 also states that the custom "is intended to stress the idea that we must not rejoice over the misfortunes that befell our foes."[29] The Birnbaum Haggadah was considered the standard traditional Haggadah for English speakers until the first Artscroll Haggadah was published in 1977[30] and, as noted above, also included this explanation. This explanation is brought in the 1959 *Passover Haggadah* by Morris Silverman,[31] a Conservative rabbi responsible for the movement's *Sabbath and Festival Prayerbook*, whose "name had become synonymous with Conservative Judaism's liturgy."[32] Rabbi Shlomo Kahn's 1960 Haggadah, *From Twilight Till Dawn*, billed "the traditional Passover Haggadah," also explains this custom as limiting our joy, reminding us that the Egyptians, "although our enemies and tormentors, were fellow human beings nevertheless."[33] This Haggadah, reprinted in 1969, is the only English-language Haggadah prior to the late seventies that "includes much longer translations of traditional commentaries,"[34] so that even a more scholarly audience was presented with this explanation.

We can say that since World War II, every American Haggadah aimed at a primarily English-speaking audience and offering an explanation for this custom provided the "incomplete joy" explanation, and in most such Haggadot it was the only explanation offered.[35] By now it is widespread

---

28 Nathan Laufer, *Leading the Passover Journey: The Seder's Meaning Revealed, The Haggadah's Story Retold* (Woodstock, Vermont: Jewish Lights Publishing, 2005), p. 92. See there his critique of this entire approach to the plagues.

29 Philip Birnbaum, *Haggadah* (New York: Hebrew Publishing Company, 1953), p. 38.

30 Hoffman and Arnow, p. 84.

31 Morris Silverman, *Passover Haggadah* (Hartforn, Conneticut: Prayer Book Press, 1959), p. 20.

32 Hoffman and Arnow, p. 83.

33 Shlomo Kahn, *From Twilight to Dawn* (New York: Scribe Publications, 1960), p. 60.

34 Gereboff, p. 283.

35 There are almost as many examples as there are Haggadot. See, for example, Sidney B. Hoenig, *The Haggadah of Passover with Introductory Notes and Supplement* (New York: Shulsinger Brothers, 1950), p. 11, "it may also show that we *symbolically* cast a tear at the mention of each plague" (italics in the original). Arthur Gilbert, *The Passover Seder: Pathways Through the Haggadah* (New York: Ktav, 1965), p. 31, writes that it is a "symbol of regret that the victory had to be purchased through misfortune visited upon God's creatures, the Egyptians." This seems to be based on Finkelstein's phrasing. Alfred J. Kolatch, *The Family Seder – A Tra-*

and better known than the original one. It is even the explanation given on the Wikipedia entry for "Passover Seder"![36]

This approach is found in more scholarly Orthodox literature as well.[37] It is particularly prevalent in works written by people connected to English-speaking countries, where this explanation was most widely popularized. It is included, for example, in R. David Feinstein's *The Kol Dodi Haggadah*[38] and Rabbi Yaakov Wehl's *The Haggadah with Answers*, in both the Hebrew and English versions.[39] Rabbi Yechezkel Abramsky discusses

ditional Passover Haggadah for the Modern Home (New York: Jonathan David Publishers, 1967), p. 38, states, "This practice has been explained as an expression of our unhappiness over the misfortune suffered by the Egyptians…The thought of rejoicing over the suffering of others is alien to Judaism, even where punishment may be justified." Zev Schostak, *Why is This Night Different?* (New York: Artscroll Studios, 1977), p. 57, writes, "As we recall the downfall of our enemies, we recall that they were creatures of God and our joy is incomplete." The famed Maxwell House Haggadah does not mention this explanation, nor did it even note the custom in its earlier editions. Later editions instruct that wine be removed from the cup but offer no explanation. The "incomplete joy" explanation is also brought in Yiddish in the Yiddish-and-English-translated *Passover Haggadah* by Nathan Mandel (New York: 1954), p. 65, the source given as "I have heard." This explanation is featured in other translated Haggadot from this time period as well, and is the only one offered in the French *La Haggadah de Paque* by Joseph Bloch (Paris: 1950), p. 36. It is also the only explanation found in the National Jewish Outreach Program's *Beginners Passover Haggadah* (New York: NJOP Publications, 2010), p. 18.

36 "With the recital of the Ten Plagues, each participant removes a drop of wine from his or her cup using a fingertip. Although this night is one of salvation, the sages explain that one cannot be completely joyous when some of God's creatures had to suffer." http://en.wikipedia.org/wiki/Passover_Seder.

37 To name a few, it is brought in the name of Abarbanel in Yaakov Weingarten, *ha-Seder ha-Aruch, volume 2* (Jerusalem: Machon Otzar HaMoadim, 1992), pp. 178, 179; it is brought without attribution in R. Ephraim Greenblatt, *Rivevot Ephraim, Orach Chayyim, volume 2* (Brooklyn, NY: Deutsch Printing and Publishing Co., 1978), siman 137, p. 361; R. Moshe Zvi Holzberg, "*Biur Makkot Mitzraim*" in *Kovetz Beit Aharon* 33, Shvat-Adar 5751/1991, p. 50; and in the name of Abarbanel in R. Yoel Friedman, "*Yayin Shel Shvi'it b'Leil haSeder,*" in *Emunat Itecha* 3, Shvat-Adar 5755/1995, reprinted in R. Yoel Friedman, ed., *HaTorah v'HaAretz* (Jerusalem: Chemed, 2001), p. 227.

38 R. David Feinstein, *The Kol Dodi Haggadah* (Brooklyn, New York: Mesorah Publications in conjunction with Mesivta Tifereth Jerusalem, 1990), p. 106. There it is stated that the wine is removed "in consideration for the losses caused by the plagues." This appears in the Hebrew original (New York: Tiferet, 1970), p. 21, as the somewhat more ambiguous "נוהגים ששופכים לאיבוד המכות."

39 R. Yaakov Wehl, *The Haggadah with Answers* (Brooklyn, NY: Mesorah Publications, 1997), p. 143. Not attributed to any authority, it is introduced by "It is also

it and explains, "The four cups were instituted by the Sages as a demonstration of our joy over having been redeemed from Egyptian servitude and our becoming God's chosen people in the process. In order to ensure that there is no trace of other emotions involved in our celebration of the Exodus, so that there will be no gloating over the misfortune of the Egyptians rather than joy at our own good fortune, some wine is spilled as we recount the frightful plagues that were visited upon our former tormentors. The spilled wine represents a symbolic reduction in the tone of our joy, to remind us to keep our celebrations within the limits of propriety and sensitivity."[40] The Bostoner Rebbe, Rabbi Levi Yitzchak Horowitz, gives a similar explanation: "Our cup is also lacking when God strikes them."[41] The "incomplete joy" explanation is the only one offered in some Modern Orthodox Haggadot. The *Yeshivah University Haggada* brings it in the name of Abarbanel.[42] Rabbi Jonathan Sacks calls it "the most beautiful" explanation for the custom, and does not offer alternative explanations.[43] Rabbi Shlomo Riskin includes it in his Haggadah, stating that "it symbolizes our sadness at the loss of human life—even that of our enemies."[44] It is also found on Orthodox "Ask the Rabbi" forums on the Internet.[45] By now it appears in many mainstream scholarly Hebrew Haggadot, one version brought in the recently published Haggadah based on

---

possible to suggest another reason..." The Hebrew original, *Haggadat Ki Yishalcha Bincha* (Brooklyn, NY: Tova Press, 1993), p. 202, introduces the explanation with "לכאורה אולי יש לומר."

40 R. Yaakov Blinder, *The Haggadah of the Roshei Yeshivah – Book Two* (Brooklyn, NY: Mesorah Publications, 1999), pp. 136, 137, translated from Asher Bergman, *Haggadah Shel Pesach – Arzei haLevanon – volume two* (Bnei Brak: Mishor, 1999), p. 154; Yaakov Abramsky, *Chazzon Yechezkel* (Bnei Brak: 2009), p. 398.

41 *Seder Haggadah Shel Pesach – Ezrat Avoteinu* (Jerusalem: New England Chassidic Center, 1997), p. 146.

42 Steven Cohen and Kenneth Brander, editors, *The Yeshiva University Haggada* (New York: Student Organization of Yeshiva, 1985), p. 19.

43 R. Jonathan Sacks, *Rabbi Jonathan Sacks's Haggadah* (New York: Continuum, 2010) p. 36.

44 R. Shlomo Riskin, *The Passover Haggadah* (New York: Ktav, 1983), p. 90.

45 This is the answer given in the Ohr Somayach "Ask the Rabbi" question on "Drops of Wine": "While we rejoice at our salvation, we nonetheless retain our sensitivities to the suffering of the Egyptians by diminishing our joy, if only in the mildest extent." <http://ohr.edu/ask_db/ask_main.php/273/Q3/>. It is worth noting that the Chabad "Ask the Rabbi" site gives not the "incomplete joy" explanation, but one more closely resembling the original explanation: "The Ten Plagues, describing the affliction of the Egyptians, represent negative energy that we would rather not bring into our system. So after reading each plague we spill wine from the cup, banishing the forces of punishment and its curses,

the teachings of Rabbi Yosef Shalom Elyashiv.[46]

Abarbanel and Avudraham

Some Haggadot attribute this explanation to Abarbanel. The earliest such attribution seems to be in the "*Fun Unzer Alten Otzar*" column of the Warsaw newspaper "Hajnt" from March 26, 1937.[47] This was a column, considered innovative at the time, that Moshe Bunem Justman (1889–1942) began writing in 1930, collecting short Torah ideas related to the weekly portion or upcoming holiday.[48] These were later collected in the "*Fun Unzer Alten Otzar*" series of books. In the Haggadah of this series, published in Warsaw in 1938, the "incomplete joy" explanation is brought in the name of Don Isaac Abarbanel, as it appeared in the newspaper column a year before.[49]

This explanation is included in a Hebrew translation of material on the holidays and Pirkei Avot compiled from Justman's books, *MeOtzareinu haYashan*,[50] first published in 1965, and from there has made it to various collections of material on Pesach.[51] The same explanation, worded slightly differently, also appears in the name of Abarbanel in the "overwhelmingly popular"[52] Hebrew *Yalkut Tov* Haggadah by R. Eliyahu Kitov, first published in 1961 and many times since.[53] From there it was copied word for word in *Yalkut l'Moadim: Haggadah Shel Pesach*, compiled by Rabbi Chaim

and leaving the cup with only blessings. The spilled wine should then be discarded, for drinking it would be drinking in the plagues." http://www.chabad.org/holidays/passover/pesach_cdo/aid/1814212/jewish/Why-Do-We-Spill-Wine-on-Passover-Night.htm.

46 Moshe Israelzon, *Haggadah Shel Pesach* (Jerusalem: Machon Keren Reem, 2006), p. 106. There it is brought as "ואפשר לומר" and suggests that God is unhappy because of the death of the Egyptians.

47 *Fun Unzer Alten Otzar*, Hajnt, March 26, 1937, p. 6.

48 H. Justus (Justman), *MeOtzareinu haYashan – Bereishit* (Tel Aviv: Mofet, 1976), p. 8.

49 B. Yoashson (Moshe Bunem Justman), *Haggadah shel Pesach mit a Modern Yiddish Iberzetzing – Fun Unzer Alten Otzar* (Warsaw: Yehudiah, 1938), p. 57. It was republished in New York by Saphrograph in 1947.

50 Shimshon Meltzer, translator, *MeOtzareinu haYashan* (Tel Aviv: Modiin, 1976), p. 109.

51 To name two, the exact formulation is copied in Chaim Zuckerman, *Birkat Chayyim al Moadim – vol. 2* (Tel Aviv: 1971), p. 133, and Chanan Levi, *be-Shvilei ha-Chodashim* (Rechasim: Tiferet Ram, 2001), p. 923.

52 Introduction to the Feldheim English translation of the Kitov Haggadah (Jerusalem: Feldheim, 1999), p. vi.

53 Rabbi Eliyahu Kitov, *Haggadah Shel Pesach: Yalkut Tov* (Jerusalem: Alef, 1961), p. 79.

Becker, published in 1968,[54] part of a series of books he wrote collecting short ideas related to each holiday. From there it was copied for later collections.[55] R. Kitov is also the source used by the 1977 Artscroll Haggadah.[56] These two slightly different Hebrew texts of this "quote" from Abarbanel seem to be based on different ways to rephrase Justman's original Yiddish misattribution.

In the 1978 Artscroll *The Haggadah Treasury* this explanation is given in the name of Avudraham,[57] an approach followed in *Rabbi Jonathan Sacks's Haggadah*.[58] Since this idea does not actually appear in the writings of either Avudraham or Abarbanel,[59] scholarly works that bring this explanation are generally careful not to attribute it to a particular early rabbinic authority, instead attributing it to ambiguous "later sources"[60] or

---

54 R. Chaim S. Becker, *Yalkut l'Moadim: Haggadah Shel Pesach* (Jerusalem: Hatechiya, 1968), p. 103. He also copies the *Mesech Chochma* brought right after from the Kitov Haggadah, as well as the same exact formulation of the Maharil's explanation. The book *Yalkut l'Moadim: Haggadah Shel Pesach* was not very meticulous about citing references. On the same page he gives the Vilna Gaon as the source for the explanation found in *Sefer Matamim* that the custom symbolizes the diminishing of the Egyptians, an idea not found in the writings of the Vilna Gaon. See R. Yosef Eliyahu Halevi Movshovitz, editor, *Haggadah Shel Pesach im Perush haGra* (Jerusalem: Mossad Harav Kook, 2009), p. 63. The source of the confusion, it seems, is Yosef Leser's *Haggadah Shel Pesach – Ma'atayim Shloshim v'Shemoneh Peirushim* (Cracow, Poland: 1905), p. 39, where two paragraphs in small print are found under a large print heading "From Rabbenu the GRA," but the second paragraph actually begins with the words "In the name of *Sefer haMinhagim*" and gives the explanation found in *Sefer Matamim* in the name of *Sefer Minhagim*.

55 Two examples: Bezalel Landau, *Haggadah Shel Pesach – l'Avot ul'Banim* (Jerusalem: Mifal Torah miTzion, 1972), p. 49; Meir Cohen, *Sefer Pesach ke-Halacha* (Ashdod: 1997), p. 130.

56 R. Kitov is listed in the bibliography of the Artscroll Haggadah, and in a footnote to the explanation of Abrabanel the Artscroll Haggadah brings an idea from the *Mesech Chochma*, which in *Yalkut Tov* is also brought right after the Abarbanel.

57 R. Nosson Sherman, editor, *The Haggadah Treasury* (New York: Mesorah Publications in conjunction with Zeirei Agudath Israel of America, 1978), p. 92.

58 R. Jonathan Sacks, *Rabbi Jonathan Sacks's Haggadah* (New York: Continuum, 2010) p. 36.

59 David Arnow, *Creating Lively Passover Seders* (Woodstock, Vermont: Jewish Lights Publishing, 2004), p. 192, correctly notes that it is "widely (but questionably) attributed to Isaac Abrabanel."

60 Joseph Tabory, The JPS Commentary on the Haggadah: Historical Introduction, Translation and Commentary (Philadelphia: Jewish Publication Society, 2008), p. 27.

"the opinion of some,"[61] or stating that "it is commonly said."[62] In later additions to the commentary of Abarbanel on the Haggadah,[63] the "incomplete joy" explanation is also absent. Modern English-language Haggadot that give Avudraham or Abarbanel as the source for the "incomplete joy" explanation seem to be using these Artscroll Haggadot from the 1970s as their source.

The Earliest Sources

What is the actual origin of this explanation for the custom? Since it seems to smack of political correctness, some claim that this particular interpretation was started by Reform rabbis, an idea propagated by the Reform movement itself. It was claimed that this "beautiful and moving interpretation" of the removal of drops of wine as symbolizing "the diminishing of our joy at our own redemption as we recall the sufferings of our oppressors" was "originated by Rabbi Herbert Bronstein in the 1974 CCAR Haggadah."[64] We have seen, however, that this interpretation was already popular decades before that.

In his introduction to his 1947 commentary to the Haggadah, Daniel Goldschmidt writes that "in recent times an attempt has been made to explain this custom in a more ethical manner, and give it a meaning that is appropriate for modern sensibilities, as if we are symbolically lessening the joy of the holiday due to consideration of the downfall of the Egyptians, based on the verse "If your enemy falls do not exult" (Proverbs 24:17)." In a note he attributes this explanation to Rabbis S. R. Hirsch and Eduard Baneth.[65] We do not find this reason for the custom of taking out

---

61 R. Menachem Kasher, *The Passover Haggadah* (New York: 1957), p. 159.

62 Lawrence Hoffman and David Arnow, editors, *My People's Passover Haggadah: Traditional Texts, Modern Commentaries, volume 2* (Woodstock, VT: Jewish Lights Publishing, 2008), p. 45.

63 Israel Meir Perser, *Haggadah Shel Pesach Abarbanel – Zevach Pesach* (Jerusalem: Mossad Harav Kook, 2007), p. 13.

64 "Selections From *The New Union Haggadah,*" *The Reform Advocate*, volume 6, number 1, Spring 2014, p. 3.

65 Daniel Goldschmidt, *Haggadah Shel Pesach* (Tel Aviv: Schocken, 1947), pp. 20-21. This is also noted in the English-language Passover Haggadah edited by Nahum Glatzer, published in 1953, which incorporated Goldschmidt's comments, "in recent times an attempt has been made by S.R. Hirsch and Eduard Baneth to interpret this custom as a symbolic tempering of the joy of the evening in order to show sympathy for the misfortune of the Egyptians." Nahum Glatzer, editor, *The Passover Haggadah* (New York: Schocken Books, 1953), p. 41.

drops of wine in the writings of R. Hirsch,[66] but we do find it in the writings of Baneth. Eduard Ezekiel Baneth (1855–1930) studied at the Rabbinical Seminary in Berlin and was ordained by Rabbi Israel Hildesheimer.[67] He served as the rabbi of Krotoszyn, Poland, and later was a professor of Talmud at the Lehranstalt für die Wissenschaft des Judentums in Berlin, where he was succeeded by Chanoch Albeck.[68] Baneth was known in Germany as a *talmid chacham* and an academic. While he was completely observant and a member of *Mizrachi* (he was one of the founders of the weekly national-religious Hebrew newspaper "*Ha-Ivri*"),[69] he was not considered part of the official Orthodox establishment due to his position at the Lehranstalt für die Wissenschaft des Judentums, a liberal institution.[70] Today Eduard Baneth is mostly remembered for giving a score of "Good" to Regina Jones' paper "Can a woman hold rabbinical office?" shortly before his death. Regina Jones went on to be the first

---

66 In the original German edition of his Schocken Haggadah, *Die Pessach-Haggada* (Berlin: Schoken, 1937), pp. 23, 24, Goldschmidt attributed this explanation to R. Hirsch but did not provide a source for that attribution. R. Hirsch did not write a commentary to the Haggadah, as noted in the introduction to the Feldheim *Hirsch Haggadah*. He does discuss the idea "If your enemy falls do not exult" (Proverbs 24:17) in his commentary to *Pirkei Avot* 4:23, but does not connect it with this Passover custom. In the material on this verse brought in the collection of R. Hirsch's writings on Proverbs, *From the Wisdom of Mishlei* (New York: Feldheim, 2000) there is also nothing related to Passover. The explanation is also brought in the name of R. Hirsch, but likewise with no actual reference, in Yehuda David Zinger, *Ziv haMinhagim* (Jerusalem: Kollel Ziv haMinhagim, 2000), p. 125.

67 *Jewish Encyclopedia – volume 2* (New York: Funk and Wagnalls, 1906), p. 489. A photo of Baneth can be found in *The Universal Jewish Encyclopedia vol. 2* (New York: Universal Jewish Encyclopedia, Inc., 1948), p. 63. An early Hebrew-language Haggadah with this explanation, but without any attribution, is R. Zev Klein, *Haggadah shel Pesach – Chochmah im Nachalah* (Buenos Aires: Julio Kaufman, 1948), p. 38. It is significant that R. Klein was a member of Kahal Adass Yisroel in Berlin, led by R. Hildesheimer, and often quotes R. Hirsch in his Haggadah.

68 Dan Cohn-Sherbok, *Dictionary of Jewish Biography* (New York: Continuum, 2005), p. 22.

69 Baneth's connection to Mizrachi may have contributed to the inclusion of this explanation in the German guidebook on the Seder for Mizrachi Youth. Bernhard S. Jacobson, *Pesach: Arbeitsplan und Stoffsammlung* (Hamburg: 1936), p. 25. Bernhard Jacobson would go on to write the *Netiv Bina* series on the prayers as Yissachar Yaakovson.

70 Mayer Bar-Ilan, *From Volozhin to Jerusalem - volume 2* (Tel Aviv: Pilei, 1939), p. 394 (Hebrew).

woman ordained as a rabbi in 1935.[71] Eduard Baneth mentions the "incomplete joy" explanation for taking some wine out of the cup at the Seder in his lecture on the Pesach Seder, "*Der Sederabend: Ein Vortrag,*" published in Berlin in 1904, a work considered significant in its time.[72] There he writes that when he was "still a boy, the strange custom was explained" to mean that wine is a symbol of joy and because each plague caused our tormentors to suffer on our account, we diminish our joy over our own liberation. He notes that "whether this explanation may make claim to historical truth" is an open question, but "one must recognize the poetic truth" and that it "breathes the spirit of Judaism" as reflected in the midrash quoted in *Beit Yosef* O.C. 490.[73]

One of Baneth's contemporaries, Rabbi Eliyahu Klatzkin (1852–1932), the famed "ilui from Shklov" who served as Chief Rabbi of Lublin from 1910–1928,[74] also mentions this explanation. Rabbi Klatzkin authored many books, and was considered a major halachic authority, particularly in the area of releasing *agunot.*[75] He was also known for his knowledge of medicine, pharmacology, mathematics, history, and geography, and was conversant in Greek, Latin, German, French, English, Russian and Polish.[76] *Kuntres l'Dugma* is a 24-page booklet of miscellaneous material from works that Rabbi Klatzkin began writing but never completed. The beginning section has homiletic material related to the weekly

---

71 See Michael Meyer, "Women in the Thought and Practice of the European Jewish Reform Movement" in Marion Kaplan and Deborah Dash Moore, editors, *Gender and Jewish History* (Bloomington, Indiana: Indiana University Press, 2011), p. 152; Tiffany Wayne, editor, *Feminist Writings from Ancient Times to the Modern World: A Global Sourcebook and History* (Santa Barbara, CA: ABC-CLIO, LLC, 2011), p. 504; George Kohler, *Reading Maimonides' Philosophy in 19th Century Germany: The Guide to Religious Reform* (New York: Springer, 2012), p. 8, note 22.

72 Glatzer considered it worthy of "special attention." Nahum Glatzer, editor, *The Passover Haggadah* (New York: Schocken Books, 1953), p. 14. It is noted as "a penetrating analysis" in Goldschmidt, "Studies on Jewish Liturgy by German-Jewish Scholars," *Leo Baeck Institute Yearbook* (1957) 2 (1), p. 129.

73 Eduard Baneth, *Der Sederabend: Ein Vortrag* (Berlin: Poppelauer, 1904), pp. 28-29.

74 Jacob Klatzkin, "Eliyahu Klatzkin," in Leo Jung, editor, *Jewish Leaders, 1750–1940* (New York: Bloch, 1954), p. 340. Aviad Hacohen, *The Tears of the Oppressed* (Jersey City, New Jersey: Ktav, 2004), p. 62, note 125.

75 See, for example, Shimon Yosef Meller, The Brisker Rav: The Life and Times of Maran HaGaon HaRav Yitzchok Ze'ev HaLevi Soloveichik zt"l – volume one (Jerusalem: Feldheim, 2007), p. 233, note 2.

76 Shnayer Z. Leiman, "Rabbinic Openness to General Culture in the Early Modern Period in Western and Central Europe," in Jacob J. Schacter, editor, *Judaism's Encounter with Other Cultures* (Northvale, New Jersey: Jason Aronson, Inc., 1997), p. 213, note 178.

Torah reading, and in the section on *Parashat Ve'era* he writes that "We do not act like the Gentiles who are joyous at the downfall of their enemies when they...kill them, rather we follow the ways of the Holy One Blessed be He (B. Sotah 14a), and it is written, "The Holy One Blessed be He is not happy at the destruction of the wicked...He said to them 'My handiwork is drowning in the sea and you sing before me'" (B. Sanhedrin 39b), and when we mention and tell of the plagues...we pour out and diminish the cup through dripping out drop by drop..." He continues that in addition to the original reason for the custom given by the Rokeach, "it makes sense to say that it is also to show that...when we recall this we are pained...and to remember the pain mixed with joy, we take away from the cup..."[77]

Both Klatzkin and Baneth indicate that this explanation is not the historical reason for the custom, an assessment echoed in the *Schechter Haggadah*, which, after giving Abarbanel as the author of this explanation, states that "although it does not seem that this is the origin of the custom, it is a notion connected to Pesach in classical rabbinic sources" and goes on to quote the midrashim mentioned earlier.[78] It should be noted, however, that although this idea might be connected to Pesach in general, until the innovation of the "incomplete joy" explanation, the message of the plagues was understood to emphasize that "only the exercise of overwhelming force...ultimately succeeded in freeing the Jewish people from slavery."[79]

While it is clear that the latter formulations of this idea were derived from Eduard Baneth, as they make reference to the reciting of the partial Hallel, an idea noted in the discussion of the custom by Baneth but not mentioned by Klatzkin, we now see that the "diminished joy" idea was being stated by learned Orthodox rabbis in the early 1900s. Seeing as Eduard Baneth was only three years younger than Eliyahu Klatzkin, it is clear

---

77 R. Eliyahu Klatzkin, *Kuntres l'Dugma* (Lublin: 1921), pp. 4, 5. Rabbi Klatzkin moved to Jerusalem in 1928, and this explanation is included in his name in Haggadot that focus on the rabbis of Jerusalem. See, Shabbtai Rosenthal, *Haggadah Shel Pesach – Geonei v'Chachmei Yerushalayim* (Jerusalem: Mifal Moreshet Yerushalayim, 1996), pp. 95, 96; Shlomo Verner, *miShulchanam Shel Gedolei Yerushalayim* (Jerusalem: Machon Keren Re'em, 2008), p. 121. Both books change the order of the sentences in Rabbi Klatzkin's original formulation, but are otherwise true to the source material. R. Klatzkin is also quoted in Pinchas Issac, *Pninei Pardes – Haggadah Shel Pesach* (Rishon LeZion: 1995), pp. 87, 88.

78 Joshua Kulp and David Golinkin, *The Schechter Haggadah: Art, History and Commentary* (Jerusalem: Schechter Institute of Jewish Studies, 2009), p. 233.

79 Laufer, p. 98.

that Klatzkin was not the source of the explanation that Baneth heard as a young boy at the Seder.

The True Origin

Is there any way of determining who originated the idea that was told to a young Eduard Baneth? The book *Divrei Yirmiyahu – Drashot* is a collection of the drashot of R. Yirmiyahu Löw (1812–1874), compiled by his grandson, R. Binyamin Zev Lev (Löw). In the last pages of the book, some extra material is added "in order not to leave blank pages." There, the author, R. Binyamin Zev Lev, brings the "incomplete joy" explanation in the name of his grandfather, indicating that it was a nice idea that his grandfather originated.[80] He writes that his grandfather explained that "since the Jewish people are merciful, and since through the rescue from Egypt many of God's creations were destroyed and drowned, although it is a great joy for us that God took us out of Egypt and redeemed us, it is still painful for us that through this others were destroyed…and if God would have rescued us without the destruction and death of others it would be a greater joy for us. Therefore our joy is a little diminished, and to show that Israel are merciful and the children of merciful, we pour out a little at every plague."[81]

Although this book was published in 1934, making Baneth's record of this explanation published in 1904 the earliest, this represents the earliest legitimate named attribution for this explanation, placing its origin in the 1800s. This explanation does not connect the drops of wine to the midrashic explanation for the abbreviated Hallel; that connection was made by Baneth. In the formulation of R. Yirmiyahu Löw, there is nothing inherently unethical or inappropriate about celebrating the destruction of their enemies, but "since the Jewish people are merciful" and "to show that Israel are merciful and the children of merciful," we go beyond normal moral standards and express diminished joy because of the deaths of the Egyptians. This aspect was also stressed by Klatzkin, who emphasizes

---

80 He writes that his grandfather "gave a nice explanation" (נתן טעם לשבח).

81 R. Binyamin Zev Lev (Löw), *Sefer Divrei Yirmiyahu – Drashot* (Satmar: Meir Lev Hirsch, 1934), 42b. In Shaul Yechezkel Weiss, *Haggadah Shel Pesach – Otzar Divrei Hamefarshim* (London: 2010), p. 321, he mistakenly attributes this explanation to R. Elazar Löw of Santov in the name of his own grandfather, but the writer of this particular section is the compiler of the book, R. Binyamin Zev. It is clear that he is referring to his own grandfather, whom he calls זקני הקדוש ז"ל, as distinct from his great grandfather, R. Binyamin Wolf, whom he refers to as זקני הקדוש בעל שערי תורה ז"ל in the very next paragraph.

that not expressing joy at the death of enemies is a particularly Jewish trait. It would seem that the ultimate origin of the "incomplete joy" explanation is R. Yirmiyahu Löw. Although the "incomplete joy" explanation seems to express modern sensibilities and possibly political correctness, R. Yirmiyahu Löw was not known for these characteristics, and in fact was known as a "recognized leader of Hungarian Orthodoxy" who was a vigorous opponent of Hasidism, Reform[82] and Haskalah.[83]

Eduard Baneth was nineteen years old when R. Yirmiyahu Löw passed away, and it is reasonable that a member of the Baneth family related an explanation heard from Löw. The rabbinical figures in the Löw and Baneth families were connected for generations. R. Yirmiyahu Löw's grandfather, R. Elazar Löw (1758–1837, author of *Shemen Rokeach*), became the rabbi of the Moravian community of Triesch at the recommendation of his friend, the famed R. Mordechai Benet of Nikolsburg (1753–1829),[84] and his aunt Gittel married R. Mordechai Benet's son Yishayahu.[85] Benet gave one of the *haskamot* to the first volume of his father R. Binyamin Wolf's *Shaarei Torah*.[86] Most significantly, both R. Yirmiyahu Löw and his brother studied under R. Mordechai Benet.[87] R. Mordechai Benet's cousin Joachim Markus (Yaakov) Banet (1750–1812) was the

82 *The Universal Jewish Encyclopedia vol. 7* (New York: Universal Jewish Encyclopedia, Inc., 1948), p. 213.

83 See Yechiel Michel Stern, *Sefer Gedolei haDorot* (Jerusalem: Minchat Yisrael, 1996), p. 690, and David Halachmi, *Chachmei Yisrael* (Bnei Brak: Tiferet Hasefer, 1980), p. 303.

84 Zahava Stessel, *Wine and Thorns in Tokay Valley: Jewish life in Hungary* (Cranbury, New Jersey: Associated University Presses, 1995), p. 120. R. Mordechai Benet also recommended to R. Elazar Löw not to rewrite his commentary on *Choshen Mishpat* after the manuscript was lost once, then rewritten and burned in a fire. R. Benet said this should be taken as a divine sign not to rewrite this work so that scholars would have to study the original source material, p. 121.

85 Moshe Samet, *haChadash Assur Min haTorah* (Jerusalem: Carmel, 2005), p. 272; Zahava Stessel, *Wine and Thorns in Tokay Valley: Jewish life in Hungary* (Cranbury, New Jersey: Associated University Presses, 1995), p. 126.

86 Yitzchak Yosef Cohen, *Chachmei Hungaria v'haSafrut haToranit Bah* (Jerusalem: Machon Yerushalayim, 1997), p. 254.

87 Stessel, p. 124; Yirmiyahu Feldman, *Divrei Yirmiyahu – Kiddushin* (Jerusalem: Machon Yerushalayim, 1984), p. 12.

great grandfather of Eduard Baneth.[88] Thus it is possible that young Eduard Baneth heard the explanation of R. Yirmiyahu Löw through a relative at a family Seder.

Many of the elements found in the "incomplete joy" explanation as stated by Löw, Klatzkin and Baneth are found in the book *Meshech Chochma* by their contemporary, Rav Meir Simcha of Dvinsk (1843–1926). In his commentary to Exodus 12:16,[89] Rav Meir Simcha explains that the Israelites were told about the holiday on the seventh day of Pesach while still in Egypt "to teach that the holiday is not due to the downfall of the Egyptians at the sea, for God commanded them before the Egyptians drowned…and so it is explained in *Yalkut Shimoni* (*remez* 654), that this is the reason that *simcha* is not written by Pesach and we do not complete Hallel all seven because "If your enemy falls do not exult" (Proverbs 24:17)." He specifically states that other nations establish holidays to celebrate the downfall of their enemies, but Jews do not do this, an element also stated by Löw and Klatzkin. Although he does not refer to the custom of dripping out wine, there is a clear affinity of this commentary of *Meshech Chochma* to the "incomplete joy" explanation, showing that the general gist of this interpretation was "in the air" during this time period. This connection was noted by Kitov, who included it in his Haggadah right after bringing the explanation from "Abrabanel."[90] Seeing as the first part of *Meshech Chochma* was published decades after the death of R. Yirmiyahu Löw,[91] Löw remains the earliest representative of this interpretive approach.

It remains unclear how the explanation offered to the young Eduard Baneth came to be associated with Abarbanel and Avudraham. What these authorities have in common is that their names begin with the letters אב, the same letters as the Hebrew initials of Eduard Baneth. Thus it is possible that a writer saw this explanation written in Hebrew in the name of ר' אב and misunderstood these letters as referring to the first two letters of either Abrabanel or Avudraham.

---

88 Benet, Banet and Baneth are all variant spellings of the same name and were variously used by the different members of the extended family. Benzion Kaganoff, *A Dictionary of Jewish Names and Their History* (Northvale, New Jersey: Jason Aronson, Inc., 1996), p. 131.

89 In some editions it is attached to the comments on Exodus 12:15.

90 Kitov, p. 79. It also appears there in the 1977 Artscroll Haggadah, which used Kitov as a source.

91 The earliest any part of the *Mesech Chochma* was printed was 1902. See the introduction to the *Mesech Chochma* by Avraham Avraham in the Feldheim edition.

We have seen that the modern popularity of the "incomplete joy" explanation can be traced back to an approach originating with R. Yirmiyahu Löw and related to the young Eduard Baneth, and reported by him years later in a lecture. Eduard Baneth is the earliest written source for this explanation. Although sometimes claimed to originate with Reform rabbis, it actually originated with an Orthodox rabbi in the 1800s. It resonated with the sensibilities of English-speaking American Jews in particular, and was popularized through being presented as the only explanation for the custom in American Haggadot from the 1940s and on. This explanation came to be seen as more humane and understandable than the original explanation that this represents the 16-faceted sword of God, and by now has eclipsed the original meaning of the custom, certainly in the English-speaking Jewish world.[92] ☙

92 Thanks to R. Beinish Ginsburg for asking me about the source of this explanation, an inquiry that led to the writing of this article; Claudia Bollag for helping translate German material; and my students, Ephraim Hollander, Eli Genauer and Avi Hoffman who helped me go through all the Haggadot at the Hebrew Union College library. Special thanks to my friend Avi Levine for all-around help and for the many stimulating conversations we had about this issue, which opened up new areas of research.

Divine Providence and Natural Forces: Conflict or Harmony?

By: MICAH SEGELMAN

Tension appears to exist between the ideas of *hashgacha pratis, teva,* and *bechira.*[1] Do natural laws, and the choices made by others, impact people's lives in a causal sense? Alternatively, does divine providence lead to a predetermined outcome irrespective of these forces? Perhaps nature and the actions of others are utilized only as a tool for carrying out the divine will in a way that obscures *HKBH's* intervention, but do not influence the ultimate outcome.

Denying the causal impact of natural forces seems to contradict the intuitive notion that one can understand and utilize natural forces in order to influence the ultimate outcome. On the other hand, limiting the scope of *hashgacha* appears incompatible with religious experience. How is one to thank *HKBH* for His "miracles that are with us every day" in *Modim* thrice daily? On what basis is someone who is faced with danger, or afflicted with adversity, to respond with *teshuva* and *tefillah*? How does one find meaning in suffering?

Contrary to approaches that minimize either *teva* or *hashgacha*, I will argue for an approach that acknowledges the important roles of both *teva* and *hashgacha.*

Since the very notion of *hashgacha* seems to presuppose the existence of miracles, I will begin by discussing miracles and distinguishing between miracles based on their "hiddenness"—the degree to which they are consistent with nature. I will demonstrate that, although different opinions may exist on some of the details, hidden miracles as a usual phenomenon and natural forces as causal are widely accepted ideas, and I will explain

1 The author gratefully acknowledges the comments offered by Rabbi Yitzchak Adlerstein and Rabbi Ahron Lopiansky to earlier versions of this manuscript and expresses sincere thanks to Dr. Aharon Wolf for engaging in discussions and offering feedback throughout the process of writing this paper. The author also thanks R' David Guttmann from the *Ḥakirah* editorial board and two anonymous reviewers for their comments. The author bears sole responsibility for the final product.

Rabbi Micah Segelman studied in Yeshiva Chofetz Chaim (Rochester and Queens) and is currently a PhD candidate in Health Services Research and Policy at the University of Rochester.

why they are not mutually exclusive. Because natural laws have causal impact, I will distinguish between outcomes that are caused by natural forces where *HKBH* could intervene but does not (*mikra*), and those caused by direct divine intervention. I will show that many sources reflect this distinction, and consider the differences between direct intervention and *mikra*.

Three Types of Miracles

Ramban differentiates between open miracles, such as those that occurred during the exodus from Egypt, and hidden miracles. He says (*Bereishis* 17:1 and *Shemos* 6:2), for example, that different names of *HKBH* reflect these different types of miracles, and that open miracles are few and far between—they are not performed "in every generation and for each wicked person" (*Shemos* 13:16).

Furthermore, Ramban (*Vayikra* 26:11) maintains that not all hidden miracles are equivalent. He writes (*Vayikra* 26:11):

> והטעם בזה כי הברכות אע"פ שהם נסים הם מן הנסים הנסתרים שכל התורה מלאה מהם כאשר פירשתי והם אפילו ליחיד העובד . . . וימלא ימיו בטובה. אבל אלו הברכות שבפרשה הזאת הן כלליות בעם והן בהיות כל עמנו כלם צדיקים . . . וכבר בארנו כי כל אלה הברכות כולם נסים אין בטבע שיבאו הגשמים ויהיה השלום לנו מן האויבים ויבא מורך בלבם לנוס מאה מפני חמשה בעשותינו החוקים והמצות ולא שיהיה הכל הפך מפני זרענו השנה השביעית. ואע"פ שהם נסים נסתרים שעולם כמנהגו נוהג עמהם אבל הם מתפרסמים מצד היותם תמיד לעולם בכל הארץ . . . יוודע לכל כי מאת ה' היתה זאת . . .

All hidden miracles share the characteristic that the natural order is seemingly maintained. Yet some hidden miracles involve patterns that, when thoughtfully observed, can be seen to be indicative of divine intervention.[2] Discrete events, each one plausibly explainable as random, taken together become difficult to explain as chance occurrences. We can say that these miracles, though hidden, are "less hidden." This is reminiscent of how scientists use statistical methods to draw conclusions from data. Scientists declare that a finding is statistically significant if it is unlikely to have been produced by chance alone. Ramban in *Shemos* (13:16)[3] refers to this idea as well.

---

2 See *Michtav M'Eliyahu*, Volume 2, *Purim*, *Neis Nistar,* who draws a similar distinction.

3 At the very end of the piece where he refers to hidden miracles becoming publicized.

Ramban (*Shemos* 23:25 and *Vayikra* 26:11) provides examples of the two types of hidden miracles. A totally hidden miracle would be if food is "blessed" to be of superior quality and this leads to good health. Ramban stresses that when a righteous person has a long, healthy life as a result of this miracle, nothing seems unusual—evil people can also lead long, healthy lives. In contrast, it is very improbable for one land and one nation to be constantly blessed with abundant rain, peace, plenty, and tranquility. It is equally improbable for the rains to completely cease when the *shemitta* year is violated.

There are thus three categories of miracles:

1. Miracles that are completely hidden (e.g., a righteous person is blessed with good health)
2. Miracles that are "less hidden"—they don't openly violate nature but are more difficult to attribute to random chance (e.g., peace and plentiful rain in response to the righteousness of the Jewish people)
3. Miracles that openly violate nature (e.g., the splitting of the sea)

Ramban (*Vayikra* 26:11) places an important restriction on the "less hidden" miracles—they apply only when the entire nation is righteous (or wicked). The completely hidden miracles, however, apply even to individuals (see quote above where this is stated explicitly). Ramban goes on to say that when the entire nation is righteous, these "less hidden" miracles are at play to the extent that medical cures are not needed. Ramban points out that this situation is clearly not the norm[4]—the Torah itself presupposes that medical cures are needed as it requires a damager to pay doctor's fees.

Completely Hidden Miracles

Given the limited applicability of both open miracles and "less hidden" ones, it becomes extremely important to explore the parameters of the completely hidden miracles. *Hashgacha*, except in the unusual circumstances in which the other forms of miracles are at play, is realized through completely hidden miracles.

Rabbi Dr. David Berger[5] highlights several passages in Ramban's writings to argue for limiting the scope of hidden miracles/*hashgacha pratis*. In one of these passages, Ramban (*Devarim* 11:13) limits miracles in two

---

4 See also *Taz YD* 336:1.

5 Berger, David. Miracles and the Natural Order in Nachmanides. <http://zootorah.org/assets/media/MiraclesNahmanides.pdf>, accessed Dec 3, 2013.

ways: they occur only based on the actions of the nation rather than those of the individual, and they occur for exceptional people (righteous or wicked) rather than for ordinary ones[6]. He writes:

> ובאור הענין כי השם לא יעשה הנסים תמיד לתת מטר הארץ . . . רק על מעשה רוב העם אבל היחיד הוא בזכותו יחיה והוא בעונו ימות . . . ודע כי הנסים לא יעשו לטובה או לרעה רק לצדיקים גמורים או לרשעים גמורים אבל הבינונים כדרך מנהגו של עולם יעשה בהם טובה או רעה כדרכם וכעלילותם.

To what sort of miracles is Ramban referring? If all miracles are included, then Ramban indeed maintains a very limited view of *hashgacha.* This is Dr. Berger's reading (Berger p. 8): "The assertion that miracles are performed only for the absolutely righteous or wicked is couched in general terms and appears to include every variety of miracles. Hence, ordinary people are excluded from the regular operation of hidden miracles and are left, as in the *Commentary to Genesis*, to the customary, natural order."

However, it appears that this passage of Ramban in *Devarim* is not referring to all miracles and in fact does not apply to completely hidden miracles. According to Ramban in *Vayikra*, the limitation of hidden miracles to the nation rather than to the individual applies only to the "less hidden" miracles—not to the completely hidden miracles. **Ramban in *Vayikra* says explicitly that "less hidden" miracles apply only when the whole nation is righteous (or wicked) but that completely hidden miracles apply even to individuals.** Ramban in *Devarim* is consistent with Ramban in *Vayikra* only if one understands Ramban in *Devarim* to refer to "less hidden" miracles.[7] This point is reinforced by the examples of miracles that Ramban in *Devarim* uses for illustration: rain falling or being withheld. These are specifically the "less hidden" miracles to which Ramban refers in *Vayikra.*

Another indication of Ramban's intent is that he says that an individual "lives based on his merits and dies based on his sins" and that ordinary

---

6 There is actually a disagreement whether Ramban requires that both criteria be met for miracles to occur or if he means that they can occur for exceptional people even though typically they don't occur for individuals. The latter reading is adopted by the *Mizrachi* and perforce by Dr. Berger as well. See the commentary on Ramban, *Devarim* 11:13 in Ramban, *Commentary on the Torah*, Volume 7, *Devarim* (NY: Mesorah, 2008), pp. 262–264.

7 If one adopts the first reading of Ramban referred to in the prior footnote, Ramban in *Devarim* is adding a condition to what he wrote in *VaYikra*—that less hidden miracles occur only for exceptional people.

people are dealt with both within the natural order and also "in accordance with their actions." This again seems to indicate that completely hidden miracles apply to ordinary people.

Additionally, there are the famous words of Ramban in *Shemos* (13:16). Ramban's words, which emphasize hidden miracles while deemphasizing the natural order, strongly militate against limiting hidden miracles to the select few.[8] Furthermore, Rabbenu Bechaya (Introduction to *Ki Sisa*) is more explicit. He paraphrases this Ramban in *Shemos* and adds the comment that "there is not a single Jew who does not unknowingly experience hidden miracles every day."

Thus, I conclude that according to Ramban and Rabbenu Bechaya, hidden miracles are a usual and not a rare occurrence. Although their approach is not necessarily universal—Rambam's position on miracles and *hashgacha*, which has been the subject of much discussion,[9] may differ—I will demonstrate in a later section of this essay entitled "Sources That Seem to Reject *Mikra*" that many other authorities agree. Nonetheless, I will now argue that this does not preclude accepting *teva* as causal.

Natural Forces and *Hashgacha*

I have made an argument that Ramban does not limit completely hidden miracles to the select few and that they are a reality in the life of even the average Jew. Yet two other passages in Ramban's writings seem to imply otherwise. Ramban (*Bereishis* 18:19 and Job 36:7) asserts that people who are distant from *HKBH*, **even if they do not inherently deserve to be**

---

8 The words of the Netziv, though not specifically based on Ramban, leave the reader with a similar impression. The Netziv (*Haamek Davar Shemos* 17:7 and 17:14) stresses the centrality of the belief in *hashgacha pratis* taking place within the natural order, even asserting that the essential feature of *Amalek* is that they deny that there is any divine intervention in the natural order.

9 Relevant sources include: David Guttman, "Miracles in Rambam's Thought—A Function of Prophecy," *Ḥakirah*, Vol. 3 and David Guttman, "Divine Providence—Goals, Hopes, and Fears; *Ki Kol Drachav Mishpat*," *Ḥakirah*, Vol. 5; Langermann, Y. Tzvi, Maimonides and Miracles: The Growth of a (Dis)belief, *Jewish History*, Vol. 18, No. 2/3, Commemorating the Eight Hundredth Anniversary of Maimonides' Death (2004), pp. 147–172, available at <http://www.academia.edu/2483441 /Maimonides_and_Miracles>; Rabbi Gil Student, <http://hirhurim.blogspot.com/2010/04/rambam-on-miracles.html>; Rabbi Natan Slifkin, <http://www.rationalistjudaism.com/2010/06/manna-and-maimonides.html>, who also cites a number of additional sources. Several other sources cited in the present paper are relevant as well. I return briefly to Rambam's approach to *hashgacha* at the very end of this paper.

punished for their sins, can be abandoned to *mikra*—to the vicissitudes of nature. Ramban says this is in fact why the Torah insists that the Jewish people use natural means to prepare themselves for war. Ramban (Job 36:7) also approvingly cites Rambam in *Moreh Nevuchim* (3:18) who explains that the degree of *hashgacha* received by each individual varies based on their merits, and that people who are distant from HKBH are subject to *mikra* "like one who walks in the dark who will certainly stumble." Being vulnerable to *mikra* seems to conflict with the assertion of *hashgacha pratis.*

Comments of Rabbenu Bechaya appear equally contradictory. Although Rabbenu Bechaya (Introduction to *Ki Sisa*) maintains that every Jew experiences hidden miracles, he also (*Bereishis* 18:19) endorses the comments of Ramban (*Bereishis* 18:19) that people who are not righteous can be abandoned to *mikra.*[10]

I believe that these apparent contradictions demonstrate that accepting the existence of hidden miracles, even frequent ones, does not imply a belief that people are immune from the forces of nature. I will now demonstrate that many thinkers, though they may differ on nuances, maintain that natural forces are causal. I suggest that Ramban and Rabbenu Bechaya accept this as well, and will now explain why there is in fact no contradiction between embracing hidden miracles as typical phenomena and believing that *teva* is causal.

The *Sefer Hachinuch* (*Mitzva* 546), in discussing the *mitzva* of *maakeh,* asserts that *HKBH* embedded natural forces into the world and that people, with the exception of the exceptionally righteous, are subject to these forces. The Ralbag (Samuel I 26:10) explains the *mitzva* of *maakeh* similarly. Similarly, Rambam in *Shemoneh Perakim* (*perek* 8) says that many *mitzvos* in the Torah are based on the premise that *teva* and *bechira* are causal and can truly have an impact on other people. He says this is why there is

---

10 Furthermore, Rabbenu Bechaya's (*Bereishis* 18:19) assertion that many people do not merit to be saved from *mikra* seems to conflict with his statement (Introduction to *Shelach* and *Bereishis* 6:15) that the reason that the Jewish people are commanded to use natural means to fight wars is because *HKBH* performs miracles only when natural means have been fully utilized. The Ralbag (I Kings 17:3) similarly says that *HKBH* minimizes miracles and works through natural means as much as possible. I would suggest that Rabbenu Bechaya is offering this approach to explain why the Jewish people must utilize natural means even when they in fact receive special protection. He is discussing sending spies, an action that seems unnecessary since the war to conquer Israel was based on the spiritual standing of the Jewish people and not on natural considerations. Rabbenu Bechaya could agree that in other situations, natural means are needed for warfare because we may not merit divine protection.

a mitzvah of *maakeh*, an exemption from war given to those who have begun certain activities without completing them, and limitations on the taking of collateral. Rambam in *Moreh Nevuchim* (3:12) furthermore attributes suffering to natural causes inherent in the physical world, to free willed choices of others, and to overly indulgent, unhealthy lifestyles. In his *Perush Hamishnayos* (*Pesachim* Chapter 4), Rambam compares medicine curing an illness to food "curing" hunger.

Rabbi Yehuda HaLevi in *Kuzari* (5:20) says that all phenomena can be traced to HKBH in one of two ways: directly or through intermediaries which include *teva*, *mikra*, and *bechira*. It is implied by the context— and specifically by his assertion that wicked people can be the incidental beneficiaries of beneficial *mikra*—that *teva*, *mikra*, and *bechira* can result in different outcomes than if all phenomena resulted from the direct influence of *HKBH*.

The Maharal in *Gevuros Hashem* (*Perek* 61) says that the world is usually managed indirectly through *teva*. One who recites *Hallel* every day (*Shabbos* 118b) assumes constant direct intervention and this makes it impossible to explain the phenomenon of *tzadik ve'ra lo, rasha ve'tov lo*. Clearly, the Maharal feels that direct intervention results in different outcomes than indirect *teva*.

The *Drashos HaRan*[11] explains that ***HKBH* runs the world through forces that operate at the global rather than at the individual level** and that HKBH is reluctant to intervene with these forces. The Ran cites, as an example, the plague of the firstborn in Egypt, when even the Jews, who did not inherently deserve to be punished, needed to stay in their houses to avoid being affected by the plague.

That natural forces play an independent, causal role in determining events is implied by the Ramchal in *Mesillas Yesharim* (*perek* 9). The *Mesillas Yesharim,* based on the *gemara*[12] (*Pesachim* 8b), says that a person must protect himself against dangers. If he fails to do so he can be harmed. The *Mesillas Yesharim* explains that the harm is both a punishment to the careless person for not following the Torah's requirement to exercise caution and a natural consequence of his exposure to danger.

Hashgacha pratis (and hidden miracles as a usual phenomenon) and natural forces as causal are not mutually exclusive ideas. Natural forces, whether they relate to physics, medicine, etc., must be reckoned with.[13]

---

11 *Drush Shlishi* "*Amnam.*"

12 This *gemara* is based on I Samuel 16:2. See Malbim on I Samuel 16:2.

13 Ramban would include *kochavim* and *mazalos* in the same category as natural forces. See Ramban (Devarim 18:9). His discussion of *kishuf* is entirely consistent with the idea that these forces are independently causal—subject of course to divine intervention.

These global forces will impact an individual—unless *HKBH* intervenes. And whether *HKBH* will intervene to save a person from harm is a different question than whether *HKBH* would have directly imposed this harm. Hidden miracles can protect an individual against natural forces, but at times *HKBH* does not perform hidden miracles—and *mikra* prevails. **Natural forces are always in effect—and *HKBH* always oversees, deciding person by person and case by case when to intervene and when to let nature run its course. *Mikra* is a part of the system of *hashgacha.*** A similar approach to Ramban as suggested here is adopted by Rabbi Simcha Zissel Ziv[14] (the *Alter* of Kelm), Rabbi Chaim Friedlander,[15] Rabbi Aryeh Leibowitz,[16] and Rabbi Ezra Bick.[17] Rabbi Menachem Mendel Schneerson[18] offers this as a possible approach to Ramban as well.

It is important to emphasize that vulnerability to *mikra* is not all or nothing—there are many gradations on the continuum of vulnerability. This is apparent from Rambam (*Moreh Nevuchim* 3:18). Despite whatever differences may exist between the approaches of Ramban and Rambam, I believe Ramban accepts this position of Rambam as indicated by his endorsement (Job 36:7) of Rambam's approach to *mikra.* Otherwise I do not see a way to reconcile the ideas of average people being both subject to *mikra* and yet beneficiaries of hidden miracles. Similarly, Rabbi Moshe Cordovero (Ramak)[19] says that someone's level of righteousness determines his degree of vulnerability to natural forces and illustrates with an example of a capsized ship. One person may not be sufficiently righteous to be saved although in the absence of the danger would not be punished. A person with greater merit may be worthy of being personally saved. His merit may or may not extend protection to his possessions and may or

---

14 Cited in the commentary on Ramban on *Shemos* 13:16 in Ramban—Nachmanides / Commentary on the Torah Volume 3 *Shemos* / Exodus (NY: Mesorah, 2006), pp. 300–301.

15 *Sifsei Chaim, Emunah V'Hashgacha, Maamarei Hashgacha Pratis U'Klallis,* Section 5.

16 Aryeh Leibowitz, *Hashgacha Pratis* (Southfield: Targum Press, 2009), Part One, Chapter Three.

17 Rabbi Ezra Bick, "The Purpose of Signs and Miracles According to Ramban," < http://www.vbm-torah.org/pesach/pes67eb.htm>.

18 *Shaarei Emunah*, Chapter 18. <http://hebrewbooks.org/15822>, accessed May 7, 2014.

19 *Shiur Komah*, section 54, category 3. <http://hebrewbooks.org/43949>, accessed May 7, 2014.

may not preclude suffering in the context of being saved. A third individual's merit may warrant saving not only himself but also others impacted by the same forces.

Bechira as a Type of *Mikra*

The question of whether one person's actions can affect someone else is known to be controversial[20]—and the *Ohr Hachaim*[21] (*Bereishis* 37:21) and Netziv,[22] commenting on the story with Yosef and his brothers, adopt the position that the actions can in fact have this result. The Malbim,[23] commenting on David's choice to suffer a plague rather than a defeat in battle, as well as the *Metzudos Dovid* (Daniel 3:26), noting that Hananiah, Mishael, and Azariah waited for Nebuchadnezzar's invitation to leave the furnace, similarly acknowledges the power of *bechira* to impact other people. Passages from Rambam[24] also imply that one person's actions can impact someone else.[25]

In light of the previous discussion, there seems to be an obvious mechanism through which one person's actions can affect another person. *Bechira* should not be inferior to other types of natural forces. If people are made susceptible to natural forces then they should also be susceptible to *bechira*. In fact, one of the examples of being subject to *mikra* that I cited above is vulnerability to war and thus the necessity of a Jewish army. War is a result of *bechira*. Thus if one acknowledges the existence of *mikra*, one must simultaneously allow a role for *bechira*.

The *Ohr Hachaim*, Netziv, and *Metzudos Dovid* are actually going a step further and asserting that even someone who is not subject to *mikra* in general may be susceptible to the *bechira* of another person. **A greater degree of merit is needed to protect someone from *bechira* than from other types of *mikra*.**

---

20 See the discussion in Leibowitz, Part two, Chapter three.

21 See *Sifsei Chaim, Emunah V'Hashgacha, Maamarei Gezeira U'Bechira* sections 2-3 for a lengthy discussion of the *Ohr Hachaim* that includes an alternative reading.

22 *Harchev Davar Bereishis* 37:2.

23 II Samuel 24:14; I comment further on this Malbim below.

24 *Shemoneh Perakim, perek* 8 and *Moreh Nevuchim* 3:12. This is in contrast to how Rabbi Leibowitz interprets these passages in Leibowitz, Part two, Chapter three. In my opinion, the former passage implies that if a victim is predestined to die it would be difficult to understand why his murder is a crime. And the latter passage implies that one of the reasons evil exists is because of free-willed choices.

25 I am citing the view of these authorities to provide context, not to argue that others (such as Ramban) share that view.

Two Distinct Processes

Having demonstrated that a wide range of thinkers accept natural forces as causal, I now point out an important corollary to this idea. It seems to follow that adversity[26] can result from two distinct processes.[27] There are direct divine punishments that can take the form of either an open or a hidden miracle. On the other hand, there are indirect punishments that result from *HKBH* not offering protection against natural forces. While all adversity is "from *HKBH,*" two different processes are at work. Many sources accept this basic distinction (though the approaches of these thinkers may differ in some respects).

Pesukim in *Vayeilech* (*Devarim* 31:17-18) describe *hastaras panim*—the Jewish people suffering because *HKBH* "conceals His presence." Rambam in *Moreh Nevuchim* (3:51) interprets this to mean that the Jewish people's actions distance *HKBH* with the result that they are abandoned to *mikra*—just like animals.[28] The Ramak[29] similarly understands these *pesukim* as referring to a removal of the protection of *HKBH,* resulting in vulnerability to *mikra.* The Ohr Hachaim, Malbim, and Netziv (*Haamek Davar*) also describe these *pesukim* as referring to *mikra.* Furthermore, the Abarbanel distinguishes between direct punishment and *hastaras panim* in explaining these *pesukim.*[30] Finally, the Ramchal in *Daas Tevunos* (*siman* 142) distinguishes between the *hastaras panim* described in these *pesukim* and the standard system of reward and punishment.[31]

---

26 Many thinkers would contend that not all adversity fits into these two categories, and that adversity may not be a punishment at all. For example, the *Daas Tevunos simanim* 166- 170 explains that many divine acts which result in misfortune are an expression of *hanhagas hamazal,* bringing the world closer to its perfection, and are not expressions of punishment which emanates from *hanhagas hamishpat. Hanhagas hamazal* is unrelated to what an individual deserves and thus provides an important explanation for *tzadik ve'ra lo, rasha ve'tov lo.* Note that presumably, *hanhagas hamishpat* can also lead to indirect effects similar to what I now describe above. A person cannot know if an adversity was a direct punishment, a direct expression of *hanhagas hamazal,* or an indirect punishment.

27 While I focus on adversity, one could similarly distinguish between direct reward and beneficial *mikra.* See *Kuzari* 5:20, cited above.

28 Rambam previously maintained (*Moreh Nevuchim* 3:17) that individual animals are completely abandoned to *mikra.*

29 *Shiur Komah,* section 54, category 10.

30 The Abarbanel offers two interpretations of these *pesukim*—that they could refer to either *hastaras panim* or direct punishment.

31 Interestingly, the *Meshech Chochma* (*Devarim* 31:17) faults the Jewish people for attributing their predicament described in *Vayeilech* to a lack of *hashgacha.* He says that instead, they should interpret their suffering as a direct punishment from

Many commentators explain events in Tanach based on the distinction between direct punishments and *mikra.* Rav Saadya Gaon[32] explains that David initially interpreted a famine as due to *mikra* as opposed to a direct punishment and therefore delayed searching for a spiritual cause. The Ralbag (Joshua 7:1) and Malbim (ibid.) explain that the consequence of Achan's sin was a removal of *hashgacha.* The resultant exposure to danger led to the deaths of 36 soldiers who did not themselves deserve to be directly punished for Achan's sin. Inversely, the Ralbag (Judges 4:8) explains that Barak requested that Devora accompany him to fight against Sisera in order to enhance the level of *hashgacha* provided to the Jewish people. The Ramak[33] says that due to sin, otherwise righteous people can be left vulnerable to the forces of nature. Yaakov was afraid that due to sin he would be vulnerable to brother Esav's attack. According to the Ramak, this potential vulnerability to nature provides an explanation for *tzadik ve'ra lo, rasha ve'tov lo* and also a rationale why a person can be saved from danger by natural means.

The concept of *mikra* is utilized by the Maharal[34] in one of his explanations of the *gemara* (*Rosh Hashanah* 16b) which explains the judgment of *Rosh Hashanah.*[35] The Maharal says the judgment is whether a person is protected from *mikra.* The righteous person is protected from *mikra* and allowed to live the lifespan allotted to him, while the wicked person is subject to *mikra,* which may or may not result in his premature death.

HKBH. Does the *Meshech Chochma* reject the concept of *mikra*? Perhaps the *Meshech Chochma* means that although sometimes it is unclear whether to interpret an event as direct *hashgacha* or as *mikra*, there are times, such as when the impact is very substantial, when it must be interpreted as direct *hashgacha.* The Abarbanel (*Bereishis* 45:1–5) asserts that an example of this was when Yosef was sold into slavery. Yosef rejected viewing this as *mikra* and insisted that a direct act of *hashgacha* was responsible for placing him in a position where he could help prepare for the impending famine. The *Kuzari* (5:20) similarly says it is unclear whether phenomena are the result of direct *hashgacha* or intermediaries but advises attributing them to hashgacha—certainly "for major events such as death, victory, war, success, failure, and so on" (The Kuzari In Defense of the Despised Faith Newly Translated and Annotated by Rabbi N. Daniel Korobkin. Jerusalem, Israel: Feldheim Publishers, 2009, p581).

32 Cited in Radak, II Samuel 21:1.

33 *Shiur Komah*, section 54, categories 9 and 10.

34 *Chiddushei Aggados Rosh Hashanah* 16b, "*Shlosha Sefarim.*"

35 The Maharal cites Samuel I 26:10 as a source for the concept of death due to *mikra.* The Kuzari (5:20) and Ralbag (Samuel I 26:10) understand this verse similarly.

What are the differences between the processes of direct punishments and *hastaras panim*?

Direct divine punishments seem to be "worse" than *mikra* in that they are inevitable. Abandonment to *mikra* seemingly leaves open many possibilities and does not necessarily result in adversity.[36] Rather, a person is "on his own"—and has to live with the natural consequences of his actions and predicament. One of Ramban's (Job 36:7) examples of *mikra* is that the Jewish people must use natural means to fight wars. Surely the uncertainty of fighting a war with natural means is better than certain destruction!

In another sense, however, *hastaras panim* is "worse" than a direct punishment. *Mikra* means that harm can befall a person that based on the regular rules of justice he doesn't deserve. Someone may not deserve to specifically suffer adversity—yet may also not merit to be saved from natural forces. This may be the intent of the Abarbanel (*Devarim* 31:17-18) who says that *hastaras panim* is worse than the other punishments in the Torah.

An illustration of this point is the choice made by David to suffer a plague rather than a famine or defeat in battle. The Malbim (II Samuel 24:14) explains that a famine involves natural forces and a battle involves the *bechira* of the enemy. Overcoming these forces requires a greater degree of divine intervention. In contrast, a plague is a divine act and is thus most likely to be mitigated by divine mercy.

Direct punishments contain an element of mercy and love that is absent in *hastaras panim*. The Ralbag (I Kings 19:11-12) interprets one of Eliyahu's prophecies as saying that *HKBH* brings direct punishments only if they can accomplish a positive purpose. The message to Eliyahu was that when direct punishments failed to arouse the Jewish people to *teshuva*, the punishments stopped. The next step was to abandon them to *mikra*—to be "like a target for arrows." The implication is that abandonment to *mikra*, unlike direct divine punishments, is not carefully measured to achieve a purpose.

This element of mercy that is present in direct punishment and absent in *hastaras panim* is further reflected in a comment of the Ohr Hachaim to the *pesukim* in *Vayeilech*. The Ohr Hachaim (*Devarim* 31:17) writes that if *HKBH* would "pay attention" to the travails of the Jewish people then He would have mercy and stop their suffering. Therefore He "hides His face"—allowing for more destructive consequences than direct punishment would inflict.

---

36 See, however, the above Abarbanel for why *hastaras panim* may in fact result in inevitable suffering.

The Ramchal in *Daas Tevunos* (*simanim* 138, 142, 166) contrasts when *HKBH* runs the world with *hanhagas hamishpat* and when *HKBH* distances himself and the world is run with *hastaras panim*. He says that *mishpat* comes from HKBH's love and that "revealed rebuke originates from hidden love." As a result, punishments are delivered with love and mercy. There are times, however, when based on *hanhagas hamishpat* the world would not deserve to be sustained. During these times, the world is nonetheless allowed to continue. But such a world is run with *hastaras panim* and there is no *mishpat*—and thus no discernible love and mercy.

Sources that Seem to Reject *Mikra*

There are sources that seem to challenge the understanding of *teva* and *mikra* that I have put forward.

Rabbi Aryeh Leibowitz[37] demonstrates that various thinkers, including Hasidic thinkers and the Vilna Gaon, maintain that *hashgacha pratis* encompasses even non-humans (in contrast to Rambam, Ramban, Rabbenu Bechaya,[38] and others who say it does not). He refers to their approach as the "Expansive Approach." This expansive approach to *hashgacha pratis* seems to contradict the notion of *teva* being causal.

Similarly, Rabbi Menachem Mendel Schneerson understands that the Baal Shem Tov connects the concept of *hashgacha* to the concept that *HKBH* constantly renews the creation.[39] This is why *hashgacha* encompasses everything, even inanimate objects, plants, and animals. He even suggests[40] that Rambam could be consistent with this approach.

Seemingly in contrast to the Ramchal in *Mesillas Yesharim* (*perek* 9) cited above, the Ramchal in *Daas Tevunos* (*siman* 36) stresses that the will of *HKBH* alone—and not *teva*—determines what happens in the world: "...that He alone supervises with individual providence and nothing occurs in His world except through His will and His hand, not though chance, not through nature, and not through *mazal*..." Also, he writes in *Mesillas Yesharim* (*perek* 19), based on the *gemara* (*Berachos* 60b), that everything that HKBH does with respect to each person is beneficial to him.

Rabbi Abraham Isaac Kook[41] writes that miracles demonstrate that *HKBH* is in complete control and thus natural laws do not result in unin-

37 Leibowitz, Part One, Chapter Four.

38 Ibid.

39 For more on this concept see Korobkin, p. 586 footnote 178.

40 *Shaarei Emunah*, Chapter 19.

41 *Ein Aya Brachos* 9:1-2.

tended consequences—"even small details are intentional." Even small details should not be considered *mikra,* mere collateral damage—"even something that could possibly be attributed to mikra, one should realize that it has a constructive purpose."

The Chazon Ish[42] similarly defines *bitachon* as the belief that "there is no *mikra*—all that happens is declared by Him."

I would suggest that there need not be a contradiction between these ideas and the notion that natural forces are causal.[43] *HKBH* created the world (or continually creates the world) with an ordered system of natural laws. **These laws have a causal impact in the sense that they can result in a different outcome compared with if *HKBH* did not will that these laws operate. The natural laws alter the decision calculus of what will ultimately happen.** If, however, given all relevant considerations, there was no constructive purpose in allowing nature to "take its course," then, according to some opinions, *HKBH* would in fact intervene.[44]

The Ramchal is not arguing that *teva* (or *mazal* for that matter) has no causal role—only that the will of *HKBH* is the ultimate determinant. While there is a system of laws through which *HKBH* runs the world, these laws are fully subject to the will of *HKBH.* As the Ramchal in *Daas Tevunos* explicitly writes a few lines later: "…and all of the systems of justice and all of the laws that he embedded—are all dependent on His will, and He is not forced by them in any way." It is the will of *HKBH* that these laws operate.[45]

---

42 *Emunah U'Bitachon* beginning of *Perek* 2, Section 1.

43 I am only suggesting that these sources accept the basic premise of *teva* as causal. For example, some of the sources cited earlier may not agree that *HKBH* will intervene such that every outcome ultimately has a constructive purpose. But the disagreement is limited to under what circumstances *HKBH* chooses to intervene—all can agree that the natural order is causal.

44 I believe that what I am suggesting here differs from what Rabbi Aryeh Leibowitz suggests in Leibowitz, Part One, Chapter Five. If I understand him correctly, he equates *hanhagas hayichud* with *teva*—"G-d's governance through the system of *hanhagas ha-yichud* is called nature, *teva* …The system of nature, *teva*, is really the mask that hides an unfolding G-dly process of divine revelation (Leibowitz, pp. 105-106)." I am arguing that *teva* can be a mask for *hanhagas hamishpat* just as it can be a mask for *hanhagas hayichud* and furthermore that neither *hanhagas hayichud* nor *hanhagas hamishpat* precludes that *teva* can also be causal.

45 The purpose of these laws, according the *Daas Tevunos* (siman 36), is to enable the ultimate revelation of the Oneness of HKBH: "It emerges that the revelation of this Oneness is what The Supreme Will desired, and based on this intention He embedded laws to govern His creations."

Rav Kook in fact seems to accept the causal role of *teva* in describing the negative health impacts of overindulging in food and also describes *teva* as a force that is balanced by opposing, spiritual forces.[46]

Rabbi Eliyahu Dessler[47] describes *teva* as nothing more than an illusion that is not causal, and strongly criticizes the belief that *teva* is causal by characterizing those who adopt this perspective as guilty of believing that "by my own might I have achieved all of this." He interprets[48] Rambam (*Moreh Nevuchim* 3:18) and *Seforno* (*Vayikra* 13:47), who appear to limit *hashgacha*, as drawing a distinction between *hashgacha pratis* and *hashgacha klalis*. In Rav Dessler's approach, those who do not deserve *hashgacha pratis* are not abandoned to the vicissitudes of nature. The difference between someone who receives *hashgacha pratis* and someone who receives *hashgacha klalis* is that the former is judged with respect to their own role in furthering the purpose of creation, while the latter is treated as an instrument in enabling the righteous to further that purpose—but everyone is guided by continuous *hashgacha*. Rav Dessler's approach seems to be inconsistent with my assertion that natural forces are causal.

Adopting the Proper Perspective

I have argued that a far-reaching belief in *hashgacha pratis* does not conflict with a causal understanding of *teva* and *bechira*. *Teva* can be causal, and this provides a sound basis for the need to engage the world using natural means. At the same time, the existence of hidden miracles (and the fact that hidden miracles are a usual phenomenon) offers a solid basis for a spiritual response to danger, adversity, and suffering. When faced with danger, one can and ought to bear in mind that nothing precludes the possibility of divine intervention.

Even if adversity is due to *mikra*, vulnerability to natural forces reveals a lack of divine protection, and this is due to spiritual causes. The Abarbanel (*Devarim* 31:17-18) says that the Jewish people, having been abandoned to *mikra*, are faulted for not realizing that their abandonment to *mikra* is a consequence of their attachment to *avodah zarah*. The Ralbag (I Kings 19:12) also stresses that the Jewish people are supposed to view a lack of *hashgacha* as a consequence of sin.

Rambam in *Mishna Torah* (*Taaniyos* 1) cautions against interpreting misfortunes as simply the result of natural forces—rather, these misfortunes should be an impetus to *teshuva*. I would suggest that this indicates

---

46 *Ein Aya Brachos* 6:34 and 9:131, respectively.

47 *Michtav M'Eliyahu*, Volume 1, *HaNes V'Hateva, HaTeva—Hester Nissim.*

48 *Michtav M'Eliyahu*, Volume 2, *Yamim Noraim, Shnei Yomim Shel Rosh Hashanah.*

that Rambam agrees[49] that vulnerability to *mikra* is an expression of *hashgacha*—and is thus a call to *teshuva*. Rabbi Yosef Dov Soloveitchik[50] also understands Rambam that susceptibility to *mikra* needs to be understood as reflecting a spiritual lack and is thus an opportunity for growth:

> The fundamental of providence is here transformed into a concrete commandment, an obligation incumbent upon man. Man is obliged to broaden the scope and strengthen the intensity of the individual providence that watches over him. Everything is dependent on him; it is all in his hands. When a person creates himself, ceases to be a mere species man, and becomes a man of G-d, then he has fulfilled that commandment which is implicit in the principle of providence.

ƆƦ

49 See earlier footnote (#9) for sources that provide perspective on Rambam's approach to miracles and *hashgacha*.

50 Soloveitchik, Joseph B., *Halakhic Man*. (Philadelphia: The Jewish Publication Society, 1983), pp. 123–128.

חקירה

כרך י"ט – שנת תשע"ה

חקירה

כרך י"ט – שנת תשע"ה

תוכן עניינים

הלכה

השקפה

לדרכו של השופט המנוח פרופ' מנחם אלון בהעצמת[ה] המשפט העברי: יחסי הורים וילדים כמשל

מאת: ישראל צבי גילת

א. פרשנותו של מנחם אלון ליחסי הורים וילדים בדיני התורה

אין אחד בדורנו המזוהה כל כך עם הטמעתה של ההלכה היהודית בציבוריות הישראלית בכלל ובעיני המשפטנים בפרט כמו השופט פרופ' מנחם אלון ז"ל. שיטתו הייחודית שנפרסה בפסקיו, במאמריו בהרצאותיו ובספרו המונומנטלי המשפט העברי – מקורותיו תולדותיו ומקורותיו[1] הוסברה על ידו בפירוט רב. דומה כי גם היום, מנחם אלון משמש השראה לכל מי שנזקק למציאות המורכבת של "יהדות ודמוקרטיה" שבה משמשים בכפיפה אחת "משפט והלכה". מנחם אלון, שטרם הגיעו לעולם המשפט, היה חניך של שני בתי מדרשות הפכיים: ישיבת "כנסת ישראל", שיסודה בסלבודקא שבליטא, המכונה "חברון" שבירושלים, מחד גיסא, והחוג לתלמוד שבאוניברסיטה העברית בירושלים, מאידך גיסא, השכיל לבנות מסילות בלבם של אנשים הרחוקים מדת וממסורת - שאינם רגילים בדואליות של "מחקר טהור" עם "תורה לשמה" – להסכין ולקבל את יציקת תכניה של ההלכה היהודית העתיקה בכליו של המשפט המודרני הנוהג בישראל. במפעלותיו הרבים – תחילה, כמשנה ליועץ המשפטי לממשלה לענייני חקיקה בתחום המשפט העברי, בהמשך, כפרופסור בפקולטה למשפטים וכמיסדו של המכון למשפט עברי והעומד בראשו, וכשופט בית משפט עליון ומשנה לנשיא עד לפרישתו לגמלאות – הביאו לכך שקיים מנחם אלון למעשה מה שהגו ברעיונם אנשי חברת המשפט העברי בכינוסם הראשון בבית הכנסת הגדול במוסקבה, להציע סינתזה של דין לאומי עצמאי המשלב מסורת יהודית עתיקה, קנאית באורחותיה, במסורת משפטית אזרחית, ליברלית חילונית.

---

[1] (מהד' 3, ירושלים: הוצאת מאגנס,) = M. Elon, *Jewish Law: History, Sources, Principles* (Philadelphia and Jerusalem: 1994).

ישראל צבי גילת, פרופסור-חבר בבית הספר למשפטים שליד המכללה האקדמית נתניה, מלמד דיני משפחה וירושה, משפט עברי ותחיקה סוציאלית. כמו כן מלמד בבית הספר לחינוך באוניברסיטת בר-אילן דיני המינהל החינוכי. גילת כתב את ספרו: דיני משפחה: יחסי הורים וילדים (2000) וכן מאמרים בכתבי עת ובספרים מדעיים. בשנים 2002-2003 עמד גילת בראש וועדת ייעוץ ציבורית לשר העבודה והרווחה דאז "בעניין 'וועדות החלטה' והתנהלותם של פקידי הסעד למיניהם מולן" ('וועדת גילת').

תרומתו של מנחם אלון ראויה למחקר מעמיק וקוהרנטי, וחוששני כי קרובים אנו מדי אליו בכדי להעריך את מפעלו בפרספקטיבה היסטורית.[2] אך בקעה קטנה אחת, דוגמאטית, אני מעונין להתגדר בה, והיא הערתו עלי בספרו האחר מעמד האישה. שם כותב אלון:[3]

> ...לדעת גילת אין להשוות את עמדתו של המשפט העברי בנושא זה להוראת חוק הכשרות המשפטית והאפוטרופסות גם לפי הגישה שחלה בעולמה של ההלכה בימינו לפי המקורות שעמדתי עליהם לעיל....אך עדיין נראה לי, גם סביר וגם ראוי, להביא למגמה משותפת של האמור בחוק הכשרות המשפטית והאפוטרופסות והגישה בעולמה של ההלכה בימינו, כפי שהיא באה לכלל ביטוי בפסקי הדין האמורים , כ"פרשנות יוצרת" העולה מתוך המקורות גופם (הדגשה במקור – יצ"ג)....

הערתו של מנחם אלון מתייחסת לפסק דין מנומק היטב שכתב בפרשת נגר נ' נגר[4]. שם הגן אלון על כבודו של בית הדין הרבני במעטפת הפרוצדוראלית (התנגד לשלילת פסקיו על ידי בית המשפט המחוזי ב"תקיפה עקיפה"), תוך ביקורת לא מוסווית על תוכנו המהותי של פסק הדין הרבני שקבע כי לאב, ולא לאֵם, הזכות הבלעדית לקבוע את מקום החינוך של ילדיהם. באותה פרשה היה סכסוך ממושך בין שני הורים שנסב, בעיקרו, על דרך חינוכם של ילדיהם. ההורים מתחילה היו חילוניים באורחותיהם ושלחו את ילדיהם לבית ספר ממלכתי כללי. לימים האב, חזר בתשובה, וחפץ היה להוציא את ילדיו מבית-הספר שבו למדו, ולהכניסם לבית-ספר מהזרם הממלכתי-דתי. האֵם, שילדיה היו בהחזקתה, רצתה שילדיה ימשיכו ללמוד בזרם החינוך הממלכתי הכללי. האב פנה לבית הדין הרבני וביקש לצוות על מקום חינוכו של הילד.

בית-הדין הרבני שדן בעניינם קבע שהילדים ילמדו לפי רצון האב בבית הספר הממלכתי-דתי, ובלשונם:[5]

> מאחר ובהתאם לדין על האב מוטלת חובת החינוך של בניו, מוצא בית הדין שהוא הוא הזכאי לקבוע את צורת החינוך של ילדיו. לאור זאת פוסק בית הדין: על הנתבעת (האֵם – יצ"ג) להכניס את שני בניהם המוחזקים אצלה לבית ספר דתי בסביבת מקום מגוריה, רמת גן. התובע זכאי לפעול בעירית רמת גן לבצע החלטת בית הדין.

---

2 (השופט) אליקים רובינשטיין, "על השופט מנחם אלון: אנושיות, משפט עברי במדינה יהודית וצדק במדינה יהודית ודמוקרטית" הסניגור 192, 4 (2013); אביעד הכהן "מנחם אלון: חכם המשפט וחכם במשפט" שערי משפט ו 9 (תשע"ה).

3 (תל-אביב: הוצאת הקיבוץ המאוחד, 2005) בע' 104-105, ה"ש 17.

4 ביד"מ 1/81, פ"ד לח(1) 365.

5 תיק 13355/שם מיום 31.8.80

האֵם פנתה לבית המשפט המחוזי בתל-אביב ובקשה מתן צו שיורה על רישום ילדיה בבית הספר הממלכתי הכללי בו למדו בשנים עברו עד פרוץ הסכסוך. האב התנגד. השופט חיים פורת שישב בעניינם, תקף החלטה זו של בית-הדין הרבני והורה לרשום את הילדים כרצון האֵם, כשבין יתר נימוקיו – כי בית הדין הרבני חרג מסמכותו ולא שקל את טובתם של הילדים כראוי. ובלשונו:[6]

> שחייבים להגיע למסקנה, שבית-הדין הרבני לא דן בענייננו בחינוך ולימוד כענף של אפוטרופסות, אלא בזכות הורית - זכות האב על-פי ההלכה לקיים מצות תלמוד תורה. בענין זה חזקה על בית-הדין שישקף את עמדת ההלכה, אך הוא לא דן ולא פסק בענין של 'אפוטרופסות', וממילא דן ופסק בעניין שלא הוסמך לדון על-ידי המחוקק (החילוני), פסקו חסר נפקות משפטית ...[7]

כאמור, השופט אלון ישב בראש ההרכב של בית הדין המיוחד, ומעבר להכרעתו שיש לדחות את "התקיפה" של בית המשפט המחוזי על בית הדין הרבני (מטעמים פרוצדוראליים, שאינם לענייננו), תמה על ניסוח הכרעתו של בית-הדין הרבני, שנטה לרצונו של האב לחייב את הילדים ללמוד בבית ספר ממלכתי-דתי נגד רצונה של האם רק בשל זכאותו של האב על פי ההלכה לחנך את ילדיו , ובלשונו:[8]

> בכך עדיין לא בא הפתרון למקרה המסוים שלפנינו, אשר בו אירעו ובאו דברים לידי כך, שלכל אחד מההורים אורח חיים שונה מבחינת שמירת תורה ומצוות, ומתוך כך שונות הם תוכן הלימוד וצורת החינוך, שכל אחד מהם מבקש להנחיל לילדים, במקרה זה חזר האב לחיי תורה ומצוות; אבל אותה בעיה יכולה שתתעורר

---

6 תמ"א 342/81, נגר נ' היועמ"ש, פ"מ תשמ"ג(1) 232, 242 (1981).

7 ניתן לומר שההנחה של השופט פורת הייתה כי בית הדין הרבני לא עסק באפוטרופסות הילד משום שלא דן ב'טובת הילד' משמע שלא התחשב בשיקול זה בכלל. אך דומה כי השופט פורת הלך אחר גישתו של השופט זילברג כי כל דיון בענייניו של ילד חייב לחתור אחר שיקול יחיד בלעדי והוא טובת הילד, וכלשונו של השופט זילברג בפרשת ע"א 209/54, שטיינר נ' מד"י, פ"ד ט 241, 242 (1955):

> מבחן טובת הילדים, לדעתי, לא ימלט בו אחד מן השניים: או שאינו שיקול רציני כלל או שמתחשבים בו ובו בלבד. פשרה לא תתכן כלל: הוא אינו ניתן לחלוקה, ואין למזגו ולערבבו באיזה שהוא שיקול אחר. כי משהתרומם המחוקק לדרגת התפיסה המודרנית - ובתפיסה מודרנית זו נוקטים חכמי ישראל זה עידן ועידנים - כי הילד אינו 'אובייקט' של שמירה והחזקה להנאתו או לטובתו של אחד ההורים אלא הוא עצמו 'סובייקט', הוא גופו 'בעל דין', בשאלה חיונית זו, הרי לא יתכן להתעלם מן האינטרסים שלו בשום צירוף מסיבות שהוא, ולא יתכן כי נדחה אותם מפני 'זכות' של מישהו אחר, ויהא זה האב או האם שלו. לכן צדק המחוקק הישראלי בקבעו - וזהו לדעתנו מובנו הנכון של סעיף 3(ב) - כי טובת הילדים תהא השיקול הסופי והמכריע [הדגשה שלי - יצ"ג] הן בהתנגשה עם זכות האפוטרופסות האמורה בסעיף 3(א) והן בהתנגשה עם הוראות חוק זר...

8 שם, עמ' 407.

במקרה הפוך - שהאב אינו שומר תורה ומצוות, והאֵם חזרה לאורח חיים דתיים, האם גם במקרה אחרון זה היה כבוד בית-הדין הרבני האזורי משתמש בכלל, שחובת החינוך של הבן מוטלת על האב, ולכן הוא זכאי לקבוע את צורת החינוך?

אך מעבר לתמיהתו, אלון קבע כי בית הדין הרבני שגה בקביעה כי חובת החינוך חלה רק על האב וכי מצות תלמוד תורה אינה שייכת לאֵם. לשם כך נזקק אלון למקורות הלכתיים, מהם ראשוניים, לאשש את הנחתו כי עמדתה של ההלכה אינה קופאת על שמריה וכי ניתן ליישב אותה עם אורח החיים המודרני, שבה לאם ולאב יש זכות שווה לעצב את חינוכם של ילדיהם. פסק דין נגר הוזכר הרבה בפסיקה המאוחרת, וגם אלון עצמו מצטט פסק דין זה באריכות בספרו המשפט העברי, בפרקים "המשפט העברי במערכת המשפט הכללי", ו"המעמד האישי והמשפט העברי במדינה".[9] דומה בעיני כי פסק הדין היא פרדיגמה ממנה ניתן להבין כיצד השופט והחוקר, באישיותו של אלון, מפרנסים זה את זה. הן בפרשה זו והן במקומות אחרים אלון מדגיש את היטמעותם של דיני התורה ביחסי ההורים והילדים עם הוראות חוק הכשרות המשפטית והאפוטרופסות, תשכ"ב-1962 ועם חוק לתיקון דיני משפחה (מזונות), תשי"ט-1959 עד כדי הפיכתם ל"בשר אחד". כך סבור אלון כי ההורים הם "אפוטרופוסים טבעיים" לא רק לפי חוק הכשרות אלא גם לפי ההלכה , מאחר שלפי ההלכה אין הקטנים יכולים לזכות ולהתחייב בעצמם וכי גם בהלכה "טובת הילד" היא "עיקרון-על" ו"חזקת הגיל הרך" לקוח מ"כבשונה של ההלכה".[10] מכאן גם הגיע אלון בפרשת ניר נ' ניר, לפריזומציה הבאה:[11]

> דומה עלי, אפוא, כי אין מקום להבחין בסוגיה זו בין עמדת המשפט העברי לדבר המחוקק בסעיף 25 לחוק הכשרות המשפטית והאפוטרופסות. נראה לי, שלא זו בלבד **שלא קיים הבדל** מהותי בין גישת שתי מערכות משפטיות אלה, אלא דעתי נוטה לומר שאף מבחינת הרמת **נטל הראיה אין משום הבדל** של ממש ביניהם; בשתיהן הכלל הגדול הוא, ששומה על בית המשפט לבדוק, מיוזמתו הוא, בכל מקרה ומקרה טובת הילד מהי, ואין לו להסתפק בהסתמכות על הנחה זו או אחרת ולפסוק על-פיהן בלבד, ללא כל בדיקה נוספת (הדגשות שלי – יצ"ג).

דרכו זו של אלון מחייבת את בחינתם של דיני התורה עצמם, האם מקורות ההלכה העוסקים ביחסי הורים וילדים, הם "כפטיש יפוצץ סלע, מה פטיש זה מתחלק לכמה ניצוצות אף מקרא אחד מתחלק לכמה טעמים",[12] ומכאן שניתן לדרוש מבתי הדין הרבניים לעגן את פסיקתם, בפרשנות יצירתית של המקורות, כפי שהיטיב אלון לעשות? או שמא

---

9 עמ' 1399-1398, 1488-1479, 1515-1508, 1535-1534.

10 שם, עמ' 1398, הערה 173. המכתם הוא מפיו של שר המשפטים דאז, פנחס רוזן, בעת הבאת הצ"ח לקריאה ראשונה בד"כ 32 (תשכ"ב), 48.

11 ע"א 458/79, פ"ד לה(1) 518, 523 (1980).

12 סנהדרין, לד ע"א.

יש בפרשנותו של אלון "שבירת כלים" היינו, העמדתה של אלטרנטיבה מודרנית בכסות עתיקה, שאז ניתן לראות בקריאתו מעין "תקיפה ישירה" על דיני התורה בשל חריגתם מהתקינות הליברלית הרווחת בישראל? כדי לענות על שאלה זו חייבים אנו לפנות למקורותיהם של דיני התורה בטהרתם, החל מהספרות התלמודית והמשך בפסיקותיהם ובביאוריהם של חכמי ההלכה הראשונים והאחרונים, ולא רק במופעיהם בפסיקות בתי הדין הרבניים הממלכתיים בישראל. על עמדתה הטהורה של ההלכה הרבנית עמדתי בספרי דיני משפחה – יחסי הורים וילדים ומכאן שההפניות למקורות ההלכה ולניתוחם יובאו בצמצום ובקצרה בהערות השוליים.[13]

ב. גישתה הטהורה של ההלכה בעניין יחסי הורים וילדים

1. האפוטרופסות אינה תיאור הזיקה בין הורים לילדיהם

במקורות התלמודיים לא נמצא את המונח אפוטרופסות כבא לתאר את היחס המשפטי של האב כלפי בניו ובנותיו. אין האפוטרופוס בדיני התלמוד אלא שליח שמונה להשגיח על נכסי הזולת, שחייב, כנאמן, לנהלם לטובת האיש שמינהו. לרוב, האפוטרופסות שבתלמודים היא השגחתו של אדם על נכסי יתומים, שבאה לו אם מכוח מינויו של אבי היתומים לפני מותו, אם מכוח מינויו של בית-הדין ואפילו מכוח סמיכתם של היתומים אליו, שהוא מינוי למעשה. יחד עם זאת מצינו בכמה מקומות בתלמודים שאדם ממנה אפוטרופוס מטעמו לפקח על נכסיו בעודו בחיים ולתפקד כשלוחו לביצוע המשימות שיוטלו עליו. ניתן איפוא לשער, שאין האב ממונה מטעם בית-דין על נכסיהם של בניו ובנותיו, ומשום כך אין הוא מחויב לפעול בהם כפי שמחויב האפוטרופוס בנכסיהם של היתומים או בעבור כל מי שהוא נתמנה לפעול לטובתו.[14]

אף מתוך עיון בראשונים, שנזקקו למונחי "אפוטרופסות האב" כדי לתאר את היחסים הממוניים שבין האב ובין בניו ובנותיו, עולה בבירור שאין האב משמש אפוטרופוס טבעי, כפי שהוא משמש בשיטות משפט מודרניות, וממילא אין מוטלת עליו חובה לנהוג בנאמנות כלפי נכסי בניו כזו המוטלת עליו בשיטות המשפט המודרניות, אלא במקרה הצורך, כשיש לקטין רכוש או איזו זכות המגיעה לו, "אין בית דין נזקקין לקטן שיש לו אב אלא כל מה

13 (תל-אביב: חושן למשפט, 2000)(להלן: ספרי).

14 ראו בהרחבה שלום אלבק יסודות בדיני הממונות בתלמוד (רמת-גן: אוניברסיטת בר אילן, תשנ"ד) 210, 215 [=מחקרי משפט ט (תשנ"ב) 7, 13, 17]. בתרגומים מצינו אפוטרופוס גם כפקיד ממונה בשמו של המלך, ראו: תרגום ירושלמי בראשית, מא, מ; שם, שם, לד. כן ראו סוכה, כז ע"א "אפוטרופוס של אגריפס המלך". פסיקתא דרב כהנא (מנדלבוים) נספחים, פרשה ה; ספר העיטור אות פא (רמא"י, ע' עח). ועיינו משנה כתובות ט:ד, כתובות, פו ע"ב; אנציקלופדיה תלמודית: בערכו כרך ב, עמ' קכא; יעקב ק' רייניץ "האפוטרופסים מכוח יתומים שסמכו אצל בעל הבית" מחקרי משפט א (תש"ם) 219

שיעשה האב בנכסי בניו הוא עשוי ואין בית דין מדקדקין אחריו", כלשון הרא"ש.[15] כלומר, בית-דין רשאי להאמין לאב שינהג בתבונה ובהיגיון בנכסים של בניו ובנותיו ויפעל למענם. אך אין באמירה זו כדי להטיל חובה קטיגורית על האב לנהוג כך. הריטב"א אף שולל אפריורית את מינוי האב לאפוטרופוס על נכסי בניו מן הטעם שהאב הינו "קרוב הראוי ליורשו" את הקטן. וכמו ש"אין מורידים קרוב בנכסי קטן", כך אין ממנים את האב לאפוטרופוס על נכסי בניו.[16]

2. חובת האב לזון את ילדיו תמורת זכויותיו הממוניות בהם - גמול למתנדב

מאחר שאין האב משמש כאפוטרופוס לבניו ולבנותיו, ולא כל שכן שאין הוא נחשב לאפוטרופוס טבעי על ילדיו הקטנים לפי ההלכה היהודית, על מה נסבה אחריותו ההלכתית כלפי בניו ובנותיו? נפתח ונאמר שבמקורות העוסקים במזונות הילדים יש שניוּת, לכאורה. יש מקורות המטילים על האב לזון ולפרנס את בניו ובנותיו כחובה עצמאית, אם מתקנת אושא ואם מטעם צדקה. ויש סוגיות תלמודיות לא-מעטות שעולה מהן כי חיוב האב לזון את בניו ובנותיו הוא חיוב משני, הטפל לזכויותיו הממוניות של האב בבניו ובבנותיו. חיובו של האב לזון את בניו ובנותיו נובע מזכותו לקבל רווחים שהפיקו ממעשה ידיהם, ממציאות שמצאו, או אף מתשלומי נזק שהגיעו להם. ויכול אפוא האב לוותר על זכויות נרחבות אלה, ולוּ רק כדי להיפטר מן החובה לזונם ולפרנסם. חיוב האב, לפי סוגיות אלה, נתון לרצונו הסובייקטיבי, והוא יכול להיפטר ממנו בהינף יד בכל שעה שירצה. המקורות התלמודיים עצמם וכן פרשני ההלכה הבתר-תלמודית סותמים ואינם מבארים את פִּשרה של שניוּת זו.[17]

דומני שאחריות האב הולכת וסובבת סביב ציר אחד - חפצו של האב לדאוג לבניו ולבנותיו, לזונם ולכלכלם. לאמור, בבסיס של יחסי הממון של האב עם בניו ובנותיו אין האב אלא מתנדב לעשות טוב עם בניו ובנותיו, לזונם ולפרנסם לפי רצונו. לפי אסכולה

---

15 תשובות הרא"ש, כלל פז, סימן א. ברוח זו ראו גם תשובותיו, כלל פב, סימן ב, שכתב "וששאלת עם מי תשב הבת אצל אביה או אצל האפוטרופוס שהוא אבי אמה, דבר זה ראוי להתברר על מי שמכירין את שניהם, אבל לכאורה נראה שהבת יש לה קורת רוח אצל אביה והממון יישאר ביד האפוטרופוס אבי אמה אם יראה לדיינים שהממון שמור יפה בידו. ואם האב בעל אחריות שיוכל למשכן קרקעות כדי ממון הבת טוב הוא שנתן הכל לידו ויפרנסנה וישיאנה באותו ממון". ראו פירוש תשובה זו בדרכי משה, חו"מ, סימן רצ, ס"ק ה; הגהות רמ"א, חו"מ, סימן רפה, סעיף ח; סמ"ע, שם, שם, ס"ק לג. ראו גם תשובות זכרון יהודה (לר' יהודה בן הרא"ש) תשובה לה. גם מתרומת הדשן, חלק התשובות, תשובה ש, עולה דבר דומה. אך שם הוא מוסיף: "... דכיוון דאביו קיים עדיין אין בית דין מצווין לפקח על נכסיו 'דארוד ילדה ואביה"ד דינא שדיה' ולאו כל הימנו שישקט את עצמו ויטיל את הטורח על בי דינא ..." נראה שדברים אלו אינם מראים על חובה משפטית אלא על דבר הראוי שיעשה. וראו גם רבצמ"ח עוזיאל שערי עוזיאל חלק א, שער א, פרק ב, סעיף א והערה א.

16 תשובות הריטב"א (קאפח), תשובה קסב. מובא בשינויי נוסח בב"י, חו"מ, סימן רצ.

17 עיינו בספרי, עמ' 155-163 והמקורות המשוקעים שם.

אחת בבבלי ובירושלמי, שהתקבלה על דעתם של פוסקים רבים, כדי להמריץ את האב לזון ולפרנס את בניו ובנותיו, קבעו חכמים שהאב "העושה טוב" עם בניו ובנותיו יהיה זכאי בזכויות הממוניות שיפלו לידי הבנים והבנות כל עוד הם סמוכים על שולחנו.[18] אך גם תקנה-המרצה זו אינה "גזרת הכתוב", אלא היא נשענת על גמירות-הדעת של האב, מתי בדעתו לסמוך את הבנים על שולחנו, לזונם ולפרנסם, רק אם יזכה ברווחיהם הממוניים, ומתי בדעתו לזון ולכלכל את בניו ובנותיו אף אם לא יזכה ברווחים הממוניים. התנדבותו של האב אינה נמדדת לפי דעתו הסובייקטיבית של כל אב ואב לחוד, אלא לפי אומד הדעת הכללי של האבות. חכמי ההלכה, בתקנותיהם ובגזרותיהם, ירדו איפוא לסוף דעתו של האב מתי, במה ובאילו תנאים הוא גומר בדעתו להתחייב כלפי בנו. כך קבעו, למשל, שהאב מקפיד על רווחי הבנים והבנות הבאים ממציאה שמצאו, שאם לא יזכה בהם, יימנע מלסומכם על שולחנו, ומשום כך מציאת הבנים והבנות הללו - לאביהם. לעומת זאת, בתשלומי נזק המגיעים לבנים, בניגוד למציאה, האב מוכן לא לזכות מהנימוק שתשלומי נזק "אית להו צערא דגופייהו" [= יש להם לבנים צער הגוף], ומשום כך אין האב נמנע מלפרנס את בניו ובנותיו גם אם לא יזכה בתשלומי נזקם. אך גם בתשלומי נזק עצמם יש להבחין אם אותם תשלומים באים מגורם שלישי שהזיק לבנים או אם אלה תשלומי נזק שהאב מחויב לשלם בעבור מה שהוא הזיק בעצמו לבניו, שכן "כי קא קפיד במידי דחסר...". כלומר, האב מקפיד מאוד על חסרון ממונו אף אם בנו מצטער, ומהחשש שמא יימנע מלסמוך את בנו על שולחנו, פטרוהו חכמים מלשלם לבנו דמי נִזקו. מכאן שהבן יכול להחליט שאין הוא מעוניין להיות סמוך על שולחן אביו, ולוּ רק מן הטעם שהוא רוצה לקבל דמי נזקו.[19] מכל האמור עולה שאין הזכויות הממוניות של האב בבניו ובבנותיו עומדות בפני עצמן כביטוי לאדנותו של האב על בניו, אלא הן רק משפיעות על האב לגמור בדעתו להתחייב בחיובים שונים כלפי בניו ובנותיו. דעתו של האב להתחייב כלפי בניו היא אפוא העומדת בבסיסן של ההלכות השונות, ואין חכמי ההלכה כופין את האב להתחייב כלפי בניו ובנותיו מעבר למה שאבות גומרים בדעתם להתחייב כלפי בניהם ובנותיהם.[20]

---

18 בב"מ, יב ע"ב; ירושלמי ב"מ פ"א ה"ה; ירושלמי פאה פ"ד ה"ה(ו); רש"י ב"מ, יב ע"ב, ד"ה 'אדר' חייא'. טעמו של הסמ"ע חו"מ, סימן רע, ס"ק ב.

19 על מובאות ומראי מקום מדויקים עיינו בספרי, עמ' 71-101.

20 גם האסכולה האחרת, התולה את זכויותיו הממוניות של האב ברווחיהם של בניו ובנותיו הקטנים בהיעדר הדעת של הבנים והבנות הקטנים לזכות לעצמם, אינה עניין לאפוטרופסות, אלא נובעת מן הנוהג הכללי שהקטן המוצא מציאה "בשעה שמוצאה מריצה אצל אביו ואין מאחר בידו". משום כך, כשהבן הקטן הוא בן שש או בן שבע (ולדעות אחרות בגיל מאוחר יותר - מהגיעו לגיל עשר), ודעתו חריפה, מציאה שמצא שייכת לעצמו, ולא לאביו. עיינו בספרי, עמ' 62-70.

3. עיצומה של חובת האב לזון את בניו ובנותיו - חיוב משלים

מנגד, קיימים מקורות המטילים על האב חובה לזון את בניו ובנותיו, חובה שאינה תלויה במידת "התנדבותו" של האב לזון ולפרנס כדי לזכות ברווחים הנופלים לידי בניו ובנותיו. אף חובה זו אינה חובה ראשית, הנובעת מחובה אפוטרופסית של האב, הבאה להיטיב עם הילד בלבד, אלא, בעיקרה, קיום מצוות צדקה על-ידי האב. כפי שעמדתי במקום אחר,[21] מצוות צדקה בכללה היא חיוב דתי שאינו ניתן לאכיפה, מאחר שהיא כולה אחוזה ודבוקה ברצונו למי ייתן וכמה ייתן, ומכאן שאין לעני הנזקק כל זכות תביעה לקבלתה. רק בשני מקרים ניתן לכפות על הצדקה, ואף שניהם תלויים, לאמיתו של דבר, באומד דעתו האמיתית של הנותן: האחד, כשאדם נדר לתת צדקה מממונו, כופין את המסרב לתת את הסכום שנדר מטעם של מצוות "מוצא שפתיך תשמֹר ועשית".[22] והאחר, כאשר הצדקה ניתנת כחלק מחיובי אנשי העיר, והם כאותם תנאים סוציאליים שמתנים אנשי העיר, אלה עם אלה, לתת לקופה של צדקה לצורכי ביטחון ולשאר הצרכים החיוניים ביותר. וכשם שאין צורך בהסכמה סובייקטיבית של כל בני העיר לתת לצורכי הביטחון של אנשי העיר, מכיוון שיש הסכמה מאומדת של רובם המוחלט של אנשי העיר, הנמצאים בעיר שהם נהנים מכך. אף בעניין מתן צדקה לקופה של צדקה יש אומד הדעת של רובם המוחלט של אנשי העיר שהם מסכימים לכך מאחר שהם נהנים מקופה של צדקה אם יירדו מנכסיהם.[23]

ומן הכלל אל הפרט. לפי המקורות התנאיים, מזונות הבנים הקטנים הם מצווה דתית של צדקה, ותו לא. מהפסוק "עֹשׂה צדקה בכל עת", שדרשו "רבותינו שביבנה", "זה הזן בניו ובנותיו כשהן קטנים", דרשו גם "זה המגדל יתום ויתומה בתוך ביתו ומשיאן", "זה הלומד תורה ומלמדה", "זה הכותב תורה ונביאים וכתובים ומשאילן לאחרים".[24] וכשם שאלה האחרונים, לא נשמע מעולם שניתן לאכוף אדם את עשייתם, אף מצוות הזנת הבנים כן. ברם, במקורות האמוראיים התגבש חיוב של האב לזון את בניו ובנותיו. מכמה מן המקורות - לא מכולם - עולה שזו מתקנת אושא, אך גם מהמקורות המאזכרים זאת אין הדבר ברור אם תקנה זו התקבלה להלכה פסוקה, אם תקנה זו תופסת לגבי כל הבנים הקטנים, או רק לאותם "קטני קטנים". ההנחה האחרת, סמויה יותר, היא שחיוב האב הוא מטעם צדקה, ומכאן שיש להבחין בין אב אמיד לבין אב שאינו אמיד. אלא שלא הוברר אף בין פוסקי ההלכה הבתר-תלמודיים אם חובת הצדקה משלימה את תקנת אושא או מחליפה אותה, אם יש הבדל בין מזונות בנים קטני קטנים עד גיל שש למזונות בנים מעל גיל זה. שיערנו איפוא, במקום אחר, שחיוב האב לזון את בניו הוא העתקה של חיוב בן עיר לתת צדקה לקופה של צדקה. חיוב הצדקה הוא תקנת חכמים לפי אומד דעת האב, כנהוג בין

21 "האמנם מצות צדקה 'שמתן שכרה בצידה' אין בית דין מצווה על קיומה?", סיני קיד (תשנ"ד) ריז, עמ' רכא-רכז.

22 דברים, כג:כד.

23 עיינו ר' שלום אלבק, דיני ממונות בתלמוד (תל-אביב: דביר, תשל"ו), עמ' 514-515.

24 כל הציטוטות הן מבבלי כתובות, נ ע"א. הפסוק מתהלים, קו:ג.

הבריות, מאחר שדעתו קרובה אצל בניו הקטנים. ואף הדירוג בין חיוב האב לזון את בניו הקטנים לבין חיובו לזון את בניו קטני הקטנים תלוי באומד דעתו המשתנה של האב. חיוב האב לזון את בניו קטני הקטנים הינו מוחלט, ואינו תלוי בעושרו של האב, מאחר שאומד דעתו של האב לדחוק עצמו ביותר ולזון את בניו קטני הקטנים מכיוון שאינם יכולים לצאת ולהתפרנס בעצמם ממעשה ידיהם. לא כן בבנים קטנים שיכולים לצאת ולהתפרנס בדוחק ממעשה ידיהם, אפילו מהכנסות מזדמנות, אין אומד דעת של האב לזון ולפרנס אותם אלא רק אם יש לו משלו, אך לא כשהוא דחוק בעצמו. לפיכך, רק אב שהוא אמוד לנו בעשירותו כופין אותו לזון את בניו הקטנים, ואין כופין את האב שאין לנו אומד על עשירותו.[25]

ולא רק עיקר החיוב של האב תלוי באומד דעתו האובייקטיבית, אלא אף שיעור החיוב במזונות הבנים והבנות תלוי באומדן זה. דעתו של אדם לדחוק עצמו לזון את בניו קטני הקטנים, ולשם כך הוא מוכן להשכיר עצמו למלאכה נוספת - רק באשר לצורכיהם ההכרחיים ביותר. אך מעבר לכך, בענייני מותרות, אין דעת האב לדחוק עצמו כל-כך, וממילא אין לחייבו לצאת ולהתפרנס ממלאכה נוספת. הדבר הברור מרובם הגדול של פוסקי ההלכה (כולל מדעתו של מהר"ם מרוטנבורג) הוא שכל אימת שיש לבנים אף קטני הקטנים נכסים משלהם, נכסים שיכולים להרוויח מהם, אין האב חייב לזון ולפרנס אותם משלו, אלא הם מתפרנסים משלהם.[26]

ניתן איפוא לשער שחיוב האב בדיני התורה לזון את בניו לעולם אינו חיוב העומד בפני עצמו, כשהזכויות הממוניות של האב בבניו ובבנותיו טפלים לו, דוגמת הקיים במשפט האנגלי וביתר שיטות המשפט המודרניות, אלא הוא חיוב המשלים את פרנסת הבנים כשאין להם משלהם. שכן, כשיש לבנים משלהם, האב יכול, לפי בחירה, לסומכם על שולחנו, לזונם ולפרנסם, ולזכות בשל כך בזכויותיהם הממוניות; ויכול להיפטר מהם ולהעדיף לא לסמכם ולא לזכות בממונם.[27]

25 ועיינו בספרי, עמ' 196-200.

26 בתשובות הרשב"א, חלק שני, תשובה שצא - הדברים נאמרו במפורש. אך הדבר עולה גם מתשובות מהר"ם מרוטנבורג (דפוס ברלין) (בלאך), רמב, 241-242; ובקיצור מופיעה תשובה זו בפסקי הרא"ש, כתובות, פרק ד, סימן יד; בעל הטורים, אבן העזר, סימן עא. ועיינו כיצד מבארים האחרונים בשיטותיהם השונות בספרי, עמ' 179-181 ומה שנראה לעניות דעתי, שם, עמ' 200-202.

27 מאחר שחיוב המזונות הוא חיוב משלים ונובע מטעם צדקה, קיימים הבדלים בין מקרים שונים בהם לא מבדילים בין מזונותיהם של קטנים לקטני קטנים, ועיינו בפרוטרוט במובאות שבספרי, עמ' 199-200, 206-207.

4. טיב היחסים הממוניים שבין האב לבתו הקטנה והנערה - "רשות"

לא רק בבנים ובבנות שאינן מצויות ברשות האב מתפרשות הזכויות שיש לאב לפי אומד דעתו, אלא אף זכויותיו המרובות של האב בבנותיו הקטנה והנערה שהן ברשותו, כפי שהאשה ברשות בעלה והעבד ברשות רבו, נתפרשו זכויות אלה - הממוניות ושאינן ממוניות - אצל חכמים כביטוי לאומד דעתו של האב. אין גִדרן והיקפן של זכויות אלה נקבע אלא לפי אומד דעתו של האב, במה הוא סבור לזכות מבנותיו אלה ובמה אין הוא סבור. מכיוון שהבת ברשות אביה לקדשה ולהשיאה לכל מי שירצה מבלי לקבל את הסכמתה, הרי שכל "שבח הבא מחמת גופה", כלומר, ממעלות גופה ונפשה, שייכים לאב, ולא לבת. משום כך האב זוכה בכסף קידושי בתו ובמעשה ידיה, שהם זכויות הנובעות במובהק ממעלות גופה ונפשה של הבת הקטנה והנערה. לעומתן, מן הצד האחר, זכות "אכילת פירות" (שיש לכל בעל בנכסי אשתו) אינה קיימת לאב, מאחר ששבח זה אינו בא ממעלות גופה, אלא מחמת נכסיה. ביחס למציאת הבת הקטנה והנערה ולמתנה שקיבלה מצאנו מחלוקות בין הראשונים והאחרונים. יש הרואים באלה זכויות צדדיות שהגיעו לבת באקראי ואין הן נובעות משבח נעוריה של הבת, ולכן אין האב זכאי בהן. חכמים אחרים סוברים לעומתם שגם מציאה ומתנה שייכות לאביה, שכן סגולות אלה לחפש ולמצוא מציאות או לשאת-חן בעיני נותני המתנה אף הן בעקיפין "שבח נעוריה" הבא ממעלות גופה ונפשה של הבת. אף על תשלומי הנזק המשתלמים עקב חבלת הבת מצינו חילוקים מסועפים בין האמוראים בתלמוד לבין הראשונים בשאלת זכאותו של האב בהם, ונראה ששורשם של החילוקים הללו בא מראיית נזקי הבת כחבלה ב"שבח נעוריה".[28]

מעיקרו של הדין, זכותו של האב לקבל את מעשה ידי בתו היתה חד-צדדית, ללא קשר לזכות הבת להיות ניזונה ממנו. אלא שמהמורה זו נרפאה במקצת על-ידי תנאי כתובה עתיק שהתחייב אדם לאשתו לפני הנישואין: "בנן נקבן דיהווין ליכי מנאי, יהוין יתבן בביתי ומתזנן מנכסי, עד דיתנסבן לגברין" (= בנות נקבות שיהיו לך ממני יהיו יושבות בביתי וניזונות מנכסי עד שיילקחו לאנשים).[29] התנאי הזה נהג כהתחייבות מפורשת בכתובה שכתב אדם לפני שכנס את אשתו, אלא שבמשך הדורות נעשה תנאי זה נפוץ ומקובל על הכל כ"תנאי בית דין", כלומר, כחיוב מכללא. ההתחייבות הייתה כלפי הבנות דווקא, לזונן ולפרנסן, משום שרק הן היו משועבדות לאביהן, ליתן לו את מעשה ידיהן מבלי יכולת להשתחרר ממנו לפני בגרותן. לא כן הבנים הסמוכים על שולחן אביהם, שאין הם מחויבים למסור את מעשה ידיהם לאביהם, ויכולים להעדיף להתפרנס מעצמם ולא למסור לו מעשה ידיהם - לא ניתקנה תקנה זו כלפיהם. ברם, גם תנאי זה איבד הרבה מתוקפו, שכן באינטרפרטציה יוצרת - "מדרש דרש" - ביאר ר' אלעזר בן עזריה את תנאי

---

28 עיינו מאמרי, "זכויותיו הממוניות של האב בבתו הקטנה והנערה – סיבותיהן והשלכותיהן" שנתון המשפט העברי כ עמ' 49-101(1995-1997).

29 משנה כתובות, ד:יא.

הכתובה הזה שלא כפשוטו - כמחייב את יורשי האב לזון את הבנות רק לאחר מיתת האב, בצמצום, עקב צוק העיתים.[30] דרשנות-פרשנות זו לא היתה יחידה בהיקפה, שכן כמה מתנאי הכתובה פורשו בצמצום עקב צוק העיתים.[31] רק במקורות האמוראיים בבבלי מצינו כי זכות למעשה ידי הבת היא קורלטיבית - רק למקרים שהאב זן את בנותיו אלה.[32]

5. מעמדה של האֵם ביחס לבניה ולבנותיה - חוסר בהירות

מאחר שזכויות האב משמשות מניעים לגמירות-דעתו לזון את בניו ובנותיו ולפרנסם, לא נתקנו כל זכויות לאֵם, מפני שהאם, כל עוד היא נשואה לאביהם, משועבדת היא לו למעשה ידיה ולמלאכות הבית, ואף מנכסיה שקיבלה במתנה או בירושה - הבעל אוכל את פירותיהם. משום כך, מדרך הטבע, אין האם גומרת בדעתה לזון ולפרנס את בניה, ומצד אחר, אין היא זוכה בזכויות הממוניות בבניה ובבנותיה כדרך שהאב זוכה. אך גם אם מת האב, אין האם זוכה בכל זכות ממונית מבניה, אלא הבנים יורשים את אביהם, ואין הם זקוקים לה ואין מזונותיהם תלויים בה. ולהיפך, היא האלמנה זכאית לעיתים לתבוע את מזונותיה מהם. וגם במקרה שהתגרשה האם ואין היא משועבדת לבעלה כלל, אין היא גומרת בדעתה לזון ולפרנס את בניה אפילו בתמורה לקבלת רווחיהם מהם, שכן האֵם, כאישה, רוצה בכל שעה ושעה להינשא בשנית ולהשתעבד למי שיכניסה לרשותו.[33]

ההנקה, שהיא אקט נשי מובהק, התפרשה במקורות ההלכתיים בעיקרה כחובה של האֵם הנשואה כלפי בעלה, חובה שאינה ישירה של האֵם כלפי תינוקה. האֵם, כל עוד היא נשואה לאבי התינוק, משועבדת לו למלאכת ההנקה.[34] שעבודה של האם לבעלה, אִם לאביהם של הילדים ואִם לאדם אחֵר לאחר נישואיה בשנית, גרם להדגשת פטורה המוחלט של האֵם מהזנת בניה. אין האֵם חייבת לזון את בניה ובנותיה, בין קטנים ובין קטני

30 משנה כתובות, ד:ו ועיינו חנוך אלבק השלמות, 842; בירושלמי כתובות פ"ד ה"ח (ליברמן, 68) מובאת דעתו של ר' יוחנן בן ברוקא לפיה חיוב האב מתחיל עוד בחייו, אך בבבלי כתובות מט ע"א-ע"ב מובאת גירסה שונה שלפיה אין ר' יוחנן בן ברוקא חולק על דרשתו של ר' אלעזר בן עזריה. ועיינו שאול ליברמן, תוספתא כפשוטה, כתובות, עמ' 245

31 עיינו אמו"ר יצחק ד' גילת "מדאורייתא לדרבנן" ספר זיכרון לפרופ' ב' דה-פריס (ירושלים, תשכ"ט) 84 (=פרקים בהשתלשלות ההלכה (רמת-גן: אוניברסיטת בר-אילן, תשנ"ב)), 242 והמקורות שהביא בהערות 11-12.

32 כתובות מג ע"א. ועיינו במובאות נוספות בספרי, עמ' 111-113, 125-127 והמקורות המשוקעים שם.

33 עיינו שם, עמ' 244-248.

34 זו היא דעת בית הלל. לדעת בית שמאי אין האישה משועבדת ש"אין אישה אלא ליופי". כך עולה מתוספתא כתובות פ"ה ה"ה (ליברמן, 73); מכתובות נט ע"ב; מירושלמי כתובות, פ"ה ה"ו. הלכך "אין להטריחה בטורח קשה כזה לטחון ולאפות ולהיניק, כל הנך דכתיבי במתניתין, לפי שיופיה מתמעט", כלשון ר"ש משנץ בתוספותיו, כתובות נט ע"ב (ליס, עמ' קס), ד"ה 'אין אישה'.

קטנים.[35] נמצא שאם התגרשה מבעלה, אינה חייבת להיניק.[36] ויתר על-כן, אם נישאה בשנית, בעלה השני יכול למנוע אותה מלהיניק את בנה "שיש לה מאיש אחר", כלשון בעל הטורים.[37]

מחוץ לשעבודה לבעלה, הטילו חכמים חיוב על האם להיניק את ילדה שמכירה וחש קרבה אליה "מפני הסכנה", היינו שאם יימנע מלינוק מאישה אחרת שאינו מכירה יסתכן בחייו. מלכתחילה הוחל האיסור בתוספתא ובברייתות על כל מינקת שנשכרה להיניק, ואין האֵם שאינה משועבדת לבעלה יוצאת מכלל זה.[38] גם המינקת וגם האֵם מחויבות להיניק רק אם שילמו להן שכר ראוי. ברם, בזמן האמוראים הבדילו בין המינקת שאסורה להינשא כל עוד היא מיניקה בפועל לבין אֵם שאסורה להינשא לאדם אחר, גם אם אינה מניקה בפועל, י"ח חודשים מיום הולדת התינוק, משום גזרה.[39] מעבר להנקה, אין האֵם מחויבת לזון את הבנים והבנות אם אינה רוצה בהם, אלא "מישלכת אותן לקהל, אם אין להם אב והן מטפלין בהם", כלשון הרמב"ם.[40] מדברים אלה ניתן אפוא להסיק שחיוב הנקת הילדים הוא חיוב המוטל על האב באופן בלעדי.

באחד מפסקי הדין של בית הדין הרבני הגדול חידש הדיין ר' שאול ישראלי (שהיה דעת מיעוט), כי לאור הגישה השוויונית בין המינים הנהוגה בישראל, כאשר אימהות נשואות ולא נשואות מתנהלות בעצמאיות כלכלית, "אכן כשזה (המזונות – יצ"ג) מדין צדקה יש לברר גם את אפשרויותיה של האם, שכן גם האישה מחויבת מדין צדקה ובמקרה שגם היא אמידה, יש לדון על חלוקה נאותה של חיוב זה שמדין צדקה שעל האב והאם כאחד".[41]

35 ראו למשל רמב"ם, אישות, פכ"א הי"ח.

36 עיינו בספרי, עמ' 209-215.

37 טור, אבן העזר, סימן פ. ועיינו גם בית יוסף, שם, ד"ה ומ"ש רבנו, בשם הרמב"ם; וב"ח, שם, שם.

38 תוספתא נדה, פ"ב ה"ב וההלכות האחרות בהמשך בעלות הזיקה ביניהן: שם (מהד' צוקרמנדל, 642-643); בבלי כתובות, ס, ע"א-ע"ב.

39 וראו בספרי, תיאור השתלשלות ההלכה מהתנאים לאמוראים ומהאמוראים לראשונים, עמ' 215-244 והמקורות המשוקעים שם.

40 רמב"ם, אישות, לעיל הערה 34. דעה שונה במקצת היא של רבנו ירוחם, מישרים, נתיב כג, ה (נח ע"א). דברי רבנו ירוחם הובאו בהגהת הרמ"א על השולחן ערוך, אבן העזר, סימן פב, סעיף ה. ועיינו ביאוריהם של ר' יהונתן אייבשיץ, בני האהובה על הלכת הרמב"ם ור' מאיר פוזנר, בית מאיר על השו"ע.

41 ערעור תשל"ג/39 פד"ר ט 251, 263. דעתו של ר"ש ישראלי נדחתה על ידי שאר דייני ההרכב: ר' יוסף קאפח ור' מרדכי אליהו.

6. "מצות האב על הבן" - אינה אפוטרופסות

רשימת "מצות האב על הבן" כמו "למולו, לפדותו, ללמדו תורה"[42] אינה רשימה של ענייני אפוטרופסות שהאב מחויב בהם כלפי בניו ובנותיו. במרכז חיוביו של האב כלפי בנו ובתו עומדים, בשיטות משפט מודרניות, הבן והבת וטובתם, ואין ההורה אלא הערובה הטובה לביצועם של חיובים אלה כלפיהם. לא כן גישתה של ההלכה. במרכזן של "מצות האב על הבן" עומד האב עושה המצווה, המחויב בקיומה, ולא הנהנה. נכון שאם ילמד הבן תורה ומלאכה, ייפדה ויהא נימול, הוא ייצא נשכר עד למאוד, אך התכוונותה של "מצות הבן על האב" היא כמו התכוונותה של כל מצווה דתית אחרת - לאב עושה המצווה, וכל העולה ממנה לבן ולבת הנהנים הוא טפל לחלוטין.[43]

כך ניתן להסיק שאדם מישראל מחויב למול את בנו בעצמו ואין הוא מחויב לשכור לבנו מוהל.[44] ויתר על-כן, אם רצה האב למול את בנו בעצמו, אין האֵם, בית-הדין או כל אדם אחר מישראל יכולים למנוע אותו מכך, ואסור להם לחטוף מצווה זו ממנו אפילו אם טובתו של הבן דורשת שיהא נימול על-ידי אחר.[45] הוא הדין שהחובה המוטלת על האב ללמד את בנו תורה אינה אלא שילמדה בעצמו לפי כוחו ויכולתו, ממש כשם שחובתו של כל אדם ללמוד תורה בעצמו היא מעיקרה להגות בתורה לפי כוחו ויכולתו. משום כך נראה כי אין האב מחויב לשכור מלמד מיומן לבנו שילמד את בנו במקומו.[46] ויתר על-כן,

---

42 תוספתא קידושין פרק א, הלכה יא (ליברמן, 279); בבלי שם, כט ע"א; ירושלמי קידושין פ"א, ה"ז; מכילתא דר' ישמעאל, בא, פרשה יח, (מה' הארוויטץ-רבין, עמ' 73); מכילתא דרשב"י, יתרו כ, י, (מהד' אפשטיין-מלמד, (מה' בובער עמ' 150); ספרא אמור, פרשה א, ז, (מהד' וויס צד ע"א); מדרש תנחומא, במדבר, שלח, כו, (בובער, עמ' 71); במדבר רבה פרשה יז, א. "להשיאו אישה, ללמדו אומנות" הן מצוות שלא ממש כתובות בתורה אלא הם דרשות חכמים מפסוקי נביאים וכתובים.

43 עיינו מאמרי, "'מצות האב על הבן' - מאי משמע?" ספר השנה למדעי היהדות והרוח אוניברסיטת בר-אילן כח-כט, עמ' 371-408 (2001).

44 דין קיום מצוות מילה כדין הפרשת תרומה. כשם שיש מצוה על כל אדם להפריש תרומה ומעשר מתבואתו בנפרד מן החובה שהתבואה תהיה מותרמת ומעושרת, ואין כל חובה למנות שליח במקומו. כך מצוות המילה. יתר על-כן מדברי כמה מן האחרונים עולה כי חובת האב למול את בנו היא מצווה אישית שאינה ניתנת להתבצע על-ידי שליח. עיינו ש"ך, חושן משפט, סימן שפב, ס"ק ד; קצות החושן, שם, ס"ק (ב). ועל השפעת דעת הש"ך למעשה עיינו: תשובות דובב מישרים, חלק א, סימן סז; תשובות ציץ אליעזר, חלק יט, סימן לו. לענין פדייה מצינו כי הרמ"א בהגהתו על השולחן ערוך, יורה דעה, סימן שה, סעיף י, סבור ש"אין האב יכול לפדות על ידי שליח". ועיינו ש"ך, שם, שם, ס"ק יא, שמתנגד למסקנת הרמ"א, בניגוד מפתיע לעמדתו שלו באשר למצוות המילה, נימוקיו; וכן פתחי תשובה, שם, שם.

45 פסקי הרא"ש חולין, פרק שישי, סימן ח. עיינו גם באור זרוע, חלק ב, הלכות מילה, קז, ה; פסקי ריקאנטי (ד"צ ירושלים, תשל"א), סימן תקצב. אך עיינו מה שמובא בספר מהרי"ל, הלכות מילה (ד"צ ירושלים, תשל"ח, ע' סו, א).

46 תקנתו של יהושע בן גמלא, בבבלי בבא בתרא, כא, א; שם כתובות, נ, א, נועדה בעיקרה למי שאין לו אב, אלא לפי המסופר ש"עדיין מי שיש לו אב היה מעלו ומלמדו, מי שאין לו אב לא

אם האב רוצה ללמד את בנו בעצמו, אין האם, בית-הדין או כל אדם אחר יכולים לחטוף מצווה זו ממנו. הבנים הם איפוא מושאן של חובות האב, ואינם "בעלי זכויות" כשלעצמם. לפיכך אין פרטי החיובים של האב במצוות אלה נמדדים לפי נחיצותם לבן, אלא, כשאר המצוות, לפי כוחו ויכולתו של האב לקיימן בעצמו.

רק בראשונים, ובראשם הרמב"ם,[47] מופיעה לראשונה חובת האב לשכור מלמד לבנו. וכמה תירוצים נאמרו מפי חכמי ההלכה מהיכן נובעת חובה זו.[48] בספרי שיערתי שחובה זו של שכירת מלמד היא פיתוחה של חובת הצדקה. אותה חובת צדקה שעליה הושתתה "פרנסת הגוף" של הבנים היא העומדת בבסיסה של "פרנסת הנפש ללמדו חוקי אלוהים ותורותיו", כלשון החת"ם סופר.[49] וכשם שהחיוב בפרנסת הגוף של הבנים תלוי באומד דעתו של האב, כפי שביארנו לעיל, אף עניין שכירת המלמד כן. משום כך תלה ר' מאיר הלוי המובא בטור את החובה של שכירת המלמד ב"מנהג המדינה", או ביכולתו של האב לממן את לימודי בנו, כלומר, באמידותו של האב.[50] נוסף על כך הרחיבו את החובה של שכירת המלמד לא רק ללימוד מקרא, כפי שהבבלי מציין, אלא גם ל"משנה ותלמוד הלכות ואגדות", כשלימוד המקרא הוא בכל תנאי, ואילו לימוד תורה שבעל-פה תלוי ביכולתו של האב לשכור מלמד לבנו.

מאידך גיסא, חובת חינוך הבן לקיום מצוות, הן מצוות עשה של ציצית, לולב, והן מצוות לא תעשה כגון להפריש את הבן הקטן מאיסורי תורה של מאכלות אסורים או מעשיית מלאכות בשבת, שהן באופיין חובות אפוטרופסיות, לא נמנתה ברשימת "מצות האב על הבן", מאחר שלעניות דעתי, לא הוטלה חובה זו במקורה על האב דווקא, אלא כל אדם בישראל מחויב להשתדל שחברו יקיים את המצוות ויימנע מלעבור עבירות, והוא בבחינת ערבותו של כל יהודי לזולתו. השערתי נסמכת איפוא על דעתו של אמו"ר, רי"ד גילת, שבימי התנאים לא היה גיל אחיד לתחילת החיוב במצווה, ואף הקטנים היו מחויבים במצוות - כל מצווה היה הקטן מחויב לפי כוחו ויכולתו (אף אם לא נענש אם עבר עליה או לא קיימה).[51] לפיכך, לא הייתה מצווה זו של חינוך למצוות ודאגה להפרשת הקטין מאיסור מיוחדת לאב עצמו ביחס לבנו הקטן יותר מאשר לאם, לקרוב משפחה, לבית-דין

היה עולה ולמד", נראה שכך היה המנהג לשלוח אף שלא היתה חובה מן הדין. החובה של העמדת מלמדי תינוקות היתה חובה ציבורית כשאר צורכי העיר החיוניים, עיינו: בבלי שבת, קיט, ב; ירושלמי חגיגה, פרק א, הלכה ז.

47 רמב"ם, תלמוד תורה, א, ג; טור, יורה דעה, סימן רמה.

48 לחם משנה, תלמוד תורה, פרק א, ז המביא את סברת המהרי"ק; הגהות מיימוניות. תלמוד תורה, א, א, בשם מהר"ם מרוטנבורג.

49 ספרי, עמ' 312-301. חידושי חת"ם סופר, בבא בתרא, כא, א ד"ה 'והנלפע"ד בזה'; הנ"ל, נדרים, לז, א ד"ה 'מה'.

50 יורה דעה, סימן רמ"ה.

51 "בן שלוש עשרה למצוות?" מחקרי תלמוד א (תש"ן) 39 (=פרקים בהשתלשלות ההלכה לעיל הערה 31, עמ' 19).

או לכל אדם מישראל. ברם, מזמנם של האמוראים, כאשר התגבשה ההלכה ש"בן שלוש עשרה למצוות", נעשה הקטן שמתחת לגיל שלוש-עשרה פטור מעשיית המצוות, ואינו מחויב באיסורי תורה. משום כך, לעניות דעתי, נהפכה מצוות החינוך למצווה פרטיקולרית של האב כלפי בנו - להרגילו בקיום המצווה או להימנע מאיסורי תורה אף שאין הקטן מחויב בה כשלעצמו.[52] מסיבה דומה לא נמנתה "מצוה לזון את הבנים" "מצוה לזון את הבנות" ברשימת מצוות "האב על הבן" מאחר שלדעתם של התנאים, כנראה, לא הייתה מצווה זו יותר מאשר הנהגה ראויה של צדקה אך לא חיוב דתי בנפרד.

7. "טובת הילד" אינה שיקול "מכריע ועליון" בסכסוכי משמורת

החזקתם של הבנים והבנות (custody), שהיא חובה אפוטרופוסית מובהקת בשיטות המשפט המודרניות, שיש לשקול בה את "טובת הילד" בלבד, נידונה בספרות ההלכה במשך תקופה ארוכה כזכות טפלה של האב לחיובו במזונות. כלומר, לעיתים היה האב יכול להיפטר ממזונות בניו ובנותיו בתואנה שאינם אצלו, ולעיתים היה האב מחויב במזונותיהם אף-על-פי שאינם אצלו. בין הגאונים וחכמי הראשונים אנו מוצאים התייחסויות לסוגיה זו, אך לכלל משנה סדורה לא הגיעו. אפילו הלכת הרמב"ם, שנחשבת כיום אבן פינה לכללי החזקת ילדים, לא עסקה לאמיתו של דבר בענייני החזקת הילדים, אלא בטענות אפשריות של האב להיפטר ממזונות בנו.[53] רק החל מתקופת ראשוני האחרונים (שנדחקו בדבריו ופירשו את הרמב"ם כעוסק בענייני משמורת) התגבשו כללי החזקת הילדים לחובה אפוטרופסית מובהקת העומדת בפני עצמה, באופן הבא:[54]

א. ההלכה היהודית מכירה בזכותו הבלעדית של האב על ילדיו, הן בנים והן בנות, בעניינים רבים, ובכללם גם זכותו לקבל משמורת על ילדיו. אם הוכרה זכותה של האֵם להחזיק בילדיה, הרי שזו זכות פונקציונלית, כלומר, הזכות קיימת רק אם היא משרתת את

52 תפקידו של האב בהפרשת בנו מן האיסורים כעניין של חינוך לפי ההשקפה האמוראית, נעשה בעייתי ושנוי במחלוקת גם בימי התלמוד וגם בספרות שלאחר התלמוד. ועל מקצת הבעיות עמדתי בספרי, עמ' 331-333 ועיינו עוד מאמרי "נאמנות החבר והשלכתה על נאמנותם של בניו ובנותיו" סיני קכב (תשנ"ח) עמ' פג-צג.

53 ביאור הלכת הרמב"ם ימצאו המעיינים בספרי, עמ' 391-396, 202-202. ביאורי נסמך בין היתר על תשובת ראי"ה קוק בעזרת כהן, נז:

> אבל באמת, לשיטת הרמב"ם, אין לנו שום הלכה מקובלת ע"ד כפי' לאיזה צד שיהי' ביותר מבן שש, והכל תלוי בראות עיני ב"ד, אלא שחובת האב ליתן לו מזונות קבעו רק כשהוא אצל אביו, ואם אמו מעכבת היא חייבת ליתן המזונות, ואם אין לה, או שאינה רוצה ליתן לו מזונות, בודאי שלא יניחו את הילד לרעוב ומחזירין אותו אצל אביו, כדי שיגדלו ויתפרנס.

54 על ניתוח תשובותיהם של חכמי ההלכה בעיצוב כללי החזקת הילדים עיינו בספרי, עמ' 439-397.

טובת הילדים מבחינה גופנית ורוחנית. זכות פונקציונלית זו של האם אינה אלא שיקול נגדי שלא לילך אחר זכותו הבלעדית של האב על ילדיו. מטבע הדברים, שיקול זה של "טובת הילד" אינו יכול להכריע את זכותו הבלעדית של האב, אלא אם-כן הוא ברור ובולט. טובת הילד אינה נשקלת באופן מקסימליסטי, לאמור, היכן יהא לילד טוב יותר, אלא באופן מינימליסטי, כשיקול נגדי: האם הפגיעה בילד מצדיקה את מסירתו לאם תוך שלילת זכות האב?

מתוך המקורות ההלכתיים עולה שההבדל בין בן קטן מתחת לגיל שש לבין בן שמעל לגיל זה אינו משמעותי מבחינה אפריורית, אלא סיכוייה של האם לזכות בהחזקה נאמדים לפי חומר העובדות: האם הילד זקוק לאימו? באותה מידה התפרש הכלל ש"הבת אצל האם לעולם" ככלל פונקציונלי שאינו משקף "אמת מוחלטת".

ב. בד בבד עם המבחן שהצגנו בסכסוך שבין ההורים עצמם, התפתחה בדיני התורה אמת-מידה כפולה לקביעת משמורת הילדים בסכסוך שבין אחד ההורים לבין צד שלישי שאינו הורה הילד. לאמור, כאשר האֵם מתה והאב דורש את החזקת ילדיו אצלו, הוא גובר על כל הטענות של קרובי משפחתה. אך אם האב מת והאֵם דורשת את החזקת בניה ובנותיה, זכותה אינה מוחלטת. לאמור, אם היריבות היא בינה לבין אדם שלישי שאינו בא מכוח האב, הסכסוך מוכרע תוך שקילת האינטרסים המועדפים של הקטין נשוא ההליך, מעין "טובת הילד המקסימליסטית" המוכרת לנו מן הפסיקה האזרחית. ברם, אם היריבות היא בינה לבין אדם שהוא קרוב משפחתו של האב, "דעשאו (האב) אפוטרופוס על כל נכסיו", "שנתן לו כוחו ורשותו", כלשון הרשד"ם וחכמי דורו,[55] כי אז זכותם של האפוטרופסים

55 תשובות הרשד"ם, אבן העזר, סימן קכג. אלון בפרשת ניר נ' ניר קובע כי "גם לפי המשפט העברי חייב בית הדין לפסוק בענייני הורים וילדים לפי עקרון-העל של טובת הילד" בהסתמכו על ציטוט מהבא:

> וכללא דמלתא כי כל זכות שאז"ל בדבורם הבת אצל האם לעולם לא אמרו כן לחוב לאחרים אלא במה שאין כופין אותה לדור אצל האחים ושאין האחים יכולים לומ' אם את אצלנו יש לך מזונות כו' אלא שיתנו לה מזונות אפי' שהיא בבית אמה ובזכותה דברו לא בזכות האם...

אך המעיין לכל אורך תשובת הרשד"ם יראה את זכותו העדיפה של האב, בסוף התשובה (הדגשות שלי – יצ"ג):

> ...ומטעם אחר וגדול הוא בעיני אני אומר שמה שאמרו הבת היא אצל האם לעולם אינו ר"ל שיש לה כח להוציאה ולהוליכ' למקום שתרצ' האם שהרי שנינו בפ' נערה שנתפתת' האב זכאי בבתו בקדושי' בכסף בשטר ובביא' זכאי במציאת' ובמעש' ידיה ובהפרת נדריה כו' וכל אלו הזכיות הם מן התור' לבד מציאתה שהיא תקנת רבנן משום איב' ורשאי למוסר' מה"ת למנוול ומוכה שחין ואח' אשר הודיע לנו ה' את כל זאת פליא' דעת ממני מי הוא זה אשר יעל' על דעתו לומר שהתור' זכת' לאב בכל אלו הזכיות ואתה רוצ' לבטלן בהבל תקנה שאמר רב חסד' זאת אומרת כו' מדיוקא דמתני' ותרצ' לבטל המשנה השלימה הנז' והתורה השלימה שאמרה בנעוריה בית אביה כל שבח נעורים ברשות אביה ואני שמעתי ולא אבין דעת הרוצי' לתקן כל זה בקש אשר ידפנו רוח שאומרי' שכבר יוכל לזכות בכל זה אפי' תהיה היא במ"ה

עדיפה, ואמת-המידה להוצאת הבנים מחזקתם זהה לאמת-המידה של הוצאת הבנים והבנות ממשמורת האב עצמו.

עוד יצוין שהשיקולים אם להשאיר את הילדים אצל אימם אינם בהכרח חומריים עכשוויים, כמקובל בפסיקה האזרחית, אלא הם באים חשבון עם עתידם הגשמי והרוחני של הילדים, כפי שהרשב"א כותב שהבת אצל האם ש"תלמדה דרך נשים ושלא תרגיל עצמה בפריצות אבל הבן יותר ראוי להיות אצל אנשים הקרובים, שהם ירגילוהו וילמדוהו דרך הלימוד ודרך האנשים יותר מן האם, שבני האלמנה דרכם דרך זר".[56]

ג. מסוף המאה השמונה-עשרה ניתן להצביע במקורות הלכתיים שונים על מבחן שונה, הוא מבחן האשמה. כלומר, מן ההורה "האשם" בפירוקו של התא המשפחתי נשללת הזכות למשמורת על ילדיו. שינוי גישה זה של המשפט העברי התהווה באופן הדרגתי ומתון. תחילה דובר על מבחני אשמה לפי קנה-מידה ערכי דתי, מבחנים הקשורים ישירות למידת "תרומתו" של בן-הזוג "האשם" לפירוקו של התא המשפחתי. אך לאחר-מכן הורחב מבחן האשמה כך שכל עבירה על מצוות הדת שעבר ההורה האחד הייתה עשויה לזַכות את ההורה האחר במשמורת הילד.

הנוסחה להפעלתו של מבחן האשמה מצביעה על הרצון להיצמד למבחנים המסורתיים של ההלכה בסוגיה זו, ונעשתה באופן הבא: כאשר האב שומר תורה ומצוות

> והאב במקום רחוק ממנה ואני משיב להם הנה שראובן גרש את אשתו והיה לו בת ממנה וחביבה אצלו ואתה נותן רשות לאם שיוליכנה לעבר הים ולמקום שתרצה ובאותו מקום שהאם הולכת אינו מקו' תוכל הבת להרויח דבר ואם תעמוד במקום האב תרויח ה' לבנים או יותר בכל יום ואתה אומר להפסיד לאב זכות זה שהתורה זכהו...

בתיק (ת"א) תשי"ד/226 שעובדותיו יובאו להלן בהערה 55 פסק ר' אליעזר גולדשמידט בדברים הבאים (עמ' 157):

> והסבר הדברים הוא, כי ההלכות בדבר החזקת ילדים אינן הלכות בטובת ההורים, אלא הלכות בטובת הילדים, אין הבן או הבת חפץ לזכויות אב או אם. אין כאן זכויות לאב או לאם, רק חובות עליהם ישנן כאן, שמחויבים הם לגדל ולחנך את ילדיהם. ובבוא ביה"ד לקבוע בדבר מקומו של הילד, בדבר המגע בינו ובין הוריו, רק שיקול אחד נגד עיניו והוא, טובתו של הילד אצל מי תהיה ובאיזו אופן תהיה, אבל זכויות אב ואם, זכויות כאלו לא קיימות כלל.

ברם עיון בעובדות המקרה מצביע בעליל כי לא "טובת הילד" כפשוטה הייתה כאן אלא הדרת תובע מהסדרי ראייה בשל אי ההכרה באבהותו.

56 תשובות הרשב"א המיוחסות לרמב"ן, סימן לח. גם תשובה זו, המצוטטת על ידי התומכים בדעתו של אלון, מצביעה בעליל על ניגוד בין ההלכה למוסכמה של המשפט המודרני לפיה זכות האם כהורה גוברת על זכויותיו של כל מי שאינו הורו של הילד. גם הציטוט של אלון מדברי הרדב"ז בתשובתו חלק א, קכג "כללא דמילתא, הכל תלוי בראות בית דין, באי זה מקום יש תקנה לולד יותר" אינה מלמדת בהכרח על דרכו של הרדב"ז שכן בתשובתו בחלק ג, סימן תתנא, עולה ההיפך שלאב יש זכות יתרה על משמורת הבן מאשר לאם, בין היתר בהנמקה הבאה: "דהא מאי דאמרינן הבן אצל אמו כל זמן שהוא צריך לאמו מדרבנן בעלמא הוא דמן התורה 'לבית אבותם' אמר קרא והאם כלי בעלמא" (הדגשה שלי - יצ"ג).

והאם אינה כזאת, חכמי ההלכה מדגישים את זכותו העקרונית והבלעדית של האב; ואילו כאשר האב הוא פורק עול תורה ומצוות והאם נחזית להיות אחרת, מודגשת יותר ויותר יכולתם וזכותם של הדיינים לשקול אם למסור את הילדים למשמורת האם.[57]

ג. הניתן להתאים את "דיני התורה" בסוגיות יחסי הורים וילדים לימינו?

ניתן אפוא להניח כי מנחם אלון במפעלותיו ביקש להטעים את ההלכה היהודית המסורתית למשפטנים המודרניים ולתת לה "פנים שוחקות" של מכובדות ליברלית דמוקרטית, ולשם כך חתר בכל פסקי הדין שכתב ל"אקטיביזם" שבו יתיישבו המסורות העתיקות של דיני התורה עם אסכולות מודרניות במשפט.[58] ברצוני לטעון כי גם אם נקבל את הצורך בשינוי

---

57 ראי"ה קוק בתשובות עזרת כהן, נז קובע הדברים הבאים באשר לדרך קביעת משמורת הילד בסכסוך שבין הוריו:

> שכל הדברים לשיטת הרמב"ם והשו"ע לא נאמרו כ"א ע"ד חובת המזונות וסילוק החובה, אבל בעצם הכפי' לא נאמרו דברים ע"ז בדברי רבותינו ז"ל. ומ"מ ראוי לסמוך ע"ד הח"מ שהבן יותר ראוי שיהי' אצל האב, שהוא שייך לו בעניני חובותיו על חנוכו ולמודו, אבל לקבוע בזה מסמרים א"א, כגון אם יראו ב"ד שאצל האב יתקלקל הבן בעניני יהדות, ואצל האם יחונך ביהדות, וכיו"ב בשארי ענינים, אז אפי' אם נפקפק אם ב"ד יכולים להוציא את הילד מאביו, אבל עכ"פ אין ב"ד נזקקים לעזור לאביו בזה.

השיקול הדתי עולה בעקיפין מערעור 1/2/704, אוסף פסקי הדין, כח (הרכב: הרבנים עוזיאל, הרצוג, קלמס) שם נקבע (בע' לב) שהמשמורת תהא אצל האם וכי "אין החלטה זו עומדת בניגוד להלכה, כי הדין שילד זכר של למעלה משש שנים הולך אחרי האב... הרי דין זה מכיל רק הסדר כללי ואינו נוטל מידי ביה"ד רשות לסדר השארת הילד באופן אחר". ברם עיון בעובדות שהניעו את ביה"ד להכריע כפי שהכריע, מראה כי אישיותו של האב - כפי שתואר בפסק הדין הנ"ל (ע' כח): "הוא שונא את בנו, מכה אותו בלי שום סיבה... גם יחסו של הנתבע לגבי דת הוא שלילי... שהנתבע הוא כופר בעיקר וקרקפתא דלא מנח תפילין ואינו מתפלל לעולם אפילו בחגים ובימים נוראים, אוכל נבילות וטריפות ומחלל שבת בפרהסיא ואולם היא התובעת שומרת דת היא ומחנכת את בנה ברוח זו" - היא זו שהכריעה את הכף.

58 כך נהג בע"א 1354/92 פלוני נ' היועמ"ש, פ"ד מח(1) 711 (1994) בו אסר בדיקת רקמות בשל חשש של ממזור הילד, אף שנטען כי המידע ישמש רק לשם קביעת זכאותה של הילדה למזונות. אלון חשש "פיצול הסטאטוס" של אבהות, למרות שגם אלון מודה בהכרעתו כי בתי הדין הרבניים עצמם היו אמורים שלא להסתמך על בדיקת רקמות כראיה לשם קביעת ממזרות. לענ"ד אלון בחששו מרעיון האבהות המפוצלת הביע עמדה טהרנית יותר מפסיקת בתי הדין הרבניים. לשם השוואה עיינו בפרשת תיק (ת"א) תשי"ד/226 פד"ר א 145. (הדיינים: אליעזר גולדשמידט, קרליץ, בבליקי). מדובר היה באישה נשואה שקיימה יחסי אישות גם עם גבר זר. היא עברה לגור עם הגבר הזר, ומפעם לפעם הייתה מתראה עם בעלה ומקיימת יחסי אישות גם עימו. האישה ילדה בת ואחרי שהיא נולדה היא התגרשה מבעלה, והמשיכה לחיות עם הגבר יחד עם הבת. לאחר מספר שנים היא הסתכסכה גם עם הגבר, ואז הגישו הגבר והאישה תביעות הדדיות: האישה תבעה בשם בתה מזונות מאותו גבר בבית-הדין הרבני, והגבר הגיש תביעה בה הוא מבקש שהבת תצא מרשות האם ותעבור לפנימייה כדי שהוא יוכל להתראות עימה יותר זמן. גם הגבר וגם האישה טענו שהבת הזו היא בְּתָם. בית-הדין הרבני פסק שהוא איננו יכול להוציא את הילדה מהאם ואינו יכול לצוות שהילדה תראה את הגבר משתי סיבות משלימות: האחת "רוב בעילות אחר הבעל" – היא נולדה לפני

ההלכה, לא ניתן לטעון כי חל שינוי ב"עולמה של ההלכה בימינו". כפי שיראה המעיין בפרק הקודם, הלכות עתיקות ונידחות ששום אדם בעל מסורת ליברלית יכול להסכין להן, הן הן התשתית להכרעות בבתי הדין הרבניים בתחום יחסי ההורים וילדים. מנגד, מונחים בסיסיים הרווחים בשיטת המשפט בישראל, כמו "אפוטרופסות ההורים", "טובת הילד", "חזקת הגיל הרך", "אימוץ ילדים", "ציות להורים תוך כדי כיבוד ההורים", "חינוך הילד" או שהם אינם קיימים כלל בדיני התורה אף בימינו, או שקיימים אך במשמעות אחרת, רדיקלית, של ערכים דתיים שאינם מתפשרים.[59] גם השופט מנחם אלון היה מודע בפסקיו לקשיים ההלכתיים ביישום מונחים אלו בפרשנותם המודרנית.[60]

שהאישה התגרשה מבעלה, והם מפעם לפעם התראו. השנית, אומנם גם הגבר וגם האישה אמרו שהיא בתם, אך בעניין זה הכלל בהלכה היהודית הוא כי "אין אדם משים עצמו רשע". ברם, לגבי תביעת המזונות אמר בית-הדין שמאחר ומזונות היא תביעה ממונית, והגבר הודה שהבת הזו היא בתו : "הודאת בעל דין כמאה עדים דמי", ולכן עליו לשלם לה מזונות. כלומר לבת קטנה יש שני אבות סימולטאנית: אב אחד לעניין הסדרי הראייה (שהיא סניף של החזקת הילדים) ואב אחר לעניין מזונות.

59 ראו מה שכתבתי בפרק לעיל. על כיבוד אב ואם עיינו מאמרי, "'עד היכן כיבוד אב ואם?' - על סובייקטיביות ואובייקטיביות באשר לחובות הילדים כלפי הוריהם" עיונים ובירורים במצות כיבוד אב ואם, עמ' 229-244 (אלון שבות, 2005). המעניין הוא כי גם מונחי המשפט משתנים עקב שינוי הערכים. הנה בעקבות אמנת האו"ם בדבר זכויות הילד שנעשתה בשנת 1990, ואושררה בישראל ביום 2 לנובמבר 1991 הוקמה ועדת ייעוץ שבראשותה. הועדה שמונתה על-ידי שר המשפטים "לבחינת עקרונות יסוד בתחום הילד והמשפט" הגישה דו"ח מפורט (דו"ח ועדת רוטלוי) בו הוצעה רפורמה מקפת של הדין הישראלי ובראש ובראשונה בהטמעתן של 'זכויות הילד' בתור אנטיתזה להגמוניה של עקרון 'טובת הילד'. ברוח זו המליצה הועדה להמיר את המונח "אפוטרופסות ההורים" "אפוטרופסות טבעית" בעל קונוטציה 'אדנותית' של ההורים לילדיהם הקטינים, במונח "אחריות הורית". גם "חזקת הגיל הרך" שאלון ראה בה מורשת יהודית (מכלליו של הרמב"ם) עומדת להשתנות בעקבות דו"ח הועדה לבחינת ההיבטים המשפטיים של אחריות ההורים בגירושין" (דו"ח ועדת שניט). על הרנסנס של ההלכה היהודית בעקבות שינוי הערכים ראו מאמרי: "The renewed insights of the U.N. Convention on Children's Rights: The Renaissance of "Ancient Jewish law," *Jewish Law Association Studies: The Bar-Ilan Conference,* 2006 Vol. 18, pp. 88-101(2008).

60 כך בפרשת בג"ץ 268/80, ינסן זוהר נ' זוהר פ"ד לה(1) 1 (1980)בו נחטף ילד שנולד לאב יהודי ואם גיורת שנישאו בישראל והגרו לנורבגיה ומשם חטף האב את ילדיו לישראל תוך שהוא מטיח אשמות באם על רצון להחזיר את ילדה לחיק הנצרות, קבע השופט אלון כי "כאשר מרכז חייו של הקטין הוא בישראל, והוא נלקח על ידי הורה אחד, שלא בהסכמת ההורה האחר ממקום מגוריו שבחוץ לארץ, הרי עם כל הסלידה שיש לסלוד ממעשה זה של עשיית דין עצמית, חסר כאן האלמנט של חטיפת קטין מהמקום, שבו נולד וגדל לארץ זרה לו, כי אם להפך – שב הוא למרכז חייו". "מרכז חייו" של הילד הם שיקולי הזהות הלאומית של הילד לעומתו, השופט בייסקי מכריע כי הייתה חטיפה בשל הרחקתו של הילד מ"מרכז חייו" שהוגדר בלשונו: "...כי כשם שמרכז חייו של יונק הוא לצד שד אמו -כך מרכז חייו לילד בגיל רך, בו המדובר כאן, הוא קרוב לחיק אמו ולידה המלטפת. ולא רק מבחינה מליצית וסנטימנטלית. עקירת פעוט מחיק אמו היא גם עקירה מרכז חייו." לענ"ד שיקולים דתיים

נחזור אפוא לפרשת נגר נ' נגר. קביעתו של אלון כי "המגמה המקובלת בעולמה של ההלכה בימינו" מצדדת בזכותה של האם לקבוע את חינוך ילדיה, נוסחה על ידו בלשון הבאה:

> סיכומו של עיון. כפי שראינו, ההלכה, שהאב חייב ללמד את בנו תורה והאישה פטורה מכך, יסודה בהלכה, שהאב חייב בעצמו בלימוד תורה והאישה פטורה מלימוד עצמי, על פי הכלל שכל החייב ללמוד - חייב ללמד. בימינו אנו, משחל שינוי כה מהותי, שלא רק שאין איסור, אלא אף נקבע חיוב האישה בלימוד תורה, והאישה לא רק שלומדת היא לעצמה אלא מלמדת היא אף בניהם של אחרים, דומה שמתבקשת מכך גם המסקנה, שהחיוב ללמד הבן תורה צריך שיהא מוטל שווה על האב ועל האם, על פי העקרון ההלכתי היסודי, שכל החייב ללמוד - חייב ללמד.

השופט אלון אישש את מסקנתו כי חל שינוי באסמכתאות שונות, כפי שיראה המעיין.[61] ברם, לעניות דעתי, המקורות שהביא השופט אלון לא קבעו נורמה הלכתית המעניקה זכות לאם לחנך את בנה בדומה לזכותו של האב, ולא הניחו שיש לאם חובה ללמוד תורה באותה מידה שחובה כזו קיימת לגבי האב. כל שהניחו שם המקורות הוא

בדבר זהותו של הילד הם שהכריעו את אלון ליצור זיקה משפטית בינלאומית-פרטית בלתי מקובלת. בפרשת ניר נ' ניר, לעיל קבע השופט אלון כי "חזקת הגיל הרך" נוסח החוק אינה הולכת אחר ההלכה הקובעת ש"הבת אצל אימה לעולם". ובע"א 488/77 פלוני ופלונית נ' היועמ"ש, פ"מ לב(3) 421 (1978) קבע השופט אלון כי האימוץ החוקי בישראל אינו עוקב אחר כללי ההלכה.

61 ואלו המקורות שהביא השופט אלון (כפי שהוזכרו שם): מאירי בית הבחירה נזיר, כח ע"ב; רש"י, חגיגה ב, ע"א ד"ה איזהו קטן; תוספות, עירובין, פב ע"א ד"ה קטן בן שש; חיי אדם, הלכות תפילות וברכות, כלל סו, ב; ערוך לנר, סוכה, ב ע"ב; אגרת התשובה (לר"י גירונדי) אות עב; של"ה, שער האותיות אות דרך ארץ; רבנו ירוחם, נתיב כג, ג; ערעור לג/39, פד"ר ט 251, 259; תיק תשכ"ד/42, פד"ר ז 10, 17; קידושין, כט ע"ב; רמב"ם, תלמוד תורה א:א, א:יג; משנה סוטה, ג:ד; בבלי סוטה, כא ע"ב; תוספתא, כלים ב"ק, ד:יז; משנה ב"מ, א:ו; בבא בתרא, קיט ע"ב; סיבוב הרב פתחיה מרגענסבורג (קלעטער) ג, ב; תשובות רשב"ץ, חלק ג, עח; תשובות מהרש"ל, כט; שם הגדולים (לחיד"א), מערכת גדולים, קונטרס אחרון, ערך: רבנית; שולחן ערוך יורה דעה, סימן רמו, סעיף ו; ר' שמשון ב"ר רפאל הירש, ספר חורב, פרק עה; ליקוטי הלכות (לר' ישראל מאיר הכהן מראדין) סוטה, כא; תשובתו של הנ"ל התפרסמה על-ידי אהרן גרינבאום, "החינוך הדתי לבנות בישראל" בשבילי החינוך (ניו-יורק, תשכ"ו) 24, 35; ר' זלמן סורוצקין, מאזניים למשפט (תשט"ו), סימן מב; ר' בן-ציון פירר "בענין לימוד תורה לבנות" נעם ג (תש"ך) עמ' קלא; תשובות מקוה המים (לר' משה מלכה), חלק ג, יורה דעה, כ; תשובות עשה לך רב (לרח"ד הלוי) חלק א, סימן מא; ר' אהרן ליכטנשטיין האשה וחינוכה (כפר סבא, תש"ם) 158-159, 345; אליקים ג' אלינסון, בין האשה ליוצרה (ההסתדרות הציונית העולמית, מהדורה 2, תשמ"ב), 143-165. אציין את מאמרו של שמחה פרידמן, "תלמוד תורה לנשים בימינו" הגות (מאסף למחשבה יהודית, תשמ"ג) 53.

שהאם שותפה למעשה החינוך של הבן מבחינה מציאותית, מאחר שהיא נמצאת שעות רבות בבית עם בנה, אף יותר מאשר האב עם בנו.[62] גם המקורות שקבעו כי יש חובה לחנך את הבת לקיום מצוות או ללימוד תורה לא קבעו זאת אלא כדי להציל את הבת מהתדרדרות דתית ו"להשריש אמונה טהורה",[63] אך אין להסיק מהם כי הבת מחויבת ללמוד כמו הבן, ושזכותה וחובתה של אם לחנך וללמד את בנה שוות-ערך לזכותו ולחובתו של האב. ההסתמכות על דבריהם של החכמים, כר' ישראל מאיר הכהן מראדין בעל "החפץ חיים" או ר' זלמן סורוצקין, כדי לאשש מסקנה כי לאם זכות שווה לאב לחנך את הבנים והבנות וללמדם, אינה משקפת את דרכם של חכמים אלה, אלא היא "פרשנות יוצרת" של השופט אלון עצמו.[64]

אפשר היה ליישב את דרכו של אלון בפרשת נגר עם המסורת הרבנית, בתובנה שעומדת ביסודה של הבנת הרמב"ם והרמ"ה המובא בטור, כי חובת האב לשכור מלמד לילדיו היא משתלשלת מחובת המזונות שחייב האב לילדיו, לפרנסם ב"פרנסת הנפש" ללמדם "חוקי אלוהים ותורותיו",[65] על כן בימינו שנשים נשואות, קל וחומר אימהות שאינן נשואות, עומדות ברשות עצמן ומפרנסות עצמן ממעשה ידיהן, מחויבות אף הן באותה צדקה רוחנית לילדיהן, כפי שמחויב האב.[66] משום כך לא רק הבן מחויב בלימוד תורה אלא גם הבת. לא רק איש מישראל יכול לעסוק באותה צדקה רוחנית, אלא גם אישה, שלעתים מיומנת במתן סעד רוחני יותר מהאיש. אך בפרשת נגר לא עצם זכותו של האב ללמד את ילדיו בעצמו עמדה בבסיס המחלוקת, שייתכן שלא היה בר-הכי, ואפילו לא "שכירת מלמד" לילדיו, אלא רק רישום הילדים בבית ספר ממלכתי-דתי, שהוא מוסד מוכר ורשמי וששכר לימוד ההוראה נשען על תקציב המדינה באופן בלעדי.

אך אלון בהמשך פסק דינו בפרשה, קובע כי לפי ההלכה "טובת הילד" היא עיקרון-על, וכי על בית הדין הרבני היה להתחשב ברצונם של הילדים ובעצם באיבתם כלפי שינוי מקום לימודיהם. בזו הלשון מובאת קביעתו:

---

62 מהשל"ה ומר"י גירונדי לא ניתן ללמוד על נורמה הלכתית, שכן ספרים אלו נכתבו כספרי יראים, המלמדים דרך-ארץ ומוסר, אך לא באו לחרוץ קביעה על הזכות ההלכתית של האם לחנך את בנה. קשה אפוא להסיק מהם קביעה נורמטיבית שהאם עדיפה במקרים של יריבות עם האב.

63 הציטוטים מר"ז סורוצקין, בהערה קודמת, סוף דבריו.

64 השופט אלון מסתמך גם על שני פסקי-הדין הרבניים: תיק תשכ"ד/42, פד"ר ז, 10; ותיק לג/39, פד"ר ט 251. באשר לתיק הראשון דומה כי ר"א שפירא חזר למעשה מעמדתו הנחרצת שצוטטה בפסק-הדין נגר, בע' 403, והביע עמדה מתונה יותר בסוף פסק-דינו הקובעת שלו היה האב חפץ באמת ללמד בניו תורה בעצמו ולא רק להיפטר ממזונותיהם, הייתה לו לאב זכות עדיפה. באשר לפסק-הדין השני, שם דובר בבני זוג חילוניים ולכן שיקול החינוך למצוות לא תפס אצלם. משום כך לא הועדף בן-זוג אחד על פני האחר.

65 עיינו לעיל הערה 48.

66 ראו דעתו של הדיין ר' שאול ישראלי לעיל הערה 40.

קנה המידה האחד והיחיד לפתרונה של בעיה קשה וסבוכה מעין זו, שנוגעת בבבת עיניהם של הורים וילדים, הרי הוא רק ביישום נכון ונבון של עקרון טובת הילדים, שהן בית הדין הרבני והן בית המשפט האזרחי מצווים עליו ודנים לפיו. יישומו של עיקרון זה הרי הוא בראש ובראשונה עניין שבקביעת ממצאים ועובדות - כיצד ישפיע שינוי מגמת החינוך על נפשם של הילדים, מהו גילם של הילדים, מה טיב בית הספר שלמדו בו עד עתה ואיזהו בית הספר שמוצע להם מכאן ואילך, וכיוצא באלה שאלות, שלהכרעתן ייעזר בית המשפט ובית הדין בחוות-דעתם של מומחים לכך. במקרה שלפנינו מצויות חוות-דעת שונות וסותרות; יש המצביעים על הנזק שעלול להיגרם לילדים כתוצאה משינוי מגמת החינוך, בפרט שנמצאים הם בחזקת האם שאינה מקיימת אורח חיים דתי, ויש המצביעים על החיוב שבלימודם בבית-ספר דתי, שבאווירתו הכללית תואם הוא את אורח חיי הילדים בני גילם בכל סוגי בתי הספר, פרט לעניין שמירת מצוות וקיומן, כשעל-ידי כך יישמר הקשר בין הילדים לבין אביהם, המקפיד על אורח חיים דתי, ובחינוכם לא תתקפח "דמות האב", דבר שחיוני הוא בגידולו ובחינוכו התקינים של הילד.

בכך לענ"ד העביר השופט אלון על מידתם של דיני התורה המסורתיים. מסתבר אפוא כי לפי ההלכה, אין לראות ב"טובת הילד" עקרון-על מכריע ובלעדי.[67] אכן, "טובת הילד" היא עיקרון חשוב הרווח בספרות ההלכתית מתקופת הגאונים ועד זמננו, אך אין היא חזות הכל. לצידו של שיקול "טובת הילד", אף בפירושו ההלכתי, קיים שיקול עצמאי נוסף, והוא השיקול הדתי.[68] השיקול הדתי המשמעותי ביותר, הוא הפרשתו של הקטין מאיסורים ומעבירות על מצוות הדת, מניעתו מלעבור איסורי תורה, כגון חילול שבת ואכילת מאכלות אסורים. זו, כפי שהצבענו בפרק הקודם, אינה חובתו הפרטיקולרית של אב, אלא היא מוטלת על כל אדם מישראל המחויב להפריש את הקטן מאיסורי תורה.

סכסוכים אלה סביב "השיקול הדתי" מתבררים בערכאות שיפוטיות שונות בין הורים שנפרדו דרכיהם או שעומדים לפני פירוד. לעיתים הם אומנם פרי יריבות אידיאולוגית

---

67 על קביעה זו של השופט אלון יצא עורר ר' יוסף קאפח שישב בהרכב בפרשת נגר, בעמ' 412, שקבע כי "קשה לי להסכים לגמרי עם קביעה פסקנית זו, נראה כי אין ההורים חפץ דומם".

68 בגישה אחרת מתאר פנחס שיפמן במאמרו, "'טובת הילד' בבית הדין הרבני" משפטים ה (תשל"ד) 421, 429, את גישתם השונה של בתי הדין הרבניים מזו של בתי המשפט האזרחיים: "...השאלה מה היא טובת הילד במקרה המסוים היא הכרעה ערכית לגביה יתכנו חילוקי דעות עקרוניים בין השופט האזרחי והדיין הדתי, שסולם הערכים שלהם אינו זהה כיוון שהמחוקק מסר את השיפוט בענייני אפוטרופסות לסמכותם המקבילה של שתי הערכאות, עלינו לומר, כי אף המושג טובת הילד הוא מושג רחב, מסגרתי, הכולל תכנים שונים. מושג זה מתאר את המטרה אליה יחתור בית המשפט או בית-הדין, אך לא את שיקוליו במקרה הקונקרטי." כן ראו בספרו, דיני המשפחה בישראל (מהדורה 2, המכון למחקרי חקיקה ולמשפט השוואתי ע"ש סאקר, תשמ"ט), בע' 250.

קשה, כגון שהורה אחד "חזר בתשובה" ובגלל זה נפרד מבן-זוגו שנשאר עיקש ב"חילוניותו", אך לרוב, נימוקים "אידיאולוגיים" אלה מאולצים לפי טקטיקה שההורה האחד בוחר לו נגד ההורה האחר, אם מדעת עצמו ואם בעקבות עצה שנטל מעורך-דינו. תכליתה של יריבות זו היא לסבר את אוזני השופט או הדיין כי אכן קיים מתח אידיאולוגי בין בני-הזוג, שאינו ניתן לפשרה, מאחר שכל פשרה עלולה להזיק להתפתחותו הנפשית של הילד; שהרי, למשל, לא יוכל להתחנך בזרם חינוכי דתי או חרדי אם תהא החזקתו אצל ההורה שאינו שומר תורה ומצוות.

אך אם ערכאות השיפוט האזרחיות מגלות יחס אדיש כלפי עניינו של השיקול הדתי ורואות בו רק סניף לשאלת ההיזק הנפשי שיבוא עקב ההכרעה בסוגיות אלה,[69] הדיינים בבית-הדין הרבני מחשיבים עד למאוד את השיקול הדתי הזה, ומכריעים בענייני ההחזקה, הלימוד והחינוך, לעניות דעתי במידת האפשר, לטובת ההורה האמון על קיום תורה ומצוות, תוך שלילת זכותו של ההורה ה"חילוני" להטביע את חותמו על עיצוב אישיותו של בנו הקטין ועל לימודו וחינוכו.

ברם, השיקול הדתי אינו מסתיים בשקילת זכויותיהם וחובותיהם של ההורים בינם לבין עצמם, אלא גם בזכויותיו וחובותיו של הדיין עצמו. לאמור, בניגוד לשיקול העוסק ב"טובת הילד", בו השופט מצווה להינתק מן ההורים היריבים ולשוות לנגד עיניו את טובתו של הקטין, בשיקול הדתי הדיין מחויב להינתק הן מן הקטין והן מן ההורים היריבים, ולשקול מהי חובתו הדתית שלו בקביעת עתידו הרוחני הדתי של הילד. שכן, אם יכריע הדיין ביחס לילד משהו המנוגד לערכי הדת, הוא עצמו עלול לחטוא בחטא דתי, שלפעמים יהא "מעוות לא יוכל לתקון". הדיין היושב בהרכב בסכסוך כזה מצווה באופן אישי מבחינה דתית לדאוג שהקטין יקבל חינוך לתורה ולקיום מצוות, ובאופן מיוחד למנוע בכל כוחו את הקטין מלעבור עבירות או מלהפר איסורים דתיים.

ניתן לחלק "שיקול דתי" זה בין שתי קבוצות-גיל עיקריות:

- קטין שלא הגיע לגיל החיוב במצוות, דהיינו בן שהוא למטה מגיל י"ג שנים ובת שהיא למטה מגיל י"ב שנה (בהלכה מכונה בן זה – קטן.)
- קטין שהגיע לגיל החיוב במצוות.

אם הקטין לא הגיע לגיל החיוב במצוות, ההלכה הרווחת מזמנם של האמוראים היא ש"קטן האוכל נבילות אין בי"ד מצוין להפרישו".[70] הלכה זו שוללת לכאורה את הנחתנו, שבית-הדין מחויב לפסוק בענייני המשמורת או החינוך לטובת ההורה שנחזה לקיים תורה ומצוות ולחובתו של ההורה שאינו שומר תורה ומצוות.

---

69 ע"א 238/88, יחזקאלי נ' יחזקאלי פ"ד מג(2) 467 (1989).

70 יבמות, קיג, ע"ב-קיד, ע"ב.

ברם המעיין בספרות ההלכתית, הן במקורותיה של ממרה זו והן בפרשנותה ההלכתית על-ידי חכמי ההלכה בדורות מאוחרים, ייווכח לדעת כי לא רק שממרה זו אינה שוללת את חובתו של בית-הדין להפריש את הקטן מאיסור, אלא שהיא אף מסייעת לעמדתנו מהנימוקים הבאים, אם במצטבר ואם לחלופין:

א. דינו של "קטן אוכל נבלות" היה שנוי במחלוקת בתקופת האמוראים הראשונים. בעוד ר' יוחנן "ספוקי מספקא ליה",[71] ומכוח ספק זה היה ניתן לחייב את בית-הדין להפריש את הקטן מאיסור, הרי שמפסק-דינו של רבי פדת, במעשה שבא לפניו, השתמע כי אין חובה להפריש קטין מאיסור.

כך היה המעשה שהובא לפני רבי פדת:[72]

> "רב יצחק בר ביסנא אירכס ליה מפתחי דבי מדרשא ברשות הרבים בשבתא, אתא לקמיה דרבי פדת. אמר ליה זיל דבר טלי וטליא וליטיילו התם, דאי משכחי להו מייתי להו."

(- לרב יצחק בר ביסנא אבדו מפתחות בית-המדרש, ברשות הרבים בשבת. בא לפני רבי פדת. אמר לו (רבי פדת), לך קח קטן וקטנה שיטיילו שם, שאם ימצאו (המפתחות) יביאו אותם.)

לפנינו אירוע חד-פעמי. הוראתו של רבי פדת באה לפתור בעיה שהתעוררה בדיעבד, ואשר לפתרונה נזקקו באי בית-המדרש והלומדים בו. מסיפור הדברים נראה כי רבי פדת לא התכוון לקבוע הלכה לדורות, שהרוצה להעביר חפץ ברשות הרבים יוכל להשתמש בקטן לצורך כזה. לפי זה אין להסיק כלל ממעשהו של רבי פדת לענייננו. חובתו של בית-הדין הרבני להפריש את הקטן מאיסורים שהוא עלול לעבור עליהם שנים רבות על-ידי קביעת משמורתו או חינוכו אצל ההורה שומר תורה ומצוות.

כך קבע מפורשות ר' יחזקאל לנדא בספרו "נודע ביהודה"[73] שעה שדן בבעיה מה לעשות בקטן שנולד מחוץ לנישואין להורים חסרי יכולת שלא חפצו להחזיק בוולדם. החשש היה "כי יצא הפקודה ליקח הילד לבית עניים שלהם עפ"י דתיהם, שכל ולד שאין מי שיחזיקנו יוקח שמה". וזה לשונו:

> "לענ"ד נראה דאף דבר זה דאין ב"ד מצווין להפרישו לא מצינו רק באיסור שהוא לשעתו, אבל איסור שאנחנו יודעים שאם יבוא לזה בקטנותו ישאר בזה לעולם, היכן מצינו שאין ב"ד מצווין להפרישו תיכף".[74]

---

71 שם, קיד ע"א. אך ראו ב"י, טור או"ח, סימן שמג, שסבור היה, כי לבעל הטורים הייתה גרסה אחרת לפיה לא ר' יוחנן הוא זה שהסתפק.

72 שם, קיג ע"ב.

73 תשובות נודע ביהודה (תנינא), אהע"ז, סימן לד.

74 יצוין כי בסוף התשובה השאיר ר"י לנדא את ההכרעה בענין מסירת התינוק לשיקול דעתו של השואל, מאחר שהיו שם כמה עניינים אחרים שאינם רלוונטיים לכאן.

ב. קביעה דומה נמצאת בתשובות מלמד להועיל[75] לר' דוד צבי הופמן שעה שנידונה שם שאלת הפרשת קטן מאיסור שבת.

"שדווקא במילתא דלא שכיחא, כמו איבוד מפתח וכיוצא בו מתירין משום מצוה, אבל במקום דשכיחא מילתא כמו במקום שאין כאן תיקוני חצרות ומבואות ועירוב ושיתוף ובכל שבת צריכין לעשות כן, הוי מילתא דקביעא, דחיישינן דילמא אתי למיסרך."[76]

כלומר, מלבד ההבדל בין ארעיות האיסור על מעשה המבוצע על-ידי הקטן לבין קביעות הביצוע, עליו העיר ר' יחזקאל לנדא, רד"צ הופמן מדגיש את תכליתו של מעשה הקטן: אם "מעשה האיסור" בא לשם מצווה, כמו לימוד בבית-המדרש, שיש מקום להתיר; אך אם מעשה הקטן בא רק לספק את הנאתו של הבוגר, מצווים אנו להפרישו. לאור זאת ניתן לשאול: איזו מצווה מוטלת על בית-הדין למסור את הקטן למשמורתו של ההורה שאינו שומר תורה ומצוות או לחינוכו?

ג. בסוגיית הבבלי ביבמות[77] ובשבת[78] התעוררה שאלת התאמתה של הלכת רבי פדת להלכה שבמשנה "קטן שבא לכבות אין שומעין לו, מפני ששביתתו עליהן".[79] התשובה לשאלה זו היא: הלכת רבי פדת עוסקת בקטנים שאינם יודעים כלל כי הם עוברים איסורי שבת וכי העצה "זיל דבר טלי וטליא וליטיילו התם דאי משכחי להו מייתי" נאמרה כשהקטנים לא יודעים על אובדן המפתח; לעומת זאת, ההלכה שבמשנת שבת דנה "בקטן העושה על דעת אביו",[80] כלומר, בקטן שיודע להבחין שהכיבוי נוח לאביו ועושה בשבילו, "דהוה כאילו מצווהו לעשות".[81]

כך מבחין המאירי בחיבורו:[82]

"כל קטן שראינוהו עושה על דעת אביו או על דעת איזה גדול, כגון שהיה אביו עומד על גביו וראינוהו לתינוק צופה לאביו ומביטו ותנועותיו מורות שהוא מכיר שנוח לאביו בכך אסור, שהרי הוא כמי שמצוהו לעשות ... (ולא שרינן אלא באינו

---

75 תשובות מלמד להועיל, מחברת ראשונה, סימן נח, 72.
76 שם, 75.
77 יבמות קיג ע"ב.
78 שבת קכא ע"א.
79 משנה שבת, טז:ו.
80 שבת, קכא ע"א.
81 רש"י שם, ד"ה על דעת אביו.
82 מאירי בית הבחירה, יבמות, קיד ע"א (אלבק, 426).

עושה על דעת אביו),[83] וכמעשה של מפתחות שזכרנו שלא הודיעו לתינוק שנאבדו שם שלא יתבוננו שנוח לו בכך ..."[84]

נדמה כי רוב המקרים בהם בית-הדין הרבני פוסק בענייני משמורת הילד או בקביעת מקום חינוכו ביריבויות שכאלה רחוקים מן הסיטואציה של הלכת רבי פדת.

ד. הלכתו של רבי פדת נאמרה רק לגבי קטן שלא הגיע לגיל חינוך, אך בשום פנים ואופן אין ללמוד ממנה על קטן שהגיע לכלל חינוך. כך קובעים מפורשות התוספות בשבת:[85]

"דבאיסורא דרבנן מוכח בפרק חרש דאין בי"ד מצווין להפרישו ונראה דמיירי בקטן שלא הגיע לחינוך, דבהגיע לחינוך כיון שחייב לחנכו כ"ש (כל-שכן) דצריך להפרישו שלא יעשה עבירה".

ה. ישנם מן החכמים הסוברים[86] שחידושו של רבי פדת נאמר דווקא לגבי איסורי שבת, אבל לא לגבי איסורי טומאה כגון טומאת כוהנים, טומאת שרצים או טומאה של אכילת דם.[87] בשלושת האיסורים הנ"ל, ובאלה בלבד, נדרשו הפסוקים הן בספרא והן בבבלי "להזהיר גדולים על הקטנים",[88] ועל-כן יש חובה על בית-הדין או על כל אדם החייב במצוות להפריש את הקטנים מאיסור. העובדה שאיסורי הטומאה עומדים בפני עצמם מוסברת על-ידי ההנחה שהחכמים בכל הדורות סברו כי עשייתם על-ידי הקטין יכולה להזיק לו באופן נפשי ורוחני, ולכן יש למונעו מהם מעל ומעבר למשקלן ההלכתי של עבירות אלה.[89]

---

83 השלמה של ר"ח אלבק, שם.

84 כך גם כותב רבינו ירוחם, ספר תולדות אדם וחוה נתיב א, א: "קטן אוכל נבלות אין בי"ד מצווין עליו להפרישו וה"ה לשאר איסורין ודוקא כשעושה על דעת עצמו, אבל אם מוכח מילת' שעושה ע"ד (על דעת) גדול, שמבין הקטן שגדול נחת רוח לו בכך, אסור ומצווין עליו להפרישו", כל גדול במשמע, לאו דוקא אביו.

85 שבת, קכא ע"א ד"ה שמע מינה קטן אוכל נבלות.

86 ראו תשובות רא"ם, סימנים עט-פ.

87 ראו יבמות, קיד ע"א.

88 ראו שם, שם. וכן ספרא דבי רב (א"ה וויס) שמיני, פרשה יב (ב) שם, אחרי מות פרשה ח, (ו).

89 כך למשל רש"ל בים של שלמה, יבמות, פרק יד, סימן ז (ד"צ ירושלים, 69) סובר שיש להפריש קטן מאיסור בעניני טומאה אפילו טרם הגיעו לחינוך, וזה בניגוד לשאר איסורים. רש"ל מסתמך, בין היתר, על חכמי הקבלה שכתבו "שאכילת שקצים ודומיהם מטמטמין הלב והשכל", כן בתשובות חת"ם סופר (לר"מ סופר) או"ח, סימן פג, בתשובה לשאלה אם מותר להכניס קטן שוטה שלא הגיע למצוות למוסד של נכרים שיש חשש שיאכילוהו אוכל בלתי כשר. אף-על-פי שלדעתו אין בהכנסתו של ילד כזה למוסד ספייה של איסור, נטה לאסור בהנמקה הבאה: "... ומ"מ העידו קדמונינו ז"ל שע"י מאכלות אסורות בנערות מטמטם הלב ומוליד לו טבע רע, עדיין אני אומר מוטב שיהיה שוטה כל ימיו וכו'".

ו. מן האמור לעיל יוצא כי בית-הדין מצווה באופן ישיר להפריש את הקטן מאיסור, וכי יש בהימנעותו של בית-הדין מלקבוע שהילד יהיה במשמורת ההורה שומר תורה ומצוות משום אי-הפרשתו של הקטן מאיסור.

הנחות אלה מבוססות על שיוכן של ההלכות הבאות לסוגיית "קטן אוכל נבלות". כך נאמר: "בן חבר שרגיל לילך אצל אבי אמו עם הארץ אין חוששין שמא יאכילנו דברים שאינם מתוקנים. מצא בידו פירות - אין זקוק לו";[90] "בן חבר כהן שרגיל לילך אצל אבי אמו כהן עם הארץ אין חוששין שמא יאכילנו תרומה טמאה. מצא בידו פירות - אין זקוק לו".

בשתי הלכות אלה לא נאמר מי הוא הפטור מלחשוש להאכלתו של הקטין באיסור. סביר להניח שאילו הייתה קיימת חובה להפריש קטן מאיסור, הייתה חובה זו מוטלת גם על בית-הדין, ולא רק על האב; וחובה זו לא הייתה מצטמצמת רק לסיטואציות בהן "מצא בידו פירות",[91] אלא הייתה מקיפה גם מקרים שהיה בהם חשש שהקטין ילך לאבי אימו עם-הארץ.

אך גם אם נניח, כהשקפת האמוראים, שרק האב הוא המחויב לחנך את בנו הקטן, ומכוח זה הוא המחויב הבלעדי להפרישו מאיסור, החובה מוטלת עדיין על בית-הדין להפריש את הקטן מאיסור - לא בגלל הקטן, אלא כדי שההורה שאינו שומר תורה ומצוות לא יחטא בילד. כך הסיק הרדב"ז[92] מהלכותיו המרובות של הרמב"ם בסוגיה זו, שנראו כסותרות זו את זו:

> "נמצאת למד ג' דינין בקטן. אם הוא עובר על דברי תורה אין ב"ד מצווין להפרישו, אבל מצוה על אביו לגעור בו. הרי שלא גער בו אלא הניחו, ב"ד ממחין ביד האב, ואומרים לו מדוע אין אתה גוער בבנך שלא יחלל שבת. ואם עובר בדברים שאין בהם אלא משום שבות, אעפ"י שמצוה על אביו לגעור בו מ"מ אם הניחו לעשות, אין ב"ד נזקקין לאב, כיון דאיסורו מדברי סופרים הקלו. ולהרגילו בידים, אסור אפילו באיסורין דרבנן, ואם האב הרגילו בכך, ב"ד ממחין בידו של אב, דהא איסורא עבד להרגילו".[93]

90 יבמות, קיד ע"א. בתוספתא דמאי, פ"ג ה"ג (ליברמן, 74) קיימת מקבילה: "בן חבר שהיה הולך אצל אבי אמו עם הארץ אין אביו חושש שמא מאכילו דברים שאינן מתוקנין, היו בידו פירות אינו חושש שמא אינן מתוקנין. אומר לו האכילנו מעשר ומאכילו."

91 "מצא בידו פירות" היא הסיפא של שני האירועים שהובאו כאן "בן חבר" ו"בן חבר כהן".

92 תשובות הרדב"ז, חלק חמישי, סימן אלף תלב.

93 תירוץ דומה מובא על-ידי ר' יוסף קארו בב"י, או"ח, סימן שמג בשם חותנו ר' חיים אבן אלבלג; כסף משנה, שבת, כד, יא; שם, מאכלות אסורות, יז, כז-כח. אך ראו ב"ח, או"ח, סימן שמג, שדחה תירוץ זה.

רעיון זה למד ר' חיים עוזר גרודז'ינסקי גם מממרתו של רבינו ירוחם בספר תולדות אדם וחוה,[94] לפיה הפטור מלהפריש את הקטן מאיסור הוא: "... ודוקא דלא שייך בר חיובא באיסור הקטן, אבל שייך בר חיובא באיסור הקטן מצווין עליו להפרישו".

וכך ביאר רח"ע גרודז'ינסקי ממרה זו:[95] הפטור מלהפריש את הקטן מאיסור על-ידי בית-הדין הוא דווקא אם הקטן עושה זאת מעצמו, ואין אדם גדול המאכיל אותו את הקטן. ברם אם הגדול מאכיל את הקטן "בכה"ג (=בכי האי גוונא) ששייך בזה בר חיובא על-ידי שהוא ספה האיסור לקטן, ובי"ד מצווין להפריש הקטן בכדי להציל את הגדול מאיסור לא תאכילום".[96]

ז. אך דומה, כי אף-על-פי שהִנחנו עד כה הכרעתו של בית-הדין לא למסור את הקטין לידי ההורה שאינו שומר תורה ומצוות היא הפרשה מאיסור או אף פחותה מזו, מביאורם של חכמים אחרים עולה כי הכרעתו האפשרית של בית-הדין למסור את הקטין לידי ההורה שאינו שומר תורה ומצוות, תיחשב לספייה בידיים.

כך, למשל, כותב ר' יצחק בלאזר בתשובות פרי יצחק:[97]

> אולם, לענ"ד נראה דלומר לעובד כוכבים להאכיל לקטן דבר איסור... גם זה הוי כמו דספי ליה בידיים ממש. דהנה בעיקר הדבר דילפינן מקרא דלהזהיר הגדולים על הקטנים ומוקי לה בגמרא דלא ליספו להו בידיים אין הכוונה להאכיל אותם בידיים ממש 'ליספו להו כתורא', אלא דאף לומר להו שיאכלו אסור וכמבואר בסוגיה שם לא יאמר אדם לתינוק הבא לי מפתח, וכ"כ בראשונים ... ועיין במ"ל (=במשנה למלך) סוף הלכות מאכלות אסורות דאפילו להטעות לקטן ולומר על דבר איסור שהוא היתר אסור, דהוי כמו ספי ליה בידים ועכ"פ הרי דכל שיאכל התינוק ע"י גרמתו הוי ג"כ כמו דספי ליה בידים.

הבסיס עליו משתית ר"י בלאזר את חידושו זה, כפי שהוא עצמו אומר, כתוב בראשונים ומצוי אף בתירוצים שהבאנו לעיל. אך דומה שר"י בלאזר מגדיר לראשונה כי "ספיה" פירושה גרימת אכילה, אפילו כשהקטין מקבל בפועל את מאכלו מצד שלישי, הוא הנכרי.

---

94 ספר תולדות אדם וחוה נתיב א, א.

95 ר' חיים עוזר גרודז'ינסקי, תשובות אחיעזר, חלק שלישי, סימן פא, ס"ק ט.

96 באותו קטע שם, "וא"כ כשנתן (גדול - יצ"ג) האיסור לקטן אף דמצד הקטן קיי"ל דאין בי"ד מצ"ל (מצריך ליה) מ"מ יהיה מצ"ל (מצריך ליה) מצד הגדול המאכיל שתתבטל הספיה ולא יעבור על האיסור".

97 תשובות פרי יצחק, חלק א, סימן יב, (ע' כא).

דבריו אלו של ר"י בלאזר הינם דברי פולמוס כנגד עמדתו של ר"מ סופר בתשובות חת"ם סופר,[98] שקבע על-סמך הלכתו של מהר"ם מרוטנבורג[99] (כפי שצוטטה בים של שלמה), כי אין באמירה לנכרי שיאכיל את הקטן דבר איסור משום ספייה בידיים.

הלכתו של ר"מ מרוטנבורג הנ"ל כפי שצוטטה בים של שלמה היא כדלקמן:[100]

> תינוק, נראה שאסור לסוך גופו בחלב וחזיר שאין זה אלא תענוג אבל יניח לעכו"ם לסוכו ולהאכילו, ולהזהיר גדולים על הקטנים אין אסור אלא דוקא כי ספו להו בידים.

ברם ר"י בלאזר מבאר אותה כך:[101]

> מה שכתב הסמ"ג בשם רבינו ברוך אבל יניח לעובד כוכבים לסוכָן ולהאכילן, אינו רוצה לומר שיהיה מותר לומר לעובד כוכבים לסוכן ולהאכילן, דזה בודאי אסור, כנ"ל. אולם הכוונה הוא דאם העובד כוכבים מעצמו סוכָן ומאכילן יניח לו.

האם קביעת בית-דין רבני כי הקטין יהיה במשמורתו של ההורה שאינו שומר תורה ומצוות, או שיתחנך בזרם ממלכתי אין בה משום ספיה בידיים, בדומה לאמירה לגוי להאכיל הקטן איסורים? שהרי זו כזו גורמות ישירות לקטין שיעבור על איסורי תורה. יתר על-כן, סמכותו של בית-הדין הרבני לפי החוק בישראל, לפיה הכרעתו של בית-הדין מחייבת, גורמת שכל הכרעה של בית-הדין שהילד יהיה במשמורת ההורה שאינו שומר תורה ומצוות יש בה ממש ספיה בידיים.

כאשר הקטין הגיע לגיל החיוב במצוות, הרי הוא גדול, וכשם שיש חובה ומצווה על אדם מישראל למנוע מחברו לחטוא, אם יש בידו לעשות זאת, כך בית-הדין מצווה למנוע בכל כוחו קטין כזה מלעבור על איסורים, ומוטלת עליו החובה להפרישו מאיסורים.[102] מקורה של הלכה זו הוא או משום הלאו של "ולפני עוֵר לא תתן מכשֹל"[103] או משום האיסור לסייע לעובר עבירה. האיסור לסייע לעוברי עבירה אינו ברור כשלעצמו, ורבו עליו הביאורים של החכמים.[104]

---

98 תשובות חתם סופר, לעיל הערה 89.

99 שם, ע' כט.

100 יבמות, פרק יד, בשם הסמ"ג.

101 לעיל הערה 93, שם.

102 על יחס זה בין חובתו של אדם מישראל להפריש את חברו מאיסור לבין חובתו של בית-הדין ראו בהרחבה שלום אלבק בתי הדין בימי התלמוד (בר אילן, תשמ"א), 25-19, והערות השוליים שם.

103 ויקרא, יט, יד, על היקף האיסור ראו תשובות הר צבי (לרצ"פ פרנק) יו"ד, סימן קכה.

104 עיינו למשל, רא"ש שבת, פרק א, הלכה א. תשובות מלמד להועיל מחברת ראשונה, סימן לד, נו. ר"מ פיינשטיין דברות משה, שבת, סימן ב, ועוד.

דומה שמכל האמור במאמר זה יש כדי לשער כי לו בפרשת נגר היה האב ההורה שאינו שומר תורה ומצוות והאם היא הייתה ה"חוזרת בתשובה", בית-הדין הרבני היה קובע את מקום החינוך והמשמורת של הילדים נשוא הסכסוך אצל האם השומרת תורה ומצוות.

ד. מפעלו של מנחם אלון: בין פרשנות 'יצירתית' ל'יצירה פרשנית'

נחזור לראשית המאמר, הקריאה ה"הרמוניסטית" שהציע אלון בהשגה עלי למציאת "מגמה משותפת" בין דיני התורה לבין המשפט הנוהג בישראל היא מאלפת ומלמדת על דרכו. אין מנחם אלון קורא את המקורות בקריאת אומן, ואין הוא משתדל ליישב את הכתובים רק מכוחם, אלא מתוך השקפה אזרחית ובעיקר מתוך מגמה יישומית של דיני התורה בישראל המודרנית. כך רעיון "אפוטרופסות ההורים", שאלון מחשיבו מאוד, לא הוכר מעולם בהלכה, "חזקת הגיל הרך" לקוחה "מכבשונה של ההלכה" היא לא הכרחית והרבה חכמים סברו כי בכלל אין לאב זכות לדרוש משמורת הבן לכשעצמו אלא הוא תלוי ברצונה של האם, או של הבן והבת הקטנים. מכאן גם ניתוחו של אלון כי קיים גיל בגרות קבוע בהלכה של שתיים עשרה/שלוש עשרה שנה ורק לצורך עניינים כלכליים הוקדם הגיל לגיל שש או שבע, אינה מדויקת. ומעניין לעניין, קביעתו של אלון כי אין לערוך כלל בדיקת רקמות לקטינה שאימה הרתה אותה בעת היותה נשואה בשם "טובת הילד"- בשל החשש שיצא עליה קול שהיא ממזרה – למרות היותה בשל תביעת מזונות בממונית, היא מוסרנית מודרנית, אך ההלכה הטהורה מכילה בקרבה ללא כל רגש אבהות "דיפרנציאלית": יש אב למזונות ויש אב לצורך הכרה בסטטוס.

במבט לאחור, גישתו של אלון הופכת להיות אט אט מיושנת. כך באמנת האו"ם בדבר זכויות הילד שהרבה מדינות חתומות עליה, ביניהן ארצה"ב וישראל, הומרה ה"אפוטרופסות" ההורית ב"אחריות הורית". כך גם "חזקת הגיל הרך" בוטלה בהרבה שיטות משפט מודרניות הסבורות כי אין להעדיף את החזקת הילד בגיל הרך אצל האם על פני החזקתו אצל האב, וגם בישראל קמים קולות רבים הדורשים את ביטולה של חזקה זו.

***

"אין עושין נפשות לצדיקים דבריהם הם הם זכרונם", אמרו בירושלמי. לא קבלת קביעותיו של מורה הדרך השופט פרופ' מנחם אלון המנוח, ללא עוררין, כ"נפש", ראויה למורשתו. דווקא העיון והדיון בדבריו הוא הוא הזיכרון האמתי של דמותו החיה והפועמת בליבנו. ☙

רדיקאליות פילוסופית בעולם הישיבות: הרב יצחק הוטנר על השואה

מאת: גמליאל שמלו

באוקטובר 1977 פרסם הירחון *The Jewish Observer*,[1] השופר הפופולרי של אגודת ישראל בארה"ב, מאמר[2] על משמעות השואה מאת הרב יצחק הוטנר, ראש ישיבת מתיבתא ר' חיים ברלין בברוקלין וחבר מועצת גדולי התורה של אגודת ישראל בארה"ב באותה תקופה. המאמר הוא תרגום לאנגלית של הרצאה שערך הרב הוטנר ביידיש לפני כמאה מחנכים שהתאספו בבית מדרשו, שעסקה בשאלות שהופנו אליו על לימוד נושא השואה בבתי ספר חרדיים בארה"ב.

המאמר עורר תגובות ביקורתיות רבות ומכתבים רבים שנשלחו למערכת. בצעד יוצא דופן עורכי הירחון ראו לנכון לפרסם מאמר הבהרה מאת אחד המתרגמים, שנועד להבהיר כוונותיו של הרב הוטנר.[3] שלוש שנים לאחר מכן התפרסם מאמר בכתב העת *Tradition* מאת לורנס קפלן, שבו הוא תקף את דבריו של הרב הוטנר הן על העובדות ההיסטוריות המוצגות בהם והן על הנחות היסוד של המחבר בנוגע לציונות ולמושג "דעת תורה" שעמד במרכז המאמר.[4]

אין מחלוקת על כך שדבריו של הרב הוטנר היו חריפים ופולמוסיים, אולם הסערה שהתעוררה סביב מאמרו התמקדה דווקא בנושאים המשניים. הרב הוטנר דיבר אמנם על חלקה של הציונות בעידוד האנטישמיות ובגרימת השואה, אולם טענות אלה לא עמדו במרכז דבריו. הרב הוטנר ביקש להסיט את תשומת הלב מהחיפוש הקבוע אחר הסיבות לשואה, ולהעבירה לתורה דיאלקטית והיסטורית מחודשת. במאמר זה אציג את החדשנות והייחודיות בתורתו התיאולוגית וההיסטוריוסופית של הרב הוטנר, שהיתה די מודרנית

---

1 *The Jewish Observer* היה שופר פופולרי שיצא לאור ע"י אגודת ישראל בארה"ב בין השנים 1963-2010. כתב העת כלל מאמרי דעה והדרכה המופנים ליהדות החרדית האמריקאית. נושא השואה עלה לעתים קרובות על דפיו.

2 Rabbi Yitzchok Hutner (1977), "'Holocaust' - A study of the term and the epoch it is meant to describe," *The Jewish Observer*, XII (8), 3-9.
המאמר הודפס באוסף מקורות *Wrestling with God: Jewish Theological Responses During and After the Holocaust*, (2007), Steven T. Katz (ed.) New York, 557-565.

3 Yaakov Feitman (1978). *The Jewish Observer*, XIII (1), 11-12.

4 Lawrence Kaplan (1980). "Rabbi Isaac Hutner's 'Daat Torah Perspective' on the Holocaust: A Critical Analysis," *Tradition*, 18 (3), 235-28.

גמליאל שמלו הוא המנהל החינוכי של Meor NYU ומרצה למחשבת ישראל במכללת שטרן לנשים שעל יד ישיבה יוניברסיטי. הוא פרסם מאמרים במחשבת ישראל והלכה.

ומתונה ביחס למה שקדם לה בעולם הישיבות, וייתכן שהיה לה חלק במיתון התנגדותם של בני הישיבות הליטאיות לציונות ולהשכלה.

א. מידה כנגד מידה: הגישות הנפוצות בקרב חשובי הרבנים המתנגדים ומחנכי הישיבות הליטאיות לפני השואה ולאחריה

הן הרבנים שניבאו על העומד להתרחש והן הרבנים שעסקו בחשבון הנפש בדיעבד לאחר השואה העמידו את החטא ועונשו במרכז הדיון, ובכך הם דבקו במאמר חז"ל:

> אמר רבא ואיתימא רב חסדא אם רואה אדם שִׁסורין באין עליו, יפשפש במעשיו, שנאמר נחפשה דרכינו ונחקורה ונשובה עד ה'. פשפש ולא מצא, יתלה בביטול תורה שנאמר אשרי הגבר אשר תייסרנו יה ומתורתך תלמדנו. ואם תלה ולא מצא, בידוע שִׁסורין של אהבה הם שנאמר כי את אשר יאהב ה' יוכיח.[5]

לפי חז"ל, אדם העובר ייסורים חייב לערוך חשבון נפש נוקב בחיפוש אחר חטאיו. רק מי שנקי מכל רבב יכול לחפש אחר גורמים אזוטריים יותר לסבלו, ולבסוף תולה בייסורין של אהבה. גם במקרה זה, המונח "ייסורין של אהבה" אינו ברור מהו. הרמב"ם דחה רעיון זה בשתי ידיים וטען שהוא רק דעת מיעוט,[6] וגם הרמב"ן סבר שייסורין של אהבה באים רק כדי לכפר על חטא הנסתר מעיניו של אדם צדיק (אם כי הוא אינו "צדיק גמור").[7] גישות אלה נסמכות על דברי חז"ל: "אין מיתה בלא חטא ואין ייסורין בלא עוון".[8] אדם העובר ייסורים ומתעלם מהחיפוש אחר חטאיו, מחמיץ את ההזדמנות לתקן את דרכיו ולהינצל ממכאוביו. בכך לא זו בלבד שהוא מתאכזר לעצמו, אלא שכאשר הקהילה כולה סובלת, ההתאכזרות היא גם כלפיה.[9]

תפיסה זאת היא אבן היסוד שעליה התבססו רבנים, ראשי ישיבות, ומחנכים ממחנה המתנגדים ועליה הם בנו את תורות התיאודיציה שלהם. רבים מהם הוסיפו ופירשו מאורעות ואסונות בחייו של אדם על פי מאמר חז"ל הידוע, "מידה כנגד מידה". לפי

---

5 תלמוד בבלי, מסכת ברכות, דף ה', עמ' א'.

6 **מורה נבוכים**, חלק ג', פרק י"ז.

7 שער הגמול (רישא). **כתבי הרמב"ן**, כרך ב', ירושלים, תשכ"ד, עמ' רס"ט-ר"ע.

8 **תלמוד בבלי, מסכת שבת**, דף נ"ה, עמ' א'.

9 על פי הרמב"ם, **יד החזקה**, הלכות תעניות, פרק א': "אבל אם לא יזעקו ולא יריעו אלא יאמרו דבר זה ממנהג העולם אירע לנו וצרה זו נקרה נקרית, הרי זו דרך אכזריות וגורמת להם להִדבק במעשיהם הרעים ותוסיף הצרה צרות אחרות. הוא שכתוב בתורה (ויקרא כ"ו) והלכתם עמי בקרי והלכתי עמכם בחמת קרי, כלומר כשאביא עליכם צרה כדי שתשובו, אם תאמרו שהוא קרי אוסיף לכם חמת אותו קרי".

עיקרון זה ישנה התאמה בין החטא לעונש (ובין המעשה הטוב לשכר) בעוצמה[10] ובאופן שבו הם מופיעים.[11] אחד המקורות לעיקרון זה נמצא במשנה במסכת סוטה:

> במידה שאדם מודד, בה מודדין לו. היא קישטה את עצמה לעברה, המקום ניוולה. היא גילתה את עצמה לעברה, המקום גילה עליה. בירך התחילה בעברה תחילה ואחר כך הבטן, לפיכך תלקה הירך תחילה ואחר כך הבטן, ושאר כל הגוף לא פלט: שמשון הלך אחר עיניו, לפיכך ניקרו פלשתים את עיניו... אבשלום נתגאה בשערו, לפיכך נתלה בשערו. ולפי שבא על עשר פילגשי אביו, לפיכך נתנו בו עשר לוּנְבִיות...[12]

נראה כי עיקרון זה הובא לא רק כדי להסביר את דרכיו של הא-ל אלא גם כדי להזהיר מפני העתיד ולהדריך את החוטאים בחיפושיהם אחר שגיאותיהם בדיעבד: מי שחוקר את הייסורים, יבין מתוכם את שעליו לתקן.

בשנות השבעים כתב הרב שלמה וולבה מאמר קצר 'על מעמקי השואה'. הרב וולבה, יליד גרמניה (1914-2005) ותלמיד ישיבת מיר בליטא, הושפע מהמשגיח הרוחני הרב ירוחם הלוי ליבוביץ, שהיה תלמידו של הסבא מסלובודקה. לימים כיהן הרב וולבה כמשגיח הרוחני של ישיבת מיר בירושלים. דרכו היא דרכה של תנועת המוסר, והוא הרבה לצטט מדבריו של מייסד התנועה, הרב ישראל מסלנט. גם בנושא השואה התבסס הרב וולבה על דברי הרב ישראל שנאמרו כבר באמצע המאה התשע עשרה:

> ובוא וראה ראייתם הבהירה של גדולי ישראל יחד עם ההנהגה של "מידה כנגד מידה" הפועלת בהיסטוריה שלנו. בשנת התר"ד התקיימה בעיר בראונשוויג בגרמניה האספה הידועה לשמצה של הרפורמיים שבה פירקה תנועה זו מעצמה עול המצוות המעשיות של התורה עד כדי "התרת" נישואי תערובת. כאשר שמע על זה הגאון רבי ישראל סלנטר זצללה"ה, אמר: "הם חיברו שולחן ערוך חדש שבו התירו נישואי תערובת. יבוא זמן והגויים יחברו שולחן ערוך משלהם ובו ייאסרו נישואים עם יהודים, ואוי ואבוי ליהודים משו"ע זה...!" והנה בדיוק תשעים שנה אחרי אספת בראנשוויג באו חוקי נירנברג הידועים לשמצה, בהם קבע היטלר ימ"ש עונש מוות

---

10 בנוגע לעוצמת העונש/השכר, חז"ל קבעו: "לעולם מידה טובה מרובה ממידת פורענות" (**תלמוד בבלי סוטה**, דף י"א, עמ' א').

11 ראה פירוש רש"י, שם, ד"ה "דבאותה מִדה".

12 **משנה מסכת סוטה**, פרק א', משנה ז'-ח'. במשנה ט' הובאו דוגמאות המראות כי העיקרון פועל לא רק לשבט אלא גם לחסד. לונביות הן חניתות.

ליהודי שבא במגע עם גויה! זה היה בשנת תרצ"ד. זהו פרט אחד של מידה כנגד מידה.[13]

קטע זה ממחיש את דבקותם של בני האסכולה הליטאית בעקרונות שמרניים אלה המופיעים בעקביות בקרב מנבאי השואה הראשונים ועד אחרוני מפרשיה.[14] כמאה ועשרים שנה חלפו מהתקופה שבה נאמרו דבריו של הרב ישראל ועד התקופה שבה נכתב מאמרו של הרב וולבה, שנים של דם ואש ותמרות עשן, בצד תחייה לאומית ותחייה דתית מסוימת, אולם מפתח התיאודיציה של הרב וולבה לא השתנה דבר. הרב וולבה ציין את המשניות במסכת סוטה הנ"ל וכתב שגם בעת "הסתר פנים" אין מקרה בעולם, אלא הא-ל ממשיך לתקשר עם בריאותיו דרך המאורעות הנוראיים ועלינו להשתדל להבין את דרישותיו. "מידה כנגד מידה" היא המפתח להבנה הזאת, מכיוון שהעיקרון פועל לא רק במישור הפרט (כפי שנאמר במפורש בחז"ל), אלא על פי הרב וולבה הוא פועל גם במישור הלאומי.[15]

אזהרה דומה לזו של רב ישראל, המבוססת על עקרון "מידה כנגד מידה", נכתבה על ידי הרב יעקב מזא"ה, רבה של מוסקבה, בשם המגיד מקלם. על פי המגיד, הגרמנים התנהגו כיראי שמים בעוד שבמציאות הם היו שונאי ישראל גדולים:

> מחוצף פנים כגייגלעיל יימח שמו, יכלה להיות לו תקומה רק בגרמניה... כי הדייטשעלע לא ירדוף את היהודים סתם בעלמא, ולא יהא פשוט מיצר לישראל בשעת שירים ראש, אלא הוא יעשה משנאת ישראל מין שולחן-ערוך ר"ל. מורי ורבותי! שימו זאת על לבכם (בנגון אמר זה), כי על חטא השולחן ערוך של גייגר'ל יקום לנו שולחן ערוך חדש נוסח גרמניה נגד כלל ישראל, ושם, ר"ל, יהא כתוב: "טוב שביהודים הרוג (בנגון) טוב שביהודים הרוג!" ישמרנו ה' ויצילנו![16]

גם הרב מאיר שמחה כהן מדווינסק (1843-1926), מחבר הספרים **אור שמח** ו-**משך חכמה**, הזהיר בראשית המאה העשרים מפני ההשכלה וההתבוללות התרבותית. לדבריו, כל אסון העוקר את עם ישראל ממקומו בא בעקבות ההתבוללות. כאשר ההתבוללות מאיימת להשריש את העם הנבחר באדמת נכר וכאשר היהודי מכריז כי "ברלין היא ירושלים", באה הסערה להזכירו שזאת אינה ארצו וזה אינו עמו.[17] דברים אלה נכתבו כאזהרה על ידי הרב מאיר שמחה עשרות שנים לפני השואה, ואחרים חזרו

13 הרב שלמה וולבה (תשל"ו). **בין ששת לעשור** (עמ' ע"ח, 'על מעמקי השואה'). ירושלים. מאמר נוסף ברוח דומה מאת הרב וולבה הופיע בירחון *The Jewish Observer* בקיץ 1987.

14 לעניות דעתי אליעזר שביד המעיט בחשיבותו של עקרון מידה כנגד מידה. ראה: שביד, א' (1994). **בין חורבן לישועה**. בני ברק: הקיבוץ המאוחד, עמ' 11.

15 הרב שלמה וולבה (תשל"ו). **בין ששת לעשור**. ירושלים, עמ' ע"ה.

16 הרב יעקב מזא"ה (תרצ"ו). **זכרונות** (כרך ד', עמ' קנ"ה-קנ"ו). תל אביב.

17 **משך חכמה**, ויקרא, פרק כ"ו פסוק מ"ד.

עליהם כהסבר והצדקת הדין גם אחריה. באוקטובר 1973 תרגם *The Jewish Observer* את דבריו לאנגלית ופרסם אותם. ביוני 1974 התפרסם בכתב העת מאמרו של הרב מרדכי גיפטר (1916-2001), ראש ישיבת טלז בארה"ב. במאמרו חיזק הרב גיפטר את דבריו של הרב מאיר שמחה[18] ולדעתו יש ללמוד אותם בכל ישיבה כחלק אינטגרלי ממערכת הלימודים שלה. על פי הרב גיפטר, לא רק שהאזהרה שהועלתה לפני השואה תקפה כהסבר להתרחשותה, אלא שיש לפרש כל חורבן על פי הכללים העולים מחורבן הבית,[19] שהוא הפרדיגמה לכל חורבן בישראל. הנביאים שחיו בתקופת החורבן הנחילו לנו את משנתם במדרשים ובקינות. לנו אין את הסמכות לחדש קינות לאסונות שאנו חווים, אך גם אין צורך בכך, שכן ניתן לייחס את הקינות המסורתיות לשואה באותה מידה שהן מתייחסות לחורבן הבית.[20] כשהנביא לימד שחורבן הבית נגרם מפני חטאי הדור, המאמין מבין שאין חורבן שאינו עונש, ואין עונש נפקד ללא עוון.

הרב ישראל מאיר הכהן מראדין (החפץ חיים, 1838-1933) הגיב למצוקת דורו על בסיס אותם כללים תלמודיים. הוא חיפש את החטא והטיף לתיקונו:

> אכן באמת כבר גילו לנו חז"ל כל זה ברוח קודשם, כדאיתא בשבת ל"ב: "על עוון ביטול תורה וחילול שבת חרב וביזה באים לעולם" (ובעוה"ר יחד עם ביטול תורה מהחדרים נתרופף למאוד גם שמירת הש"ק [שבת קודש], שהוא יסוד דת קדשנו). והנה ידוע מה שאמרו חז"ל "על מה העולם קיים, על הבל פיהם של תשב"ר", ובעוה"ר כהיום, אשר אלפים ורבבות ילדי ישראל נתרחקו מהחדרים של תורה, ותחת הבל פיהם של תורה לפנים, מלא פיהם כביום דברי הוללות וליצנות ושירי הבל, מתרופפים כל העמודים שבעולם קיים עליהם, ומצוקות הזמן מתגברות מיום ליום.[21]

מלחמת העולם הראשונה, שהיתה רצחנית באופן שלא היה לו תקדים, המצב הכלכלי הקשה, ועליית האנטישמיות הובילו את בעל החפץ חיים למסקנה כי "ובוודאי הלא הוא מאת ה' שחטאנו לו".[22] הצרות באו על כלל ישראל ועל העולם כולו (למשל, רעידת אדמה

---

18 עמ' 82 במאמרו של הרב מרדכי גיפטר, שהתפרסם שוב בגיליון מיוחד של *The Jewish Observer* בפברואר 1989 לציון 25 שנים לכתב העת.

19 שם, עמ' 80.

20 גם הרב יוסף דב סולוביציק השמיע דברים דומים. ראה:
Jacob J. Schacter (2008). "Holocaust commemoration and Tisha Be-Av: The debate over 'Yom ha-Sho'a'," *Tradition* 41 (2), 177-178.

21 מאמרו של הרב ישראל מאיר הכהן 'חינוך הבנים' (אלול תרצ"ב), התפרסם בספר **חפץ חיים על התורה**, בני ברק, עמ' שי"ד-שט"ו.

22 מאמרו של הרב ישראל מאיר הכהן 'זכרו תורת משה' (ניסן תרפ"ה), שם, עמ' רצ"ז.

באמריקה) כתוצאה מפריקת עול התורה בכלל, ובעיקר בגלל חילול השבת, זלזול באיסור נידה והפקרת חינוך הבנים לשיטות ההשכלה.

בשנות השלושים, ככל שהאיום באירופה ביחס למצבם של היהודים התקרב, בני האסכולה חידדו את הביקורת שלהם ופירטו את החטאים שעל העם לתקן. המאמר החריף 'עקבתא דמשיחא' של הרב אלחנן וסרמן (1874-1941), תלמידו של בעל החפץ חיים, נכתב על ידו כמה שנים לפני רציחתו בידי הנאצים. לא ברור ממאמר זה, שנכתב ברוח רבו, עד כמה התכוון הרב וסרמן לעורר את החזרה בתשובה כדי לעצור את האסון הקרב ובא, ונראה שבאותם הימים הקשים הוא ביקש רק לספק פשר לכאב ולחזק את אמונת עדרו באל ובצדקתו. יש "בעל הבית", אין מקרה ואין הפקרות, הכל התפתח כצפוי על ידי ההשגחה העליונה ובהתאם למצב הרוחני העגום של עם ישראל בימים ההם, ימי עקבתא דמשיחא. כמו רבו, הרב אלחנן הצביע על נטישת החינוך המסורתי ועל ההשכלה ("השכלת ברלין")[23] כגורמים למה שהוא הגדיר כ"חשכה". הוא התריס נגד האידיאולוגיות השקריות, ה"איזמים" שאומצו במקום האמונה בתורה,[24] והסביר, תוך שהוא נשען על דברי הגאון מווילנה[25] והרב ישראל מסלנט,[26] מדוע דווקא פורקי עול התורה הגיעו להנהגת העם באותה תקופה. ובווריאציה וירטואוזית על המוטיב "מידה כנגד מידה" הוא כתב:

> בימינו אלה בחרו להם היהודים בשתי עבודות זרות אשר להן יקריבו את קרבנותיהם, הרי הם: הסוציאליזם והנציונליזם. את תורת הנציונליזם החדש אפשר להגדיר בקיצור נמרץ: נהי' ככל הגויים. אין דורשים מיהודי אלא את ההרגשה הלאומית. השוקל את השקל והמזמר את "התקווה" פטור מכל מצוות שבתורה. ברור כי שיטה זו נחשבת כעבודה זרה לפי דעת התורה. שתי עבודות זרות אלה הרעילו את המוחות ואת הלבבות של הנוער העברי, לכל אחת מטה ראשי של נביאי שקר בצורת סופרים ונואמים העושים את מלאכתם בשלמות. קרה מעשה נסים: בשמים הרכיבו את שתי העבודות הזרות לאחת – נציונל-סוציאליזם, יצרו מהן מטה זעם איום, החובל ביהודים בכל קצווי ארץ. הטומאות, להן סגדנו, הן החובלות בנו. "תיסרך רעתך".[27]

עד היום מאמר זה הוא מקור מרכזי בתודעת השואה בישיבות הליטאיות בארץ ובחו"ל. לפני כעשור הוא הודפס מחדש כספר כיס וחולק במחיר מסובסד על ידי "המוסד

---

23 הרב אלחנן וסרמן (תשנ"א). **קובץ מאמרים**, ירושלים, עמ' קי"א.
24 שם, עמ' ק"ח.
25 שם, עמ' ק"י.
26 שם, עמ' קט"ו.
27 שם, עמ' קי"ט.

לעידוד לימוד התורה, ספריית בני תורה המרוכזת" ובתמיכת הישיבה הירושלמית שנוסדה על שם המחבר, ישיבת אור אלחנן.

בשנת 1939 כתב הרב חיים עוזר גרודזנסקי (1863-1940), אב בית הדין של וילנה ומי שנחשב לגדול פוסקי ההלכה באירופה, על המצב ההולך ומחמיר שכבר אז "לא היתה כזאת גם בימי הביניים אשר כל הגולה כמדורת אש".[28] למרות ההרג, בתי המדרש וספרי התורה שעלו באש, הגזרות הקשות המתחדשות נגד דתו ושערי מדינות המקלט הנעולות בפני עמו, אמונתו באל לא נחלשה, וזאת מכיוון שהיה ברור לו מהיכן יצא הקצף.

> אכן עתה בעוה"ר רפתה האמונה ובארצות המערב הכה הריפורם שורש מכבר זה איזה דורות ובאו הרבה עי"ז לידי טמיעה והתבוללות ממש, ומשם יצאה הרעה כעת לרדוף באף להחרימם ולגרשם מן הארץ, וארס השנאה לאחב"י התפשט על ידם גם בשארי ארצות, וגם במדינות המזרח רבו התועים והמתעים אשר ללא אמונה גברו בארץ להטות את המון בית ישראל מדרך התורה, ועוד יתרה עשו חלק מן העם לחלל קדשי העם בפומבי, לא עמדו בניסיון ופרצו פרצות בקדושת השבת... בכל זאת עדיין לא בא העם לידי הכרה לדעת מה זה ועל מה זה נרדפנו ככה, הוכה העם בסנוורים ונמס כל לב ורפו כל ידיים וכשל כוח הסבל...[29]

הרב חיים עוזר מצא את "שורש המחלה" בחינוך החילוני "בבתי ספר חופשיים ללא תורה וללא אמונה" וקרא לחיזוק החינוך התורני והקמת בתי ספר דתיים וחדרים ללמוד גמרא.

הרב אברהם גרודזינסקי (1884-1944), המשגיח הרוחני של ישיבת המוסר הדגול בסלובודקה ובעל ספר תורת אברהם, גם כן פירש את האסונות שנגרמו ליהודים בדרך מידה כנגד מידה. כאשר הרוסים פלשו לליטא והפכו את בניין הישיבה למקום בידור, הוא פירש זאת בכך שכנראה תלמידי הישיבה בעצמם התייחסו לבית מדרשם כמקום בידור כבר מזמן: "מן השמים גילו כי הישיבה היתה מקום נופש – אכלו ושתו, נחו ובאו לישיבה להשתעשע קצת בפלפול התלמידים... תמיד חשבנו, כי קיימנו את התורה מעוני, והנה נוכחנו לדעת כי ביטלנו אותה מעושר".[30] מול "שתים עשרה סיבות שהמיטו, בגזרת עליון, את השואה על עם ישראל" ואת כניסת הנאצים לליטא והקמת הגטו בסלובודקה, הציג הרב אברהם בפני בוגרי הישיבה רשימה של שנים עשר נושאים שבהם עליהם להתמקד

---

28 הרב חיים עוזר גראדזענסקי (1939). **אחיעזר**, חלק ג'.

29 שם.

30 הרב אברהם גרודזינסקי (תשל"ח). **ספר תורת אברהם**. בני ברק, עמ' ט"ו (על פי **משנה אבות** פרק ד' משנה ט').

כדי לערוך תיקון ומהם הם ישאבו חיזוק, כגון: אמונה, חינוך בדרך התורה, שמירת שבת, שמירה על כשרות ועוד.[31]

גישה זו חיה עשרות שנים לאחר השואה. בספרו **בין ששת לעשור** חזר הרב שלמה וולבה, חתנו של הרב אברהם והמשגיח הרוחני של ישיבת באר יעקב, על דברי חותנו ועל רשימתו.[32] לדעתו, רק מי שסבל בעצמו רשאי לערוך דין וחשבון על דור השואה,[33] אבל העיקרון שלפיו הייסורים באו מחמת החטא ובמידה כנגד מידה עמד גם אצלו.

אם כן, נמצא קו מחשבה עקבי משותף לרבנים המתנגדים. החטא מזמין פורעניות, והפורעניות אמורות לדחוף לחיפוש אחר החטא הגורם. המפתח לחיפוש הזה הוא העיקרון של חז"ל "מידה כנגד מידה". החטאים שהרבנים הצביעו עליהם היו הן חטאים פרטיים, כחילול שבת ואי הקפדה על כשרות, והן חטאים כלליים, כציונות חילונית ונטישת החינוך המסורתי לטובת חינוך ברוח ההשכלה.

דברים אלה שנאמרו לפני השואה הובאו במאמרים ובשיחות גם אחריה והם מבטאים דבקות ואמונה בגישת "מידה כנגד מידה", שלא השתנתה מול המאורעות הקשים שחווה העם היהודי. הרב אליהו דסלר (1892-1953), המשגיח הרוחני של ישיבת פוניבז' בבני ברק בשנות החמישים, סבר שהשואה נפלה על היהודים בעקבות ההתבוללות. האמנציפציה נועדה לתת ליהודים את מנוחת הנפש, השמחה, ורוחב הדעת הדרושות לעלייה רוחנית וביאת המשיח, אך הם השתמשו בחופש החדש כדי "להתערב בגויים וללמוד ממעשיהם".[34]

הרב יעקב קנייבסקי (1899-1985), בעל ספר **קהילות יעקב**, כתב שבדומה ל"פריקת עול ר"ל" שנולדה בגרמניה והתפשטה לשאר הארצות, כך גם הגזרה לטבוח ביהודים יצאה מגרמניה והתפשטה לארצות נוספות.[35] דברים דומים נאמרו ב-1991 לפני מלחמת המפרץ על ידי המנהיג הרוחני של הציבור הליטאי בישראל, הרב אלעזר מנחם מן שך (1899-2001) מישיבת פוניבז'. לפי הרב שך, ההשכלה הכתה קשות גם בערים היהודיות במזרח אירופה, ובכל מקום שבו היהודים התקרבו לתרבות האירופית האנטישמיות גברה.[36] הא-ל מאריך אפו, אבל כשהדין האלוקי דורש את הפירעון, אין

31 שם, עמ' י"ז.

32 הרב שלמה וולבה (תשל"ו). **בין ששת לעשור**. ירושלים, עמ' ע"ח.

33 שם, עמ' ע"ז, כנראה על פי הרב אברהם גרודזינסקי (תשל"ח). **ספר תורת אברהם**. בני ברק, עמ' י"ז.

34 הרב אליהו דסלר (1987). **מכתב מאליהו** (חלק ד'), ירושלים, עמ' 124-135.

35 הרב יעקב קנייבסקי (תשל"ב). **ספר חיי עולם**, עמ' ל"ז.

36 הרב אלעזר מנחם מן שך (תשנ"ג). **בזאת אני בוטח**. בני ברק, עמ' צ"ב. הרב שך ניסה להתגבר על הבעיה ההיסטורית המונעת לדעתו את השימוש בעקרון מידה כנגד מידה, והיא שהשואה פגעה במיוחד באזורים שבהם היתה דבקות גדולה ביותר במסורת. ראה שביד, א' (1994). **בין חורבן לישועה**, עמ' 11-12.

ויתור: "מאריך אפֵּיה וגבֵּי דיליה".[37] הרב שך השתמש במוטיב זה לא רק לפירוש השואה אלא גם כדי להתריס נגד מה שהוא ראה כחילוניות גוברת בחברה הישראלית בכלל ובממשלת ישראל בפרט, ולהזהיר ערב המלחמה מסכנות ההתבוללות התרבותית. עבור הרב שך, דבריו היו "אמת לאמיתה, האמת הטהורה כמו שהיא ללא כל רבב",[38] גם אם הם לא יהיו לרוחם של השומעים. הסיבה לשואה "ברורה עד למאוד". השואה היתה עונש מן השמים, ומי שלא מקבל גישה זו "כופר בעיקר".[39]

שיאה של שיטת מידה כנגד מידה התבטא בספרו של הרב אביגדור מילר (1908-2001) *Rejoice O Youth*. הרב מילר נולד בבולטימור, למד בישיבה יוניברסיטי בניו יורק ואצל הרב יעקב יוסף הרמן. יחד אתו למדו הרב נתן ווכטפוגל, שלימים כיהן כמשגיח הרוחני של הישיבה הגדולה בלייקווד, והרב ברוך קפלן, מייסד מערכת בתי הספר "בית יעקב" בארה"ב. בשנת 1932, בהיותו בן 24, הגיע הרב מילר הצעיר לאירופה כדי ללמוד בישיבת סלובודקה של הרב נתן צבי פינקל ("הסבא מסלובודקה") ועם חתנו, הרב חיים יצחק אייזיק שר. ב-1938 חזר הרב מילר לארה"ב. היכרותו עם עולם התורה המזרח האירופי הניבה לפחות שנים עשר ספרים באנגלית רהוטה, וכאלפיים מהרצאותיו הוקלטו והופצו בקהילה החרדית.

בשנת 1944 פנה הרב הוטנר לרב מילר בבקשה שיכהן כמשגיח הרוחני של ישיבת חיים ברלין. בישיבת חיים ברלין הִרבה הרב מילר לשוחח על השואה ובספרו הראשון *Rejoice O Youth*[40] הוא נתן מקום מרכזי להתמודדות עם השואה. הספר, שהובא לדפוס בשנת 1962 ויצא לאור שנה לאחר מכן, הוא דיאלוג בין דמותו של ה"חכם" לדמות ה"צעיר", כנראה תוך התבססות על השיחות שהתנהלו בישיבה. מטרת הספר היתה להבדיל בין האמת, שהיא דעת התורה, לבין השקר, שאותו הוא זיהה עם התרבות הפופולרית, העיתונות והאוניברסיטאות (מדעי החברה והרוח בפרט)[41] המאיימים להוציא את הצעיר מכותלי בית המדרש. הספר פונה ליהודי האמריקאי הצעיר והמתלבט בראשית שנות השישים, שאחד הדברים המערערים את אמונתו הוא השואה. כבר בפתיחת הספר ה"צעיר" שואל:

> אילו יכולתי להשתכנע באמיתות התורה, הייתי משתחרר ממשא נפשי גדול. המחשבות האלה העסיקו את תודעתי לאורך זמן מה, אבל לאחרונה ביתר שאת. אירע דבר מה שהטריד אותי עמוקות. קראתי את הספר "הכחדת ששת המיליונים".

---

37 מארמית: מאריך את אפו וגובה את שלו. שם, עמ' צ'-צ"א. על פי **מדרש בראשית רבה** סי' ס"ז פסקה ד'.

38 שם, עמ' פ"ט.

39 שם, עמ' צ"א.

40 A. Miller, (1962), *Rejoice O Youth*,. New York, pp. 1-2.

41 שם, עמ' 4-9.

הרשעות חסרת ההבחנה הזאת של האומה הגרמנית והסבל האיום של עמנו עוררו בי אי שקט עז. אני חש דחף בלתי נשלט לרדת לחקר העניינים האלה. מה המשמעות של כל זה, כיצד עליי לראות זאת ומה עליי לעשות בעניין זה?[42]

במהלך הדיאלוג, דעתו של הצעיר נחה מהסבריו של החכם והוא משתכנע שאין מקרה בעולם וכי הכל מודרך בהשגחה פרטית.[43] על בסיס מאורעות הגלות, החכם הוכיח שהא-ל תמיד מלווה את עמו בדרך נסית. למשל, בניגוד למצופה המתבוללים היו שנואים יותר על האנטישמים לעומת היהודים שלא התבוללו.[44] כך שמר הא-ל על היהודים מפני התבוללות, שכן היהודים לא היו חזקים דים כדי לעמוד בניסיון.[45] דוגמה נוספת: הא-ל בחר לתת את הר הבית לישמעאלים מכיוון שפסלים, האסורים בדת היהודית, אינם חלק מפולחנם ואין סכנה שהם יכניסו אותם למקום הקדוש. ובכלל, הא-ל מסר את הר הבית לאויבי ישראל כדי להרחיק משם את היהודים, שעלולים להתנהג בקלות ראש במקום הקדוש "with their women and their cameras and their lunches".[46]

לאחר הצגת המשניות ממסכת סוטה[47] מפרט הרב מילר בספרו רשימה של חטאים ועונשים על משקל מידה כנגד מידה. על פי מוטיב זה מידת ההתבוללות של היהודים בגרמניה היתה הגדולה ביותר ועל כן הפעולות שננקטו שם לזיהויים כיהודים היו המתוחכמות והמרושעות ביותר:[48] הנאצים פיתחו קטלוג לרישום השמות הגרמניים החדשים שהיהודים אימצו,[49] וקבעו שעליהם להוסיף לשמות אלה את השם "שרה" או "ישראל",[50] והכריחו אותם ללבוש את טלאי מגן דוד הצהוב.[51] דוגמה נוספת למידה כנגד מידה: מברלין יצא מבול של זרמי התבוללות, כולל תנועת הריפורם, שקלקל את היהודים באופן חסר תקדים, ועל כן ברלין היא המקום שממנו יצא מבול של שנאה שהחריב את ישראל באופן חסר תקדים.[52] הרב מילר גם ערך רשימה מפורטת של הסברים העומדים מאחורי מעשי הזוועה שנעשו כלפי היהודים בשואה:

---

42 שם, עמ' 2.

43 שם, עמ' 1.

44 שם, עמ' 40.

45 שם, עמ' 146-147. הרב מילר העמיד את השואה מול גירוש ספרד, שם אמונתם של היהודים היתה חזקה יותר והם עמדו בניסיון: "Only a small group remained, and even these continued to be Jews in secret".

46 שם, עמ' 146. ליהודים אסור לעלות להר הבית מכיוון שהם לא יכולים לקיים בו את תנאי הטומאה והטהרה, ואילולא המחסומים העומדים בפניהם, הר הבית הקדוש היה הופך למוקד תיירות.

47 שם, עמ' 348.

48 שם, עמ' 350.

49 שם, עמ' 147.

50 שם, עמ' 147, 349.

51 שם, עמ' 147.

52 שם, עמ' 349.

... כיוון שיהודים אירופים רבים כל כך נפלו קרבן לטעות של הערצת הגרמנים וחיקויים, אלוקים הרשה לגרמנים לעשות ככל שיכלו כדי להראות מי הם היו באמת. אותם יהודים, שהתחילו להתעלם מהנשמה, ובחיקוי של הגרמנים השקיעו את מאמציהם אך ורק לצורכי הגוף, נאלצו לראות איך מאמציהם הוליכו להחרבת הגוף הגרועה ביותר שהיתה בהיסטוריה...

כיוון שיהודים רבים כל כך חיקו את הגויים וסירבו לנוח ביום השביעי, הם אולצו לעבוד שבעה ימים בשבוע בעבודות כפייה הורגות.

כיוון שהיהודים שלחו את ילדיהם לבתי ספר לא יהודיים או לבתי ספר חילוניים וחדלו להעניק לילדיהם לימודי תורה, הנאצים הורשו להרוס לחלוטין את הילדים היהודים.

כיוון שהנשים היהודיות חדלו לכסות את שערן לראשונה בהיסטוריה, הגרמנים גילחו את ראשיהן במחנות המוות.

כיוון שהיהודים זלזלו במעלות הלבוש וההתנהגות הצנועים, הגרמנים הצעידו אותם עירומים לתאי הגזים והנשים היהודיות נאלצו לסבול משלל התנהגויות מגונות ברבריות לפני שהרגו אותן...

כיוון שהם כל כך העריצו את הרופאים, בייחוד המומחים הגרמנים, היהודים נפלו קרבן לניסויים ועינויים מרושעים שהרופאים הגרמנים ביצעו בהם.

כיוון שהיהודים נטשו את מצוות התורה, הגרמנים הטילו עליהם את חוקי נירנברג, ששללו מהם את כל הזכויות שאנשים אחרים נהנו מהן...[53]

הרב מילר ניסה להראות שככל שהיהודים ינסו לבגוד ביהדותם או להסתיר אותה, כך הם ייחשפו למעשים קשים נגדם החושפים את מה שהם מנסים להסתיר - והכל תחת הכוונתו של הא-ל.

רשימתו של הרב מילר, שהשפעתו על היווצרות השקפת העולם הפופולרית בקרב הקהילה החרדית בארה"ב היתה משמעותית ביותר[54] אם כי היא טרם נחקרה, ייחודית וחריפה בספרות השואה והיא כמעט לא משאירה מקום לחידושים נוספים. על רקע ספר זה, שיצא מבית מדרשו של הרב הוטנר, אדון במאמרו של הרב הוטנר.[55]

---

53 שם, עמ' 350-351.

54 וכדי להמחיש: בשנת 1988 כשהייתי אורח לשבת אצל משפחה חרדית בניו יורק סיפרתי לאבי המשפחה שאני עומד לסיים את התואר הראשון בלימודי פילוסופיה. הוא אמר לי שאם אני מתעניין בפילוסופיה, "You must read Rabbi Avigdor Miller!".

55 לעיל, הערה 2.

ב. שיטתו של הרב הוטנר

הרב יצחק הוטנר נולד בשנת 1906 בוורשה, למשפחה הקשורה לחסידות קוצק.[56] כצעיר היה לו קשר ישיר עם משנת הרב מנחם מנדל מקוצק, אחד מבעלי המחשבה הרחבים והיצירתיים ביותר במאה הקודמת, בשל קרבתו לדודו, הרב בן ציון אוסרובר, שהיה תלמידו של הרב מנחם מנדל. בגיל חמש עשרה נשלח יצחק הוטנר הצעיר לישיבת סלובודקה, שם למד במשך ארבע שנים בפיקוחו של הסבא מסלובודקה. בשנת 1925 הוא עלה לארץ ישראל ולמד במשך ארבע שנים בסניף הישיבה החדש בחברון. בתקופה זו הוא התקרב לרבנים רבים, ובהם הרב יוסף חיים זוננפלד, הרב שלמה אליעזר אלפנדרי, הרב איסר זלמן מלצר, ובייחוד לרב אברהם יצחק הכהן קוק, עליו הוא אמר לתלמידו הרב שלמה פריפלד ששורש נשמתו היה גם זה של הרב קוק. הרב הוטנר התרשם משליטתו של הרב קוק בספרות ההלכה, הקבלה והמוסר, ומיכולתו לשלב את הידע הזה יחד, והתפעל מעדינות נפשו של הרב קוק, רוחו הפיוטית ורוחניותו הדינאמית. "אלמלא נפגשתי עם הרב", הוא אמר לרב משה צבי נריה, "היו חסרים לי חמישים אחוז מהוויותיי!"[57] בשנת 1929 חזר הרב הוטנר לוורשה ומאוחר יותר נסע לגרמניה שם למד לזמן קצר באוניברסיטה בברלין באופן לא רשמי. בשנת 1933 הוא התחתן ובשנת 1935 עבר לגור בניו יורק, שם הוא ייסד את ישיבת ר' חיים ברלין.

כמקובל, ההרצאות שלימד בישיבה היו על התלמוד, אך הוא גם הקדיש תשומת לב למחשבת ישראל, ובשיחותיו בלטו תורותיהם של המהר"ל מפראג והגאון מווילנא. גם החסידות ואפילו הפילוסופיה הלא-יהודית השתלבו יחד במשנתו, אם כי בדרך כלל הובאו ברמיזה וללא ציון מקורם.[58] אמנם שמו של הרב קוק לא הופיע במאמריו, אבל היה ברור שהרב התכוון אליו כאשר הוא הביא רעיונות מאת "קדושי עליון" של הדור הקודם.[59] נקודת המבט שלו היא הסתכלות על דפוסים חוזרים באירועים ובתהליכים היסטוריים בתולדות עם ישראל, המובילים לגאולה. יש אומרים כי גישתו זו טעונה במשיחיות.[60] הדגש על ההיסטוריה והציפייה לגאולה בא לידי ביטוי גם במאמרי ההגות שכתב על היחסים בין בני ישראל לבין בני עשיו, שבע מצוות בני נוח והנצרות, וגם ביצירותיו ההלכתיות. דומני שספרו הראשון **תורת הנזיר** (שהוא פירוש על 'הלכות נזירות' של

---

56 פרטי הביוגרפיה של הרב יצחק הוטנר לקוחים מ:
S. Schwarzschild, (1993). “Isaac Hutner,” *Interpreters of Judaism in the Late Twentieth Century*. Washington DC: B’nai B’rith Int’l Continuing, p. 154.
M. Greenblatt, (2001). “Rabbi Yitzchak Hutner—The Vision Before His Eyes,” *Jewish Action*, 61 (4).

57 משה צבי נריה (תשנ"ג). **חיי הראי"ה**. בני ברק, עמ' רנ"ח.

58 Schwarzschild, "Isaac Hutner," p. 155.

59 Greenblatt, M. (2001). “Rabbi Yitzchak Hutner – The Vision Before His Eyes”. *Jewish Action*, 61 (4).

60 Schwartzchild, “Isaac Hutner,” p. 158.

הרמב"ם) מתבסס על גישה זו, פיתוח סוגיות השייכות לעבר הרחוק, ולעתיד המשיחי המיוחל. ספר זה, שיצא לאור בברכתו של הרב קוק, נכתב ברוח ספרו של הרב קוק **שבת הארץ**, שבמרכזו עיסוק הלכה למעשה בהלכות שמיטה. השפעתו של הרב קוק על הרב הוטנר בולטת במיוחד במאמר שכתב הרב הוטנר על השואה.

הרב הוטנר התנגד לשימוש במילה "שואה" כמונח המתאר את רצח העם שבוצע על ידי הנאצים, והעדיף את המונח "חורבן אירופה". לדעתו, מונח זה ממקם את השואה ברצף היסטורי תיאולוגי וארוך טווח של חורבן-גלות-גאולה, בעוד שהמילה "שואה" מבליטה את השוני שבמאורע ומוציאה אותו מהרצף הזה.[61] במאמר תמיכה ברב הוטנר מינואר 1978, הוסיף הרב פייטמן הסבר:[62] במשך אלפי שנים למדו ילדי ישראל אודות "חורבן הבית", "חורבן ירושלים", "חורבן ביתר", והשם "חורבן אירופה" מכניס את השואה לתוך המסורת הזאת באופן המעורר פחות ספקות תיאולוגיות מיותרות. כל מונח אחר עלול להוציא את השואה מן הכלל, כאילו קיים סוג של חורבן שאינו חלק מתוכנית האלקית. הסכנה גדולה אף יותר כשידוע שמטבע הלשון החדש הוטבע על ידי כופרים בתורה.[63] בשל אותה סיבה הוא התנגד לקביעת יום זיכרון מיוחד לשואה במקום שתיכלל באבל של תשעה באב.[64]

על פי הרב הוטנר ישנה תוכנית אלוקית שלפיה אסונות וייסורים מובילים לגאולה, והשואה היא צעד בהליכה הדיאלקטית והבלתי נמנעת לקראת הגאולה. את המקור המקראי לתוכנית הקוסמית הזאת הוא מצא בספר דברים ל"א.[65] הדיאלקטיות ההיסטורית של הרב הוטנר אינה מוגבלת למסגרת הכוללת של חורבן-גלות-גאולה, אלא ישנן התפתחויות דיאלקטיות בעידן הגלות עצמה. השואה פרצה בגלות כחלק מתהליך חינוכי שבו עם ישראל אמור ללמוד שאין לבטוח בגויים ("אלוהי נכר הארץ") אלא בא-ל בלבד.

זהו כיוון חדש בתולדות עם ישראל בגלות. עד האמנציפציה חוו היהודים על בשרם את היחס הקשה מהגויים וידעו למה לצפות. האמנציפציה שניתנה להם הבטיחה להם שוויון, והם נתנו בגויים אמון ושמו בהם את מבטחם ואת תקוותם. בשואה הכל קרס. היהודים נבגדו והזכויות שהובטחו להם נגזלו מהם. עם השואה חלה קריסה נפשית. התקווה הפכה לבגידה באמון.

> הראשון בסימני שינוי העידן האלה כרוך במעתק מדיכוי לאורך דורות רבים, אשר גם אם אנו מצטערים עליו, היה צפוי והמדכאים אף הצהירו עליו בגלוי – בעידן

---

61 .Rabbi Yitzchok Hutner, *The Jewish Observer*, XII (8), 9

62 .Yaakov Feitman (1978). *The Jewish Observer*, XIII (1), 11-12

63 ראה גם שם, עמ' 9.

64 שם, עמ' 9.

65 .Rabbi Yitzchok Hutner, *The Jewish Observer*, XII (8), 4

> שבו ניתנו, ואחר כך הופרו, הבטחות לשוויון, הוענקו זכויות שנשללו אחר כך, התעוררה ציפייה לחסד, שהתרסקה לנוכח זדון אכזרי.
> התוצאה הסופית של התקופה הזאת לנפש היהודית היתה משמעותית, ואף מכרעת. האמון בעולם של הגויים פינה את מקומו לגינוי באמון. בתקופה היסטורית קצרה יחסית, האכזבה מהעולם הלא-יהודי הוטבעה עמוקות בנשמה היהודית.[66]

לפי הרב הוטנר, עם ישראל בגלות למד לבטוח בגויים ודומה שאפילו היכולת לצפות לרדיפות עקביות בתקופה שקדמה לאמנציפציה נחשבה למעין "ביטחון". עם ישראל למד לשרוד בגלות והתאקלם. השואה שברה את הביטחון הזה מכיוון שהיא הפכה את קערת האמנציפציה על פיה: כגודל ההבטחה כן גודל האכזבה. מכאן שנוסף על התהליך הדיאלקטי של חורבן-גלות-גאולה ישנו בגלות עצמה תהליך חינוכי דיאלקטי: יציבות ומעין "ביטחון" ביחסים עם הגויים, אמנציפציה וביטחון מלא בהם, רצח עם ואכזבה גמורה, ביטחון בא-ל בלבד ותשובה שלמה.

בניגוד לדעותיהם של הרבנים שהחזיקו בגישת מידה כנגד מידה, הרב הוטנר אינו סבור שמדובר בחטא מסוים שגרם לעונש הנורא, אלא בזווית ראייה מעוותת של העם, הדורשת תיקון. אף לא מדובר בפלג אחד חוטא – הפלג החילוני, הציוני, הסוציאליסטי – אלא בבעיה הנמצאת בקרב העדה כולה. אמנם בהמשך דבריו הרב הוטנר דיבר על אשמה ועל הצורך לחזור בתשובה,[67] אך נראה לי שכוונתו היתה להצביע על בעיה מופשטת הרבה יותר מהחטאים שהוצגו בגישות אחרות. חידוש נוסף של הרב הוטנר הוא שיותר משהאסון הוא עונש, הוא נועד לתקן את ההסתכלות על עם הנכר, להסב את הביטחון בגויים לביטחון בא-ל בלבד ולסלול את הדרך לתשובה שלמה. הרב הוטנר הסתייג מהחיפוש אחר חטאים ספציפיים. היו פגמים בעם, שנדרש בהם תיקון, אך זה ייעשה באופן דיאלקטי וטבעי על ידי הייסורים עצמם. אין כאן "תוכחה המביאה לתשובה", אלא צרה הנראית כתוכחה ("tochacha phenomenon"), המביאה לתיקון גם באופן תת-הכרתי, כפי שקרה למשל בתנועת החזרה בתשובה של שנות השבעים.

תחת הכותרת המשנה "Tochacha vs. Specific Guilt" כתב הרב הוטנר:

> בנקודה זו למותר לציין שכיוון שחורבן יהדות אירופה היה תופעה של תוכחה, פעולה של נזיפה וגינוי, ש'כלל ישראל' נושאים על כתפיהם כחלק אינטגרלי מהיותם העם הנבחר, אין לנו הזכות לפרש את התופעות הללו כסוג כלשהו של **עונש ספציפי על חטאים ספציפיים**. התוכחה היא היבט מוטמע באופיים של כלל ישראל עד בוא המשיח, והיא נשלחת לכלל ישראל כרצונו של הבורא, ומסיבות הידועות ומובנות **אך ורק לו עצמו**. צריך להיות נביא או תנא כדי לטעון להבנת הסיבות הספציפיות למה שאירע לנו; כל מי שנופל מהנביאים או התנאים הטוען

66 שם, עמ' 4.
67 שם, עמ' 6.

להבנה כזאת, רומס לשווא את גופיהם של הקדושים שמתו על קידוש השם, ומשתמש לרעה בכוח לפרש ולהבין את ההיסטוריה היהודית.[68]

מול גישתו של הרב הוטנר, ראש ישיבת חיים ברלין, עמדה השקפתו של הרב אביגדור מילר, המשגיח הרוחני של הישיבה. בספרו של הרב מילר *Rejoice O Youth*[69] הוזכרו חטאים ספציפיים רבים והעונש עליהם – מידה כנגד מידה. הרב מילר פרש מישיבתו של הרב הוטנר בשנת 1964 ועובדה זו אומרת דרשני. נראה כי הרב הוטנר, שאיבד בשואה קרובי משפחה שהיו צדיקים וקדושים, ראה בגישה של הרב מילר הקצנה של השיטה המסורתית. מסופר בחוג הישיבה[70] שדודו של הרב הוטנר, שהיה כה רגיש לכבודה של התורה, מת מהתקף לב כשראה חייל נאצי יורק על ספר התורה. אין להסביר את מיתתם של קדושים כאלו באופן כל כך גס במשקל מידה כנגד מידה, ועל כן הרב הוטנר חיפש פרשנות חלופית.

גישתו זו היתה חריגה בעולם הישיבות, אם כי היו תקדימים. אחד מהם נמצא בדפי *The Jewish Observer* עצמו. בשנת 1974 הודפס באותו כתב עת מאמרו של ראש ישיבת טלז בארה"ב, הרב מרדכי גיפטר. לפי הרב גיפטר יש לפרש את השואה כמו חורבן הבית. הוא למד משיטת הנביאים בתקופת הבית, שהטיפו על דפוס מסורתי של חטא ועונש, ויישם אותה על השואה, אך גם ריכך במקצת את ביטוייה של מידה כנגד מידה.

> הנביא מסביר שהגלות מירושלים היא תוצאה של החטא – יחס בין עבירה לעונש – **בין שאנו מבינים את החטא ובין שאיננו מבינים אותו.**[71]

הרב גיפטר לא ניסה לפענח את החטא או להבין את משמעות העונש. ברור לו שהיה חטא, אך הוא לא התיימר להצביע עליו. הדגש במאמרו היה חיזוק האמונה בא-ל ובהשגחתו על ידי הכרת גודל האסון, שחרג מדרך הטבע.[72] הרב גיפטר הציע משמעות חלופית לשואה, אישית יותר, שאינה מדגישה את הסיבות לשואה. הוא לא שאל "למה זה קרה לנו?", אלא "מה נוכל ללמוד ממה שקרה לנו?".[73] הרב הוטנר התרחק צעד נוסף

---

68 שם, עמ' 9. ההדגשה במקור.

69 Miller, A. (1962) *Rejoice O Youth*. New York. pp. 1-2:

70 שמעתי על כך מהרב ברל גרשנפלד, שהכיר את הרב הוטנר כשעלה לישראל בסוף חייו.

71 עמ' 80 במאמרו של הרב מרדכי גיפטר, שהתפרסם שוב בגיליון מיוחד של *The Jewish Observer* בפברואר 1989 לציון 25 שנים לכתב העת. ההדגשה שלי.

72 שם, עמ' 82.

"For if ח"ו Hashem would have forsaken us, this *Churban* could never had occurred. The Churban itself is evidence and testimony to the fact that "we have a father in heaven."

73 בכך שיטתו דומה לזו של הרב י"ד סולוביצ'יק במאמרו 'קול דודי דופק' (תשנ"ב), מתוך **איש האמונה** ירושלים. ראה במיוחד עמ' 68 ועמ' 72.

מהדרך המסורתית וטען שאיננו מסוגלים להבין את מניעיו של הא-ל בקשר לחטא ועונשו אך אפשר להשיב על השאלה "למה" בלי להזדקק לסוגיית החטא ועונשו. אם כן, הרב הוטנר הציע לא רק משמעות חלופית לשואה – מהו הלקח שאנחנו יכולים ללמוד מהשואה? – אלא גם פירוש חלופי לשואה – למה השואה התרחשה? – ותשובתו היא שהשואה היתה חלק מתהליך היסטורי דיאלקטי.

באחד ממכתבי התגובה הרבים למאמרו של רב הוטנר נשאלה שאלה המחדדת את הייחודיות בשיטתו: האם סביר לטעון שהא-ל יעניש את בניו מבלי שהם יוכלו לדעת במה חטאו ומה עליהם לתקן? "האם ירביץ האב לבנו ויאמר לו בו בזמן 'אל תשאל למה, שכן הדבר גדול ממך'?"[74] יש להניח שגם הרב הוטנר סבר שאב רחמן וצודק לא יתנהג באכזריות כזאת, והתשובה לשאלה זו מונחת במאמרו: החורבן אינו עונש בלבד, והוא יביא לתיקון שיתרחש ממילא (אכזבה מהגויים ומדרכיהם, ביטחון בא-ל בלבד), ומכאן שאין בו אכזריות:

> שלב ה-*teshuva* יבוא כתוצאה ישירה של כל ה"רעות והצרות", אשר, כפי שפירשנו את הדברים על פי אונקלוס, באים עליהם בגלל האמון שהם נותנים בגויים. התוצאה של האסונות הגדולים של ימינו רחוקה מלהיות רק עונש על העוולות: היא תתקן את האמון שניתן בעבר שלא כראוי ותכין את הדרך לתשובה אמיתית.[75]

ה-*teshuva* היא תיקון שיוביל לשינוי ביחס לגויים ולדרכיהם, והיא תבוא כתוצאה ישירה מהייסורים. ניכרת כאן השפעתו של הרב קוק על תורתו של הרב הוטנר. הרב קוק התבונן בהיסטוריה בצורה דיאלקטית, ומהתבוננות זו נבעה גישתו החיובית כלפי הציונות בכלל וגם כלפי הציונות החילונית (אם כי לא כמתן אישור לציונות החילונית).[76] הרב הוטנר לא קיבל את גישתו של הרב קוק לציונות, אך הוא כנראה אימץ את דרך ההסתכלות הדיאלקטית שלו על תהליכים היסטוריים והשתמש בה כדי לפענח את השואה. בדומה לו גם הרב צבי יהודה קוק, בנו של הראי"ה קוק, השתמש בתורתו הדיאלקטית של אביו כדי לפרש את השואה כ"ניתוח שמימי" המטהר את עם ישראל מטומאת הגלות.[77] אף שטומאה זו קשורה גם לתרבות הגויים,[78] היא קשורה בעיקר לאדמת נכר.

74 התגובות למאמרו של הרב הוטנר הופיעו ב-*The Jewish Observer*, ינואר 1978, עמ' 9.

75 Rabbi Yitzchok Hutner, *The Jewish Observer*, XII (8), 6.

76 ראה רביצקי, א' (1997). **הקץ המגולה ומדינת היהודים**. תל אביב: עם עובד, עמ' 141-152.

77 שם, עמ' 152, מתוך הרב שלמה אבינר (תש"ם), **שיחות הרב צבי יהודה**. מושב קשת. עמ' 11, וכן שם, עמ' 176.

78 ראה: רוזן צבי, י' (תשס"ב). 'החולה המדומה - צידוק השואה במשנת הרב צבי יהודה קוק וחוגו'. **תרבות דמוקרטית**, 6, 172, הערה 14.

ראה גם: Achituv, Y. (2005). "Theology and the Holocaust". In S. Katz (ed.), *The Impact of the Holocaust on Jewish Theology*. New York, pp. 275-286.

בשונה מדבריו של הרב קוק האב, ההתייחסות של הרב הוטנר אינה לאדמת הגויים אלא לאמונה בגויים ובדרכיהם. התיקון יבוא לא מניתוק של עם ישראל מאדמתם של הגויים אלא מאכזבתו מאמונתו בהם. הן הרב הוטנר והן הרב צבי יהודה למדו מהרב קוק לקרוא את ההיסטוריה באופן דיאלקטי ודטרמיניסטי לקראת גאולה, אך השואה מפורשת על פי אידיאולוגיות שונות: עבור הרב צבי יהודה הציוני, השואה חיזקה את הציונות, ועל פי הרב הוטנר החרדי, השואה חיזקה את ההיבדלות מהגויים.

שיטתו של הרב הוטנר ושל הרב צבי יהודה קוק נבדלות ביניהן גם בעניין הבא: לפי הרב צבי יהודה, השואה היתה מעין ניתוח המפריד את עם ישראל מהטומאה שבאדמת הגויים. אף שהניתוק הזה היה אכזרי, הרי שכמו כל ניתוח זהו מעשה חיובי, כמעשה תיקון.[79] ישי רוזן-צבי מפרש גישה זו של הרב צבי יהודה – השואה איננה זוועה מזעזעת, אלא מעשה ריפוי שיש לברך עליו למרות הצער הכרוך בו – כנגזרת מתפיסתו שלפיה עם ישראל מצוי בעיצומה של הגאולה.[80] כאשר הגאולה היא סיפור העל, כל מאורע חייב להתפרש לאורה – לחסד ולא לשבט.

בניגוד לפרשנות זאת, פרשנותו של הרב הוטנר מניחה את השואה ואת בגידת הגויים באמון שעם ישראל נתן בהם כמעשה של שבט ודין, כזוועה שלילית ולא כדבר מה שיש לברך עליו. גם כאן התפיסה דטרמיניסטית – התיקון יבוא בתגובה לייסורים בשלב הדיאלקטי הבא, אבל אין להגדיר את הייסורים עצמם כמעשה תיקון. הרב הוטנר דחה את הקביעה שזהו זמן של תחילת הגאולה, ועל כן הוא לא פירש את החושך הנורא כאור חדר הניתוח.

נראה שגישה זו היא נקודת מפנה משמעותית מתורתו של הרב קוק, אביו של הרב צבי יהודה קוק ומורו של הרב הוטנר. לרב קוק היו תפיסות פנתיאיסטיות שהגיעו אליו בעיקר דרך חב"ד.[81] השקפות פנתיאיסטיות מובילות בדרך כלל לשקט נפשי, לסבילות, כמו השַתקנות של הקווייקרים.[82] כאשר ההוויה מלאה באלוקות, אין דחף להסתכל מעבר להווה. אך לפי רביצקי, כשהפנתיאיסט, הרואה התגלות אלוקית בכל דבר, פונה להיסטוריה, הוא יראה את הא-ל גם בה ויתפוס את ההיסטוריה כהתגלות בזמן, קרי "גאולה". גם כשהמאורעות נראים קשים ביותר, הא-ל מופיע בהם, ועל כן הם לא יכולים

---

79 ראה רביצקי, א' (1997). **הקץ המגולה ומדינת היהודים**. תל אביב: עם עובד. עמ' 176.

80 שם, עמ' 183-182.

81 רביצקי, א' (1999). **חירות על הלוחות**. תל אביב: עם עובד. עמ' 110-107.

82 ראה: Baltzell, E. D. (1979). *Puritan Boston and Quaker Philadelphia*. Boston: Beacon Press. pp. 97-98.

להיות אלא מעשי תיקון אלוקי בדרך לגאולה. כך פירש הרב קוק את זוועות מלחמת העולם הראשונה[83] וכך פירש בנו, הרב צבי יהודה קוק, את השואה.[84]

לדעתי, ראש הישיבה הליטאי הרב הוטנר שאב מאת הרב קוק את הדטרמיניזם ואת המבט הדיאלקטי, אך הוא הרבה פחות פנתיאיסטי בתפיסותיו, ובשואה הוא ראה רק הרס והרג, ולא גאולה. הוא האמין שהתיקון יבוא, אך רק כשלב שני התלוי בשינוי בתודעת עם ישראל, שינוי שלא יבוא מבחירה חופשית אלא כתוצאה מהזעזוע והאכזבה שהוא יספוג.

רוזן-צבי מבקר את גישתו של הרב צבי יהודה, שלפיה הזוועות שהתרחשו בשואה הן מעשים חיוביים בתהליך של גאולה. לדעתו, גישה זו אינה מתקבלת על הדעת. אמנם דברים אלה אינם תקפים להשקפתו של הרב הוטנר, אך בביקורת אחרת של רוזן-צבי הוא טוען שהרב צבי יהודה ותלמידיו "התגברו" על הזעזוע של השואה רק על ידי דחיקה לשוליים של סבלם של הקורבנות הבודדים ממרכז תשומת הלב התיאולוגי. השחקן הראשי בתפיסתם ההיסטורית הוא האומה, ועל כן זעקתם של הבודדים נשמעת פחות בסיפור העל של ריפוי הקולקטיב. כמו כן, הרגש והמוסר והחשיבות בבחירתו החופשית של האדם בטוב או ברע נדחקים הצידה על ידי הבלטת התיאולוגיה הדטרמיניסטית.[85] נראה שגם שיטתו של הרב הוטנר אינה מצליחה להתעלות מעל הביקורת הזאת.

מאמרו של הרב הוטנר על השואה משך תגובות חריפות ביותר בעיקר משום שהמגיבים ראו בדבריו שנכתבו בהמשך האשמה עקיפה, אם כי לא מכוונת, של הציונות בגרימת החורבן.[86] במאמר טען הרב הוטנר שבשואה התגלו שני מוטיבים חדשים בהתפתחות הגלות: המוטיב הראשון הוא התהליך הדיאלקטי שבו העם התאכזב מהגויים ומדרכיהם, והמוטיב השני הוא שיתוף הפעולה חסר התקדים בין בני ישמעאל (הערבים) לבין בני עשיו (המערב) ברדיפה וברציחה של היהודים. לפי הרב הוטנר, למופתי בירושלים לא היה עניין ביהודי אירופה והוא שמר על יחסים טובים עם יהודי היישוב הישן, אולם העלייה לארץ הקודש איימה על קהילתו והוא הפך להיות "התגשמותו של מלאך המוות" והשפיע על היטלר להשמיד את כל היהודים.[87] לדבריו, השפעתו של אל הוסייני על היטלר היתה מכרעת לגבי "הפתרון הסופי" וההחלטות בוועידת ואנזה.[88]

מבקריו של הרב הוטנר טענו כי מהמוטיב השני עולה האשמה של הציונות שדחפה כביכול את המופתי האג' אמין אל הוסייני לידי אנטישמיות שטנית, קשירת קשר עם הנאצים ועידוד רצח העם. לכאורה עולה מדברי הרב הוטנר שלציונות יש אחריות כבדה

---

83 ראה: הרב אברהם יצחק הכהן קוק (תש"ן). **אורות**. ירושלים, עמ' י"ג; וראה: רביצקי, א' (1997). **הקץ המגולה ומדינת היהודים**. תל אביב: עם עובד, עמ' 152-151.

84 שם.

85 ראה רוזן-צבי, י' (תשס"ב). 'החולה המדומה - צידוק השואה במשנת הרב צבי יהודה קוק וחוגו'. **תרבות דמוקרטית**, 6, 172, עמ' 171-168, 174, 178.

86 ראה: Schwarzschild, "Isaac Hutner," p. 164 (no. 6).

87 Rabbi Yitzchok Hutner, *The Jewish Observer*, XII (8), 8.

88 שם, עמ' 8-7.

לשואה, אך הרב הוטנר עצמו[89] והרב יעקב פייטמן,[90] מליץ היושר של הרב הוטנר, הסתייגו מפרשנות זו והדגישו שאין להטיל את האשמה על היהודים, אלא יש להבחין בין סיבה ומסובב, מחד גיסא, לבין חטא ועונש, מאידך. הציונות היתה סיבה לשואה, אבל לא חטא שהביא את השואה כעונש. הרב הוטנר לא התייחס לקשר שבין המופתי לבין היטלר כתוצאה של חטא שביצעו היהודים, אלא כחלק מתהליך דיאלקטי הנגזר מראש שממנו היהודים מתאכזבים מהגויים ולמדים שאין להם על מי לסמוך אלא על הא-ל בלבד.

קפלן לא מקבל זאת. במאמר ביקורתי הוא ציטט אמירות של הרב הוטנר בדבר "culpability of the forerunners of the state"; "guilt" ו- "shameful episode"[91] שמהן עולה שהציונות אינה גורם נטול אשמה, אלא היא שהביאה את החורבן על היהודים. "What is Rabbi Hutner doing if not placing the blame of the Mufti's greatly exaggerated influence on the final solution on those who fought for the establishment of the State of Israel?", הוא תהה.[92]

אמירות אלה של הרב הוטנר אכן מעוררות תהיות, לא רק בגלל שקשה להגן על טענותיו בדבר הקשר שבין המופתי לבין היטלר באופן היסטורי, אלא מכיוון שלא ברור כיצד הן מתיישבות עם שיטתו הכוללת. הרב הוטנר בנה מערכת דיאלקטית שאינה תלויה בחטא ועונשו בכלל ובמידה כנגד מידה בפרט, ושהורידה מעל כתפו של עם ישראל את האחריות לחקור אחר עוונותיו. האם מי שמחזיק בגישה כזו יכול לסתור את עצמו ולהאשים את הציונות בצורה כה בוטה? האופן שבו הרב הוטנר מפרש את ההיסטוריה היה תלוי בהשקפת עולמו,[93] ולכן גם אם העובדות ההיסטוריות היו מצביעות על אשמה ברורה של הציונות ועל קשר שבין המופתי להיטלר, נדמה לי שהרב הוטנר עדיין לא היה

---

89 שם, עמ' 9.

90 Yaakov Feitman (1978). *The Jewish Observer,* XIII(1), 13.

91 Lawrence Kaplan, (1980). "Rabbi Isaac Hutner's 'Daat Torah Perspective' on the Holocaust: A Critical Analysis," *Tradition*, 18 (3), 244.

92 במאמר מאוחר יותר של קפלן, שבו הוא חוזר וחוקר את משנתו של הרב הוטנר על השואה, הוא מנתח את מאמרו בפחד יצחק על ראש השנה. נראה כי בממצאיו החדשים של קפלן ישנה ראייה חדשה של גישת הרב הוטנר שלפיה אין להטיל אשמה על גורם כלשהו בקרב היהודים. ראה: L. Kaplan, (2010). "A Righteous Judgment on a Righteous People: Rav Yitzhak Hutner's Implicit Theology of the Holocaust," *Ḥakirah*, 10, 101-116.

93 ראה למשל בספרו של הרב יצחק הוטנר (תשמ"א). **פחד יצחק אגרות וכתבים**. ירושלים, עמ' קס"ג: "... שכל אלה שהם בני היכלא בגופי תורה, ותושבים קבועים באהלי התורה, הרי תורתם יוצרת בלבבם מין **תחושה** מיוחדת להבנת דברי ימיה של האומה. ואפילו בלי הזדקקות לפרטי הדיונים של מאורעות הזמנים, ומבלי הזדקקות לדיוקי העובדות שבשלשלת בתקופה..."

סוטה משיטתו הדטרמיניסטית ולא היה מטיל את האשמה על הציונות. על כן יש לשאול מדוע נוצר הרושם שהוא האשים יהודים על סמך טיעונים היסטוריים כה קלושים?

הטענה העיקרית של הרב הוטנר בנוגע למופתי אינה קשורה לאשמתם של הציונים. הרב הוטנר התייחס להתערבותו של המופתי ביצירת "הפתרון הסופי" כדי להמחיש את התגלמותה של הנבואה המקראית כפי שהיא באה לידי ביטוי בבראשית פרק כ"ד פסוק ט'. על פי הנבואה, בשלב קריטי בתולדות ישראל, ישמעאל (הערבים) יחבור לעשיו (המערב) כדי להרוג את ישראל.[94] נבואה זאת משתלבת בהיסטוריוסופיה הדטרמיניסטית של הרב הוטנר, והתגשמותה היא בלתי נמנעת:

> כיוון שמעשיהם של האבות הם סימן למה שיקרה מאוחר יותר לבנים, ולכל מעשה המצוין בחומש יש משמעות נצחית, נוכל ללמוד מהפִיסקה הזאת **שמן הנמנע** היה שכוחותיהם של עשו וישמעאל יתאחדו. עתה אנו חיים בתוך רגע המפנה הזה בהיסטוריה היהודית.[95]

לפי הרב הוטנר, שיתוף הפעולה שבין בני ישמעאל לבין כוחות המערב נגזר מראש. אולם מדוע הוא הדגיש את חלקה של הציונות בשידוך השטני הזה?

לעניות דעתי, הסטייה מההסבר הדטרמיניסטי של הרב הוטנר נועדה לצרכים פולמוסיים בלבד ולהגנה על כבודם של גדולי התורה. מנהיגים ציוניים יצאו נגד גדולי התורה בטענה שהם גרמו לאסון בכך שלא עודדו את העלייה לארץ. הרב הוטנר מתייחס לכך בהקדמה לקראת דבריו על המופתי. טענות אלה של יוצרי דעת הקהל בישראל הן מסולפות ובגדר כתם שיש להסירו, מכיוון שהאשמה זו מוטעית לא רק ברמה העובדתית אלא גם ברמה התיאולוגית, מכיוון שאין לנו (לשיטתו של הרב הוטנר) להטיל אשמה כלל.

ביקורתו של הרב הוטנר כלפי הציונים הובאה רק כדי להמחיש את הפגם שבגישתם, המבוססת על היסטוריוגרפיה פוליטית וחברתית, בעוד שיש להתעלות להיסטוריוגרפיה מסוג אחר. מאחורי דבריו של הרב הוטנר עומדת הטענה שאילו חיפשנו את הסיבות החברתיות והפוליטיות לשואה במעשי היהודים, היה עלינו לבקר את העולים עצמם, ובעיקר את אלו שפעלו לקידום ההתיישבות היהודית בארץ ישראל, שאיימה כל כך על הערבים בארץ באותה עת. "לשיטתכם", יאמר הרב הוטנר לציונים התוקפים, "שלפיה אתם מחפשים את הגורם האשם ומטילים את האחריות על גדולי התורה, אפשר באותה מידה להטיל את האשמה דווקא עליכם בכך שההתיישבות היהודית היתה גורם לחץ שהוביל את המופתי לחפש דרכים שימנעו את עלייתם של היהודים באמצעות חבירה להיטלר".

כך עולה גם מהבהרתו של הרב פייטמן, העולה בקנה אחד עם המערכת ההיסטוריוסופית-תיאולוגית של הרב הוטנר:

---

94 ראה הגר"א ל**ספרא דצניעותא** פרק ד'. וספר **אפיקי ים** למסכת ב"ב, דף ע"ג, עמ' ע'.

95 Rabbi Yitzchok Hutner, *The Jewish Observer*, XII (8), 8 (הדגשה שלי).

> מובן מאליו שיש כאן יחס סיבתי – אבל לא יחס של חטא ועונשו... אם נבקש לשאול למה לפתע אנו טרודים כל כך בהבנת הסיבות לקטסטרופה הזאת שאירעה לאחרונה בהיסטוריה היהודית, בו בזמן שאת קודמותיה (לדוגמה, פרעות ת"ח ות"ט [1648] של חמלנצקי), אין אנו מציעים פשר סיבתי, התשובה פשוטה: הדיון של ראש הישיבה לא היה בשום אופן תרגיל בחיפוש אחר מישהו **להטיל** עליו את האשמה, אלא נועד **להסיר** אותה ממי שמגיע להם יותר כבוד.[96]

מכאן שעל אף דבריו הנוקבים של הרב הוטנר, הוא לא ביקש להאשים את הציונים אלא לבטל את שיטתם. נדמה לי שנקודה זו נדחקה לשוליים על ידי קפלן, אולי בגלל הסגנון הפרובוקטיבי של הרב הוטנר והטיעונים שהוא הסתמך עליהם.

לסיכום, קיים קשר רעיוני בין שני המוטיבים שהרב הוטנר תיאר – המהלך הדיאלקטי שבו עם ישראל יתאכזב מהגויים, ושיתוף הפעולה האנטישמי בין המערב לבין בני ישמעאל. בשניהם ההיסטוריה מתפתחת בצורה דטרמיניסטית, והלקח בשניהם הוא שאין לסמוך על הגויים. בזמני רדיפה היהודים הצליחו תמיד למצוא אלטרנטיבות בארצות ששימשו עבורן חוף מבטחים, אולם בשואה הם לא הצליחו לעשות זאת בשל הקשר שבין עשיו וישמעאל. אם אין לסמוך על הגויים, המסקנה המתבקשת היא שעל עם ישראל לסמוך רק על אלוקי ישראל ועל נביאיו וחכמיו. הציונות הציעה שאם אין לסמוך על הגויים - עלינו לסמוך רק על עצמנו, אולם לפי הרב הוטנר מסקנה כזאת עלולה להוסיף חוליה מיותרת ואולי אף טראגית לשרשרת ההיסטוריה הדיאלקטית, ועל כן היא מסוכנת ויש לדחותה.

ג. רישומי שיטת הרב הוטנר על ההגות החרדית

אביעזר רביצקי הצביע על דבקותם של ראשי הישיבות הליטאיות בתורתם של הרב וסרמן והחפץ חיים, שלפיה כל סטייה מתורה וממצוות גורמת לאסון כפי שקרה עם החילונים בשואה. לדבריו, עולם הישיבות הוא כה שמרני עד שלא היה בכוחה של השואה כדי לשנות השקפת עולם זו, למרות הממדים חסרי התקדים שלה.[97] ואולם גישתו של ראש הישיבה הליטאי, הרב הוטנר, מנהיג בעל השפעה בעולם החרדי, מראה כי מתפתח שינוי בהשקפה המקובלת בעולם החרדי בעקבות השואה. השואה והבעיות התיאולוגיות העולות ממנה יצרו דרך חשיבה חדשה בשיח הליטאי שהוביל הרב הוטנר. במקום החיפוש אחר החטא על פי "מידה כנגד מידה", עלינו לחפש במאורעות טראגיים או שמחים מהי התכנית של הא-ל בהכוונת ההיסטוריה הדטרמיניסטית והדיאלקטית. כראש ישיבה דגול אי אפשר

---

96 Yaakov Feitman, *The Jewish Observer*, XIII (1), 13.

97 רביצקי, א' (1997). **הקץ המגולה ומדינת היהודים**. תל אביב: עם עובד, עמ' 243-244.

היה להתעלם מדרכו החדשה של הרב הוטנר. יתרה מכך, חידת השואה קוראת לפתרונות יצירתיים, ועל כן העולם החרדי קיבל את גישתו כדעה לגיטימית.[98] בדרכו הצנועה והשקטה הצליח הרב הוטנר, אדם בעל עולם עשיר ורקע מגוון, להחדיר לעולם השמרני הזה מרוחו ומדרכו החדשנית של רבו הרב קוק, ויש לזקוף לזכותו את התרומה לעיסוק הגובר בלימוד אגדה ומחשבה בישיבות.[99]

תורת הרב הוטנר סטתה מהדרך המקובלת בעולם הישיבות ובכך הוא חשף את עצמו לביקורת מבפנים. יש להניח שבאמירות החריפות שלו נגד הציונות והדגש שהושם על המושג "דעת תורה" – אותו מושג שעמד במרכז הכתיבה של הרב אלחנן וסרמן שייסד את ההשקפה הישיבתית[100] – הרב הוטנר התכוון (בין היתר) להוכיח את נאמנותו לעולם הישיבות, גם בזמן שהוא פותח פתח לכיווני חשיבה מחודשים ופילוסופיים יותר.

על אף התרסתו נגד הציונות[101] נראה כי גישה זו, המתעלה מעל האשמה של צד זה או אחר, יכולה למתן את ההתנגדות המסורתית של חרדים כלפי הציונות, התנגדות המבוססת על מה שנתפס כמרידה נגד הדת והאחריות לעונש המר שפקד את העם בעקבות מרידה זאת.[102]

השתתפותו הגדלה של החוג החרדי בחיים הפוליטיים במדינת ישראל מצד אחד, בו בזמן שהתנגדותו העקרונית לציונות נותרה בעינה מצד אחר, יוצרת מתח פסיכולוגי וסוציולוגי שמבקש פתרון. סביר להניח שעם הזמן גישות חדשות ייפתחו שיגשרו על הסתירה לכאורה בין השקפות אנטי ציוניות מחד גיסא וחיים פוליטיים פוריים במדינת ישראל מאידך גיסא. אין ספק שקולו של הרב הוטנר יצר פתח להשתתפות הפוליטית ההולכת וגדלה של המחנה החרדי במדינת ישראל. ☙

---

98 ראה י' שוורץ וי' גולדשטיין (ללא תאריך). **השואה.** ירושלים, עמ' 103-104. וכן ראה מכתב ה"הסכמה" של הרב אהרן פלדמן, ראש ישיבת נר ישראל בבולטימור, מרילנד, וחבר מועצת גדולי התורה של אגודת ישראל בארצות הברית, בספרו של Joseph Elias, *Tragedy and Rebirth: Transmitting the History and Messages of Churban Europa to a New Generation* (2012) New York. הרב פלדמן תומך בשיטה המסורתית, אך מכיר גם בלגיטימיות של גישות אחרות.

99 ראה: Schwarzschild, "Isaac Hutner," p. 153, 163.

100 ראה גם שביד א' (1994). **בין חורבן לישועה**, עמ' 18-22.

101 ביקורתו של הרב הוטנר כלפי הציונות היתה נוקבת - ראה גם שם, עמ' 161-163 , אך אין ספק שהיא חריפה פחות מזאת של הרב אלחנן וסרמן לפני השואה ושל הרב שך אחרי השואה.

102 ייתכן שמאמרו של הרב הוטנר, שמקורו בהרצאה שנשא בקיץ 1976, אף תרם להצטרפותה של אגודת ישראל לקואליציה עם החילונים בקיץ 1977. במסגרת המהלך הפוליטי הזה, אחד הנושאים הנידונים היה בקשתה של אגודת ישראל להעביר את יום הזיכרון לשואה מחודש ניסן לחודש אב שבו אנו אבלים על חורבן הבית, וכפי שהציע הרב הוטנר במאמרו. ידיעה זו התפרסמה בעמ' 9, בצד מאמרו של הרב הוטנר:
The Jewish Observer, XII (8), 9.